CLARA VYVYAN

*Edited and Introduced by I.S. MacLaren
and Lisa N. LaFramboise*

Foreword by Pamela Morse

The Ladies, the Gwich'in, and the Rat

*Travels on the Athabasca, Mackenzie, Rat, Porcupine,
and Yukon Rivers in 1926*

 The University of Alberta Press

Published by
  The University of Alberta Press
  141 Athabasca Hall
  Edmonton, Alberta
  Canada   T6G 2E8

Printed in Canada 5 4 3 2 1
Copyright © The University of Alberta Press 1998

Canadian Cataloguing in Publication Data

Vyvyan, C. C. (Clara Coltman), 1885-1976.
    The ladies, the Gwich'in, and the Rat

    Includes bibliographical references and index.
    Previous ed. has title: Arctic adventure.
    ISBN 0-88864-302-0

    I. Vyvyan, C. C. (Clara Coltman), 1885-1976—Journeys—Canada, Northern. 2. Smith, Gwendolen
Dorrien, 1883-1969—Journeys—Canada, Northern. 3. Canada, Northern—Description and travel. 4.
Women travelers—Canada, Northern. 5. Frontier and pioneer life—Canada, Northern. I. MacLaren, I. S.,
(date) II. LaFramboise, Lisa N., (date) III. Title. IV. Title: Arctic adventure.
FC3205.3.V9 1998   917.1904'2   C97-910999-X
F1060.9.V9 1998

Colour scanning by Elite Lithographers, Edmonton, Alberta, Canada.
Printed and bound by Friesens, Altona, Manitoba, Canada.
∞ Printed on acid-free paper.

The University of Alberta Press acknowledges the financial support of the Government of Canada through
the Book Publishing Industry Development Program for its publishing activities. The Press also gratefully
acknowledges the support received for its program from the Canada Council for the Arts and the Alberta
Foundation for the Arts.

COMMITTED TO THE DEVELOPMENT OF CULTURE AND THE ARTS

Contents

For Margaret

Foreword

Thirty-three years have passed since I first read Clara Vyvyan's *Arctic Adventure* in 1965. Published four years earlier, the book formed some of the required reading for our party of six, preparing to canoe the Rat-Bell-Porcupine route through the Richardson Mountains. Vyvyan's was one of the few books about the route available to us. When I made that trip, with G.H.U. Bayly, J.W.L. Goering, W.A.E. Sheppard, D. Woods, and my husband, Eric, I was forty-one, about the same age as Clara Rogers (as she then was) and Gwendolen Dorrien Smith during their 1926 journey. Coincidentally, the interval between their trip and the publication of *Arctic Adventure* is now matched by that between my trip and the present.

During the past half-century, recreational canoeists have attempted the route in gradually increasing numbers, although not always with success. It is not a comfortable trip. It requires strong motivation, which for some people is found in its geographical significance, as a link in a transcontinental journey between east and west. For others, it is the lure of crossing the Rockies or the challenge of a difficult expedition, while for yet others, the attractions of wild scenery and remoteness from civilization are paramount. Vyvyan's writings make clear that she and Gwen were in the last category: all her life, she was impelled to seek wilderness and solitude.

I have been glad of the opportunity to read *Arctic Adventure* again, not only to compare the conditions of travel with our own, but also to appreciate the description of the whole journey from Edmonton to Seattle, through Alberta, the Northwest Territories, the Yukon, Alaska, and British Columbia. My earlier reading had focused on the canoe-travel section that we should ourselves be following. Now, particularly after many more travels "up North," I am struck by the quality of writing and power of observation in this woman's account of her first impressions of northern Canada and its people. Writing of the leisurely travel by passenger-boat, and the visits to northern communities, Vyvyan captures well the adjustment to the different pace of life in the North, no longer dominated by the clock. There have been many accounts of early travel on the Mackenzie and the Yukon, but Vyvyan's ranks high among them, peopled as it is with characters whose stories and dialogue she catches with perception and accuracy. The lure of the North, and tales of what has brought people "In," and what has kept them from going "Out," fascinate her. Yet, the book might have been just another travelogue, albeit lively and perceptive, were it not for the section that sets it apart: the canoe trip through the mountains.

In her autobiographical writings, published later in her life, Vyvyan describes the McDougall Pass journey as a remarkable experience, unlike any other in her life, distinguished though this was for exotic travel. She recalls the vastness, the remoteness, and the sense of achievement. One does not easily forget, however, and nor did she, the mosquitoes of the Rat River, which are grim even by northern standards. Although Clara and Gwen had been warned, the onslaught came as a shock, and the mosquitoes form a recurrent theme in the book. To make matters worse for them, their tents were evidently not bug-proof. Even for our party, most of us with several seasons' experience of northern bugs, and with good protective gear, the mosquitoes of the Rat were a sore trial. I remember a sense of complete outrage at the way those clouds of insects zoomed in on the exposed parts of my anatomy when necessity forced me to lower my pants. Bitterly, I envied the men their less vulnerable plumbing arrangements. Whenever one was motionless, the creatures would be piled thickly on one's clothing, creating a stress that was more psychological than physical. A slap of the hand yielded a black, soupy mess, on which the next cohorts quickly descended to probe and jostle. Eating was a problem; like the Vyvyan party, we would use the smoke of a fire for protection, or eat standing up to catch what breeze there was.

Unfortunately, most of our party found it impossible to wear headnets when working the canoes upstream, for they precluded the accurate judging of distances, depths, and underwater hazards. I often thought, as we toiled up the rocky Rat, of Clara and Gwen trudging on shore while their two guides manhauled the laden canoe upstream. But I did not envy the two women. Except where there was a narrow beach to walk on, they had to plunge through the tangle of spruce, poplar, willow, and alder, arousing more mosquitoes in clouds. The footing was difficult and tussocky, whereas we in the water were at least cool, and the business of working upstream holds its own fascination—a form of intellectual exercise akin to that experienced by mountain climbers. Snap decisions had to be made about which shore to follow, where and when to cross the river, and which of several channels to take. There was plenty of discomfort, and sometimes considerable alarm. More than once, I was swept off my feet. Even so, rather that than a laborious tramp on shore, which for me would have lacked the compensating delight that Clara and Gwen, both accomplished naturalists, could take in spotting plant life.

Our trip shared a misfortune with Clara and Gwen's: we too had rain in the first few days, resulting in a two-foot rise in the water level. We were able to make some progress each day, but it was slow and arduous, as the beaches needed for tracking the canoes were submerged. We took desperate measures then, poling and pulling ourselves upstream by grabbing branches leaning from the bank. We were often flirting with danger.

The Rat River has, I imagine, inflicted a "low" on most who have attempted to travel up it. For us, having been misdirected to start up the river's southern branch, the nadir came on the very first day. Words cannot describe the misery of our eighteen-hour paddle through a maze of muddy ditches and pools, the current at times undetectable, and the river no longer conforming to the map. It was a frightening experience. For Clara and Gwen, the low point came when they thought they were without guides (and food), having become separated from Lazarus and Jim by the braiding, swollen river. Vyvyan's narrative conveys a sense of the real fear and shock that can strike when an apparently safe situation suddenly turns to one of menace, out of control. It must have required great self-discipline for the two women to stay put, hoping for the guides to find them, rather than flounder around in the bush and swamp.

There were joyful times as well. Reaching the summit of McDougall Pass has inspired euphoria in every party I know of on this route. And more joy lay ahead for the women—four days when they were really on their own after Lazarus and Jim left them and returned to Fort McPherson and Aklavik. The two women had picked up enough competence with the canoe to be able to manage, and Gwen's boating experience was an asset. Their unhurried journey downstream with a fast current became a time of bliss that shines as the emotional pinnacle of the entire book. They were lucky they did not encounter any serious head-winds during those days, or anywhere else, for that matter. The Bell and Porcupine are wide rivers with long reaches, and head-winds have slowed or stopped many a stronger party on this route. But fortune smiled, and Clara's account is radiant.

The women were also lucky not to have swamped or capsized anywhere on their route. Their eighteen-foot canoe seems dangerously small for four adults and at least four hundred and twenty pounds of food and gear. On departing Aklavik, they appear to have had twenty packages of one sort or another, plus at least two rifles and perhaps other odds and ends. By contrast, and fairly typically for a modern recreational canoe-party, the cargo for each of our seventeen-foot canoes comprised only two people, four packs, and a maximum of two hundred and fifty pounds of food and gear. How did Vyvyan's party manage? Most of their time up the Rat, there were no passengers, but when the women had to be ferried across the stream, all four might have been aboard. To scramble into such a loaded canoe, in a swift current and with poor footing, would be quite a feat, and there can have been little freeboard.

River-crossings have to be made frequently on the Rat. Not only were they hazardous for the Vyvyan party, but hard-won ground was lost each time. An experienced canoeist would have used the technique of cross-ferrying—pointing the canoe upstream and at only a slight angle to the current. In this way, the crossing can be made without strain and without losing ground. Like most northerners by this time, however, Lazarus and Jim were motor-boat men and would simply aim the canoe at their objective across the river, presenting too much of a broadside to the current. Lacking the power of a motor, they would be swept downstream, with the risk also of being forced onto shoals or rocks. Lazarus shows his motor-boat conditioning again later in the trip, when the party bounces down rocky stretches of the Little Bell and Bell rivers, risking damage to the fragile canoe. He admits one night that his experience of fast waters has been on the alluvial Husky and Peel channels, and that he had been up the Rat in summer only once before, at which time he had vowed never to do so again. Nevertheless, he was probably the best guide available, physically strong, with good bush sense, and outstandingly conscientious and considerate. He and Jim made a good team.

Most canoeists, coming back from "another world" at the end of a wilderness trip, experience a reluctance to face people and civilization. Remarking on how well Vyvyan conveys these feelings, I have puzzled over why two such independent and solitude-loving people chose an itinerary with such a high proportion of travel either by conventional commercial means, shared by many strangers, or in the company of guides. One answer to this puzzle is that they were uninterested in proving their physical strength and stamina; moreover, the stage by canoe was initially only incidental to the whole journey. Their chief aim was to see as much as they could of Alaska's mountains and glaciers, and to do so by a one-way route—both of them hated to retrace their steps. It was an intriguing and enterprising itinerary for the time. Not until they were well on their way did they discover conditions would be far different from what they had imagined. The unexpected toil up the Rat intensified the ecstasy of emerging at the pass, and, even more, the delight of the few days on their own, idling down to Old Crow. Writing the book in her mid-seventies, Vyvyan shows why the experience remained fresh in her memory throughout her life.

Arctic Adventure has long been out of print. *The Ladies, the Gwich'in, and the Rat* performs a valuable service in bringing it back into print, supplemented with a wealth of background material, including Vyvyan's field notes and biographical sketches of the other three participants in the struggle up the Rat.

PAMELA MORSE

Acknowledgements

The research for this edition has been measurably assisted by a great many librarians, archivists, research assistants, and other individuals of good will. We wish to express our gratitude to the following people: Sandra Alston, Robarts Library, University of Toronto; Colin Beairsto, Heritage Research Officer, Vuntut Gwitchin First Nations; Diane Bessai, Department of English, University of Alberta; David Bentley, Department of English, University of Western Ontario; Theodora P. Bobrinskoy; John Bockstoce; Joan M. Hester Boucaud; Rev Sister Fernande Champagne, sgm, Archives of Les Sœurs de la Charités (Sœurs Grises), Regional Centre, Edmonton; Kenneth and Marilyn Conibear; Helene Dobrowolsky; Milton Freeman, Department of Anthropology, University of Alberta; J.W.L. Goering; Glen Gordon, Archives, Royal Canadian Mounted Police; Jeannine Green, Bruce Peel Special Collections Library, University of Alberta; Sheila Greer; Peter Harding; Ross Hastings, Provincial Museum of Alberta; Gwyneth Hoyle; Irene Jendzjowsky, Provincial Archives of Alberta; Helen Kerfoot, Canadian Permanent Committee on Geographical Names; Ingrid Kritsch, Gwich'in Social and Cultural Institute; Paddy Lamb, City of Edmonton Archives; Barbara Langhorst; Raymond Le Blanc, Department of Anthropology, University of Alberta; Paula Lucas, Archives, Royal Geographical Society; Craig Mackie, CBC North; Eli MacLaren; Milo McLoed; Peter Mitham; Eleanor Mitchell, Gwich'in Language and Cultural Centre, Fort McPherson; Sarah Montgomery, National Archives of Canada; Pamela Morse; Anne Morton, Hudson's Bay Company Archives; Elizabeth Murray; Murielle Nagy; Lawrence Osgood; Frank A. Peake, Department of History, Carleton University; Michael

Peake; Sean Peake; Sherwood, Austin, and Stephen Platt; Gwen Rempel, Northern Life Museum, Fort Smith; John Ritter, Yukon Native Language Centre, Whitehorse; Sylvie D. Savage, Rasmuson Library, University of Alaska, Fairbanks; Sarah Simon; Shirleen Smith; Kristina Southwell, Research and Public Services, The Archives of the Episcopal Church; Jonathan Stover; Marie Swanson; Fay Tangermann, Yukon Archives; D. Richard Valpy, Northwest Territories Archives; Michele Wellck, California Academy of Sciences; and the Rev Don Wootten.

Particular thanks are extended to Lady Elizabeth Bourne, Mrs Susan Lea, and Mr Fred E. Koe, who played indispensable roles in making much unpublished material by and about Clara Vyvyan, Gwendolen Dorrien Smith, Lazarus Sittichinli, and Jim Koe available. We wish, as well, to thank Sherwood, Austin, and Stephen Platt, Sherry Schellenbach, Milo McLoed, and Alden C. Hayes for making available a copy of Sherwood Platt's field notes, and Edward Zealley, whose efforts in the 1970s to republish Vyvyan's book were renewed and channelled with alacrity into the present edition.

Because it grew clear during the course of research for this volume that the holdings of the Circumpolar Library at the University of Alberta were indispensable, we wish to express our gratitude to Robin Minion and Elaine Simpson and, before them, Anita Cook, who built the fine collection of northern monographs and "grey matter" over the years. The editors gratefully acknowledge the assistance of research grants from the University of Alberta's Central Research Fund and the Social Sciences and Humanities Research Council of Canada, and a publication grant from the Alberta Historical Resources Foundation.

Finally, the colour reproduction of Gwendolen Dorrien Smith's watercolour sketches, and other aspects of this publication would not have been possible without the generous additional support of the following benefactors: Warren Baker, Lady Elizabeth Bourne, Copper Cliff Chiropractic Centre, Linda and Merrill Distad, Frontec Corporation, J.W.L. and S.H.M. Goering, Bob and Kathleen Henderson, Hide Away Canoe Club, Lois and Ted Hole and Family of St Albert, Stuart and Mary Houston, Grant and Kathleen Kennedy, George and Linda Luste, Hon. J.W. McClung, the Minsos Family (Derrick Motor Inn), Northern Books, Lawrence Osgood, Herb Pohl, Provincial Council of the Sisters of Charity (Grey Nuns) of Alberta, Fred Vermeulen, Marjorie and Max Ward, and the Wilderness Canoe Symposium.

Introduction

What was the North like 70 years ago? It has changed so much since 1926 that it might seem almost unrecognizable in a portrait drawn by strangers whose purpose was to gather impressions, not record information. That these visitors were middle-aged English women influenced what they could see, were allowed to see, and were inclined to see. They saw a western Arctic that was still governed and made into a coherent unit by representatives of various institutions—the federal Department of the Interior, the Royal Canadian Mounted Police, the Hudson's Bay Company, and the Roman Catholic and Anglican churches. They met native peoples whose lives had been transformed for many decades by contact with whites; former hunters and gatherers, the Dene and Inuit had become whalers, trappers, and traders. Some were even employees of the various institutions. Many still lived on the land, but few lived wholly in isolation from Euro-Canadian society.

Clara Coltman Rogers (1885-1976) and Gwendolen Dorrien Smith (1883-1969) came from one patriarchal society—England—to another; its agents arranged for their every need as they travelled from Edmonton, Alberta to Fort Yukon, Alaska in June and July, 1926. For three blissful days during the month of July, they enjoyed the wilderness entirely on their own. Otherwise, they were handed almost like mail from one settlement to another, one means of conveyance to another, one guide to another. Yet they managed to visit a wilderness that few people—men or women—had ventured to see. Seeing it became the most memorable adventure of their lives, even if northerners took their journey in stride. Because the brand new wireless telegraph, together with the ancient moccasin telegraph, kept everyone abreast of everything, these northerners knew all about the women's itinerary. Consequently, the visitors encountered many of the people, much of the news, and a surprising amount of the flavour of northern life in 1926. This account of the journey captures much of it.

In 1961, thirty-five years after making their trip, Rogers, who had taken the name of Vyvyan when she married in 1929, published *Arctic Adventure*. She was the "authoress," as one fellow-traveller and the "Women's Activities" page of the *Edmonton Journal* called her (Bonnycastle, Diary, 4 May; "Women"). Dorrien Smith, her friend, was the painter. Lazarus Sittichinli and Jim Koe, two Gwich'in, Canada's northernmost Dene from the lower Mackenzie River, guided them to and up against the other prominent character in these travels, the Rat River. It had as much say in their plans as any of the great institutions serving as their agents. Add two ambitious seekers after the solitude of wilderness to wilderness in the form of the "malignant Rat" and we have a singular set of circumstances: women eager to shed the identity of lady tourists and become wilderness travellers, and a river that would challenge them on whatever terms they chose.

Arctic Adventure is a story of personal adventure for two women headed north. Down the Athabasca River they went, aiming for the Pacific Ocean by steamer: across Great Slave Lake, down the length of the Mackenzie River and, later, down the Yukon River. In between, the tourists, who watched the North ease past them from their vantage point on deck, became travellers on an arduous canoe trip up the Rat River and then down the Bell and Porcupine rivers through Yukon Territory. Critic Paul Fussell has argued that real travellers (as opposed to mere tourists) have to prove themselves physically: "Etymologically a traveler is one who suffers *travail*" (39). That upriver trek through mosquito-infested bush was demanding; just as well that the two women had what one cocky young HBC man called "walks like bushwhackers" (Bonnycastle, Diary; 4 May). Seen on the broad scale of history, their adventure completed a route such as Scottish fur trader and explorer Alexander Mackenzie had hoped to find in 1789 and 1793, when he searched for a waterway leading from the interior of North America to the west coast. Such was their achievement.

Yet, neither their ambition nor their achievement was so very remarkable. Northerners aware of history and weary of many a southern snowbird's wide-eyed idea that "none had gone that way before" might marvel at how uninformed the travellers were of their whereabouts. Vyvyan and, to a lesser degree, Dorrien Smith inferred that their journey was unique, but this was only one of many presumptions they had about the North. They tended to dismiss the women of the North and revere the men—the mounties and their Dene guides, in particular. They were as expressive of casual racism as most tourists, and they generally exhibited the English sense of superiority over the frontiersmen on the edges of Empire. How could they avoid it? We might as reasonably expect Dorrien Smith to paint outside the conventions of the English tradition of picturesque landscape depiction, or Vyvyan to describe with acute understanding the first and only Inuit seal dance she would ever see. So today in *The Ladies, the Gwich'in, and the Rat*, published about thirty-five years after Vyvyan published *Arctic Adventure*, we observe these travellers with a much different awareness as they observe, pass judgment on, and enthuse over northerners and the North.

   The Ladies, the Gwich'in, and the Rat offers more than a reprinting of the text of *Arctic Adventure*. It also complements the earlier text with several new items, including photographs of the people and places encountered by the travellers. Vyvyan's complete field notes from the trip are included as Appendix One. In Appendix Two, the considerable list of flora that the women collected is collated with both classical and popular names for the plants. Editorial notes to Vyvyan's book follow Appendix Two. They also include references to both Vyvyan's and Dorrien Smith's field notes, and quotations from Vyvyan's letters to her mother. The editorial notes also assemble information from a broad range of sources, both published and unpublished, in an effort to provide an ample historical context for this journey through the western Arctic in the mid-1920s. As well, a selection of Dorrien Smith's watercolour sketches from the journey is reproduced for the first time. Thus *The Ladies, the Gwich'in, and the Rat* rounds out many of the character sketches and anecdotes recorded impressionistically by Vyvyan while on the move, and offers a picture of the routes the women followed and places they visited, from Edmonton (the gateway to the western Arctic) to Fort Yukon (the gateway to eastern Alaska), and all the points between. It remains then to introduce the characters, beginning with the route and its star—the Rat—and proceeding to the travellers themselves; a critical discussion of the book follows.

THE ROUTE

The women's transatlantic crossing aboard the SS *Empress of Scotland* brought them to Quebec City in nine days during the month of May 1926. There they boarded the transcontinental railway for the trip west, stopping for four hours at Montreal and twenty-four at Winnipeg, and arriving in Edmonton on the morning of Friday, 28 May. Staying at the Macdonald Hotel for four nights, they waited for the Tuesdays-only northbound train by completing the logistical and initiating the psychological preparations for their canoe trip. Then, on the first of June, they boarded the train to Waterways, on the Athabasca River near Fort McMurray. At that point, and after some delay, they took to water again, aboard the SS *Athabasca River*. This wood-burning sternwheeler conducted them down-river to Lake Athabasca, and down the Slave River as far as Fort Fitzgerald, Alberta. Steamers could go no farther north at that point: the rapids of the Slave were unnavigable. So, the women covered the twenty-five kilometres of the Smith Portage to Fort Smith, NWT by automobile (a few roadsters had been in service on the portage for about five years). They had to spend nearly a week at Fort Smith while the next steamer was readied for the season and the frozen route to the north thawed out. The women found the wait interminable, perhaps because they were still being treated as "ladies." In 1920, Jean Godsell had gone north on this route as the bride of a fur trade district manager. Her pithy comment is instructive: "A bride of a week, I was on my way into the Northland, in God's Wide Open Spaces where men were men and where, I soon learned, white women were placed on pedestals since they were few in number and far between" (2). The North did not know what else to do with them.

On 14 June, the women boarded the SS *Distributor*. Over the next ten days, it would steam them down the Slave River to Great Slave Lake and across to the Mackenzie River for the long trip to the part-Gwich'in, part-Inuvialuit settlement of Aklavik, sitting in the mud on the west bank of the Mackenzie's great Delta. The *Distributor* called at nine settlements before delivering them there. Then they made an unscheduled pause for two weeks, to allow time for the sprained tendons in Dorrien Smith's ankle, injured during a hike at Fort Providence, to heal.

Departing Aklavik on 7 July, they turned back upriver in an HBC motor boat, following the Mackenzie's westernmost channel, the Husky, in order to gain the deceptively languid mouth of the Rat River, which marked the start of their trip

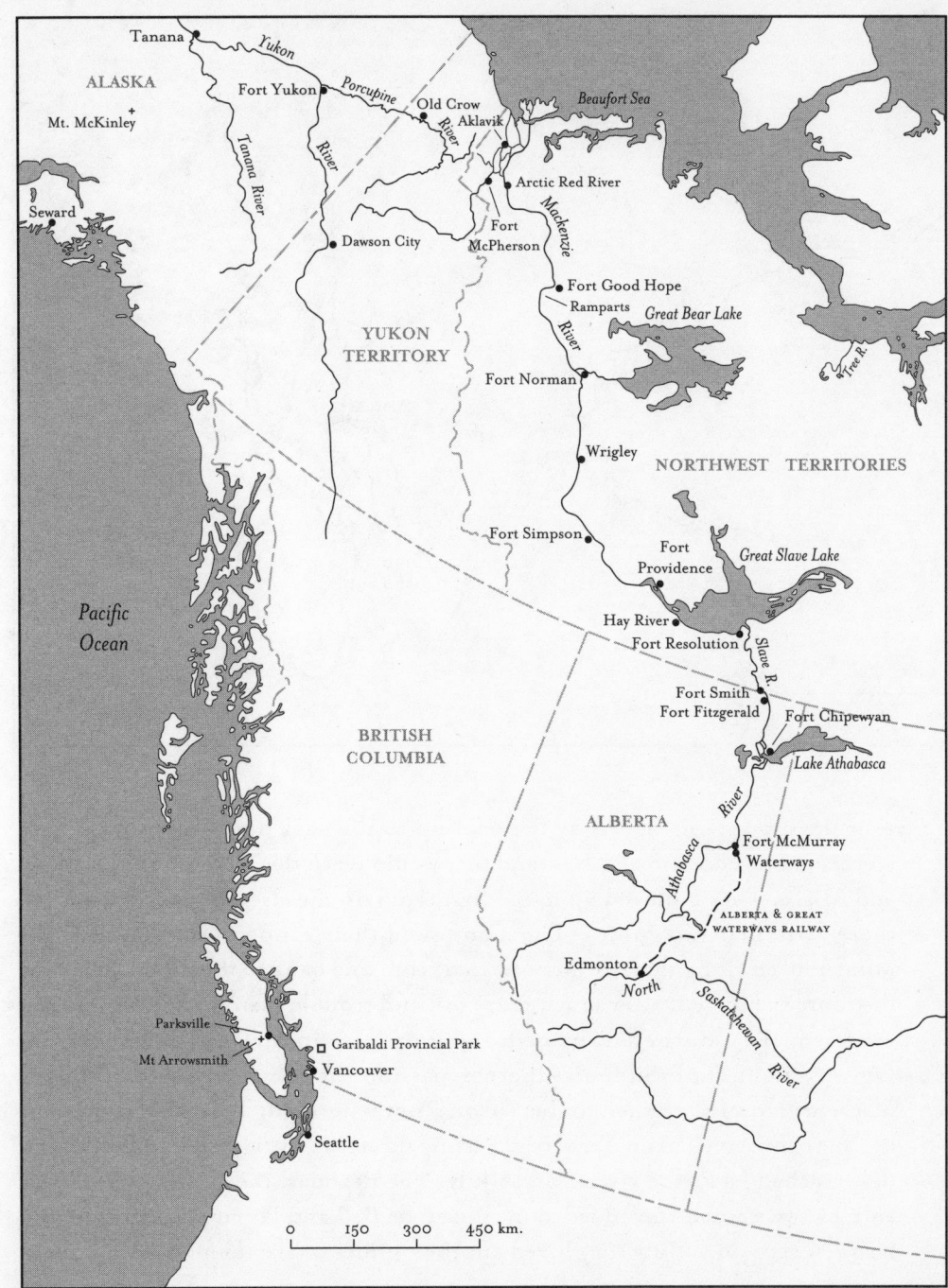

Western and Northern North America in 1926.

ALASKA

Tanana

Yukon

Fort Yukon

Porcupine

Old Crow

Aklavik

Beaufort Sea

+ Mt. McKinley

River

Seward

Tanana River

Arctic Red River

Dawson City

Fort McPherson

Mackenzie

Fort Good Hope

Ramparts

Great Bear Lake

YUKON TERRITORY

River

Tree R.

Fort Norman

Wrigley

NORTHWEST TERRITORIES

Fort Simpson

Fort Providence

Great Slave Lake

Pacific Ocean

Hay River

Fort Resolution

Slave R.

BRITISH COLUMBIA

Fort Smith
Fort Fitzgerald

Fort Chipewyan

Lake Athabasca

ALBERTA

Athabasca River

Fort McMurray
Waterways

ALBERTA & GREAT WATERWAYS RAILWAY

Edmonton

North

Saskatchewan

River

Parksville

Garibaldi Provincial Park

Mt Arrowsmith

Vancouver

Seattle

0   150   300   450 km.

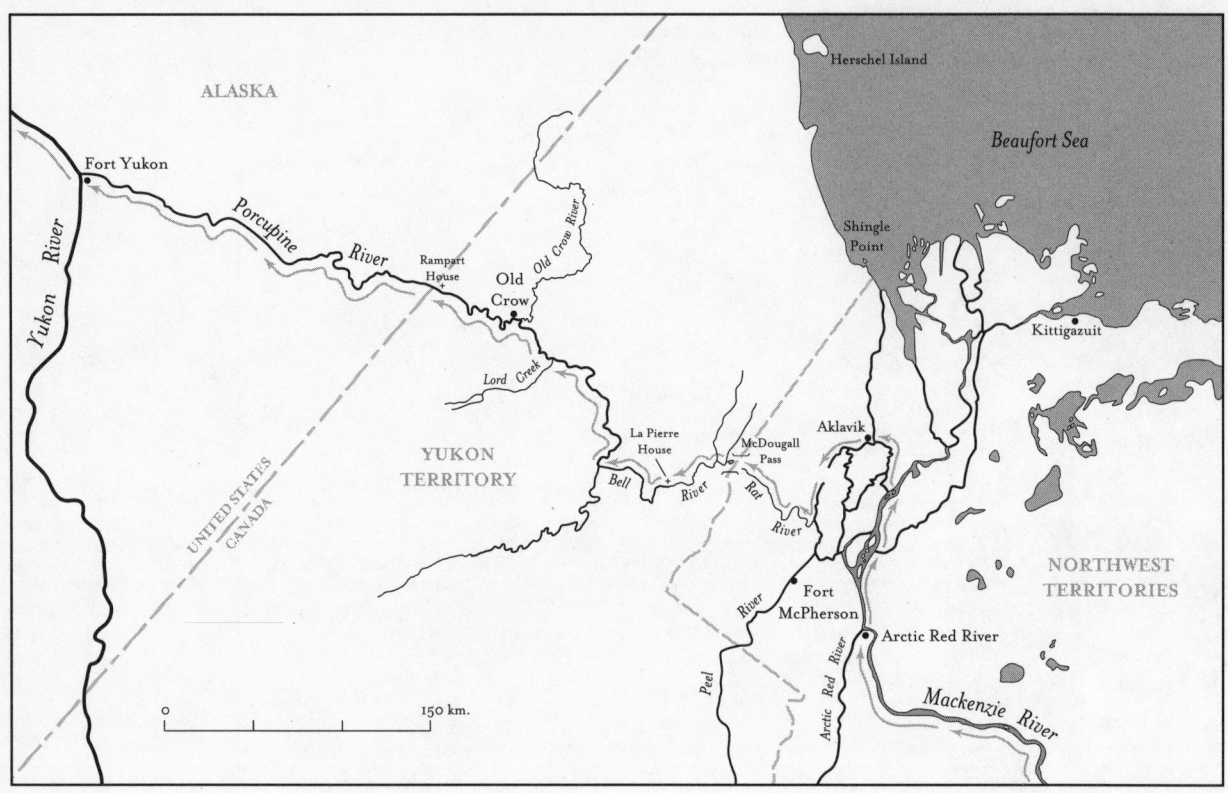

The Western Arctic in 1926.

over the mountains. Here lay the path up to the back door; open it, as gold seekers had a generation earlier, and they would reach the Yukon, the Klondike, and Alaska. They motored up to the first rapid on the river and were deposited there with their two guides. The men towed their canoe upstream while the women hiked along shore or were ferried from one bank to the other. Reaching the source of the Rat after much more toil and trouble than the sojourners had expected, they journeyed through the four lakes in McDougall Pass—Twin, Ogilvie, Long, and Summit—thereby passing the height of land from the Mackenzie River watershed to the Yukon River watershed. Then they proceeded by canoe through Yukon Territory. Passing down the Little Bell and Bell rivers, they reached La Pierre House on 16 July. The next day, the guides turned back and the two women continued alone down the Bell and Porcupine rivers to Old Crow, where on 21 July they hired another guide to take them to Fort Yukon,

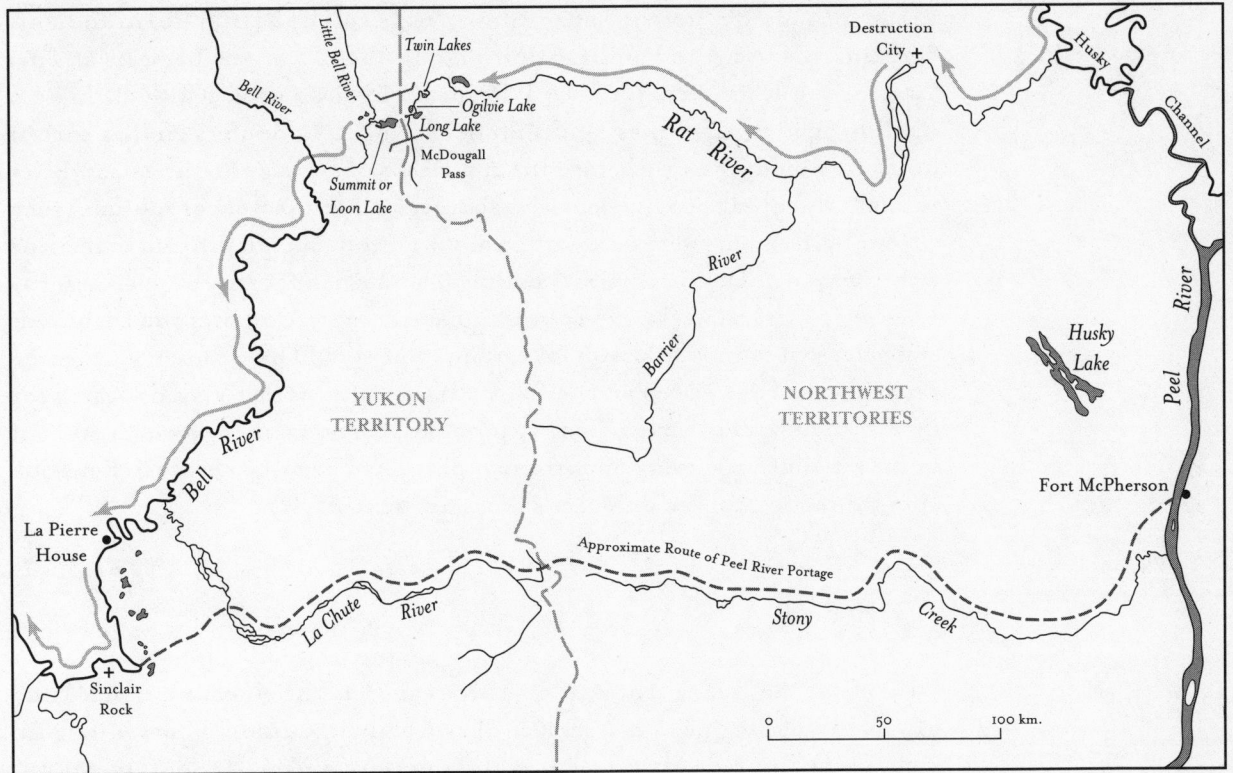

Alaska. They arrived there on 26 July, and, after several days' pause, again boarded a steamer, the SS *Yukon*; it sailed down the Yukon and up the Tanana rivers to Nenana, where the travellers, full of regret at having to revert to tourists again, took a train out to the Pacific Ocean at Seward, and then a steamer, also named SS *Yukon*, to Seattle. After a visit to Parksville on Vancouver Island, and hikes on the island and the mainland's Garibaldi Provincial Park, they boarded the transcontinental train for the East and shipped back to England in early October.

The women's steamer journey from Edmonton to Aklavik was promoted in the 1926 travel brochure of the Alberta and Arctic Transportation Company (AATC) as a thirty-five day junket: "in commodious and up-to-date steamers you may travel in absolute comfort to the very rim of the world" (*Midnight* 2). "A glorious, health-giving holiday" full of "[s]trange sights you will never forget"

Up the Rat and over the Mountains.

(2) are promised to tourists at an approximate cost of $400 return. Indians, "feasting, dancing and jollification among them," might be seen at Fort Simpson, while the arrival at Aklavik "brings us in direct contact with the Eskimo in all his native ruggedness and simplicity" (6). (No doubt a similar sort of brochure would have proclaimed the attractions of a voyage on the Yukon River in similarly appealing and jocularly racist terms.) For seekers of solitude, such voyages by steamboat were necessary means to an end, but it is difficult to imagine either Vyvyan or Dorrien Smith travelling from England merely to sit on a stern-wheeler for several weeks. No conventional transportation over the Divide was available, so it cannot be known for certain if they would have chosen to make the canoe trip had there been an alternative. What *is* clear is that Vyvyan's search for the North of Robert Service's poetry prompted forays from the steamer and out of the settlements at every opportunity. She stated her view clearly in her book after the canoe trip: "an onlooker's life is no life at all" (176).

THE RAT

What about the "malignant" Rat, as Vyvyan apprehensively calls it in her book (39, 108)? The highlight and great challenge of their journey, it owes its English name to the fur trade era's interest in its bounty of muskrat. In 1851, the 9,000 muskrats traded at Fort McPherson represented twenty-nine per cent of the HBC's total in the Mackenzie district (Anderson 11/24/1853; cited in Krech, "Interethnic" 110). Canoeing upriver is hardly anyone's idea of a trip worth crossing half the world to undertake, and the women encountered no shortage of individuals willing to predict disaster if they attempted it. But ignorance is a great scaremongerer. Less well and accurately known than it deserves to be, the Rat River is the lone manageable Canadian canoe route across the Cordillera, that system of mountain ranges extending the length of the Americas. Flowing out of McDougall Pass—a nick in the Richardson Mountains merely 317 metres (1,040 ft) in altitude—its westernmost reach lies near the headwaters of the Little Bell River, a tributary of the Bell and, in turn, the Porcupine and Yukon rivers. The Gwich'in names for the Rat emphasize this aspect of it; they are, alternatively, *Ddhah zhìt han* ("River through the mountains") or *Ddhah zhìt gwandak* ("Mountain-in-through"; GSCI no. 1). "Nowhere else in North America," wrote arctic canoeist Eric Morse, "is it as short and easy to pass over the main continental divide or to go by water from sea to sea" ("Rat-Bell" 37). However, Morse, the doyen of recreational canoeing in Canada, who made the trip in 1965 (*Freshwater* 161-80), also allowed that "[i]f anyone is looking for the most physically challenging section of old fur-trade routes to retrace today, the Rat-Porcupine trip over the mountains should satisfy him" (*Fur Trade* 108). At the very least, it is what seasoned arctic traveller Geoffrey Peake has called "an exercise in patience" (7).

The nearest settlement on the eastern slope is Fort McPherson (*Teetl'it Zheh*), NWT, which lies on the east bank of the Peel River, about thirty-eight kilometres (Benyk 7) upstream from Point Separation. That name was given to the junction of the Peel and Mackenzie rivers in 1826, a century before the women's journey, by Sir John Franklin (Franklin 93). Running across the alluvial plain that forms part of the Peel-Mackenzie Delta, the Rat River enters the Peel about fourteen kilometres below Fort McPherson (McConnell 115). Meanwhile, on the Pacific Slope lies Old Crow, at the confluence of the Old Crow and Porcupine rivers. One of only two permanent settlements in the northern Yukon Territory, the settlement dates from 1911; yet evidence of human habitation found in its vicinity is arguably the oldest in North America (Morrison and Wilson 34; Dickason 423 n26). Although the Dempster Highway passes through Fort McPherson today, McDougall Pass remains wilderness, thanks in large measure to Justice Thomas R. Berger's recommendation in the 1970s that none of the pipelines planned for the shipment of oil and gas from the Arctic Ocean to southern Canada be constructed. One of these, proposed by a consortium known as Arctic Gas, was destined to go through McDougall Pass (Berger 32).

The Rat River route, unknown to explorer Alexander Mackenzie in 1789, was familiar to native people long before Europeans began to explore the Arctic. Indeed, Old Crow and Fort McPherson, on opposite sides of the mountains, are communities of the same people, spelled "Gwich'in" in the Northwest Territories and Alaska, and "Gwitchin" in the Yukon. Mackenzie called them "Quarrellers" [195]; French-speaking employees of the North West and XY companies who were on the Mackenzie in 1804 called them "Loucheux" [Masson 1:110]; and "Kutchin" was an earlier spelling of the modern name. "Takhudh" was a name given them by Robert (*Gikhyi*) McDonald, the Ojibwa Anglican missionary from Red River who went to Fort Yukon in 1863 and ministered to them from Fort McPherson beginning in 1873; but, according to Vuntut Gwitchin Charlie Peter Charlie, this name most properly belonged only to those who dwelled around the head of the Porcupine River (*LaPierre* 93; *Rampart* 46).

"Gwich'in" is rather like a suffix; the prefix clarifies where in the region a particular group is living. Those Gwich'in living around Fort McPherson today call
themselves "Teetl'it Gwich'in" (also spelled "Tatlit"), while those from Old Crow
have taken the name "Vuntut Gwitchin" (also spelled "Vantut" or "Vunta").
Many older people still prefer to be identified as Loucheux (Kritsch; Osgood 13;
Balikci 14). These Athapaskan-speaking people knew the Rat River route but
seldom canoed over it. They preferred a more direct trail between Fort
McPherson and the upper Yukon River basin. Known as the Peel River Portage,
this trail is an ancient portage of 130 km that proceeds westward across low-lying
muskeg, up foothills, around a shoulder of La Chute Mountain, across its
glacier, and through a canyon, finally reaching the Bell River (*LaPierre* 29, 132). It
is called *Gwitoh traa taii* in Gwich'in, which means "over well used trail." When he
crossed it in July 1898, Anglican archdeacon Charles Whittaker noted a remarkable feature of it even up at the higher, less boggy, elevations: "generations of
Indians have worn into the soil. This trail was about four or five inches wide, and
four to ten inches deep. There is no splay to the Indian foot, and such a trail, or
rut, is hard walking for a white man" ("Sunrise" 56-7). Gwitchin John Joe Kaye
set its age at "1000 years or more" (*LaPierre* 132).

When it began operating in the area, the HBC regularly hired Gwich'in to
carry supplies over this trail, which became "the line that made the Company's
operations in this remote area possible" (Allen Wright 77). The trailhead on the
Pacific Slope was La Pierre House, a company staging post on the Bell River.
According to Vilhjalmur Stefansson, the company employed "no man ... who
could not make eighty miles in four days carrying in addition to the ninety-
pound piece whatever he needed in the way of food and bedding" (*Hunters* 210).
Sarah Simon (b. 1901), who has lived in both Old Crow and Fort McPherson,
travelled widely through the western Arctic during the middle decades of this
century in order to minister to her people with her husband, Anglican priest Rev
James Simon. During a conversation in 1994, she was asked if she had crossed the
mountains: "'Oh, many, many times,'" she replied. "'Mostly in winter. Once we
made it from Fort McPherson to Old Crow in ten days by dog team'" (Simon).
Indeed, almost half a century ago, she told Ethel Stewart that in January each
year, "'everyone went over the mountains for caribou'" ("Early" 41). Because the
Porcupine herd's migration route normally remains west of the Richardson
Mountains, the eastern Gwich'in could hunt this valuable animal only after a
transmontane trek (Benyk 24), although Jim Koe remembered caribou on the

eastern side of the mountains for several years beginning in 1927 (Koe 1:19). When Stefansson urgently needed to send a wireless message in the autumn of 1907, the mounties assured him he would have no trouble "in getting Indians to help [him] cross the mountains from" Fort McPherson (*Hunters* 209). Economically, this was one of two routes that were significant to the Gwich'in: the other was the north-south Mackenzie River access, which made contact with the Inuvialuit of the Mackenzie Delta possible. Through them, trade goods coming from Asia and Russia along the arctic coast reached the Gwich'in (Ethel Stewart, "Kutchin" 54-5). At least in winter, the trail is still used today; interviewed in 1995, Gwitchin Alfred Charlie mentioned that Fort McPherson people travel on it to Old Crow by skidoo (*LaPierre* 110).

The Rat River is not as direct a route across the mountains as the Peel River Portage, but Euro-Canadians have been fascinated by it for some time, often choosing it over the portage. The river is a typical mountain stream: "like any in this latitude, with but few trees in its basin and with permafrost a few inches below the soil, [it] does not sponge up water the way a river flowing through forest farther south does. Rain quickly produces a flood" (Morse, "Rat-Bell" 41). Its upper fifty-five kilometres, from the east side of McDougall Pass to Destruction City, drop more than 300 metres (Hodgins and Hoyle 194; MacGregor, *Klondike* 167). This makes for an average drop of 5.5 m/km, a prohibitive rate for paddlers. Moreover, a portion of the upper reaches takes the form of a canyon. Morse advises that the canoe trip from Destruction City to Summit Lake requires about nine ten-hour days of strenuous work—almost certainly a combination of lining, paddling, poling, and hauling ("Rat-Bell" 43; Bayly 43)—sometimes at a rate of less than one kilometre per hour (Hayes 94-5). In their first talk in Edmonton with Harry Warner of the AATC, Vyvyan and Dorrien Smith learned that "it would take ... at least ten days to track up the Rat," so they had no illusions about the time involved for this portion of their trip. Two weeks would not be unheard of; six men in two canoes took seventeen days, including some mishaps, in 1938 (Hayes 104), but in 1940 a smaller party, which benefitted from a map of the route drawn for them by Lazarus Sittichinli, reached Summit Lake on 14 July, only ten days after leaving Aklavik (Ederer 78, 80, 91, 93). A gush after a rain will elevate the river-level dramatically, as it did for Vyvyan's party, and will slow upriver progress if it does not bring it to a halt.

The only portages required on this route occur at the top of the river, from Long Lake 400 m west to the pond named McDougall Lake, and 800 m west from it to Summit Lake (Morse, "Rat-Bell" 43). The different stages of the 950-km route measure as follows: from the mouth of the south branch of the Rat near Peel River up to Destruction City, approximately 60 km of sluggish water; from there to Summit Lake on the west side of the height of land, 70 km with a touch of Hell about them; from the east end of Summit Lake to Old Crow, about 340 km; and from Old Crow to Fort Yukon, 480 km (Morse, "Rat-Bell" 44). Unless strong headwinds are met with, the trip from Summit Lake to Fort Yukon can be canoed in about eleven days.

The region was first explored by Europeans during the nineteenth century. On 3 September 1826, Franklin's men boated him part way up the Peel River, which he named after the then British secretary of state. Franklin surmised that "it was to this river the Loucheux alluded, when they told Sir Alexander Mackenzie ... that there was a river which conducted them to the sea in five days" (182). However, even though Franklin concluded that Russian trade goods came into the Mackenzie Basin by this route, the HBC did not investigate it any farther until 1839. In that year, Chief Trader John Bell traced the Peel until it dwindled to a stream. Returning downstream, he entered the Rat and canoed up it to the beginning of the strong rapids. This place, where rough and smooth waters meet, is known in traditional Gwich'in as *Tr'ih zhit tagwehdii* ("canoe landing"), because westbound people left their canoes here and then walked into the mountains to hunt (Kritsch). In English, it is known as Destruction City and marks the spot where Vyvyan's party was deposited by the HBC's motor boat. Leaving his canoe at this point, Bell walked inland twelve kilometres to the foot of the mountains. The next year, he established Fort McPherson (called Peel River Post by the HBC until 1898 [Allen Wright 47]), but the press of trade precluded further exploration; moreover, he likely found obstacles put in his way by the Peel River Gwich'in who had only recently acquired, through HBC expansion into the Mackenzie Basin, a regular supply of European trade goods. This placed them "in a strong middleman position vis-à-vis the western [Gwitchin] and the Han Indians. ... [R]ealizing the value and importance of maintaining a monopoly over a source of supply or a trading area, ... [they] did their utmost to hinder the Hudson's Bay Company's efforts" to push past them to native traders farther west" (Coates 55, 56).

Although in 1839-40 Canadian-born Alexander Kennedy Isbister traced the course of the Rat during a winter trip, he could not have learned much about the river; at least, the published version of his map, if not the original, showed it flowing straight through the mountains (Isbister, after 332). In 1842, three years after his journey up the Rat, Bell was guided by Gwich'in over Peel River Portage to the Pacific Slope and the river that bears his name today. Why had he not continued up the Rat earlier? This is a mystery, further confused in 1842 by his mistake in thinking that, although he could see that it flowed westward, the Bell River merely formed another fork of the Rat (the West Rat and East Rat remained on maps for some years). He reached the Porcupine River in that year, and the Yukon during a similar trip in 1844, thereby establishing a very profitable expansion of the company's trade (Craig 42). But Bell did not realize the significance of his discovery. Vilhjalmur Stefansson considered such a failure remarkable. He wrote of Bell in the same breath as Columbus—two great seekers of the Northwest Passage—but he regretted Bell's failure to seize on the significance of the geography he had encountered: "Clearly it did not occur to him, at least then, that the great Rocky Mountain chain here had been smoothed beneath a surface of gently sloping grasslands, to rise craggily again farther north and west." In Stefansson's view, it also did not dawn on Isbister in his published account that the men had crossed a "portage far the best that anywhere connects the Mississippi-Mackenzie central basin of the continent with Pacific waters" (*Northwest* 184, 176).

When, in 1847, Alexander Hunter Murray took over the area from Bell, he bypassed the Rat, sledging across Peel River Portage to La Pierre House, which had been established in either 1843-44 (Coutts 154) or 1846 (Coates 58). Murray's wife, Anne, three men, and another woman stayed at the post while he returned to Fort McPherson, rejoining them with a larger pedestrian party on 14 June (Murray 28). He then continued down the Bell, Porcupine, and Yukon rivers. At the confluence of the latter two, he began building Fort Yukon. Despite this achievement, which constituted an act of commercial aggression on internationally acknowledged Russian territory, Murray will be remembered as well for not discovering the water connection between the upper Bell and Rat rivers.

Finally, in 1872, James McDougall, Murray's successor, explored the pass that connects the Mackenzie and Yukon watersheds; he reported it as commercially viable and relatively straightforward (qtd in Vilhjalmur Stefansson, *Northwest* 223-25): in short, possibly preferable in summer to the long and initially swampy Peel River Portage. When, in June 1888, he surveyed it for the Geological Survey of Canada, William Ogilvie proposed that the pass be named for McDougall (Ogilvie 63, 64). The name stuck, but the HBC had already begun to curtail its interest in the route; in 1867, with the annexation of Alaska by the United States, any route that involved passing at some point through foreign territory lost its appeal.

If geo-political developments prevented the fur trade from making the Rat famous, the gold rush rectified matters at the end of the nineteenth century. "The back door to the Klondike," as it became known, served as the chosen route of some 400 of the more than 500 men and women who descended on Fort McPherson during the race for the precious metal in 1897 and 1898. "Of all the Edmonton routes to the Yukon," wrote J.G. MacGregor, "the Mackenzie-Rat River route, the longest, took the least time. It was also the easiest and by far the most practical. ... The 1898 Lamoureux contingent crossed by that route and their elapsed time from Edmonton to the Yukon was eighty-six days" (*Klondike* 166). Not all writers have agreed with MacGregor; Charles Camsell, himself a veteran of the punishing Liard-Pelly River route, considered the Rat "the most roundabout and impractical route of all. Most of those who followed it turned back and never reached their destination" (59). Certainly, not all Klondikers could match the Lamoureux' break-neck pace. Travelling over the route in the summer of 1898 with her husband, Mrs Horsfall eventually reached the Dawson area; so did Emily Craig and her husband (MacGregor, *Klondike* 59, 115, 169), but they spent two winters *en route*. (An editorial note to Chapter 15 contains more information about Emily Craig's journey [272-73].) Along with Mrs LeFrancois, Craig spent the winter of 1897-98 at Destruction City (MacGregor, *Klondike* 169). According to some, this place garnered its name because so many prospectors "had either perished by drowning or had lost all of their gear" (Zealley, "Lazarus" 3). In a memoir apparently written in 1947, Englishman Alphonso Waterer recalled that Destruction City had first been named Little Dawson; the change of name for the eleven log cabins "was most appropriate as [t]here was where the scurvy first made its appearance and where many parties came to grief" (28). (Waterer spent much of the winter, probably 1898-99 [Robert Gordon 656], at Shacktown, twenty-nine kilometres farther upstream [48]). According to other sources, about forty Klondikers, anticipating the steep ascent of the Rat, halted at the end of the slack water, and "cut down their boats. Since this place soon became littered with discarded parts of boats, the men called it Destruction

City" (MacGregor, *Klondike* 167, 168). At least one account of the Klondike Gold Rush up the Rat River had been published in England a quarter-century before Vyvyan's journey (Inman 450-59), but apparently it and its description of the Craigs and Destruction City were unknown to Vyvyan and Dorrien Smith.

Elihu Stewart, another potential source for the women, would have suggested that low water levels were typical on the Rat River in late July. Vyvyan listed Stewart's book under "Books Read May-Oct. 1926" after the last dated entry in her field notes (226), so she must have known that, in the last week of July 1906, the superintendent of Forestry for Canada chose to walk the Peel River Portage rather than confront the Rat so late in the summer, and this despite Stewart's having brought a Peterborough canoe north with him on the steamer (115-16). So timing was crucial, and, although the women had arranged to take the first steamer of the season from Fort Smith, an injury to Dorrien Smith's ankle kept them two weeks in Aklavik. When at last they reached the mouth of the Rat, however, they were still more than two weeks ahead of Stewart's schedule and found all the water they could handle flowing down the canyon.

It is also difficult to say how much the missionaries Charles and Emma Whittaker told the women in early June when the subject arose aboard the train north from Edmonton. And that difficulty is compounded by the possibility that past experience with Agnes Deans Cameron, the first woman to publish a book-length account of travels in the western Arctic (*The New North* [1912]), had put them on their guard with writers travelling in the Arctic. Whittaker, who met her at Fort McPherson, considered Cameron "a vigorous romanticist, gathering data for a vivid volume," who would produce "an intricate compound of fact and fiction, a most interesting and readable romance of travel to be sure, but hardly a reliable book for reference" (Letter; qtd in Kelcey 131-32). Although Whittaker had previously walked the Peel River Portage several times, he chose to go up the Rat River in 1900, when he had to make the trip over the Divide with his wife and their one-year-old daughter. Vyvyan mentions it in her field note for 2 June, in her letter to her mother the next day, and in the fifth chapter of her book (25), but seems not to have pursued the matter very far. The women did learn that Whittaker found himself chest deep in water, and that he had employed "four or five" guides, not two, but they probably did not hear that the journey was made only twenty-four days after Mrs Whittaker had given birth to the couple's second child. In fact, except for this, their trip a quarter-century earlier anticipated the trip that Vyvyan and Dorrien Smith would make in many respects, including taking strength from native guides and having to trudge through mosquito-infested bush along the river banks. (An editorial note to Chapter 5 contains more information about the Whittakers' journey [246-47].)

In the intervening quarter-century, trips on the route were reported by Charles Camsell, in 1905 (Camsell); by Bishop Isaac Stringer, in 1909 (Frank Peake, *The Bishop* 118-21); by Robert Service, in 1911 (Service, "In"); by A.A. Carroll, in 1913 (mentioned by Vyvyan after the last dated entry in her field notes [227]); and by Franklin Hugo Kitto, exploratory engineer in the Natural Resources Intelligence Branch of the Department of the Interior, in 1920 (Kitto, "Report"). While far from the first Europeans to travel the Rat, Vyvyan and Dorrien Smith were two of the earliest *recreational* travellers on the transmontane route, and information concerning it was still not readily obtainable. So a keen sense of adventure still prevailed. Yet, times were changing, even in 1926: although they did not know it, the women proceeded upriver only two and a half weeks ahead of a trip by four young American male undergraduates. Sherwood Platt and friends had canoed from Waterways to Fort Fitzgerald, worked aboard the SS *Distributor* in return for their passage on its second trip of the summer, started up the Rat on 25 July (the day before Vyvyan and Dorrien Smith reached Fort Yukon), experienced two snowfalls on their way upstream, returned to Fort McPherson to re-provision for their huge twenty-two-year-old appetites, and finally reached Fort Yukon on 31 August (Platt).

Since 1926, the route has become better known (see Hodgins and Hoyle 197-98). Bill Bendy and his wife, Sylva, completed it in 1936 (Bendy), Alden Hayes's party in 1938 (Hayes), Bernard Ederer in 1940 (Ederer), Kenneth Conibear and two Americans in 1947, Eric and Pamela Morse and friends in 1965 (Bayly, Goering, Morse), and the Peake brothers in 1994 (Geoffrey Peake). For his trip in 1965, Eric Morse obtained an assessment of the route by RCMP officer L.R. Bates, in command of the detachment at Old Crow. Bates reported the arrival the previous year of two Americans who "had been without food of any amount for 2 weeks" (qtd in Bayly 55); he stated further that Special Const Benjamin, who had been stationed at Old Crow for ten years, told him "almost every year there has been one or two persons travelling this route. However, each time they report in at the settlement here, there has been a shortage of food on the trip, with several being out of food for a long period of time. Some have tipped over losing all groceries and narrowly missed losing their canoes. Most have been about 2 weeks behind the schedule they had set for themselves, due to unforeseen problems such as patching torn canoes, low water, poor channel, etc." (qtd in Bayly 56). In the light of this report, it is clear that Vyvyan and Dorrien Smith were well guided.

THE GUIDES

Because of all the planning done for them by the HBC, the women stood little chance of travelling alone through the wilderness. With tourists in mind, Harry Warner had already written two memoranda about their entire route and had recommended guides for the canoe trip portion. The guides engaged at Aklavik were both Gwich'in men: Lazarus Shit'anjiinlih (1890-1988; the older and more common English spelling of Lazarus' surname is Sittichinli) and James Koe (1905-80; the surname is pronounced Koo-ee). Prior to the advent of Euro-Canadian trade with Russian and British companies, there were thought to be eight groups of Gwich'in, who "were said to comprise a unity on the basis of their own opinion, of language, of culture, and the use of Kutchin, 'one who dwells', as a terminological ending'" (Krech, "Eastern Kutchin" 215-16). Most Gwich'in/Gwitchin who traded at Fort McPherson belonged to the Peel River, Upper Porcupine River, or Mackenzie Flats groups. (Slobodin's name for the last group is Arctic Red River [516]). These were Sittichinli's ancestors, now known as Teetl'it Gwich'in (Simon, qtd in Sax and Linklater 77). Younger by less than a decade than Vyvyan and Dorrien Smith, this inveterate traveller was born at Fort McPherson and was one of only three of the twelve children born to Edward and Annie (*née* Satah) Sittichinli to survive into adulthood. His surname means "hanging food on a tree" (Simon, qtd in Sax and Linklater 75). Not only did he have vast experience in living off the land, but also he kept his father company during his journeys.

Edward Sittichinli was "one of the first full-blooded Loucheux Indians ordained by [the] Anglican Church ... He preach the gospel and we always moving round the country" (qtd in Zealley, "Lazarus" 3; see Benyk 79). According to Sarah Simon, Edward, who was baptized by Robert McDonald on 30 May 1869 (Sax and Linklater 77), was ordained deacon at Arctic Red River on 15 July 1903 (Sax and Linklater 86). He was immediately sent as catechist to La Pierre House to continue the work started in its environs by Henry Venn Ketse and continued by Rev John Ttssietla (Sax and Linklater 79). In 1910, according to Lazarus, who was travelling with him, he stood in for Archdeacon Whittaker at Rampart House when his wife Emma's poor health necessitated their departure (qtd in Sax and Linklater 82). In 1911, he was assigned to Rampart House. Later, he made Fort McPherson his mission and was the only resident Anglican minister there between 1918 and 1924 (Fumoleau 141). His itinerant ministry often required crossing from Fort McPherson to Old Crow and Rampart House, so the route was well known to his son, who would later guide mounties over the mountains from Herschel Island to Fort McPherson (Nagy 46). But most of Lazarus' crossings occurred in winter. In an interview in 1976, he told Edward Zealley that he "had only once gone up the Rat during the summer—two years previously he had guided a lawyer up the notorious river. After that arduous journey, Lazarus had promised himself that he would never attempt it again" ("Lazarus" 3). Still, Lazarus was hardly daunted by the challenge of the job. Vyvyan's field note for 10 July, the fourth day on the Rat River, records his amusement at her notion that the wilderness is full of danger: "He screamed with laughter at idea of us dying of hunger if he upset + at idea of Jimmy drowning." His laughter is not included in the book version, although her fear remains. By the end of the trip, Sittichinli had impressed Vyvyan immensely with his knowledge of wilderness travel and his powers of endurance, and even in the last year of her life she was curious to know about the welfare of her Gwich'in guide (Vyvyan to Zealley).

It is clear that everyone was in good hands with Sittichinli in charge. This includes Jim Koe, who was about twenty in 1926, when Sittichinli asked him to join the trip. In an interview recorded about forty years later, his respect for his brother-in-law dominated his memory of that summer. In 1925, he had been helping build the first wireless station at Aklavik. It opened in October of that year, and in the winter of 1926 one of the messages received at it was for Jack Parsons, the manager of the HBC post, asking him to arrange for two men to guide two women over the mountains. Parsons, who had been among the people

for many years and knew everyone … went straight to Lazarus. He was married to Old Man Firth's (an old trader) daughter—her name was Ellen. They both worked among the people for many years. Jack Parson asked Lazarus if he could be a guide to these two women that were coming in this steamboat. He agreed; he said he was willing to go and was going to get paid. Lazarus told Jack

Parson, "I will go but first I have to be paid $14.00 a day." Jack Parson said, "When those two women come, we will talk about it. In the meantime, get another man to go with you." That's when my brother-in-law, Lazarus, asked me to go on this trip with him. I couldn't say no to my brother-in-law. I told him that I would go with him. When the steamboat came, the two women arrived. They talked over the pay and the trip and everything was alright with them. They had lots of food for the long journey; also an 18 foot canoe.

When these two ladies arrived in Aklavik, one of them had hurt her leg. Her father told her to stay behind but she insisted that she was going, too. The next day we got ready. At that time, the HBC had a gas boat. They rented this boat to take us to where we were to start by land. We camped where we landed. Early the next morning, we started for the mountains following this canoe river. It was during the rainy weather and there was lots of water—the river was swift. We couldn't use track lines because of high water. I sat at the head of the canoe with my brother-in-law, Lazarus, at the stern of the canoe. One of the women who had hurt her leg sat in the canoe with us, the other walked along the shore. In some places, the water was very strong and the canoe would nearly swing with us and sometimes I would feel scared. Sometimes my brother-in-law would yell out to me to jump ashore. I would hesitate before I made the jump. Later, he would still laugh at me about this. The water was very cold, but on we went towards Loon Lake—the mosquitoes were awful. There was no such thing as mosquito dope—we only used mosquito head nets.

Further on through Fish Creek we travelled, then came to a portage to Loon [Summit] Lake. We had to pass about five portages which were long, about one mile for each portage. We packing everything, making relays and packing the canoe. Finally we reached the lake. My brother-in-law said, "I passed the worst part, from here we will be travelling downstream." When we got to the creek, the water was very low but we made it through alright. We later canoed into White Stone River. We passed La Pierre House and landed at Saintclair Rock below La Pierre House. We made camp there. This is where my brother-in-law and I started back and the two women continued on their journey. Early the next morning the two ladies gave us all the food we needed for our journey back and they paid us, too. We watched them start off and my brother-in-law, Lazarus, and I started back, too—a long journey home. I am not sure about the distance, but I think it is over eighty miles from Saintclair Rock to the other side of the mountain. This is when my brother-in-law was a strong man and he made it in one long day with me. It was hard for me to keep up with him but I never gave up. We got back to Ft. McPherson. I gave some of my money to my father. A canoe was lent to us and we departed. We paddled all day, and by evening we got back to Aklavik. (1:11-13)

Sittichinli considered his brother-in-law untutored in country living; as Vyvyan expressed it, "Lazarus would often say scornfully: 'Mission school no good, never teach Jimmy live off the country'" (140). When he was five years old, his mother died. At the request of his father and with the help of Archdeacon Whittaker, Jim was sent to the Anglican school at Hay River (Koe 1:1). This young man, who would go on to become chief of his people in Inuvik, did all he could during the Rat River trip to earn the respect of his elder relation. Although he struggled to measure up to Sittichinli's standards, he fared well, as is evidenced by the fact that his uncle, Peter Enock, hired him to help guide a fur trade company manager from Aklavik to Fort Yukon during the subsequent winter (Koe 1:13), thus taking him back to his parents' home town in Alaska (2:7). As for Koe's complaint about the mosquitoes, it compares with many other people's. Travelling in late August, Charles Camsell, a northerner by birth and a veteran traveller, found in 1905 that "the mosquito season was almost over, otherwise we would have had a still more unpleasant time. Rat River has a very evil reputation in the mosquito season, when those pests are so thick that one not only eats them but actually breathes them" (198).

Vyvyan's views of her guides are mixed. Her praise of Sittichinli's "magnificent physique" is offset by repeated expressions of anxiety that she and Dorrien Smith "were completely in their power" (97, 108, 122). In combination, these expressions introduce in the book a racial and sexual tension that probably had more to do with European ideas about the wilderness and its inhabitants than with Vyvyan's actual experience. She had no need to be anxious about Sittichinli's trustworthiness. Son and brother of Church of England ministers, he represented one of his culture's most prominent families. And the mounties found him sufficiently trustworthy to serve as a special constable. This job earned Sittichinli an undesired fame five years later, in 1931, when he helped track down the Mad Trapper of Rat River, Albert Johnson. In fact, Sittichinli would be the one to turn Johnson's bullet-filled body face-up after the posse gunned him down on Eagle River. Interviewed by novelist Rudy Wiebe in 1987, Sittichinli, by then nearly a century old, remembered the manhunt clearly but with distaste (64-5). At 67°10'55" N., 136°15'20" W., Mount Sittichinli sits astride the NWT/Yukon border forty kilometres north of the point where the Dempster Highway crosses that border (Canada 1989). It was named for Lazarus in 1973.

David Elias was the Gwitchin man hired at Old Crow to guide the women down the Porcupine River to Fort Yukon. According to his sister, Vuntut Gwitchin Elder Mary Kassi, David was the eldest (she the youngest) of fourteen children, whose parents married in 1901; thus, he would probably have been younger than Lazarus Sittichinli and a few years older than Jim Koe. Elias attended the residential school at Carcross, Yukon, where he completed grade twelve, then took one more year of schooling at Herschel Island (*Rampart* 62). By 1926, he may already have been married to Mary Chitzi. He did not live a long life. Ten years after guiding the women, he fell ill while hunting near La Pierre House and was taken by dog team to the doctor at Aklavik. He died there late in 1936. His widow remarried and lives today in Fort McPherson (Beairsto).

THE TRAVELLERS

Born in Australia, Clara Vyvyan (Rogers, as she was then) moved to England with her family at the age of two, and was raised in Cornwall (Kinsman 646-47). Given that the publication of her first book, *Cornish Silhouettes* (1924), occurred only two years before her arctic journey, it is clear that her career did not begin until she was nearly forty; but it extended more than four decades, her last book of new material, *Nothing Venture* (1967), appearing after she was eighty. In the interval, she published many articles, including six about her arctic trip, and twenty-one other books about travel, local Cornish colour, and gardening. *Down the Rhone on Foot*, her best known travel title, told the story of a walking trip made at age sixty-seven from the headwaters to the mouth of that French river. Her two-volume autobiography shows that she was a lifelong voluminous reader. Robert Louis Stevenson's writing had a strong influence. Two of his works in particular made their mark on her: *An Inland Voyage* (1878) and *Essays in the Art of Writing* (1905). His account of a canoe trip made in 1876 with Sir Walter Simpson on the Oise River through Belgium and France offered a model for the contemplative traveller. His essays, especially because of their clarity of style and encouragement of aesthetic considerations, so impressed Vyvyan that she was still recommending them to junior editors in the 1960s ("Notes"). In her field note for 18 June, she observed with evident approval that Stevenson's works were included in the impressive library at Fort Simpson.

Gwendolen Dorrien Smith was raised at Tresco Abbey, off the coast of Cornwall on the Isles of Scilly. It is not known how or when the women met or befriended one another, but a trip together to the Balkans in 1924 had confirmed their compatibility as fellow-travellers. The sixth child in a family of seven, Dorrien Smith learned a good deal about boats and sailing in her youth. Vyvyan's reader learns that "Landlubber" is her friend's darkest imprecation. According to Susan Lea, Dorrien Smith remained single and inclined to exotic travel by land and water throughout her life. She had to be pretty resourceful and

was a traveller where finances permitted but [was] not well off. She sold her pictures chiefly in order to pay for her trips—besides the Balkans, she went to N. Africa, Morocco, and South America. After the 2nd [World] War she and her sister went to Australia and New Zealand. They had lots of friends all over the world. Gwen took a tremendous interest in birds and plants and was very knowledgeable about them. Tresco Abbey Garden grew and grows plants from all over the temperate world and new plants were being brought back all the time. (Lea)

It was chiefly Dorrien Smith who made the collection of plants during the arctic trip; upon their return to England in the autumn of 1926, she corresponded with the Royal Botanical Gardens at Kew in hopes of placing the collection there.

Although she also kept field notes during the journey, Dorrien Smith was often busy painting watercolour sketches while Vyvyan wrote. Self-taught, she was a competent colourist in the English landscape tradition; as some of the reproductions in this edition indicate, she handled water and boats particularly well. The mood of repose imparted to most of the scenes encourages a quiet contemplativeness that is the hallmark of this cultural expression. It is not always appropriate to the drama of the North—one cannot imagine vertical perspectives such as mountain peaks or the drama of the Northern Lights becoming her subject matter (the latter are rather difficult to spot in summer's nearly continuous day, at any rate). But the relative gentleness of topography in the Mackenzie River valley was conducive to her style, as was the small scale of the settlements visited by the women.

When Vyvyan wrote her autobiography, the first volume of which, *Roots and Stars* (1962), appeared the year after *Arctic Adventure*, she explained that she grew up in a family particularly stultifying in its adherence to Victorian propriety. For her, attempts to escape the social constraints of upper-class Victorian femininity took the form of reading, nature-walks, and solitary travel. Again and again in her autobiography, she associates the freedom of travel with masculine activities. She describes daily outings with her "capable, Victorian, unlovable governess ... along a road confined by high earth hedges ... a dull, empty, 'there-and-back-again' walk, for those hedges were like 'don'ts', they kept you away from things that you wanted" (9). These outings she contrasts with the adder-hunting expeditions during "long holidays when, the governess being absent and our two brothers home from school, we had excitements in our everyday life" (12). With her brothers, she would walk "along the hedge-top ... like pioneers surrounded by danger" (13), or on top of the kitchen garden wall "looking down on the house and garden and farm, and the moor and Gilly wood, with the widened vision of explorers" (15).

Later, she received permission to take solitary walks by inventing social duties that would take her away from home (37) and by developing an "improving" interest in natural history (33). She was not the only English woman to gain access to travel by invoking the Victorian ethics of self-improvement and community service. In a society that identified travel outside the domestic sphere with male activity, women who wished to travel often offered socially useful excuses. Famous traveller Isabella Bird Bishop, one of the few women accepted as a member of the RGS in the nineteenth century, justified her Asian travels with the excuse of missionary work; Kate Marsden succoured lepers in Siberia; and Marianne North produced paintings of tropical flowers, which are now the property of the Royal Botanical Gardens at Kew. Botanizing, sketching in water-colours, or recording ladylike "impressions" of the exotic spaces of the world could justify an otherwise inappropriate delight in leaving home to wander abroad. In British society, the "adventure" and "freedom" promised by travel had decidedly different connotations for women than for men: as Karen Lawrence has recognized, "the female traveler's particular baggage includes the historical link between female wandering and promiscuity" (16 n18). One of the primary appeals of both travelling and reading books of travel lay in the breath-taking adventures of conventionally male heroes "conquering" wilderness that, by definition, lay outside the law, order, and consequent safety of civil society.

Meanwhile, women embodied civilization, or so it was thought; they represented the antithesis of wilderness, and thus the conventional plot of arduous physical adventure and death-defying struggles with "wilderness" and "savages" offered limited narrative potential for women's travel.

So, while Vyvyan was struggling for parental permission to take walks alone in Cornwall, her brothers were already abroad, in the military and at work on the family cattle station in Australia. Her family accorded her a role restricted to her age, class, and gender: "I was only one of many thousand victims in our day when it was considered almost criminal for a girl to follow any career except marriage" (109). After finishing school, Vyvyan endured the "aimless years" (80) of social life by taking walking tours, and before the First World War also travelled with family members to South Africa, Queensland, Switzerland, Ireland, Venice, and Orkney. Even so, she describes those travels as "purposeful journeys...with planned duration of time and confines of locality, but they brought no wider vision nor deeper understanding of the things that matter most" (80). Epiphanies of spiritual transcendence, which Vyvyan associates with solitude in nature throughout her autobiography and her travel books, rarely appear in the company of her family. Eventually, she persuaded her family to allow her to take up social work and graduated with distinction from the London School of Economics in 1913 with a degree in social science (Kinsman 646-47). At the age of twenty-eight, she was working in the London slums with the Charity Organizations Society. She describes the subsequent years as a struggle between her family's demands that she fulfil the conventional role of the "home-daughter" (*Roots* 106) and the independence that her social work as "a paid worker" gave her. That work justified her existence and fulfilled a deep personal need (111). But it did not fulfil her social and familial obligations, nor did her later war work in a canteen in France, an internment camp in Holland, and various Red Cross hospitals in England.

After the war, Vyvyan, now thirty-five, found her activities remained circumscribed by family demands. She was sent to Queensland to look after her brother, Michael, who was suffering from depression. On the family cattle station, she found herself suddenly "in another world ... travelling forward into the very heart of an unknown continent" (136). Rejecting the "lonely Martha life" (142) of women on remote stations, she nonetheless found that the wide spaces provided moments of timeless union with nature. The Australian countryside also offered adventure in the wilderness, with crocodile hunting, fishing, and her family's roots in the colonial past:

> … many a time when we were children we would persuade my father to repeat to us the tale of his uncle Frank Newbold who was forced to eat his boots after being shipwrecked on the way to Australia and of Uncle Willie Newbold who met his violent death on the Queensland plain.
>
> My mother would never speak of those great-uncles by marriage, she did not think they adorned the family pedigree but we children all felt it was a fine distinction. (147)

Vyvyan's arctic narrative is in part a search for similar stories. She might even have envied the life of Frank Foster, a trapper whom she met at Fort Yukon: his books and the solitude he enjoyed at his cabin on the lower Porcupine River appealed strongly to her (171). Because her autobiography associates the romance of the wilderness with male exploits on the fringes of empire, "the freedom to be found in bush life" (153) is directly opposed to her maternal inheritance of stifling domesticity and social relations. In Edmonton in 1926, she and Dorrien Smith grew irritated with the confines of civilization and were eager to be free of it. As late as the writing of her autobiography, she presented travel as an escape from the still-pervasive post-Victorian constraints on single women of upper-middle-class England: "to rest awhile in open country or secret valleys, out of sight of any human dwelling, would always give me an almost religious sense of contentment" (*Roots* 58). It is understandable, then, that she found herself under Robert Service's spell of the Yukon and that her book opens with her acknowledgement of his poetry as the catalyst for her northern travels.

Why did Vyvyan wait until 1961 to publish a book about this trip? In 1926, she had been in the first wave of professional travel writers going "north of sixty" into territories containing two-fifths of all Canada's land. As many have pointed out, the tradition of arctic exploration had, by the end of the nineteenth century, established the northern sublime as "a masculine realm of arduous adventure" (Lawrence 76 n4). Traditionally represented by the literatures of scientific exploration and frontier adventure, the North was, literarily speaking, new territory for women. Surely, then, the writer in Vyvyan saw the value of striking while the novelty of the moment was hot. Yet, although she published articles, her book did not appear for thirty-five years. Perhaps she had a book rejected; perhaps she did not feel confident about her knowledge of the area and preferred to write about Cornwall for a time. Perhaps her marriage in 1929 had a bearing on her interests. There is no definitive answer to this question. The complementary question is why Vyvyan published the book when she did. Given that *Arctic Adventure* appeared just before *Roots and Stars* (1962) and *Journey up the Years* (1966), one wonders if her renewed interest in the North related to her urge to write an autobiography. The first of the autobiography's two volumes ends with an account of the arctic journey, in which it is seen as "not only the most formidable enterprise but also, in a spiritual sense, the high peak of my life" (*Roots* 175).

Vyvyan did write. Her family was well to do but, as her field notes from this trip make plain, she felt obliged to manage her funds carefully so that she could travel more or less at her own expense, not her parents'. And her six articles about the trip, published between 1929 and 1938, must have yielded some financial recompense for the costs incurred. This effort at financial independence does not mean, however, that her journeys represented a rejection of the values that formed her; indeed, it is clear at points in her book that she affirmed her class's attitudes. In the tradition of women's travels, as Maria Frawley has shown, writing not only justified and helped pay for the travel, but also, under the guise of personal expression, offered women a forum for political and social commentary (33). Vyvyan's own descriptions of northern settlements and the institutional representatives and native people who live in them are not without their own politics, despite her primarily aesthetic focus. But the values exhibited set her within, not apart from, her class and culture. When she expresses surprise at spotting an unshaven bishop, she offers an implicit comment on the standards of northern society. When she expresses surprise, but does not repudiate, one northerner's vehement opposition to mixed marriages, she conveys a tacit approval of segregation. And when observing cultures other than her own—even white cultures, such as that of nuns at remote missions or of lone prospectors and trappers "on the toot"—she does not abandon the cultural baggage she brought with her. When working their way up the Rat, she and Dorrien Smith were not reading accounts of previous trips; they were reading *Macbeth*, aloud to one another. Vyvyan's taste in literature was not just of her culture, but of her culture's past, not on the cutting edge of the roaring twenties; her quotations or allusions to the poetry of the Bible, Coleridge, Wordsworth, Henry Van Dyke, and A.E. Housman, and her esteem for the writings of Robert Louis Stevenson clarify her inclination toward the perspectives and values of earlier periods of her culture. She usually tried to avoid being treated as a "lady" but cultivated it in her reading, her botanizing, and her dismissiveness about most women not of her class.

And she exploited the treatment of her as a lady when it could benefit her. Like many other women travellers, Vyvyan had some freedom of movement because she was single; and although she lacked the direct institutional affiliations that facilitated the travels of male soldiers, traders, missionaries, and explorers, she did belong to a privileged class. Accordingly, the Commonwealth-wide institutions of imperial Britain were available to aid her. Among her contacts was her neighbour, Leonard Daneham Cunliffe. A director of the HBC from 1907 to 1931 (he was elected after Sir Sandford Fleming's resignation) and deputy governor 1914-16, he could open the way to the North for her. As she puts it in her second chapter, he "kept up a lively correspondence with his friends in Canada" (7). On 6 November 1925, he wrote to P.D. Stirling, London manager of the HBC, explaining the women's interest, clarifying that because "money is an object" some information about prices was required, and suggesting that a trip on the Mackenzie River made an appealing prospect (Cunliffe). Both Angus Brabant, who was fur trade commissioner and had just become the director of the newly acquired AATC, and Louis Romanet, general manager of that company and manager of the Mackenzie district for the HBC, arrived in London in November, and their discussions with Stirling helped to shape the women's itinerary. Thought was given to their sailing in the HBC ship, *Baychimo*, but the company had not decided if the vessel would make a trip along the arctic coast east from Herschel Island in 1926 or if it would return to Vancouver at the end of the summer; besides, Stirling added in his letter to Cunliffe of 21 January 1926, "she is not fitted to carry passengers, especially ladies" (Cunliffe).

Similarly, the shorter of Harry Warner's two memoranda about the journey noted that "it may be taken for granted that the Mounted Police would not allow any women, or party of women, to cross the divide with less than two guides. Furthermore, on the drift down the Porcupine, it is possible they may insist on a lone white woman being accompanied by a man, native guide or otherwise" ("Re" 4). In the same summer that Vyvyan and Dorrien Smith travelled the Rat River, authorities had allowed the doomed party of Englishmen consisting of John

Hornby, Harold Adlard, and eighteen-year-old Edgar Christian to set off east from Great Slave Lake on an ill-considered crossing of the Barrens, which ended in their deaths by starvation the following spring (Christian). Similarly, the trip up the Rat by the four American undergraduates took place less than three weeks after the women's (Platt), yet no prior permissions for it were either sought or granted. The significant level of planning and institutional involvement in the women's journey also included the advice of RCMP officers and of missionaries. Despite Vyvyan's insistence on the freedom to be found in the empty wilderness, her travels, like those of other women, were often hedged about with much more cultural and institutional constraint than those of men. Vyvyan and Dorrien Smith might have wished to be "independent women," as Chapter 3 calls them (14), but, given the way in which she sought corporate assistance in her planning, it seems clear that she accepted the fact that their itinerary would be prepared and their role as travellers defined by men who regarded them as ladies.

THE NARRATIVE

Vyvyan's book exhibits two distinct narrative impulses and lacks another. Because she is an adroit character sketcher, individuals populate her book, and she finds adventure in conversation with them. Alternatively, however, she finds exhilaration in transcending human community, reaching beyond it to commune directly with wilderness. These two impulses render her work contradictory at times. The impulse that her writing lacks is an interest in history. Either she sketches the present or aims beyond it at the eternal, but she seldom brings an historical context to her writing.

Vyvyan is most comfortable sketching characters. This is clear in the field notes and is only heightened in the book. In fact, with her ear for dialogue and eye for colour, she punctuated all her travel narratives with portraits of those whom she encountered on the way. In the literature of Canada by English women, she thus follows in the wake of Susanna Moodie, whose own narratives of emigration and travel, *Roughing It in the Bush* (1852) and *Life in the Clearings* (1853), all but dispense with travel in order to feature the sketch. Published under her maiden name of Rogers, Vyvyan's first two books, *Cornish Silhouettes* (1924) and *Echoes in Cornwall* (1926), appeared before and during her arctic travels. Both are primarily collections of rural sketches. So it is perhaps not surprising to find that the most powerful writing in *Arctic Adventure*, one of her last books, remains the character sketches of the "old-timers" who inhabit her arctic frontier. The first half of the book narrates the long journey from England to Aklavik, focusing attention where people have congregated or been encountered. Indeed, Vyvyan tends to develop character types to represent entire communities in northern settlements. Once in the wilderness—that is, once the party begins to ascend the Rat—Vyvyan's admiring portrait of Sittichinli comes to dominate her account.

A notable example of Vyvyan's technique is her sketch of Captain McIntyre, "'a rough old sea-dog'" whose name, perhaps to protect him in case he was still alive in 1961, was altered to Captain Cameron. Captain Aklavik, he might have been called, for the way in which Vyvyan makes her chapters about that mixed-race settlement constellate around him. "I can see the old man now," writes the seventy-five-year-old Vyvyan in 1961; indeed, the full colour of his personality, combined with his censure of racial intermarriage, makes for strong moments in the narrative, but they merely exemplify and enhance the words—"a hardened old sinner with a most pictorial tongue"—in Vyvyan's field note for 26 June (below, 210). It is partly in this sense that Vyvyan found her arctic tour an adventure. A passage in Chapter 8 clarifies her point of view:

> Talk with any new acquaintance had become a real adventure. Among the 30-odd passengers with whom we travelled on our three weeks cruise, we did not meet one ordinary person, nor experience one dull moment; all the time we were onlookers at an exciting drama. There would be an anecdote or story that left us breathless and wondering; a halt at some settlement or woodpile and a visit ashore; an unknown flower; a new bend of the river; mile after mile of enclosing forest walls; a strange bird, some duck upon the water or wood-pecker among the trees, or a bell would summon us to a meal and, sitting opposite the judge, we would listen to the table-talk with renewed astonish-ment. (42-3)

The field notes do not offer a precise analogue to this passage from early in the trip, but it is interesting to find something similar towards the end. In a field note for 28 July, two days after their arrival at Fort Yukon, Vyvyan wrote that she "[s]topped + chatted in house of a swede Burgland woman + 6 kids. They trap. She is happy as a Queen in her 1 room cabin + says life in the N is all sport + adventure meals so easy no social ties +c. One of her children at least born when away trapping with no woman at hand. Every soul you meet full of tales of the North." In Burgland and his family, Vyvyan finds adventure incarnate, and that adventure is linked to tales of people encountered on the way. Like most gifted travel writers, Vyvyan sees published pages in every uncommon event and person. And perhaps a touch of jealousy surrounds this particular description of a woman who, although she has risked her own mortality in bearing children unassisted, has managed to substitute the constricted life of civilized womanhood and all its "social ties" for "sport and adventure"; even the domestic chore of meal preparation for a large family has grown "so easy" for Mrs Burgland.

Robert Service wrote an account of his trip up the Rat River in August 1911, after he had travelled north from Alberta with George Douglas (Douglas 13; Mallory 10). Given her quotation of his work at the start of her book and her reading of his *Ballads of a Bohemian* while at Aklavik (field note for 29 June), Vyvyan would no doubt have been interested to read Service's account, but, except as a newspaper article published immediately after the trip ("In"), nothing appeared until 1945, when "Book Ten—The Spell of the Yukon" formed part of Service's autobiography, *Ploughman of the Moon*. As might be expected, he provided the most literary of all early accounts. He exploited his talents as a character sketcher and used arctic disasters to cast the prospect of the Rat River trip in ominous shades. Vyvyan would have appreciated his account if she did not know it when she came to write her own book. Service tells his reader about John Hornby, Edgar Christian, and Harold Adlard perishing on the Barrens in 1927 (422), and, closer in time and space to his own Rat River trip, the tragedy of Francis Fitzgerald's Royal North-West Mounted Police (RNWMP) party perishing on the Dawson-Fort McPherson patrol in February 1911 (426). This prepares the way for the Herculean ascent of the Rat in a scow named *Ophelia*. The allusion to a literary character who met her demise by a watery suicide hardly emboldens the characters sketched colourfully by the Yukoner, but the lone "Lady" of the group of six, the skipper's wife, "was made of rare stuff" (429). The mosquitoes are the worst Service has ever seen, the labour demanded to haul upstream a scow weighing half a ton is monumental ("even the Lady lashed herself to the straining rope, pulling like a little man" [434]), and Service has as close a call with death as he would ever wish:

Four of us were on the track-line, bent low, our chests breasting the current. It was the toughest pull we had ever had. With muscles taut we inched the scow

upstream, fighting every step. Often we would be motionless, just holding our
own.

I was bent almost double in the foam, when suddenly I was jerked off my
feet. Between me and the sky was a wall of water. I was being dragged downstream, my back bumping over the boulders. I was utterly helpless, with over
me a slab of seething foam like a coffin lid. (434)

Plucked out of the water by skipper McTosh, Service drags himself onward. Their
hired guides desert them. They find they are lost. Service saves the day by discovering the faintly pencilled name of a Klondiker on a tree. This leads the party
over the Divide to the "Glory" of the promised land: "'But for my exploring
spirit you would have rotted away the winter with the snot-nosed Eskimos'," he
brays to his companions (437-38). The Rat has been conquered, and by a
consummate, if now dated, character sketcher.

Vyvyan places her own accomplishment as a traveller in the context of the annals
of adventure by men, and she wrote her journey into the traditional adventure
narrative of the North. Heather Smyth's analysis of *Arctic Adventure* notes an opposition between a rejected (feminine) domesticity and the (masculine) adventure
personae that Vyvyan creates for herself and Dorrien Smith (10-12): they prefer
male company and stories, and reject the title "ladies" (77, this edition).
Moreover, both women, but particularly Dorrien Smith, demonstrate masculine
characteristics: Gwen is stoic and courageous, with strong fists (13) and horny
hands (129), and with a gruff manner (49) and diction flavoured by the sea (71,
117). Almost equally, however, the women's performance of the role of wilderness
adventurer is made provisional by their limited wilderness skills and by Vyvyan's
final admission that gender is one of the qualities barring them from becoming
true northerners: "We felt a great longing to turn back and spend the rest of our
days wandering about the unknown, cruel, magnificent land. If destiny had
ordered our sex, our background and our characters differently, we might have
indulged such longings and become, in due course, old-timers" (178).

However, adventure for Vyvyan also lies *beyond* humans, not just among the
most colourful ones. This sketcher of local colour also craves the vastness of the
North and the experience of unpeopled nature. Lured by the spell of the Yukon
as Robert Service had imagined it, Vyvyan longed to see what others have called
"the back of beyond." To understand the essence of humanity was clearly only
one goal. To experience the power of wilderness, to come, as her autobiography

put it, to a "deeper understanding of the things that matter most" (*Roots* 80), was the other. Like an epiphany, that experience would take one outside oneself; there, one could comprehend Identity in its clearest personal and extra-human dimension. In this second of her two narrative impulses Vyvyan is quintessentially idealistic rather than realistic. She writes of the North rather as Anton Chekhov wrote of Siberia when, in 1890, he journeyed from Moscow to Sakhalin, the far eastern prison island. In her autobiography, Vyvyan attributes to Robert Louis Stevenson her awakening to the ideals of "[s]treams and trees and the sky and an unfenced road, the only companions for a perfect life" (*Roots* 39); and when she writes of the recreative power that nature effects on the paddler, Stevenson's account of his canoe trip through Belgium and France in 1876 comes to mind:

> The central bureau of nerves, what in some moods we call *Ourselves*, enjoyed its holiday without disturbance like a Government Office. The great wheels of intelligence turned idly in the head, like fly-wheels, grinding no grist. I have gone on for half an hour at a time, counting my strokes and forgetting the hundreds. ... What philosophers call *me* and *not me*, *ego* and *non ego*, preoccupied me whether I would or no. There was less *me* and more *not me* than I was accustomed to expect. I looked on upon someone else, who managed the paddling. ... I take it, in short, that I was about as near *Nirvana* as would be convenient in practical life .... This frame of mind was the great exploit of our voyage, take it all in all. It was the farthest piece of travel accomplished. (77-8)

The idealist's goal could be pursued with a certain lack of self-consciousness by people from the centre of an empire, wielding imperial pens that claim the wilderness for a quintessential "me"/"not me" experience by ignoring any previous ventures into it. So the accommodation of this narrative impulse comes at a price.

From the beginning of her book, and despite millennia of indigenous habitation (not to mention more than a century of European presence), Vyvyan presents her readers with a land where people leave no trace on the imagination: "Among all the people that we met I cannot remember any faces ... yet certain rivers, mountains, forests, glaciers, birds and rapids, remain vivid as if I had seen them this morning" (2). Even in the midst of detailed itineraries offered by the AATC, she assures her reader that knowledge of the region, represented by the atlas, that great crucible of imperialism, is faulty: "Since La Pierre House was marked in the atlas, we came to look upon it as the key pin of our expedition but actually it brought us only disillusion, as I shall relate in due course" (8). The "naked grandeur" of wilderness evoked in Service's poems is to be the space of the women's adventure, and thus Vyvyan prepares her reader almost from the beginning to enter a frontier where knowledge is uncertain and landmarks unreliable. "'Our atlas is a liar'," Dorrien Smith states flatly when the women finally reach an abandoned La Pierre House (139).

Vyvyan's disinclination to learn more about the North before publishing *Arctic Adventure* in 1961 compounds this sense of vacancy. In combination with her disposition as a character sketcher to write about the adventure of men, this disinclination leaves the representation of women almost entirely out of her picture. In particular, women travellers, either before or after 1926, are all but absent from the book. Instead, Vyvyan leaves the impression that white women, if they were there at all, did not constitute a significant presence in the North. It is true that their arrival had been fairly recent. Under the auspices of the HBC, the northern frontier was not open to them. It was thought that they had nothing to contribute to fur production, and few people in the nineteenth century travelled in the Arctic for pleasure. White women were thus not allowed into HBC territories until Frances Simpson (wife of Sir George Simpson, governor of the HBC 1821-59) arrived at York Factory in 1830 (see van Kirk; MacLaren, "Touring"). Soon after, white women began to accompany their trader, missionary, mounted policeman, or government official husbands north of sixty. The Grey Nuns' arrival in 1867 at Fort Providence marked the first institutional participation of women in the spread of European civilization into northern Canada. They were followed, over succeeding decades, by other women missionaries and settlers, then by the women of the Klondike stampede, and by teachers and nurses.

By choosing to ignore the North's past, Vyvyan distances herself particularly from the women who travelled or settled north of sixty. Elizabeth R. Taylor, who wrote a series of articles about her steamer trip to Aklavik in the summer of 1892, was one of the first women to travel in the Arctic for pleasure (Taylor). Both she and Agnes Deans Cameron emphasized the recent accessibility of the region. As well, both expressed delight in discovering that their journeys to Aklavik would take them beyond the reach of organized tourism (specifically Thomas Cook's tours in Cameron's case [4; rev. ed. 5]), beyond society's conventions and the "beaten paths" so familiar to readers of travel literature. Vyvyan's delineation of the research needed to discover even unreliable information about the area signifies that, decades later, northern travellers still needed a strength of resolve to respond to the lure of the North's untrodden spaces.

But, just as she ignored the women who preceded her up the Rat River, Vyvyan ignored the two women travel writers who preceded her to Aklavik. At the same time, her book frequently mentions the "failed" traveller, Laura Frazeur, whose mismanagement resulted in her being abandoned by her native guides, and who did not, to our knowledge, produce a narrative of her northern travels. Like Service, Vyvyan is not above mentioning others' failures in order to heighten the suspense and the stakes of her own adventure. However, Vyvyan's omissions tend to erase women's presence in the North and represent the region as a space for explicitly male adventure. Her book ignores those women whom Vyvyan mentioned with admiration in her field notes, notably Mrs Burgland and Mrs Linklater.

Among women whose travels occurred after 1926, Isobel Wylie Hutchison (b. 1889), who spent nine weeks at Aklavik in December 1933 and January 1934, would have interested Vyvyan. The Scottish doctor's first book, *North to the Rime-ringed Sun* (1934), could have told her that a complete turnover in the non-native population of the settlement had occurred between 1926 and 1933, such that none of the people whom Vyvyan and Dorrien Smith met were still there when Hutchison visited. Vyvyan would have been intrigued to learn that Hutchison travelled from Aklavik to Edmonton by scheduled airplane, a mode of travel unavailable to her only seven years before, and a mode that made other seasons than summer accessible to northern visitors. Moreover, one of the watercolours reproduced in colour in Hutchison's book echoes one of Dorrien Smith's. *The Rocky Mountains from Aklavik (Mackenzie River in Foreground)* (facing 220), which Hutchison painted at Aklavik in December or January, depicts the same scene from a similar point of view and in the same artistic tradition as *The Wood Pile*, painted by Dorrien Smith in June or July (see below, 194). Perhaps most significant, if not necessarily to Vyvyan, is the information that a single woman of Vyvyan's era could travel in the North without the help of any of the institutions that eased the passage of the two Englishwomen. As Barbara Kelcey has shown (175-78), Hutchison's independence greatly disconcerted the RCMP and federal officials, and her seven weeks' unscheduled stay at Herschel Island in a tiny cabin with a single man (see Masik and Hutchison)—an arrangement occasioned when bad ice conditions precluded travel—was not an example that men of the North wished to see emulated. By overlooking it in her book, Vyvyan inadvertently obliged this wish. Generally, although not unaware of history, Vyvyan travelled in order to capture the essence of places and people at the moment of encounter. If these had a context for her, it was the context of the enduring grandeur of nature or the unchanging human condition. It is no surprise, then, to find that she published a dated book.

In the decade following her return from the Arctic, Vyvyan wrote those six articles about her trip, including one in the *Geographical Journal* of the RGS (eighty-four years after Isbister's account of the Rat—the first—appeared in the same journal). Her autobiography identifies her early arctic journey as a spiritual adventure which set the stage for further travels. Her immediate plans included travels in Labrador (Vyvyan to R. Hinks, 13 December 1928); however, in 1929, her life changed unexpectedly when she met and soon after married Sir Courtenay Bouchier Vyvyan. His death in 1941 left her to spend much time developing a flourishing market-garden enterprise in order to pay off the estate mortgage on Trelowarren, the Vyvyan family home (J.C.T.). Travelling and writing proceeded more regularly thereafter.

The Ladies, the Gwich'in, and the Rat makes Clara Vyvyan's *Arctic Adventure* available again. It opens a window on the western Arctic, poised, in 1926, between the dogsled and the airplane. It also marks the reappearance of an important narrative of recreational travel in the western Arctic, one of the earliest accounts of women grappling with the solitude and scale of the northern landscape. If Vyvyan saw that northern journey as a turning point in her life, leading to more conventional adventures, modern readers may see it as part of a tradition of women's northern travel that continues today with narratives such as Beth Johnson's *Yukon Wild* (1984) and Victoria Jason's *Kabloona in the Yellow Kayak* (1995), a tradition testifying to the personal rewards of wilderness travel.

A NOTE ON THE TEXT

The Ladies, the Gwich'in, and the Rat reprints the text of *Arctic Adventure*. Because, in 1961, the preparation of the book for publication was flawed, errors of spelling and some punctuation have here been corrected, paragraphing has been occasionally condensed, and capitalization and forms for times, dates, and currencies have been standardized. Vyvyan's penchant for hyphenated words has been gently reined in; otherwise, the text is as she published it. Several pages of the edited typescript have survived, and these indicate that in 1960 Vyvyan strenuously resisted the suggested corrections of an enthusiastic young editor in the employ of Peter Owen, her English publisher (the book was distributed in Canada by Copp Clark), but she did trim her original typescript by some 9,800 words. The source for some of this deleted material is likely the portions of her field notes that do not appear in her book. All such passages have been set in italics in Appendix One. Readers can conveniently compare the publication to the writing done during the journey, and consider what additions and shaping into book form took place thirty-five years later.

Editorial notes based on Vyvyan's chapters and field notes appear after Appendix Two. In order not to interrupt the flow of the book, no note numbers have been introduced into the text. Instead, where a note has been prepared to widen the context of Vyvyan's text, it is introduced by the quotation (in bold) of the passage to which it relates. Of course, the notes are arranged by chapter and in order within each chapter.

Any editorial notes prompted by passages that appear only in Vyvyan's or Dorrien Smith's field notes have been placed at the end of each of the chapter divisions in the editorial notes section. They appear under the chapter whose events correspond to the date of the particular field note. To facilitate their use, the dates covered by each chapter are given in parentheses in the editorial notes, after the chapter number and title.

Lady Vyvyan's Arctic Adventure

Contents

I
Dreaming
of the Journey

In 1913 a school-friend of mine went with her father to San Francisco and thence on a tourist steamer to Alaska. She sent me, from Skagway, a volume of Robert Service's poems and a letter describing vast and desolate tracts of muskeg country.

That letter and those poems haunted my daydreams for years. There were certain lines that filled me with a yearning restlessness.

I've stood in some mighty-mouthed hollow
That's plumb-full of hush to the brim.
. . .
I am the land that listens, I am the land that broods.
. . .
Have you gazed on naked grandeur where there's nothing else to gaze on ....
. . .
Big mountains heaved to heaven ...
black mountains where the rapids rip and roar.
. . .
And the wild is calling, calling ... let us go.

As for my friend's letter, I lost it long ago but I never forgot her description of that wild and silent land.

Some 12 years later Gwen Dorrien Smith and I were sitting down with an atlas between us discussing the wild places of the earth. I quoted some of those poems and we turned the pages of the atlas to North America.

What about Alaska for our next journey? We had tried each other out in a rough trip through the Balkans in 1924 and we each considered the other to be adequately tough for a new, a longer and a more exacting adventure.

In the event we did, both of us, prove to be adequately tough, and the adventure did prove to be more exacting.

Looking back now on this journey, I find it difficult to connect it with myself at all. I see our two selves, a pair of strangely small, foreshortened figures, setting off to travel steerage across the Atlantic and second class across Canada; consorting, on a steamer journey down the Mackenzie River, with characters as remote from our own way of living as characters in some ancient book; donning breeches, puttees, Everest cotton coats, broad-brimmed hats and mosquito veils, and setting off by canoe with two Indian guides into country that held no human homes for a stretch of 300 miles. We had cut ourselves loose from all our customary habits, occupations and preoccupations.

Then I see us as two human atoms in a vast country, paddling our canoe alone down a river bathed, at midnight, in golden sunshine. Paddling whence? Paddling whither? And for what purpose? Perhaps it was for the sole purpose of remembering always the silence of the Yukon, a silence that was broken only by the echo of some northern raven croaking, and that echo travelling away from us through leagues of forest towards the North Pole and the land of permanent ice.

That journey, seen now in retrospect, does not seem to have any connection with the life that we lived before and after. We can only view the scenes dispassionately, as onlookers. Moreover, in re-reading my diary two things strike me forcibly. Among all the people that we met I cannot remember any faces except the face of Professor Innis, yet certain rivers, mountains, forests, glaciers, birds and rapids, remain vivid as if I had seen them this morning. Also I realise that there is a great gulf between the "I" of today who is writing this book in a retrospective mood and the more superficial, younger, irresponsible "I" who made that journey so many years ago.

Given this lapse in memory and this gulf in time, how can I be sure that I have dealt truly with the story, that I am not crediting the "I" of yesterday with the somewhat wider outlook of the "I" of today?

Such is the transforming influence of time that what once were actual adventures lived fully and dangerously can become, in memory, a series of flat pictures or a story related in a book about dead persons. So little of our lives do we spend in the heart of action. Before we made that journey, Alaska was only a daydream. Now it is little more than a memory.

I am only trying to recapture, with the help of letters and diaries, the middle state, the actuality of life when we made that journey from Cornwall to Alaska in the summer months of 1926, remembering, as I write, the prayer of Henry van Dyke:

"Teach me to see the local colour without being blind to the inner light."

2 We Plan the Journey

So there we were throughout the autumn of 1925, deep in study of North American maps and books.

On the Canadian side there were, we discovered, three routes into Alaska and none of them seemed to be easy; the Mackenzie River route was apparently the least difficult. As the plans for our journey became more definite, the difficulties became more evident. There was never any question of going to Alaska by sea and returning the same way, for Gwen and I shared a rooted dislike of returning on our tracks, even if it were a case of walking to our nearest village and back, so, having decided on the Mackenzie route, we planned, after crossing the Divide, to make our way west and then south to the Alaskan coast, returning by steamer down the Pacific seaboard of Canada.

At the end of that sea voyage we might visit, in Vancouver Island, an old friend of Gwen's, a middle-aged misfit who had left her family to seek freedom overseas. No doubt she would take us in as paying guests while we explored the island.

The actual route of our journey was beginning to take shape but the difficulties were legion and we began to wonder how we could possibly get information about dates, seasons, equipment and communications. When would the ice break up and let us in and when would it freeze again and prevent us getting out? Where should we obtain a time-table for steamer travel and full details about canoes and guides? Also there was the burning question of money. Would we ever be able to afford the trip? Our families were becoming extremely cynical about the project and we were becoming somewhat depressed when one kind person changed the whole outlook.

This person was our friendly neighbour Leonard Cunliffe, a Director of the Hudson's Bay Company; when he heard of our plan he gave us warm encouragement and wrote to Canada to get the information we wanted. Then one day he arrived with a letter from Winnipeg, written to Mr A. Brabant, the managing director of the Alberta and Arctic Transportation Company Limited. The letter was from Edmonton, dated January 11th 1926.

Dear Sir

PROPOSED TRIP TWO ENGLISH LADIES
TO MCPHERSON THENCE TO PACIFIC COAST

Replying to your letter asking whether it is possible to get from the Mackenzie River to the Pacific by either
  (A)   Fort McPherson, Porcupine River, Dawson and Skagway.
  (B)   Peel River, Little Wind River, Loch Lomond, Seela Pass to Dawson.
  (C)   Liard and Dease Rivers across Cassiar Mountains and Telegraph Creek down the Stikine River.
  Trip (a) which is generally known as the Peel River Portage. A tourist by the name of Mrs Laura Frazeur, who is a professor in a classical University near Chicago, went down on the 2nd trip of the *Distributor* last year and went across this Portage accompanied by two Indians whom she engaged at Aklavik. It took her six and a half days to go from McPherson to La Pierre House. At this latter point she engaged passage in a gas boat belonging to Jackson Brothers, as far as Fort Yukon, where she wirelessed Fairbanks for a plane and flew to that point. From there she went by the American Government Railway to the Gulf of Alaska and thence to Seattle. Not using plane and going upstream to Dawson from Fort Yukon and thence to Skagway and Vancouver, instead of going downstream to the American Government Railway, we estimate that the time occupied from Edmonton to Vancouver would be about 50 days provided that close connections were made with Jackson Brothers' gas boat at La Pierre House and Steamer at Fort Yukon. We estimate the cost of this trip for two ladies at thirteen hundred and fifty dollars.
  Trip (b) which Colonel Cornwall calls the Police or Fitzgerald route. Acting on your suggestion we interviewed the Colonel re this route, and he says that he never went over it, but from what he has heard about it, it is a winter route,

and then only for hardy and seasoned travellers. He states that to organise a comfortable summer trip over it supplies would have to be distributed during the previous winter, and a whole host of packers required with the tourists, which would be very expensive, if the packers could be secured, which he doubts. We think that it would be unwise to recommend this route, and cannot put a time or cost estimate on it.

Trip (c) Liard, Cassiar and Stikine River to Wrangell, Alaska. We think that it should be placed in the same category as Trip (b), therefore unwise to recommend. We have not the data to give a time or cost estimate.

We beg to attach you copy of memorandum furnished by Mr H.A.O. Warner of this city, which is very complete and we think reliable, as Mr Warner made the trip via the Rat, Bell and Porcupine Rivers. He also made the trip over the police route from McPherson, but in winter. We will endeavour to find out dates Jackson Brothers' gas boat will leave La Pierre House, calling dates of steamers at Fort Yukon, going up and downstream, and forward same to you upon receipt.

When Colonel Cornwall went across to the Yukon, he followed the same route as Mr Warner describes in attached memorandum. Apart from special clothing, the equipment for the trip would be found at our Posts.

Yours faithfully,
(sgd.) L. Romanet,
GENERAL MANAGER.

We were to find in Mr Brabant a staunch friend when we tackled our outfitting at Edmonton and in due course we were to discover that the Rat River, so cursorily mentioned in this letter, proved to be our most formidable obstacle in the whole journey. The memorandum by Mr Warner was a detailed document of 15 pages which gave invaluable information about the McPherson, Husky, Rat, La Pierre House and Fort Yukon route that we now decided to follow.

When we had both read the letter and then the memorandum it seemed as if we were already half way to Alaska. We looked at each other. Gwen remarked: "Sounds all right." I do not remember what I said but I never can forget what I felt. Was the road to the Islands of the Blest opening before us?

During the next few months Mr Cunliffe kept up a lively correspondence with his friends in Canada; he gave us an introduction to Mr Brabant in Edmonton, from which town we should have to set out for the Mackenzie River; he obtained details about expenses, dates of steamers and guides. Finally he sent a wireless telegram to the Hudson's Bay post at Aklavik on the Mackenzie Delta, to engage a canoe for us and two Indian guides who would take us up the Rat River as far as La Pierre House. This place stood on the Divide and was, we understood, an Indian settlement where we could find a guide to take us downriver into the Yukon after we had dismissed our own two guides who would walk back over the muskeg to Aklavik. Since La Pierre House was marked in the atlas, we came to look upon it as the key pin of our expedition but actually it brought us only disillusion, as I shall relate in due course.

Incidentally our good neighbour quite unconsciously smoothed the way for us in other directions. He was a man of wealth and repute and my mother was Victorian enough to regard these two attributes, especially when they were united, with veneration; she therefore changed her attitude completely. She eased my financial position by allowing me to sell out £100 worth of shares from a trust fund and then she began boasting in the village about our forthcoming journey. As for Gwen, whose parents were dead, she scraped together all her savings and collected her sketching materials, hoping that they might enable her to earn some dollars. We realised that our money must be hoarded to meet the heavy expenses of the guides and we therefore booked steerage passages in the *Empress of Scotland* from Southampton to Quebec.

As the time drew near for us to sail, England was in the throes of the great railway strike. There were anxious moments. In those days we were not accustomed to using cars for long journeys and as my mother used hers mainly for station-work and church-going, it was a major upheaval to get her to send us to Southampton. However, where others' soft persuasiveness would often fail, Gwen could manage my parent by taking much for granted with a certain abruptness of manner that was habitual to her and we duly set off for Southampton by car on the great adventure, sailing from there on May 15th.

The serious traveller can never return home unchanged, though at what particular stage of his journeying the old man is replaced by the new, it is not easy to discover.

It is almost impossible to define this spiritual change. Sometimes in a letter or a book the reader may gain a sense of unseen forms hovering like shadows in the background of the scene described. In a diary or a record of travel there is always much, of importance, that must remain for ever in that region which we call "on the wing" or "between the lines," a region where the forms are not only dim but also different. They are like forms seen in a dream and they dissolve when one tries to register them among precise memories. The journey to Alaska was certainly unlike any I had ever made before. Whether some of its spiritual value will be apparent between the lines of this record I cannot tell.

3 *Southampton to Edmonton*

Diary. May 15, 1926.

Left Southampton in SS *Empress of Scotland* 1:30 p.m. About 7 p.m. heard the engines stop and going up on deck found ourselves inside Cherbourg harbour in the embrace of two long stone piers. Gray evening, gray town, white-gray cliffs. Cold wind. SS *Aquitania* near harbour mouth silhouetted on orange sky, gigantic, four-funnelled, raised high out of the water as if she would assert her independence, funnels sloping backward made her look like some monster about to spring; wonderful picture, that ship against orange sky.

The tender was bringing on emigrants, shawled women, children in striped garments, men carrying bundles or little wooden chests, Czecho-Slovaks and other East European peoples. They berth for'ard separately under the name of "continental emigrants."

May 16th. Church in first-class saloon. Hot sunshine. Basked on upper deck.

May 17th. Cold and calm. Saw a whale, his tail came right out of water before he sounded.

May 18th. Cold. Wretched.

May 19th. Cold and less rough. How the hours drag.

May 20th. Engines stopped dead last night 2-6 a.m. At intervals a bell tolled in the mysterious silence. Weird stillness after throb of engines for days. On deck after breakfast. Gray-brown sea and gray fog and strange briny smell with a tang, as if it came from some unseen sea creature. Engines stopped again, we drifted or wallowed in that gray silent sea. Presently a very small iceberg came drifting by, snow-white and blue, with an excrescence like a tea-pot spout, rolling over and over in the waves and when nearly submerged looking like a line of foam.

The air grew deadly chill, the fog denser. Strained our eyes to horizon. Was it a line of foam or low cloud or spouts of steam changing now and then into a darker patch? A world of fog and water "without form and void." That strange form came drifting nearer, assumed a shape and then came quickly alongside; it was like a huge piece of mainland in ice, cut off and drifting, a sinister object with snow-white peaks and edges and dark caves in its face; breakers rolling up against it, hopelessly, uselessly, clouds of fog rising from the breakers. Strange that a purely cold thing could appear so diabolic and sinister. All day we were watching for those evil white wisps on the gray horizon. Cold was penetrating and we could not sit still even with three layers of clothing. Talked a good deal to a red-hot Irishman, one Digby Hussy de Burgh. Seemed as if we had been drifting for centuries when at 6 p.m. fog cleared and we steamed ahead.

May 21st. Cold but sunny. Passed Cape Race at midnight. When it was getting dark saw island of Anticosti, gray outline with snow on flattish high top and the gray face of it streaked with snow and again gray sea and gray sky; most impressive. Passengers swarming on deck and more sociable.

May 22nd. Steamed all day along Gulf of St Lawrence, right bank hidden in haze and distance, left shore a dismal country, snow patches on brown grass among brown trees, lines of huts along the bank. Saw a large whale and 11 eider-ducks.

Sunday, May 23rd. Quebec at 6 a.m., dismal, brown and rainy, deserted wharves. For four hours we were penned, herded, moved about and kept waiting for train in vast halls where YWCA, Red Cross and every other possible organization ever known had little side-rooms. Into the train at last for Montreal.

The first lap of the journey was over and we had crossed the Atlantic without extreme discomfort. Actually there were two divisions in steerage passengers and while we were all berthed aft, the East Europeans, being subject to an infectious eye disease, were kept by themselves for'ard. In fact, while we were waiting for the customs at Southampton a man had come round to all steerage passengers, approaching each one without any warning, to turn up our eyelids and examine our eyes. It was a startling experience for us both and Gwen had been highly indignant.

We had been given a two-berth second class cabin because the ship was over-crowded aft. When the stewardess came to call us in the morning she would say: "Your cabin is a little ice-box; most refreshing." Fortunately for us Gwen's fists were strong enough to open any hole porthole which was screwed down. At meal times and on deck we experienced the full flavour of our steerage companions who did not often change their clothes. The worst thing that we had to face was the stuffiness of the dining room where we had second sittings, during which the air always seemed to taste of cabbage. There was, of course, over-crowding on deck. One almost had to walk on women and children if one moved about at all. Among our fellow-travellers the Irishman, Digby Hussy de Burgh, was as delightful as his name, incurably eloquent, with a spate of scintillating ideas about things seen and unseen. Our planned journey into Alaska filled him with excitement. He was returning to his home, a small island off the coast of British Columbia and there were many other islands in that part, he told us, islands that were simply waiting for pioneers who would settle there and populate them. "I could find you an island," he said, looking at us with admiration and speaking with his easy Irish flow of words, "it's a grand life out there it is and it's grand pioneers you two girls would make." The two "girls," being over 40, did not feel like accepting his plan for populating a strange island in the Pacific or indeed any island at all.

One of the strangest things about travel is that one's memory loses so much and so many of the things seen, loses them completely or only remembers them with wavy outlines; yet those who study mind and memory aver that nothing in one's life experience is lost and each large or small event only needs the right words or the right recurrence to release it.

Hardly anything of our long journey from Quebec to Winnipeg remains with me now, although with the help of my diary I can recapture certain fragments of experience, can see through the train window glimpses of the country flying past, lakes, rivers, dark firs, green-yellow poplars just breaking into leaf, mile after mile of monotonous flat country lined with untidy shacks, a bittern standing hump-shouldered in a pool, sheets of white trillium and some beautiful *Erythronium*, birch, spruce and a maple with red flowers and many leagues of a low shrub, like heather, called *Cassiope*. I can also record the mere fact that we spent several hours in Montreal and had supper at a hostel for 35 cents, about 18 pence each, returning afterwards with reluctance to our tourist sleepers on the train. There were 28 bunks in a coach and every window was shut and the stuffy heat was infernal; only a small slit beside each bunk let in enough air to keep us alive. We dressed lying down and breakfasted in the dining car for $1.50 between us.

After two days we reached Winnipeg where we had arranged to stop at a hotel, partly owned by a Cornish cousin. We had introductions to this cousin's two friends in Winnipeg, men who proved very helpful during our 24-hours stay. One of them, Gordon Mactavish, actually came to meet our train and at once spotted what he took to be two English women but when he saw us both making for the exit as if we knew our way about he thought we could not be strangers so he refrained from making himself known. This we only discovered after supper when we had made contact with him and were sitting in our hotel lounge talking about my cousin, our Rat River journey, Arctic exploration and many other things. He was already like an old friend.

"I reckon," he said, "that two women who can walk out of a strange station with that determined look on their faces will be able to make the Rat River all right, though it's a tough journey."

This attitude we were to meet continually. Because we acted not like lost sheep but like independent women, we met with admiration that was often embarrassing to me and always distasteful to Gwen.

With our new friend we talked long into that night about the Arctic and its history, which was his favourite subject, and he was only prevented by pressing business from joining our expedition. The next day was kaleidoscopic, from the moment when he came for us at 9 until we boarded the train at about midnight.

We visited Gordon Mactavish's flat, saw his Arctic books, tasted pemmican and borrowed a rifle and a book on wild flowers. We visited two banks, the Hudson's Bay Company's office and stores, the museum and a bookshop, acquiring information all the time; we never wasted a moment. We called on the other friend to whom we had been given an introduction, Mr Christie; we found him in his office and the two men, with a charming Lady Tupper who was vital and well-read, took us out to lunch at Fort Garry. Mr Christie was a grand elderly man with rugged features; how wonderful it would have been, I thought, had Rembrandt been alive to paint him.

The parliament house and parks, a drive beside the Assiniboine River and the Red River, the sight of exciting birds, flickers, orioles, grackles, then tea in the delightful century-old Fort Garry Club; all these things are telescoped in memory but I can still recapture the sense of peace and coolness when, towards the end of that day, we dined at Mr Christie's home, with him, his wife and son and Gordon, in a beautiful room overlooking the river.

All that day we were treated like celebrities. When strangers heard that we were going alone into the Klondike by the Rat River, with two Indian guides, some expressed admiration, others horror and several said with finality: "You will be eaten alive by mosquitoes." One or two were filled with envy, but even these added that it was "a tough proposition."

Among all these conflicting opinions the enthusiasm of our new friend, Gordon Mactavish, and the quiet approval of Mr Christie were like fixed stars keeping us to our course and when, that evening, the two men put us into our tourist sleepers we both felt rather humble. We realised, for the first time, the difficulty of our undertaking and the forces of nature that would be arrayed against us. We wondered if we should have strength to overcome those forces and fulfil the expectations of our new friends. The phrase "You will be eaten alive by mosquitoes" haunted us throughout our journey across Canada. Sometimes a greenhorn used the words, each adding his own horror-tale and then we would pay little attention but when we met old-timers who had actually travelled by that route into the Klondike we could not light-heartedly forget their warnings. Next morning we woke to find ourselves passing through a lovely fresh valley with rolling slopes, a river, singing birds and a feeling of spring in the air. All day we looked out on plains and ridges. The land appeared to be richer than in eastern Canada and the pools, lakes and rivers were teeming with ducks and waders. This was a strange contrast to the bleak brownness of snow-bound Quebec.

We slept two nights on the train and early on the second morning arrived in Edmonton where we were doomed to spend four nights and days in making the final preparations for our canoe trip. At last we had reached the starting point of our journey.

4 *Outfitting in Edmonton*

We needed all our wits about us during the four days we spent in Edmonton procuring steamer tickets, information and outfits. However much hearsay or book-knowledge one may absorb about any planned adventure, the actual transition from daydream to reality will always come as a shock. Hitherto we had enjoyed our timetable journey by land and sea. Now we began to feel like pioneers about to set foot on an unknown road. Until now we had done nothing but read and dream and provide ourselves with clothes that might or might not prove suitable for our undertaking, but at Edmonton we had come to an end of spoon-fed travel and had to begin making our own decisions.

The first thing that shocked us into realising that we must now depend on ourselves was a telephone call. We were unpacking our bags in a large expensive room at a large expensive hotel. How we had landed there I do not now remember, it was not our natural milieu—perhaps our Winnipeg friends had recommended it. We were greatly surprised by this call because we had only been in Edmonton half an hour, our introductions were still in our pockets and we knew not a single person in the town. I answered the call and, putting my hand over the mouthpiece, said to Gwen: "A reporter, a woman, asking questions about our trip. You answer her."

Gwen advanced to the telephone. "Who are you? Miss Moon did you say?" A pause. "Time enough to interview us when we've done something," and she banged down the receiver. Had Miss Moon been present, Gwen would have given her what Tennyson described as "a stony British stare." She always preferred action to words.

We then set out for the Hudson's Bay Company's office, with a letter from Mr Cunliffe to Mr Brabant. We did not find in this potentate of the famous business company, isolated in his inner office like a spider at the heart of a web, a genial ready-made friend like our friends in Winnipeg, but he was consistently efficient and kind, putting us in touch with helpful people and forwarding our plans. It was thanks to him that Mr Warner came, that very afternoon, to our hotel for a long talk. Here at last was someone who could give us first-hand and recent information about the Rat. He cleared up several obscure points.

First: It would take us at least ten days to track up the Rat, the Indian guides pushing the canoe while we walked through the brushwood. It would be necessary to dismiss them at La Pierre House because even so they would have four whole days walking back to Aklavik over soft muskeg country. Yes, the mosquitoes would be bad, we must take veils and mosquito bars. Second: We could buy our paddles and tump line at Aklavik with the canoe. Third: The Indians would bring their own rifles and fishing lines. Fourth: On an average, we should need three pounds of food per person per day. Fifth: We could re-provision certainly at Old Crow and possibly at La Pierre House, so there was no need to carry food up the Rat for more than 12 days; this would allow us a margin. Moreover we might shoot a goose.

Then he warned us about our relations with the Indian guides who would not take orders from anyone; we must treat them on a friendly and equal footing. One woman had failed in this respect and they had refused to continue up the Rat with her. She had to return and take another route with another party.

During that day we spent much time in stores and shops ordering provisions from a list furnished by Mr Brabant's office. Then the manager of the great HB Company's store, Mr Dynes, drove us round Edmonton in his Buick. It is a well-placed town in wooded country on the river Saskatchewan, with fine buildings set in open spaces. Every small house is equipped with water, telephone and electric light, everything seemed cleaner and more comfortable than at home, but how much energy had been expended on cleanliness and comfort? All the energy they had? Was there any left for spiritual adventures? Such thoughts flashed through my mind while Mr Dynes was saying: "This country is just full of optimism." Canadians seemed tremendously proud of their own achievements. Too much optimism, like tropical sunshine, can make one long for the coolness of humble shade.

H.A.O (Harry) Warner (left) and Judge Lucien Dubuc, aboard SS Distributor, 1924. PAA A3709 (detail).

After supper Gwen sketched from our window while I sat dreaming on the terrace, with beautiful lights twinkling across the river.

Next day we bought rifle ammunition, brandy, mosquito bars to pitch above our sleeping bags and other oddments. Then we bought our Mackenzie River steamer tickets. They wanted us to pay for berths and meals by daily reckoning on board. Having heard that unmelted ice would often cause delays, we stood out for the original quotation and paid about £35 each for the whole trip to Aklavik. Then we cashed large cheques. Since there were no banks in the northern settlements and the expenses of the guides would be heavy, we each took with us over £100 in notes, slung round our necks in bags.

That afternoon Mr Warner came to tea again, bringing photographs and documents with information about the North.

In general conversation people spoke of "The North" without adding the word "country," merging the high latitudes of Alaska and Canada. We began to feel that this "North" was not a territory but a personality at once alluring, compelling and sometimes cruel. Mr Warner was under its spell, we could sense that as he sat in the hotel lounge telling us some of his own story and giving us hints about our journey. He was obviously not a hard-bitten pioneer nor a gold-seeker but an idealist with a passionate love for lonely places, still seeking for something that he had never found.

He had gone north as a teacher and had failed. Nevertheless he had built his own house and a boat and was full of ideas and schemes, some of which he had put forward in a memorandum written for the government, dealing with the fur trade, police, missions and Eskimos. He was eloquent about missions and missionaries.

"After 1900 years," he said, "the Church remains the most unpractical of all our institutions. If a missionary is a zealot he is 'short on practicality' and if he isn't a zealot he generally fails as a missionary."

He turned to the subject of Indians, their greed and fawning ways and the influence of the white man that had destroyed their ancient dignity. Then, reverting to personal matters, he told us about several of his own experiences. One in particular I remember. He was camping with some Indians when a grizzly bear, smelling fried bacon, came into the camp. There was the bear, quite close to them, with a red mouth in a large head and a shambling powerful body. An Indian was leaning against a tree, when he saw the bear he tried to shoot but there was no shell in his weapon. The Indian ran towards a stream and Warner followed, feeling the bear's hot breath behind him. The animal blundered into the fire, burnt his feet in hot cinders and retired. "Grizzlies will never attack," our friend assured us.

During the next few weeks we were to hear many such stories. Sometimes we felt it was a case of the old-timer drawing the long bow in order to astonish the newcomers. Yet even if we discounted some of the sensational details of these stories, their background was always so full of local colour that we could only listen with enjoyment. It was not for us to try and separate the true from the false.

North Saskatchewan River and Hotel Macdonald, Edmonton, c. 1915. NAC PA11229.

Hotel Macdonald c. 1915. NAC PA40829.

We felt that it was wonderful to meet such typically Jack-London tales, not preserved in a book, but related, face to face, by living men.

As we sat there sipping tea in the luxury hotel, we felt extremely romantic and well satisfied. We were already living through real adventures by proxy.

Next day was Sunday and we went by tram into the country near Capital Hill and wandered about looking for wild flowers. These were the beginning of a collection that Gwen had promised to bring home for a friend of hers in the Kew Gardens Museum. We little guessed then how difficult it would be to press flowers with bare hands, standing up on the edge of a river in a cloud of mosquitoes. We found a dwarf *Polygonum*, leaves of the *Linnaea borealis* and of a *Pyrola*, and many other treasures.

On Monday we lived as in a nightmare, what with last moment shopping, sociable encounters that we could not avoid and the over-heated air of the hotel. Everyone whom we met, when they heard the words "Rat River" in answer to their questions, would exclaim: "Why, you'll *breathe* mosquitoes!" or "My! but I guess you're making some trip!" Or they would repeat the old refrain: "You'll be eaten alive."

As for the shopping, some instinct bade us ignore those reported provisions at La Pierre House and Old Crow, so we bought food for the whole journey from Aklavik to Fort Yukon. We also bought beads, silk, bicarbonate of soda—which was to prove invaluable when rubbed on mosquito bites—Viscol, bandages, a tin basin, a small axe, two pillows, soap, forks, matches, a tin of Flit, cold cream and many other trifles. We sent off four suitcases of our civilized belongings to Vancouver by rail. Why, we wondered, did we travel with so much luggage when our one aim was simplicity? Our baggage for the northern journey consisted of six canvas bundles, the rifle, one despatch-case, one suitcase and a rucksack, weighing in all 175 pounds. Our food packages, three pounds a head for four persons for 21 days, weighed 252 pounds.

Early next morning we left Edmonton by taxi for Dunvegan. At the railway station there was quite a crowd to see off the immensely long train. It was heading towards "the end of steel" near Waterways; from that settlement we were to take the first steamer to go down the Mackenzie River since the ice had frozen up in the previous September.

We bundled into the train with Mr Brabant and our new companions, mounted police, an archdeacon, a French-Canadian judge, nuns, trappers, traders. The train moved off in a leisurely fashion on its 24-hours journey. In the North there is never any need to hurry.

5 *Lure of the North*

During the journey from Edmonton to Waterways all our fellow-travellers seemed to belong to a world hitherto unknown. Their talk was either of people who had gone "in" to the North or of people who had come "out." Was this country a prison or a paradise, we wondered. There was the French-Canadian judge, going to Aklavik to preside at an Eskimo murder trial. "Don't wait for an introduction," he said, as he invited us to his stateroom on the train to have a chat and a cigarette. There were North-West Mounted Police, returning to their Arctic outposts, magnificent types like so many of the men in this force. There was a rough-looking young man whom we took for a gold prospector but we discovered later that he was going to Aklavik as counsel for the defence, knowing no word of Eskimo and nothing of his client. He told us highly coloured stories of the Eskimo attitude to murder, marriage and old age. "They kill their old folk," he assured us, "it's a case of 'Dear old Ma, she's 90, go fetch your gun.'" We listened to his fantastic tales, prick-eared, silent and dubious, just as we listened to those other tales of grizzly bears and ice and starvation. Some of the Eskimo stories were, no doubt, already out of date and others were exaggerated but some were true and we soon discovered that, in the north country, truth can indeed be stranger than fiction. We were fair game to those men of the North who love to spin a yarn to the ignorant and the innocent, for we always listened eagerly.

We reached Waterways in 24 hours; the place was nothing but an enormous new shed, beside which were some slides for baggage, and a scow, and a barge lying in the river. All the 40 passengers, including nine women, sat about on

"The End of Steel."
Waterways Station, Alberta
and Great Waterways
Railway. n.d. PAA A3936.

woodpiles or wandered among willows and exquisite poplars that were very tall and slender with silver stems. Then at last a tug came up the river with another scow and took us eight miles down the river to where the SS *Athabasca* was moored.

There followed two days of delay and confusion. There were tugs and scows coming and going, upriver and downriver, fetching goods, unloading goods into the *Athabasca*; there was the king's birthday when our tug came alongside without any load; there was a bag of tools at Waterways to be fetched for the sergeant-major of police and a final delay while the engineer was having his hair cut, before, at last, we steamed off down the Mackenzie River towards the delta which lies more than 1500 miles north of Waterways.

During those two days Gwen and I wandered about the forest that hemmed us in on either shore. There were pale poplars among dark firs; there was green water, utterly still. Among those poplars there hung a silence so heavy that it seemed as if no voice had ever spoken or echoed there. There were swallow-tail butterflies and sooty terns and exciting flowers, *Trientalis, Ledum*—which is known as the Indian tea-plant—*Kalmia* and *Sisyrinchium*. Among those trees we had to wear our mosquito veils. Whenever we went ashore there was much hand-shaking and heartiness. The people of this new country gave us a most refreshing sense of equality that at once swept away our lifelong class distinctions.

The archdeacon, a fine upstanding friendly man, was the first person we met who had actually travelled up the Rat by canoe, for Mr Warner had made the journey in winter over snow and ice. The parson, with four or five guides, had towed his wife and baby upriver in an Eskimo skin boat and had made the portage over the Divide into the Yukon. Often he had been obliged to wade up to his chest in the current. We listened to his stories anxiously. Later, when we were alone, Gwen said: "No good getting the wind up." The same thought was uppermost in both our minds. If we had to take four or five guides instead of two, how would our money last out?

Once the *Athabasca* had pulled out into the river, heading north, we seemed to enter a new existence and new impressions followed each other so quickly that many of them became blurred in outline. Yet I can still recapture certain scenes and conversations that seemed to express the essence of our whole journey, of the new land wherein we were travelling and the new outlook that was so soon to become our own.

… We are heading downstream towards the great Mackenzie Delta and our great adventure, only four days out from Edmonton, but already the North has cast a spell upon us and not only on us, for every one of the motley crowd on this steamer is travelling under this same spell. Police returning to Ellesmere Land or Melville Island or northern Canada, each one summoned back to his post of duty; trappers lured back, after a spell in some city, to their solitary huts by the strength of nostalgia; legal men proceeding to the Eskimo murder trial, missionary and trader, storekeeper and nun, all are travelling north with a peculiar elation as if a light were shining there. Only three, besides Gwen and myself, are simply tourists. "I just have that uneasy feeling I want to go North," says the man from Arizona, puzzled at his own awakening imagination. The other two observe with surprise that "there's no need to hurry in the North."

This river is full of shifting sandbanks. Our shallow-draught steamer is propelled by a paddle-wheel and fed by wood fires; every few hours we have to tie up to the river bank beside a pile of logs, in order to replenish fuel. Half-breeds saunter ashore, lithe as cats, dark-skinned, clad in mechanics' overalls, green

SS Athabasca River.
n.d. PAA 12104.

gauntlet gloves for protection from splinters of wood and brightly embroidered moccasins. In single file they return up the gangway plank on board, each with a log on his shoulder. The air is fragrant with resin.

Now we have loaded up and pushed out into mid-stream. Two scows are lashed to our bows, piled with canoes, tins of gasoline and packing cases. Navigation is slow and uncertain, last year's chart always being useless, for every summer, after the melting of the ice, new shoals and sand-bars are formed and old ones are washed away. At 9 the sun has just set and we steam on towards the northern afterglow, with the river widening out ahead of us. Whither are we drifting? Into the north land? Into infinity? Who knows? Who cares? A blue haze hangs on the left bank among dark spruces. On the right are ghostly white-stemmed poplars like slender marble pillars. Ahead the water is amethyst and purple, still as death, and in the western sky there hangs one molten cloud, casting into the water a fiery reflection.

Slowly the steamer pushes on, drawing four feet of water; those barges lashed beside the bows act as feelers for the unknown channel, since they only draw three feet. Now and then there is a woolly movement underfoot as the steamer goes bumping over a sandbar. On the foremost barge two half-breeds stand with sounding poles to right and left, and each time they bring up the pole they slide one hand along to indicate the depth of water, holding it up for a second against the sunset light. The captain from his wheel-house watches them and steers accordingly. With a regular rhythm the poles are lowered and raised and lowered again, and we move slowly on. In this stretch of the river there are shifting shoals for more than 30 miles. Five feet, four feet, four feet again, three and a half. Now, those white-stemmed poplars are no longer gliding by, but are standing still and our great paddle-wheel is churning sand with fruitless energy.

"Get out the canoe ahead there," shouts the captain.

A canoe is slid over the edge of a scow and the mate steps in, followed by a lad. The mate is a dusky half-breed, tall, hawk-faced, hawk-shouldered, with a look of great strength, as if he had led a life of struggle with elemental forces. He takes the pole and stands up in the bows as the lad begins to paddle. The canoe moves forward and we watch that darkened figure sounding to right and left, holding up the pole in silence, silhouetted on the water in his fragile craft.

Sometimes a nation's story may be spellbound in one gesture, or one scene, as in that Volga boat-song scene wherein the Russian serfs are depicted straining on a rope while they chant the unending sorrow of creatures who toil without hope or joy. Here, with the silhouette of one frail canoe moving forward through uncharted waters, with the stooping figure of the mate, patient and forceful, black against the water, there is portrayed another story: the story of those pioneers who matched their strength against the unmeasured, unrelenting spaces of the ice-bound North. Now the mate has sounded where the current is 13 feet, calmly he lays down his pole and the canoe is paddled into a backwater. Then the occupants overtake and board the steamer, hauling up their little craft as we pass downstream. We move forward without haste, with a memory of that dark enduring figure silhouetted on the Athabascan twilight …

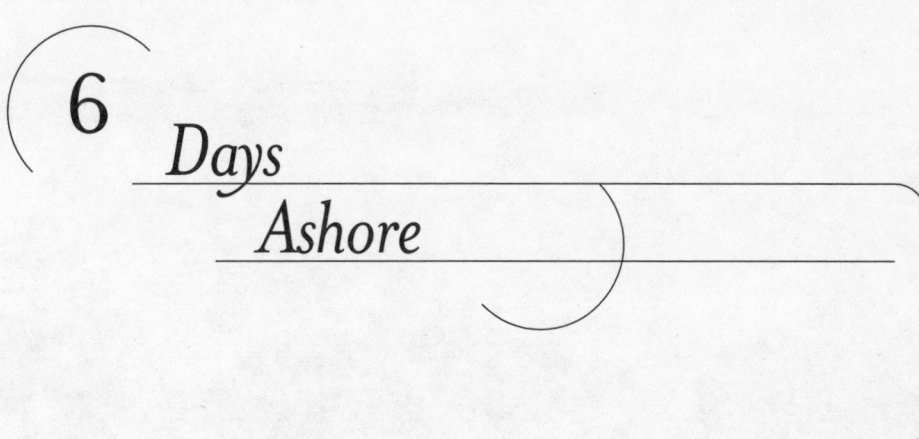

6 *Days Ashore*

We only spent a few days on board the *Athabasca* for there are unnavigable rapids below Fort Fitzgerald. Steamers have to unload there, and portage freight and passengers some 16 miles to Fort Smith where another steamer loads up for the rest of the Mackenzie River journey.

Meanwhile every hour of those few days had been full of contrasts. One day we met a sandstorm and a gale of wind and found, when we went ashore, that the mosquitoes had disappeared; we were learning to look on any breeze as a liberator. The white poplars gave way to cottonwood trees. One evening we came to deep water where the river corkscrewed between dense woods. We went up to the captain's wheelhouse to enjoy the sunset hour. The wind had died down, the sky was molten gold. The captain, a habitually silent Swiss who had come in some 45 years ago, hardly spoke at all, yet he made us feel welcome.

After passing through the western end of Lake Athabasca we went ashore for a short spell at Fort Chipewyan, a small settlement of white wood houses with rocky surroundings. Hitherto we had seen only trees and mud and grass enclosing the river. That evening we came to Fort Fitzgerald which was almost a township, though, like other inhabited places of the North it was called a settlement. It was hardly possible to believe that we had begun our river journey only a few days ago. So many new faces, so many wild stories and strange conversations, so much food for thought; the swift yet steady movement of the vast river and the thousands of trees that seemed to be passing us all the time with a mysterious greeting as they disappeared into the land of Nevermore; strange flowers and birds; the peace of dawn and sunset skies. Indeed our days had been kaleidoscopic.

SS Distributor *at*
Fort Smith, 1927.
Guy Blanchet.
NAC PA20206.

At Fort Fitzgerald and Fort Smith we became involved in an orgy of sociability. The moment after supper we hurried out to collect wild flowers and see the rapids a mile below the settlement where the Mackenzie, a vast brown river, spread out into combed and crested ripples, roaring wickedly.

We turned in early, exhausted by long daylight hours and short nights of sleep. I was ready for bed when the judge knocked at our door and summoned us to come ashore and be sociable.

"Put your clothes on over your nightgown," said Gwen. Which I did.

We went to call on the factor's wife and sat in an overheated, airless room, making conversation with our fellow-passengers since our hostess remained silent. At last the factor came in and real talk began; about moose, buffalo, trappers, trade and about a peculiar man named Hornby who had been living in the Barren Grounds on raw rabbits, eating them, fur and all, without any other meat or any fuel. At long last coffee and toast appeared and the talk dribbled on in a thinner stream about steamers, Eskimo trials, furs and the factor's new wireless.

Long after midnight we staggered out into the cool daylight world and back to bed.

Unless we arrived in the dining-saloon at 8 we got no breakfast. To gain a few minutes more in bed I would throw on a hat, coat and skirt, arriving at breakfast unwashed but, apparently, fully dressed. Gwen was indignant at such slovenly ways. "I was not brought up like that," she said. Next morning, however, as we tottered in to breakfast half sleep-bound, we noticed the frogs of the Judge's pyjamas below his half-buttoned coat. Thereafter Gwen also changed her habits and dressed in two stages, the first for show, the second for cleanliness and secu-rity.

Fort Fitzgerald was a gloomy place standing on slippery clay. We had to leave the *Athabasca* that day and hang about in a warehouse full of freight boxes and buffalo skins until we got a little roadster car to take us to Fort Smith. Away we went, bumping over black soil like a ploughed field. Our driver, half-Swede half-Eskimo, had driven buffalo teams over this portage as lately as 1911. In earlier days it took four days to drive the 16 miles through unfelled saplings. The road ended at Fort Smith in pure sand. The SS *Distributor* was still downriver in her winter quarters so we had supper at the hotel in a somewhat rough assembly of old-timers.

After supper we paid another social call with the judge and Mr Brabant.

In conversation the men of the North average one remark to five puffs at their pipe, expanding every anecdote into a full-length story, but their anecdotes are racy enough to stand the test of this dilution, their talk being rich, concentrated and highly flavoured.

The party were soon swapping yarns about mutual friends, the best story being about how old Murphy of Fort Simpson missed the priesthood, as related by himself.

"We chaps went up to the seminary at Montreal and the priest he looked us over and he sez 'All right you come back on the 23rd,' so I went away and off I goes on the toot. One day I come to meself and looks about and finds it's the 27th. 'All right,' I siz to meself, ''tis only four days late,' so I goes up to the semi-nary and sits down for a chat with the priest. Presently he sez to me, 'Do you know what day of the month it is Mr Murphy?' 'Why yes,' sez I, ''tis the 27th.' 'And do you know what month it is Mr Murphy,' sez the priest. ''Tis the month of June,' sez I. 'If my eyes serve me right Mr Murphy,' sez he, ''tis the month of August on

Conibear House
Restaurant, Hotel, and
Bakery, Fort Smith,
c. 1931–32.
PAA A7608.

Conibear Store, Fort Smith,
c. 1923. PAA 10268.

this calendar.' 'God bless me,' sez I, 'then I've been blind drunk for two months.' So I picks up me hat and out I goes an that's how I never joined the priesthood."

After the exchange of several more yarns we muttered excuses and made our escape to the river. There was the *Distributor* coming up from her winter quarters, so we retrieved our baggage from the hotel, went down to the steamer and settled into our cabin.

For six days and nights the roar of the rapids sounded in our ears while 200 tons of freight were being transported from Fort Fitzgerald to Fort Smith. For hours we would watch the pelicans, which alone range fearlessly about the waste of troubled waters, to wrest a living from the jaws of the boiling rapids. Sometimes these archaic-looking birds would huddle on a rock in mid-current, with an air of ancient wisdom, looking down their orange-coloured beaks, motionless as any Yogi in a trance. At sunset wisps of scaup and pintail would pass across the molten sky above the forest of jack pine, cottonwood and poplar on the far bank of the river.

At Fort Smith it was not a case of making friends but rather of finding them everywhere. Soon we knew many of the inhabitants, the postmaster, store-keepers, lorry-drivers, Hudson's Bay Company employees who were always courteous, Grey Nuns of the North, mounted police and the cook at the hotel. We spent much time listening to yarns with never a dull moment except when we were alone with the womenfolk. After being artificially animated for five minutes on the subjects of babies and cooking, Gwen and I would nearly expire. There would be a heavy silence while we watched the door and longed for the appearance of the men who would enliven us with tales of action and information on natural history. Among the hausfraus of the Australian bush I had often suffered a similar agonizing silence, as I sat on some verandah, hopelessly moving my body to and fro in a rocking chair until the husband should appear, full of talk about the cattle and kangaroos and wallabies, the wild birds on the plain and a large alligator in the creek, and happy intercourse would be restored.

One day we visited the hospital, a three-story building with 13 beds run by French-Canadian nuns; these Roman Catholic missions do pioneer work in growing potatoes and often they will hold on in the wilderness when the Church of England fails to do so. The Indian patients had a strange look on their faces.

On Sunday we went to the Roman Catholic church with Mr Brabant and as the Indians came along in single file he shook hands with them. We were introduced

St Ann's Roman Catholic (Grey Nuns) Hospital (est. 1914), Fort Smith, 1923. PAA 10270.

Left: Chief Pierre Squirrel, Fort Smith, 1920. NAC PA101681.

Right: A.L. McDonald, Medical Health Officer, Fort Smith, 1926. John F. Moran. NAC PA102510.

to several, including the chief, whose name was Squirrel. Mr Brabant could remember him in full war-paint and feathers, but now he wore a yachting cap and a slouching blue serge suit and had long gray hair about his shoulders. The patient expression in his glazed eyes seemed to reflect the light of ancient fires.

A bearded French priest preached in French and then in Chipewyan on the theme of "*Jesus vous aime*" in a rapid voice. Thin female voices chanted. Paper lilies and tinsel adorned the wooden church. None of the Indians appeared to be inspired or even interested. I thought of the worshippers at a mosque in the Balkans and the faces of rough Moslems for whom the heavens had opened, giving them one glimpse into a world of bliss.

Every time that we watched the pelicans we longed to visit their breeding-ground, an island near the rapids, and one morning Mr Brabant arranged for a gas boat to take us with a party upriver. We steamed across the river and anchored, then got into a canoe that danced like a cockle-shell and pulled close to an eddy below the rapids, grounding on rocks now and then until we landed on a flat pink granite islet. There was not a pelican in sight. We stood on that islet worn smooth by many floods and we looked upon that wilderness of tormented water and the debris of the forest caught and held on fangs of rock. It was a scene of utter desolation. The turbid and troubled water seemed to be flowing in all directions. There was one straight sweep of the current smooth as any pavement; here was a cauldron of brown water like a whirlpool, seething with tossed, impetuous foam; there were waves with crests flung backward against the current, and rocky islets in mid-river, each one lonely and helpless as regret. We saw neither human being nor human habitation; the only signs of mankind were some wooden frames on shore erected by Indians for drying fish and, beside our granite island, a line of floats.

On the last evening at Fort Smith Mr Brabant and the judge gave a farewell dinner, dispensing much-appreciated whisky and liqueurs. There were about 20 of us. There was much chaff about the HB Company, now more than 250 years old. At one time it had practically ruled the vast country, now it is sometimes named, in a friendly way, "Half-breed-Curse" or "Here-before-Christ." After dinner we walked over to the wireless operator's house where some danced to gramophone music while others sat smoking and exchanging yarns. Suddenly the telephone bell rang.

"All aboard," said our hosts, and we trooped back to the steamer.

A new moon looked down on the ever-troubled waters and one star shone above the spruces, but daylight still hung in the air and from the deck we could see each face in the crowd lined out on the sandbank. The roar of the rapids had become so friendly that we were hardly conscious of its voice. Slowly the half-breeds hauled up the anchor and as it came in sight they whooped and howled like wolves and laughed like children, cutting capers on the pile of boxes packed in the bows of the vessel. Last greetings fluttered to and from the shore.

"So long Bill."

"Good-bye Alice."

And then, from the whole crowd, "Hip-hip-hooray!"

In that strange northern twilight we steamed slowly out from the shore and down the river that would lead us on our long journey to Aklavik, while the friendly faces of Fort Smith receded into the land of memory.

7 Great Slave Lake

It was 9 in the evening when we came to the delta of Slave River on the shore of the great lake. The delta was dotted with islands and sandbanks. There was too much wind for our flat-bottomed vessel to venture out into the great inland sea, so we tied up in a channel no wider than a canal.

Gwen made a sunset sketch, which I still possess, brushing in the scene swiftly in parallel lines of a narrow orange bar with purple bordering lines stretched out between pale blue water and pale blue sky. Those purple borders might have been trees below and mountains above that molten glow of sunset, it was impossible to determine their nature, for the world ahead was illimitable, not broken up into any recognizable forms.

All through that night five huskies, tied up on the lower deck, were howling, passengers were stumping about outside our cabin, mosquitoes were humming in our ears.

During the next two days we made, by interrupted stages, the passage across the lake into the Mackenzie River, taking advantage of any windless hour to creep on from one lee island-shore to another, for the waters of this lake develop sea-conditions under any wind and our barge-like steamer was no sea-going craft. For one whole day we were anchored beside a wooded island where the shores were strewn with stones and timber. We landed there to collect wild flowers and found the stones were worn flat as any pavement, and decaying and decayed fragments of wood were scattered everywhere. Far away on the upper reaches of the Peace River, currents, rocks and rapids had taken toll of the forest whenever some branch or tree fell into the water and now, on this island, some of those mighty trees were no more than sawdust that would crumble in the hand.

On such a downward course a chip of wood and a whole tree trunk are tossed with equal facility. Here, on this island shore were branches, twigs, saplings and fragmentary trunks lying across each other, water-logged fragments of bark and wood, and also beds of pulpy fibrous texture into which we would sink, ankle deep, at every step. We realised, as never before, the destructive power of water and the vastness of this wild country. In the heart of the island the bush was almost free from mosquitoes. There were beds of crackling silver lichen whose moist roots are food of the caribou, and beds of deep green moss dotted with patches of the little lady's slipper, an exquisite pink *Orchis*. All about us were spruces giving out their fragrant breath in the sunshine.

We touched at Fort Resolution in the middle of the night but remained in our bunks, so we saw nothing of this trading post that is frequented by many Indians at certain times of year. Two days later we came at dawn to Hay River, an attractive settlement with Indian tents and tipis, a Church of England mission, a Roman Catholic church and the usual store, all clustered close together on the banks of the quiet lake. After an hour or two ashore there, we found ourselves moving steadily forward across the lake that was still as glass. Our world was now only sky and water in which we could detect no solid object except one seagull flying like a wraith across our bows. Far ahead, dividing sea and sky, there was a narrow green line. We could not see any break in that line, as we scanned its length, looking for the opening where the Mackenzie River flows out from the lake on its northward course.

Were we imprisoned in this fragile universe of air and water? It was one of those quintessential moments when the spirit of the world's beauty seems to come near us, saying: "Yes. You have sought me far and wide. Here I am." Certain experience, unlike harvest or coin of the realm, is not transferable, yet something impels me to try and recapture this one in words that are bound to fumble and to fail.

… We are lost in a tenuously silken web of water below and sky above where a single feather-light cloud hangs overhead. The Slave River Delta, through which we entered the lake, is out of sight and the green line of forest far ahead is rigid and unbroken. In any case, why should we wish to leave this lake? Why should we not float on for ever in a world that is so calm and beautiful? The things that we have left behind are remote and unreal, those years of dreaming and months of preparation, discomfort of travel by sea and rail, busy hours at Edmonton, new faces on the river journey. Ahead of us the unknown, mosquito-haunted and perhaps malignant Rat has no importance. We are lost in a world of clear water and clear sky which have a strange impalpable look, as if they could bear no weight and had neither beginning nor end nor purpose; no origin nor any aptitude for change. Something has touched me here and now like music on muted strings. I have come home; back to that long-lost home which, without plan or conscious purpose, I have been always seeking ...

Suddenly a voice breaks in on my reverie as I stand leaning on the rail, lost in the moment yet looking steadily toward the North. It is a harsh voice, but the words are not harsh.

"Isn't that just the quietest water you ever saw?" says a man standing beside me. I do not know if he is speaking to me or to himself, but I see that he is the man with a face like that of the villain in the drama, the man from Arizona who is travelling north on no known errand, impelled by some instinct stronger than reason. The other two tourists join us. One, a rough-spoken, hardened person whose tongue has a lash for every creed and a mocking jest for every occasion, owns to having spent a sleepless night on deck, as if in spite of himself. "That blessed sun going down behind the spruces and the light in the blessed sky all night, it just got me," he says. The other man says nothing, but his eyes have the look of a child seeing something that is not there ...

The three strolled away together and I was alone again with that stillness emanating from sky and water, that magic stillness of the North which is not the quiet of a little thing too weak to strive or cry, but the breath of a Power brooding over all.

A hush was still about us like the hush there must have been before the birth of a world. There was not a breath of wind as we steamed ahead without sense of expectation or premonition of change. There was nothing to port or starboard on which we could set foot, nothing above us that we could grasp with a hand, no familiar object within sight that we could identify. The solidity of the vessel on which we stood seemed to be an intrusion into this world. After a while the faint green line to the northward that was a narrow bar between sky and water, became more definite. A little later we could see trees fringing the lake in a dead level land that was eventually lost to sight by reason of its very flatness and immensity.

It is hard to realise the vast extent of this forested country where nature is prodigal of leagues, prodigal of trees and water and far horizons. The mere sense of spaciousness in such a country can take complete possession of a man, transmitting all his energy into that most haunting and insistent of desires, "horizon fever." Yet it can also bring him satisfaction and peace, for here, free from man-made barriers, he can embrace north, south, east and west in a glance and he feels as if he had gained in stature.

Nearer and nearer we drew to that marsh land where the Mackenzie River issues from Great Slave Lake and there, amid unnumbered shoals and islets, were ducks and loons and waders dotted on the water. We were coming back again into the world of solid forms. Meanwhile the Mother Superior of the Grey Nuns of the North, who was travelling to Aklavik to inspect a convent, had come on deck. She sat down, in her dove-gray dress and winged black coif, and when she had finished her morning meditation I joined her and we talked of many things and callings and places. Then she fell into a long silence and a little later she said quietly: "I love to look out on these spaces and feel the power of God." After that she folded her hands and fell into meditation again. I sat beside her, sharing her silence.

Just then the man from Arizona came sauntering past us. He did not utter a word yet I seemed to hear him murmuring again to himself: "Isn't this just the quietest water you ever saw." Yet the expression on his face was unchanged.

On each one of us, the great space of the North had laid its touch; on trapper, priest and tourist, clerk and trader, missionary and squaw; on those who sought for gold; on those who travelled to fulfil appointed duties; on those who travelled without purpose or desire. We were all drifting onward together, for the moment disembodied of our usual selves—onward, onward in the magic stillness of the North.

8 In and Out

The leisured tourist is an onlooker, moving so quickly from place to place that he has no time to look about him from a balanced stance. He is all too ready to invest whatever he may see with a glamorous light. Since we were mere tourists it took us some time to discover that the north country had other aspects than scenery and sunsets, but in course of time we did gain an inkling of the tragedies and hardships endured by many who dwell in that lonely land. Continually we would hear the word "in" applied to the North and "out" applied to the world we had left when we boarded the steamer; they were words indicative not merely of space boundaries or of contrast in climate but of a difference in physical and mental conditions. The mere isolation of families, is, in sickness, a major problem in the North.

One day we met a doctor who had been "in" for 15 years, in charge of a district 600 miles long.

"Don't the patients die before you get to them?" we asked.

"They do," he replied. "Sometimes they wait for me," he added drily. "For two years," he said, "I didn't like it much but now I wouldn't quit the quiet life."

Dentists are even more rare than doctors. The mother superior told me: "Oh yes, we have a doctor 600 miles down the river; there is no trouble about dentists, you see most of us have all our teeth drawn before we come in, just to make sure."

One of the Grey Nuns with whom we travelled told me her story briefly. She had come in 32 years ago in the days when there was no steamer service on the Mackenzie and the journey was made by canoe. They had shot the rapids at the peril of their lives and had often been obliged to wade ashore in their long-skirted robes when they stopped to camp for the night. "I had all my teeth out before I came in," she added, "and I have only been out once since then. Many of us do not go out at all."

One old-timer, when relating his life history, said: "I came in 40 years ago and I've never been out since. No, I haven't found no gold to speak of. Not yet." Then he added: "My mate, he came in with the Klondike rush and he just stayed around ever since."

One morning we went ashore and met a trapper living in a log hut near the woodpile that stood ready for the steamer. We fell into conversation. Times were changing for the worse in his district, he told us. "How?" we enquired. "People too thick on the ground," he said gloomily. We looked about us into the silent forest and thought of the distance to the last settlement and to the one that lay ahead. "Where's your nearest neighbour?" we asked him. "Why the settlement 200 miles down," he replied, "but now there's another trapper come in, a Belgian fellow and he's camped a hundred miles from here."

A hundred miles, it seemed, was no distance in days of winter travel by dog-team.

During a talk with a surveyor who had been living on the Barren Grounds, we realized that distance is not measurable in miles, it is a quality relative to the kind of life that one leads. Often, he had walked five miles before he had gathered enough willow shoots to make a fire for boiling tea. In that land he had seen caribou on their autumn migration, passing at the rate of some 15 to the acre for six continuous days. Apparently even the caribou like to enjoy the space of the country. Once, there had been eight inches of snow on the ground on the first of August. He seemed to have been content with that way of living.

No doubt that land is magnetic, demanding from its adherents self-sacrifice, endurance and fortitude but giving in return things that are beyond all price: strength, independence, comradeship and, best of all perhaps, the absence of any need for haste. Many a northern settler develops a sense of close unity with the land that has become his home. As for the women, their lot is apt to press more hardly on them. One does not often meet the type of a certain government official's wife who assured us that she would rather be leader in the social life of her small settlement than a mere nobody in Winnipeg or Edmonton.

Talk with any new acquaintance had become a real adventure. Among the 30-odd passengers with whom we travelled on our three weeks cruise, we did not meet one ordinary person, nor experience one dull moment; all the time we were onlookers at an exciting drama. There would be an anecdote or story that left us breathless and wondering; a halt at some settlement or woodpile and a visit ashore; an unknown flower; a new bend of the river; mile after mile of enclosing forest walls; a strange bird, some duck upon the water or woodpecker among the trees; or a bell would summon us to a meal and, sitting opposite the judge, we would listen to the table-talk with renewed astonishment. We heard much about that perennial problem of the North, mixed marriages: a practice deplored by the average white man who will go so far as to refuse to sit down at meals with the Eskimo or Indian wife of a friend.

One day, on landing at a settlement, we were introduced to Mr X, a fine upstanding Englishman with an aristocratic air. We stood on the mud bank talking with him about the Old Country, when suddenly there emerged from his cabin a shapeless squaw with an infant in a bundle on her back. He introduced her as Mrs X, and surprise cut short our flow of conversation as we shook hands with the squaw. Then we both began to talk again, in a hurry, yet trying not to betray our haste.

Many stories, in this country, are passed around like newspapers, but, unlike newspapers, they grow longer and better every time they come into new hands. One day the judge told us a tale of a mixed marriage, talking with inimitable French vivacity, flicking his eyebrows and pointing his forefinger for emphasis. After a certain mixed marriage, a formal agreement was drawn up between the two parties. Half the children were to be Roman Catholics and half Church of England; 27 children were born. Priest and clergyman ran a yearly race to get down the river first, after the melting of the ice, to assert their rights by baptism. At that time the country had no communications with the world between October and June. The bishop nearly always won the race and had acquired a majority of the little half-breeds. The births were an annual event. At last the clergyman consulted an inspector of police who advised him to get in each summer on the first steamer, taking a fire-hose, and to baptise the new infant from the deck while the bishop was stepping ashore.

Drink is another perennial problem in this country. Many a habitual drunkard has gone north in the hope of escaping from himself and his weakness, only to discover that in many settlements the sign "Prescription Drug Store" above a chemist's shop means "Drink sold here" and that there are doctors who can and will give a permit to buy liquor.

As we listened and looked about us we gained some idea of the effects of loneliness on mankind in these unpeopled latitudes; it can so easily drive a weak man to marry a native, a temperate man to become a drunkard, a sane man to madness. Later in our travels we met men who had lived so long alone that they had become "queer in the head." Thinking people will sometimes forearm themselves against the effects of solitude. There were two priests, old friends, who served lonely missions far from each other and were frozen in for many months each year. They wrote to each other weekly, leaving the letters to accumulate until such time as they could post them. They knew that reading alone cannot keep a man's mind alert, and that many a man who has always been a reader, after living alone in the Arctic for a while, will lose his interest in books. The mother superior, who spent much time in the northern convents, told me that she *had* to go out to Montreal once in every few years, to keep her mind alive.

We were beginning to learn that beyond the sunsets and the beauty of the North there was many a bitter human struggle and failure, many a slow disintegration of the human character but also many a gallant fight to retain sanity and contentment.

In my diary of our travels there are frequent references to the sky, the sunsets and their afterglow, the peacefulness of the river, also stories of men who had come "in"—and remained "in" with never a wish to revisit the busy world outside. They are brief, laconic entries, jotted down in tired moments but they awaken a whole world of memories.

Evening at Lac la Biche. An hour ashore. Beautiful lake. Smooth water. Untidy tents and half-breeds. Walked eastwards. Saw sooty terns. Cowbells. Scent of poplars. Wonderful stillness ... Had long chat with Canadian NW Policeman returning to duty on Ellesmere Land. Or he might be posted to Bernard Inlet. Interesting photographs of ice and snow. Never before met anyone who lives so near the North Pole, but he takes it as a matter of course ... Talked to a trapper returning to his solitary cabin after selling last winter's furs. These trappers talk as if they had nearly lost the power of linking one word to the next ... Perhaps they think in monosyllables. Perhaps we all think in monosyllables ... Saw wax-wing and three-toed American Woodpecker with yellow crest ... Long walk in forest. Hard to realise the vast size of this country when wandering among trees, even in a clearing no distant horizon. Trees so monotonous. No change ahead, only sometimes a glint of light between stems, light that may be sky or water. Begin to realise how a man might go mad if he walked on among trees hour after hour, day after day, at first hopefully and then hopelessly, never coming to anything else. Craving for a hill or a hummock or even one rock. We came out suddenly on the river bank at last ... Talked to an old-timer who had once walked 900 miles to stake his claim for gold and 900 miles back again. The river is the only highway, summer and winter alike ... Had a chat with a bearded Catholic priest from Rome. After living 20 years in Colombo he was now inspecting Missions in USA and the North ... Went ashore alone and on return found Gwen had acquired a new friend, a gold-toothed trapper just arrived on board with five huskies, to get his mail. Wearing breeches, high boots and an old women's jumper. Took us to his cabin nearby, neatly ceiled with brown paper. Stink of martens he had caught four alive for breeding, but the only male had died. He would have to get a Government permit to catch another. Last season he got a hundred skins, worth about $20 each ... Steamer hooted its departure signal and our talk was cut short ... Found a big party of Indians on board. Several smiling girls, sly-faced and slit-eyed, going home from school. Mixed and interesting crowd.

Indeed the crowd was almost too interesting. We longed for more mental energy so that we could listen to our fellow-passengers with greater attention, but life on the steamer in that horde of people was very exhausting. The long hours of daylight, extending to nearly midnight, curtailed our sleep and the nights were very noisy. Often we would stop at a settlement in the middle of the night, and a certain number of the passengers, nuns and officials, would have to go ashore to transact their business.

It was not, however, only lack of sleep that made us tired, nor was it only the strain of living in a crowd. This was a strange new kind of lethargy that came stealing over us both, making it almost impossible for Gwen to sketch and for me to write down word-pictures of the passing scenes. Nor could either of us summon energy enough to keep, in our diaries, a full and clear record of our experiences. We began to wonder how we should ever manage, when we arrived at Aklavik, to complete the arrangements for our canoe journey up the Rat and over the Divide. This was something more insidious than mere physical lethargy. We had left behind the unresting activity of cities and the alertness of conventional life that expresses itself in action rather than in dreams. We were in a do-nothing, dreamy state of mind that may enclose a man as surely as prison walls. One of the tourists had said, with an air of wisdom: "You may be sure if a man gets into the North and wants to stay there, then there is some weakness in him. He is unfit for competition with the world."

We began to wonder, were we ourselves becoming unfit for competition with the world, giving way to the weakness of the dreamer who makes no reckoning of time? Did we want to stay in this land that had lured us so far from our homes? Perhaps we did.

9 *From Providence to Aklavik*

Providence in this case was the name of our first port of call after Great Slave Lake, and it was there that Gwen met a disaster which threatened to wreck our Rat River expedition. We went ashore, as we always did at any stopping-place, picked our way up the rough gang-board that was set up on such occasions from steamer to mud-bank, and then along the winding track among stones and boulders to the dirt road that bordered the cluster of wooden dwellings. Thence we plunged into the forest behind the settlement, as usual, to search for and collect wild flowers and after a few visits with the judge we went to bed as usual.

Gwen woke next morning with a sprained ankle or foot that had been very painful all through the night and she could hardly put her foot to the ground. When she told me the news we looked at each other in dismay. We knew by this time that there would be no question of either of us sitting peacefully in the canoe while our guides pushed it up the river; for most of the way we should have to force open a pathway for ourselves through dense brushwood that covered the banks. However she hobbled out of our cabin to breakfast and all through that day our fellow-passengers buzzed around her, offering advice and remedies, telling tales of the sprained ankle or twisted knee or broken thigh of their brother's wife's mother-in-law, or of some first cousin long since dead from the injury; suggesting homely cures; offering an arm for support whenever Gwen moved. Among the remedies suggested and supplied, the most helpful was the application of salt and water to the foot. There was no doctor nearer than Aklavik, four or five days journey ahead.

Our next call was at Fort Simpson, a beautifully sited place on a high bank at the mouth of the Liard River. Wandering out alone I encountered bull-dog flies as well as mosquitoes and was driven back to the steamer by a thunderstorm. Later I went ashore again with the judge to visit the wireless station and the Indian agent, and then, leaving the men to their yarns for a while, I went to look at the Roman Catholic church. I stood inside it and watched two Grey Nuns who came slowly forward through doors on either side of the altar, each bearing a lighted candle. Then, each one mounted a small stool and slowly, reverently placed their lights upon the altar. A bearded priest was kneeling there, with his rosary; purple strips of paper adorned the rafters, the church was very bare. All this was a strange contrast to the scene outside where the June sunshine was pouring down on a raw settlement in which half the necessities and all the luxuries of life were wanting, where leagues of virgin forest stretched away into the distance from the river banks.

My thoughts went overseas to ancient churches in France and Italy, beautiful stone buildings deeply rooted in antiquity, with all the ornate paraphernalia of worship in their services, and then returned to the stark simplicity of this wooden building in the northern land, where the long arm of the Catholic church was reaching out into the wilderness.

Every time we arrived at a settlement of any size the scene of welcome was like some scene in a ballet. The banks were so muddy that the crowd could not assemble on them and behave as a jostling, excited crowd naturally would behave when they all hurried down to greet the first sign of outside life that had appeared in nine months. They were lined out among the stones and boulders and along the narrow duck-boards in a single file procession. The whole population would be there, old and young, lone settlers come in from their huts, nuns and priests, the Indian children of the mission with boys wearing blue corduroy suits and large white ties, with girls clad in scarlet skirts, white blouses and black boots. Sometimes the procession would be quite 100 yards long, but even so those human forms, outlined between the background of unbroken forest and the foreground of untamed river, never seemed to be any larger than mere dots on the landscape. I have seen the same effect in the mountains of Greece where hundreds of people advancing by narrow tracks towards a village, for some dance or celebration, would appear to be no larger than ants.

We awoke early next morning to see a range of hills, brilliant objects in the sunshine. We glued our eyes to the porthole in turn to enjoy that sight, for not in five whole weeks had we seen any hill worthy of the name. Gwen had had a troubled and painful night with her foot. Foreboding filled our minds and we did not dare to think too much about the Rat. I could see the anxiety in Gwen's eyes, but when I proffered sympathy she only grunted, as if to say: "We must wait and see and not worry about it." Then she grunted again and I took that sound to mean: "What will be, will be." She hobbled out to breakfast to face the shower-bath of sympathy and suggestions that assailed her. She was again stuck fast on the steamer all day, with a dozen arms stretched out to help her whenever she moved: our friendly shipmates were like buzzing bees. "I'm fed up with advice and enquiries," she said when I gave her an arm to help her in to lunch to save her from being carried, like a stretcher case, to her seat.

That day we saw ice for the first time; we stopped and large blocks of it were brought on board.

At noon we came to Fort Wrigley, a small trading post with beautiful views of the river forward and back and a few two-story buildings. The HBC manager had built his own house, with an upstairs kitchen and balcony. The scenery was becoming more varied, the river wider, and now and then a range of hills would appear above the level country. There were steep cliffs at one turn of the river and all day a lovely blue light hung over trees and hills and water.

One of the NW Police told us about his Gravel River trip in search of two missing oil prospectors; it had been in the winter and he had had no tent. He told the story, not as if it had been a highlight of adventure but rather as if he were relating the details of a routine job of work. He had met the explorer Stefansson in the far north and had not a good word to speak of him. The man was a self-advertiser, he declared, and would always grudge credit to fellow-explorers. This was not the first time, nor the last, that we heard a poor account of Stefansson's reputation in Arctic latitudes.

After midnight we came to Fort Norman and at 5:30 I got up and went for a walk along the shore; then up the bank of Bear River which flows, at this point, into the Mackenzie. Nearly all these northern settlements are built at the junction of some river with the great waterway of northern Canada. It was a fresh, beautiful morning, there was ice on the edge of the current. Bear Rock towered

THE RAMPARTS - MACKENZIE RIVER,
THE RIVER HERE IS ONLY ABOUT ONE THIRD ITS
USUAL WIDTH, BUT IS 360 FT. DEEP. IT IS FORCED
BETWEEN TWO GREAT PERPENDICULAR STRETCHES
OF SAND STONE ROCK, FROM 180 TO 300 FEET
HIGH AND CONTINUES SO FOR ABOUT
ONE MILE WHEN IT AGAIN WIDENS OUT
Photo by C.W.MATHERS, Edmonton.

The Ramparts, Mackenzie River, 1901. C.W. Mathers. From Mathers, The Far North (1902).

up on the other side and beyond that rock was a range of snow-capped mountains. On my return, I found Gwen hopping about the deck with more agility and rather less pain. We did not say much to each other about her foot, but I think we were both counting the hours to that moment when we should reach Aklavik and call in the doctor.

All that day we looked out on fine scenery, snow-capped mountains, the wide river and a great open world. Late in the evening we came to the Sans Sault Rapids, a less exciting experience than we had expected, but perhaps to get the real thrill of shooting a rapid one should be in a canoe, not in a solid, flat-bottomed steamer. An hour or two later, however, we had one moment of tense

SS Distributor *near Fort Good Hope. n.d. Louis August Romanet Papers, University of Alberta Archives 72–81, 7/1/9:485.*

excitement when, after the rocks on either side had been gradually closing in on us, we suddenly observed that our vessel was charging a wall of rock. We awaited the shock, bracing ourselves for total destruction, but the rock quietly opened a little and we slid into a narrow channel where the river had cut its way through a ridge of limestone. On either side, the cliff towered above us for some 200 feet and this channel was four or five miles long. We were in the famous Ramparts.

I find this experience narrated briefly in my diary with the comment: "a most amazing show," and am led to wonder, as one does so often wonder in old age, at the total inadequacy of human words for describing human experience. The guide pamphlet supplied by the Alberta and Arctic Transportation Co. Ltd. bears me out in this conviction, for it describes the Ramparts as "an astonishing picture of nature's force and grandeur." I find little to choose between their word "picture" and my word "show."

We came to Fort Good Hope in the night and a few miles further on entered the Arctic Circle, the Land of the Midnight Sun. Next day was cold and windy and we tied up twice to re-fuel. At the first halt I made friends with two men, a Belgian and a Swede, who lived in a cabin near the woodpile, log-cutting, trapping and now, in the summer, fishing and drying fish for their dogs. The Belgian took me out in his canoe to the fish-nets where we found corny, jackfish and bluefish. He was more than grateful for the gift of some ancient newspapers that we had brought for pressing flowers, assuring us that they would be read four times.

The second halt was in a sandstorm on a wide reach of the river that was full of sand banks and bordered by scraggy spruces. It was difficult to land, we made fast to saplings with a wire rope, but several of the saplings were uprooted before we got a hold ashore. Then the NW Police held sports on the sandy beach while I wandered about and found a semi-palmated plover's nest with four eggs and Gwen watched all our antics from the deck.

Arctic Red River, which we reached at dawn, was a cold and squalid place, full of Indians in tents, but on the shore we saw lumps of ice that were each covering quite an acre of ground. When we turned west to steam up the Peel River to Fort McPherson the waterway was most attractive; it was narrow and overhung by mud banks where ice action had hollowed out the soil. Great lumps of ice continually dropped into the water with a splash, the young poplars were a fresh green. We could see the height of land beyond the Rat River and the distant peaks that were capped with snow. Passing the mouth of the Husky River to which we should return when our real adventure began, we steamed on up the Peel River to Fort McPherson which stood on a high bank facing a fine range of mountains. This was our last port of call and in her excitement, Gwen put her strained foot to the ground, but soon withdrew it and lay back outstretched on her two deck chairs. We returned down the Peel River to the Mackenzie, turned north-east and awoke next morning to see a range of mountains on our right, then, cork-screwing in channels until they were on our left, we came to Aklavik at 8.

So, creeping northward by tortoise stages, down the Clearwater, Athabasca, Slave and Mackenzie rivers, through the Athabasca and Great Slave lakes, we had travelled by steamer, visiting those isolated northern settlements, Fort Resolution, Hay River, Fort Providence, Fort Simpson, Fort Wrigley, Fort Norman, Fort Good Hope, Arctic Red River within the Arctic Circle, Fort McPherson and finally Aklavik on the Mackenzie Delta, that splays out in a 50-mile wide triangle to mingle with the Arctic Ocean. On the next lap of our journey we should have to travel by our own exertions.

10 *Eskimos at Aklavik*

As we drew in to the Distributor's *last port* of call on her north-ward journey, most of our fellow-travellers were preoccupied with the forthcoming Eskimo murder trial to be held next day in the dining saloon of the steamer.

As for ourselves, even so strange a thing as murder or so strange a people as the Eskimos could not, at that moment, claim our interest, since our minds had been centred for five long days on the condition of Gwen's foot and its possible effect on our plans. The first thing we had to do was to get the doctor. He came on board without delay, diagnosed a strained tendon and prescribed two weeks of complete rest. He would put the foot in plaster, he said, and there was no doubt that Gwen would be able to start up the Rat River in a fortnight. When he had left us and closed the cabin door behind him, we drew a long breath and looked at each other. Both of us felt, I think, as if we were suddenly ten years younger and as if the dread Rat River journey would, after all, turn out to be one long picnic in sunshine.

"Good job I brought Eddy's army boots," muttered Gwen, "they'll be some support for the old leg when we start."

"Surely your brother's boots are too big for you," I suggested.

"Stuff 'em with grass in the toes," she said and immediately hopped out of our cabin to watch the crowd of people milling about the steamer and the shore.

Aklavik seemed to be a prosperous place, comparatively speaking, but our standards of prosperity had been lowered during the last few weeks of association with people living in wooden shacks on muddy river banks with only a dirt track

Waterfront at Aklavik,
1925. O.S. Finnie.
NAC PA100549.

Three Schooners at Aklavik:
Arctic Bluenose,
Flying Cloud, *and*
Henry Ford. *n.d. Louis*
August Romanet Papers,
University of Alberta
Archives 72–81,
7/1/9:242.

for a main street. On that day of our arrival the place was humming with bustle
and activity. The place was hardly more than a single line of houses strung out on
top of a mud bank that was about 20 feet high. The river below was a sluggish
channel of the many-branching Mackenzie River Delta. There was a beach, more
mud than sand, of considerable width and on that shore were crowds of Eskimos
encamped in tents, with over a hundred huskies tethered to posts between the
tents and the Eskimo schooners. These vessels had been brought in from the
Arctic Ocean to be outfitted for the whaling season and were either riding at
anchor in the river or propped up on the beach.

The whole population of the settlement had, of course, turned out to greet the
arrival of the steamer, an event which spelt an end to the last nine months of
isolation, for the steamer brought welcome news from outside, personal mail,
necessities, luxuries and, above all, supplies of drink.

The people were moving about like a nest of ants suddenly disturbed. There
were crowds everywhere, on deck and in the steamer's saloon, on the narrow
gangplanks and the muddy foreshore and the top of the bank. There were
Eskimos and Indians, whites and half-breeds. For two more days we could
remain on board, but we were both anxious to get the question of accommodation settled, so I went ashore and began to search the place. The Roman Catholic
mission at the far end of the settlement was too expensive. Finally I settled on a
large, airy, upper room in the convent of the Grey Nuns. It had a balcony that

Grey Nuns' Mission de l'Immaculée Conception, Aklavik, 1925. AGNRC, Album no. 1, Aklavik, 1925–1954.

Grey Nuns' Mission de l'Immaculée Conception, Aklavik, 1926, showing the balcony and staircase used by the travellers. John F. Moran. NAC PA167649.

Lazarus Sittichinli, 1926.
Clara Coltman Rogers
(Vyvyan). Collection of
Edward Zealley.

overlooked the river, and the forest stretching away to a range of hills that was often deep blue in the clear Arctic light. It also had an outdoor flight of wooden steps leading down from the balcony, by which we would be able to come and go in privacy. This privacy was to prove a great asset during the next two weeks, for when I met attractive rough characters on the beach, persons not particularly suitable for association with nuns, I could bring them in to entertain Gweń in our upper room, without any embarrassment.

Our fortnight's stay with the kindly nuns was to cost us about £17. The convent had been built by a carpenter who came in for a year and went out as soon as he had finished the job.

Having visited the HB Company's store where our canoe, bespoken by Mr Cunliffe via Mr Brabant via the wireless, was in readiness for the trip, I went back to report to Gwen, and an hour or two later the great event of the day occurred. This was nothing less than the arrival of our head guide, Lazarus Sittichinli, who was sent round by the HB Company's friendly manager to have a talk with us; he was a Loucheux Indian with wide cheekbones and a magnificent physique. After this interview we felt that our great adventure had really begun.

We could now give our full attention to the murder trial and that evening we were formally introduced to the murderer, who, with his long hair and strange face, seemed to us like a wild man of the woods personified and a very good-looking wild man. The whole business of the trial seemed cheerful and friendly, there was no sense of tragedy about this administration of justice in the Arctic. One had a feeling that we were all friends together, the judge, the prosecutor, the defence, the murderer and his supporters, the witnesses and even the dead man's family. There was no sign of sympathy or sorrow for the dead man, nor any suggestion of his ghostly presence in that crowd.

The counsel for the defence had told us the outline of the story. Without knowing a word of Eskimo he had come north to defend an unknown client; a policeman would act as interpreter. He knew, however, something of Eskimo habits and beliefs and also the main facts about this particular murder. The accused had shot a neighbour's dog. The neighbour walked off to get cartridges for his gun. The accused then shot the neighbour in self-defence, once, twice, then he was dead. It would have been certain death if the accused had waited for those shots because the neighbour had walked off without a smile and when the Eskimo stops smiling he is dangerous. The defence was in favour of lenient sentences for Eskimo murderers, because their outlook on death, so he told us, is different from ours and they are apt to kill off their old folk and their female babies in hard times. Many a baby, he assured us, is dropped in the nearest lake. There are often three men to one woman and this leads to fighting, especially when a man has three wives, one good sewer, one good cook and one good hunter. Probably not since the 1880s had old people been forcibly dismissed from this world and as for the despatch of infants, the habit was already dying out in the early part of the 20th century. We listened, however, with the deepest interest to the tales that we were told, keeping our doubts to ourselves. At a later stage of our journey we heard men of widely divergent views agreeing that Eskimo murder trials are often like a farce, being an attempt to impose on those natives a belief outside their ken. Yet no one ever suggested what should be done when an Eskimo murdered a white man. Meanwhile the judge, the prosecutor, the

Trial of Ikagena aboard SS
Distributor, *Aklavik,
24 June 1926. Canon
Edward Hester. Collection
of Edward Zealley, courtesy
Joan M. Boucaud.*

*Billie Kemaksina, trial
interpreter, 1926. Clara
Coltman Rogers (Vyvyan).
Collection of Edward
Zealley.*

defence and the clerk had all, on this occasion, travelled north in holiday frame of mind to carry out their various functions.

The trial lasted all day, with intervals for meals. The Crown lawyer prosecuted, Mr O'Connor defended, the interpreter interpreted, the clerk took notes, the six jury-men looked like a collection of the toughest ruffians imaginable, the judge presided. The evidence went round and round, off at a tangent, back again in circles and at last, although manslaughter was evident to all, a verdict of "Not Guilty" was brought in.

The chief characters in this performance were Ikagena, the accused murderer from the Coppermine district, Nalugiak and Hanergak—apparently both of them the wives of Ikagena and the dead man Ulukshuk—Panujak the witness, wearing khaki shirt and trousers with mukluks adorned by coloured tops, a man with small eyes and narrow forehead. It was a strange scene, I thought, as I watched the judge who, in black coat and white tie, sat motionless with a Union Jack behind him draped against the pantry door. Never again, I said to myself, shall I have the chance of attending an Eskimo murder trial. I began to take notes.

Sergeant: "I declare this court open in the name of the King." Interpreter stands up ready for action, in reindeer parka, white wolverine collar, moccasins, blue trousers, a man with an aristocratic face and jutting chin, alert dark eyes, gold ring on one finger, half Kanaka, half Eskimo, moistens lip with tongue, looks intently from Judge to witness who comes forward . Judge: "White man's religion in this book, see? You kiss this book and speak. Not speak truth very bad." To interpreter: "Say only tell what he knows." Questioning begins. "How many wives had Ulukshuk?" "Kookterna, Nalugiak, Nalonga." Nalonga is slit-eyed, tattooed lines on face, now fear and now anger in her expression.

Among strange questions and answers I began to lose the thread of the trial.

"Ulukshuk bad man, make plenty trouble for people?" "He in touch with spirits to make better?" "Yes, medicine man." "When Eskimo get mad what that mean?" "And he took his rifle with him." "Did the wife ever see Ikagena watch Ulukshuk when Ulukshuk was mad?" "Now I protest, my Lord, how could such a woman know a man's mental condition?"

Drums used at the Inuit dances, held by W.H.B. Hoare (left) and Rev. Canon Edward Hester (right), 1922. Miriam Green Ellis. M.G. Ellis Collection, University of Alberta Archives, Box 1, no. 226.

Lawyers began to argue points in semi-legal fashion at that point and I closed my notebooks, becoming absorbed in watching the human faces. When the verdict was given the murderer went off with his friends to celebrate; the prosecutor and I followed them into what seemed to be a large village hall, but in a few moments it was so full of people that it became a small room. The murderer was the life and soul of that evening party, being also solo dancer in one of the most amazing muscular feats that I have ever seen. During his execution of that primitive solo seal-dance I was transported back through the ages into caveman mentality, becoming unconscious of the crowd about me.

The dance was improvised, mimetic and spontaneous. There were no rehearsed nor formal steps. Ikagena began by beating, with a wooden stick, a flat, one-sided drum held by a handle. In a few moments he was no longer Ikagena, nor even a human being, he had become a seal, bending forward and shuffling sideways, with every muscle rippling in an almost fluid movement; he seemed to be endowed with flippers and encased in blubber. Curious groans and roars and hisses of encouragement rose from the audience, but however uncouth were those sounds they were obviously used for expressing delight in this scene wherein a man had become a mammal before their very eyes. I have always wished I had been able to enshrine something of that experience in words but I could

*Unidentified woman
wearing parka, 1926.
Clara Coltman Rogers
(Vyvyan). Collection of
Edward Zealley.*

not, for, like the dancer, I had left my own consciousness and gone back into some region of prehistoric time and from that far place I could bring nothing back.

I can only remember stumbling out from that room with my companion while the merriment was in full swing and making our way back to the steamer. It was 2 in the morning, but the sun had never set. The light seemed to be clear as glass and the Arctic forest beyond the river quiet as any painted thing.

When I went out for a stroll that morning after breakfast, the cabins showed no sign of life. The store was closed, the wireless office was closed, the settlement was silent as a cemetery and there was neither sound nor movement except among the Eskimos and huskies on the shore. I scrambled down the bank and began to make friends with the Eskimo women. Our only currency for exchange of thoughts or feelings consisted in smiles and more smiles and then yet more smiles. It was a good currency and for the next two weeks we used it freely every day.

The women wore either long and shapeless cotton dresses or fur-lined parkas with hoods, they carried their babies tightly swathed in bags on their backs and they walked with a waddle, toes always turned in. Their smiles were entrancing. The men wore parkas, trousers and high mukluks, or water boots, made from the skin of sea mammals. One old man wore two labrets in his lower lip. We exchanged handshakes with the men and greetings, each speaking in our own language which, of course, sounded like gibberish to the one who listened. When I tired of this form of intercourse I would always turn to the babies, pointing at them with admiration and indeed they were lovely creatures. They must have been born smiling. There was one old woman who, as I learned later, was reputed to be a wife of the explorer Stefansson.

At midday, while Gwen had her meal spread-eagled on two folding chairs, I lunched alone with an American trapper, our friends having all gone ashore to feed at the convent. This trapper was going out in the *Distributor*, after 14 years in the North, taking his Eskimo wife with him. He told me how hard it was to find two men, even two good men, who could spend a whole winter together without quarrelling, a fact which accounts for the solitary lives of so many trappers.

After lunch Gwen was carried ashore on a stretcher by four men and taken straight up to the convent balcony. Then the *Distributor* backed slowly out from the river bank and steamed away, bearing the judge and his party and many new passengers, outward bound for the South. A mixed crowd of Indians, Eskimos, whites and half-breeds cheered the departing vessel and we were left alone on our balcony with the strangest feeling of isolation. Little did we guess that very soon the Arctic wilderness would afford us moments of experience incomparably more lonely. After all, here at Aklavik we had a solid room of our own, kind hostesses and also several hundred fellow-creatures, coloured and white, within hail; moreover we had the prospect of another steamer arriving, in six weeks time, with news from the outside world.

By the end of that afternoon however we were more distressed by hunger than by loneliness, for we had lunched at noon and only later discovered that the convent clocks were always two hours slow, so that we had to wait eight hours for our supper. After supper we went to bed and slept for 12 hours.

II Harbour of Wrecked Men

Next morning, when I walked down the river bank, Aklavik was like a city of the dead.

I paid various calls on ready-made friends found during the last two days, hoping to bring in some of them to cheer Gwen in her solitary state, but not a soul was stirring. There was silence about the wireless station, silence at the store; every cabin door and window was shut and not a voice was heard. Only the missionaries were at work within their mission house, busy with washing and sewing. On my way back I met a friend, one of the North-West Mounted Police who had travelled down the Mackenzie with us, and I walked with him to the cabin where his comrades were typing, cooking, reading or sleeping. They had a good library of novels and I borrowed half a dozen volumes. When I asked him what had happened to all the inhabitants he explained the silence of the place in a few brief words.

"The steamer brought in drink," he said. "The first liquor in nine months. They are all under the covers today. Dead drunk."

Then I remembered a certain remark once made by the judge. With his typically French lucidity he always liked to place his subject in a clear light and then to define it in a telling phrase. The north country, he had observed, is "The Harbour of Wrecked Men."

Now we pondered on that remark and began to observe people's lives with new understanding and no sooner did we look for tragedy than we found it constantly. Day after day our experience would reinforce the judge's theory. It might be a face seen in a crowd, a phrase or a story overheard, a few minutes spent in a cabin interior. Any such glimpse or tale or encounter might flash on the inner eye a whole life history, some great or little tragedy enacted without spectator or human consolation.

Here is one. In a certain home, that is to say in a partitioned hut where the cracks between each log are filled with mud or moss and the roof is ceiled with brown paper, a tired little woman sits in a rocking chair with a peaky infant on her lap. The baby's eyes are black as ink, it is very small for its age. The woman has a shaded look in her eyes as if she were trying to veil some insistent secret feeling, there is no hope nor animation in her face. She is a little slip of a creature, city-born, married to a half-breed trapper, and now our steamer has brought her in the first mail received from the outside for many months. Her husband is earning a bare subsistence; drink has always been his trouble. The home has an empty air, with a floor of bare boards and on the walls nothing but two cheap coloured prints and some Indian bead-work hanging from a nail. Through the partition door we can see her kitchen with its bare, unfurnished look. One or two raggedly cut empty tins lie on the floor, shining brightly but they are the only bright objects in that home.

At every turn in this country one sees those empty tins, between the cabins and among the Indian tents, even along the earth track that serves as a main street, these unsightly objects are thrown out and left to lie there. It seems as if, among these hard-living people, no one has the leisure to beautify or even to keep tidy their home surroundings.

So that little woman sits there, week after week, all dreams of yesterday becoming dim, all hope for the morrow stillborn.

There is another home. Here also the crevices between the logs are filled with mud or moss, but inside there are rugs on the floor. There are also photographs and knick-knacks and a gramophone and several tables, and the rocking chair is upholstered. Moreover, the father of the family is a white man. The children are asleep in the next room, a cheerful meal is ready in the over-heated cabin, but the woman hardly speaks at all, there is a set look on her face, like the look of an image. One cannot imagine her glancing expectantly round any corner or facing any new road with hope. The man's talk, though slow to the point of reluctance, as if he had nearly lost the habit of human intercourse, is interesting, for it is centred on the wild life of the forest where he works as a woodcutter and there is little he does not know about wild birds and animals.

Later we learned that he only works intermittently, that on every possible occasion he "goes on the toot" and that, on these occasions, he always takes his neighbours' boots and moccasins. Such is the history of "Moccasin Bill" who, like so many others in this country, has a permit for liquor. As for "Moccasin Bill's" silent wife, she has had no history of her own, nor is she likely to have one. She is a forlorn shadow of a woman.

It takes a strong man to keep his integrity and mental powers alive in these northern solitudes. Once we asked the judge: "Can't these isolated people get books and don't they read in the long winter nights?" He told us that a newcomer would read, perhaps, during the first year, but after that he would find little interest in reading the same old books and then also the life was so hard for lonely men that they would lose all power of concentration after a while. The toughness needed in the mere struggle for survival would absorb all their energy.

It is true that the northern posts receive an occasional winter mail brought in by dog-sleigh along the frozen rivers, but when the last steamer goes south, in the early part of the fall, the people of the North do not expect to see any new face or to hear of any new event for nine long months. No wonder the first steamer of the summer receives such a welcome at every northern settlement. Long before the hooting signal is heard beyond the bend of the river, news of the steamer's imminent arrival will always be brought in, having been carried north by that mysterious Indian method of sending signals that can flash news over leagues of country. Quickly the children of the mission are dressed in their Sunday clothes, they come streaming down the bank of mud or stones and then line up like a chorus in a comic opera. Grey Nuns in their long robes come fluttering down like doves; reverend fathers or brothers in cassocks or alpaca jackets come pacing slowly forward; half-breeds and Indians cluster on the bank like bees and every Indian child, decked out with ill-assorted scraps of finery, is like a macaw with feathers blown awry. For the coming of the steamer means the coming of supplies, of newspapers and letters and strange faces from the outside world, of things desperately needed and things desperately desired. As for communications by wireless and airplane, both of them were, at the time of our journey, in their early stages of development in northern Canada. It was not possible to foresee, nor even to imagine, how much those things would change the lives of the lonely people in coming years.

There is, however, one magnificent type of manhood that stands out in the North. You will find such a type most often among the North-West Mounted Police whose work lies often in the lonely outposts beyond the white man's settlements. There they guard, among ice-floes and the Eskimos, the white man's justice and the white man's creed. When travelling by dog-team, often hundreds of miles alone, over ice and snow where winter's grip has drawn the land and sea together, when enduring physical hardship as part of the day's routine and remaining keenly alive to his duties and responsibilities, a man may rise to spiritual heights undreamed of by those who walk in trodden ways. Sometimes also one may find among the trappers and woodcutters a man who, in his isolation has kept his inner integrity. Yet for every one of such men there are many others who become, after living for a long spell alone, peculiar or crabbed or even mad.

In the end one is bound to admit that the North is, to a certain extent, a prison. Those who once go in may not easily get out, being held there by some individual weakness or by the grip of a force too great for definition or defiance. Yet even such imprisonment may confer its own kind of freedom. Two remarks that I heard will always linger in my memory. An Eskimo, just returned from a visit to San Francisco, summed up his experience. "I no like San Francisco. If I got no money I got no food. If I got no money here I go 'nother man's house, get plenty food."

Then there was the trapper, lately come in again after his first holiday in Seattle. "Towns won't do for me. I guess I can't cut down a tree out there when I want to make a fire."

12 *La Pierre House*

The doctor's verdict on Gwen's strained foot had lifted a load of anxiety from our minds, for ever since that morning after leaving Fort Providence, when she could not set foot to the ground, we had both been filled with secret gloom. Now, at Aklavik, we only had to exercise patience for two weeks and all should be well. That first day, however, when I discussed the details of our journey with the manager of the Hudson's Bay Company store, Mr Parsons, a dark cloud appeared on our horizon. From the safety of our armchair plans in Cornwall, where neither ice, mosquitoes, rapids, nor mud approaches to human dwellings played any part in everyday life, all the stages of our journey had seemed to dovetail so perfectly. How many times we had spread out maps and letters and gone over every detail!

Two Indian guides and a canoe up the Rat River; portaging over the Divide. La Pierre House, a trading station where Jackson Brothers ran a store for the large Indian settlement and for passing travellers; a place marked clearly in the atlas. There we should find, without any difficulty, a single Indian guide to take us down to Old Crow and the rapids and through the Ramparts to Fort Yukon in Alaska. There we would sell our canoe, catch a tourist steamer and travel by water and then by rail to Seward, thence by steamer past the Pacific coast fjords to Seattle. From Seattle we would cross to Vancouver Island, stay with Gwen's old friend as paying guests for as long as our money lasted and then return by the Canadian Pacific Railway across the Rocky Mountains and the prairie. It all seemed to fit in like the pieces of a jig-saw puzzle, except that our map of the Rat River seemed rather blank, showing no natural features to mark our course; but

John Ambrose Parsons,
HBC Post Manager,
Aklavik, 1931.
Glenbow–Alberta Museum.

then our guides, we assured ourselves, would know the country well and perhaps we should not need a map of the river at all.

I went over these completed plans with Mr Parsons and he said calmly, just as he might have remarked casually that there was still some ice on the river bank, "There's nothing at La Pierre House. Only one empty cabin."

"Wha-at?" I said incredulously, "why it's marked on the atlas. And they told us we could get an Indian guide there for certain."

I do not imagine that the mention of our atlas meant much to him, but he knew about the country in which he worked and he just repeated calmly: "One empty cabin. Jackson Brothers will most likely come up later in the summer once, or maybe twice, and the Indians in that country will come in to trade their furs with him. No chance of a guide there. No possible chance."

"Where *is* the next possible chance?" I asked, holding my breath and trying to speak in a casual tone. He told me it would be at Old Crow. By this time we had the maps spread out before us on the counter of the store.

"It's quite a settlement," he said, "you'd sure find a guide there who would paddle down to Fort Yukon with you."

"What about Lazarus and the boy coming on to Old Crow with us?" I enquired hopefully. He shook his head.

"They wouldn't do it," he said with decision. "The track back over muskeg country to McPherson or Aklavik is long enough when they are carrying their food on their backs."

"What's the river like between La Pierre House and Old Crow?" I asked him, and he told me that he had never been there, but he reckoned it was a stretch of about 115 miles.

"Could we do it alone?" was my next question.

"Oh, sure," he said airily, but he did not mention the question of rapids nor did he seem to know exactly where they occurred.

I returned to Gwen with the news. She began muttering to herself. Whenever Gwen muttered it was like the growl of distant thunder, one knew there was worse to come. At last it came, with the most scornful expletive in her vocabulary, which was rather a limited one except where nautical matters were involved.

"The miserable landlubbers," she said, "and they told us that La Pierre House was a certainty."

A landlubber, in her view of things, was not only an incompetent oaf but also a man who was apt to let others down and to make engagements without fulfilling them. I do not think she credited those earth-bred and earth-bound people with any virtues at all. The sea had always been the greatest thing in her island life and all her heroes were to be found among seafaring men.

We both sat on our balcony for a while, gazing with glum faces at the maps, as if we hoped to find on them a substitute for that deserted cabin with the French name. Then suddenly in the same breath we said: "115 miles isn't very far, and it's going downriver."

"Have you ever paddled a canoe?" asked Gwen. I told her I had not and asked her if she ever had. It seemed that she had only paddled a small one in the pond on Tresco, when she was a child in the Scilly islands. On the other hand I knew that she had learned to row a boat before she learned to walk.

Archdeacon Charles
Edward Whittaker. n.d.
ACC/GSA P7517-301.

"I could steer clear of the snags all right," she said, "but I'm not so sure if we come to rapids."

So there we sat like two old wise-acres faced with a problem too hard for them, discussing things about which we knew nothing at all and then we suddenly agreed that I must go out to the river bank and pick up first-hand information.

"None of your old-wives' tales," said Gwen, "don't listen to any croakers. Find men who've done that 115-mile stretch and get first-hand information about it."

I set off on my quest. Resolution came ebbing back into me like a slow tide. Of course we could and must paddle down from La Pierre House to Old Crow by ourselves. I was almost ready to dictate to Archdeacon Whittaker, when I went to get his opinion, what he should say about our tackling that reach of the river alone. Yet I could not completely dismiss from my mind the thought and the fear of rapids. The archdeacon was neither for nor against our lone journey. However, he assured me that there were no really dangerous rapids between La Pierre House and Old Crow and he sent me off to find a trader and also a trapper who had each, at different times, navigated the Rat River in summer.

After long interviews with all three of them I went back to Gwen with the result of my enquiries. They were agreed that if we had common sense and moderate courage we could certainly paddle down that stretch alone. There would be patches of swift water and we must keep a lookout for snags of fallen tree branches both above the surface of the water and below, but there were no actual rapids and as for Old Crow it was a settlement of some size and we would have no difficulty in picking up a guide there.

I rather think that they overestimated our powers. They probably believed that since we had come so far from home and had deliberately chosen the Rat River route for crossing the Divide into the Yukon, we were equipped in mind and body to face any danger or emergency. From their point of view a patch of swift water—a little less turbulent than a rapid—was hardly to be counted as a danger; for a canoe man it was all in the day's work. They could not have guessed how inexperienced we were.

Looking back on all these things from the vantage point of today, I see that the advice of those three men was an enormous help to us, although at the time we thought them rather casual. Their confidence in us, their conviction that we were seasoned travellers, encouraged us to think that we really were seasoned travellers. They helped to restore our self-confidence when it was at a low ebb.

So our resolution was taken. We made up our minds on the strength of what those three had told us about their own experience, to paddle on alone down the Porcupine River after dismissing Lazarus and the boy Jimmy, at La Pierre House. Old Crow and the unknown guide that we should find there had now become the key-pin of our canoe journey, for even those three old-timers did not think it possible for us to paddle down alone from that settlement, through the rapids and the Ramparts, to Fort Yukon.

That evening our friend Sergeant Anderton of the North-West Mounted Police came to see us and we had a long talk with him about Eskimos and other

Sgt Frederick Anderton at Fort Wrigley, 1922. Miriam Green Ellis. M.G. Ellis Collection, University of Alberta Archives, Box 1, no. 71.

local topics; also about our own forthcoming journey. He had not actually been up the Rat River in summer, but he knew the whole country well and there was a quiet confidence about him which was very infectious.

"It will be perfectly all right for you to do those hundred-odd miles alone," he assured us, "it will take you about three days or possibly less."

Three days absolutely alone in the Arctic wilderness, with our canoe and our provisions. For the first time we saw this journey not as a dream but as a sober fact. As we came nearer and nearer to it, the Rat River adventure seemed to grow smaller and more ordinary.

Sergeant Anderton went on to talk more about the Eskimos, telling us how useless is their evidence at trials, since their minds are like the mind of a 12-year-old child and only from their facial expressions can one get any reliable evidence. It had taken him a whole year to bring in to Aklavik the murderer who had just been acquitted. The mounted police, he said, go about their duties with their lives in their hands and control the Eskimos by bluffing about the numbers of the police force. Two Eskimo murderers, who had been taken out to Edmonton and imprisoned for a while, had come back deeply impressed by the immense numbers of white men in the world. Then he told us how Archdeacon Whittaker had exposed Stefansson and his "old hag of an Eskimo" wife, from a pulpit in Toronto and how Stefansson's fiancée thereupon went off and married a Yankee. He made no comment and I think we were all asking ourselves the same question: "But what about the archdeacon and the part he played?"

He himself was going for the summer to Bernard Harbour and then to range during the winter about King William Land and Victoria Island. Then, just as he rose to go, he said: "Why don't you hire a gas boat from the Hudson's Bay Company and get them to take you and the canoe and the guides up the slack water of the Rat? Save yourselves three or four days dull travel. Go as far as Destruction City."

We acted on his advice and the next morning settled the plan with Mr Parsons.

That night we went to bed exhausted, for, as we sat looking at the brown and sluggish current of the river below and the low line of forest on the other side and the distant range of intensely blue hills, we felt as if we had travelled far that day, not in space but in the world of emotions. We had been through dismay and apprehension, changing to uncertainty, and a horrible wavering between hopes and fears; then through anxiety that slowly faded away to be replaced by determination and finally by self-assurance. We had only won through to this mood of confidence in ourselves thanks to the help and encouragement of our kind friends.

Before we went to sleep we decided that I must take advantage of the idle days ahead, by finding someone who would teach me how to paddle a canoe.

13 The Unrelenting North

In the middle of that radiant Arctic night, when the prosecutor and I were walking back to the steamer after the Eskimo celebrations, I said to him: "I would give anything to meet some of those members of the jury and talk to them. They have the most interesting faces." And indeed, with that plain hard-bitten rascality writ large on human features they seemed to me unique. My companion looked rather surprised but he said nothing. Next morning I met him sauntering about that silent place where everyone was still "under the covers."

"If you really want to know one of those members of the jury," he said, "I will introduce you to their leader, Captain Cameron, before I go out. He and I fore-gathered a year or two ago on Herschel Island. He is a rough old sea-dog, but I have warned him that you are ladies and that he must curb his tongue accordingly."

"'Ladies?'" I said, in a tone of resentment, "how could you have said such a thing? Of course it will cramp his style."

"Oh you can easily take the lid off that," answered the barrister airily, "come along down to the shore and we'll look for him."

We found him on the shore, occupied with his new schooner. She was beached and lying sideways while he was putting in a new engine and outfitting her for the white whaling season, for he had piled up his last ship, the *Bonny Belle*, in a gale during the previous summer. In the days that followed he and I had many a yarn together. Taking a spell off work and puffing at his old black pipe, he would sit beside me on the mud bank above the shore where the Eskimos were encamped and the huskies were tied to posts implanted in the mud while their little fleet of

scows and schooners lay anchored in the river. Across the river were those stunted spruce trees of the Arctic forest and far away that brilliant line of blue, the Richardson range of mountains. Every day we enjoyed summer sunshine while two feet underground the earth was still frozen.

Sometimes I would persuade him to visit Gwen and would convoy him stealthily up our outside staircase, since he preferred to give a wide berth to nuns. Then he would hold us both entranced with his stories, and Gwen would forget her plastered foot and the wearisome delay and the tedium of inaction in the sheer delight of listening to him.

I can see the old man now, with his cold blue eyes and unshaven face, his black shirt, guiltless of stud or necktie, knitted brown cap running to a point, worn blue trousers and mukluks made of seal-skin reaching to his knees. We never really heard his history, but one anecdote after another would, like a series of sparks, light up bits of his past, or reflect some corner of his rugged independent mind that, in all the devious wanderings of the man, had kept a certain stiff integrity.

"My dad," he told us, "thrashed me when I was a youngster for some skylarking that I'd never done. I wasn't going to swallow that whole, so I went to him and I said: 'I'm going over the sea, dad, and I'll never come home till you ask my pardon.' The old man said: 'I'll never do that so long as I live but I'll leave the string of the doorlatch outside for ye, Robbie, dinna forget.'"

"Well, I went, and that string was always outside, you may bet your bottom dollar on that, you may. It must have been a dozen years later that I picked up a paper and saw the Glasgow bank had failed. I knew the old folks' savings was all invested in it and I wrote home and sent a cheque, for I'd made a little money that winter, trapping on the Liard River. What d'you guess the old dad did? He didn't stop to write and return that cheque, he telegraphed refusal. He wasn't going to take no help from his runaway son, not if he was down to bedrock. I can see now that Dad had the fine old covenanting spirit, he wouldn't change his ways or thoughts for any god or devil, he'd have been grand stuff for this country."

"I'd soon spent that money and 'twas the year of a big gold rush in Alaska. A bloke in Edmonton put up the grub stakes for me and for three partners and I remember we tried to get in from the Mackenzie side, with horses and grub for 12 weeks. Gosh! but I'll never forget the silence in that great basin of country, it was deep as hell and wide as the sea, but do you think we could get out of it? Not we. It was like some cruel trap we were in and every time we tried to break through the mountains, we failed. I can tell you we pretty nigh lost our reason those two years, the bigness of the country fair got on our nerves, it was like some unseen devil holding us in there and mocking at us. When the grub was through we ate our horses and then there was only the fish lines and our guns to help us. We stuck it though. In the end some Indians led us over that blamed watershed and when we got down into the Selkirk country, why, that gold rush was old as Adam and Eve."

On two burning questions, missionaries and the intermarriage of white men with squaws, Captain Cameron had a fund of stories and reminiscences. To our surprise this hardened old sinner held the most rigid notions about the impropriety of white men marrying Indians or Eskimos.

"'Tis a degradation of manhood," he asserted, "and that's all there is to it."

He himself, he told us, would always draw a line across his tent or cabin. White visitors would feed with their host on one side of that line, coloured ones on the other. Often he had found himself obliged to say to a friend: "You can eat here with me, but your wife doesn't come across that line for natives."

"A man must draw the line somewhere," he assured us with a grim smile, "and mine was always plumb across the cabin."

On the question of missionaries he had much to say and little that was good. The very word seemed to rouse him to scornful eloquence.

"One time," he told us, "I met Mr Bloom up in Point Barrow country and I says to him in a friendly way: 'Are you any relation to Mr Bloom the trader at Herschel?' He says: 'I *am* Mr Bloom of Herschel, but I'm a missionary, there's no trader of that name.' 'Is that so?' says I, 'I'm a trader myself but I never gave a sack of flour to a husky and took two fox skins off him.' I tell you that missionary-trader chap had a gawd-awmighty struggle with his lower or higher self not to murder me then and there. These missionaries, what do they do but teach the Eskimos it isn't modest to strip to the waist, as they always do inside, women and all? Well, for myself I never was comfortable that way, I always like to keep a sweater on, but as for the women, well, if a lad's 21 and doesn't know the shape of a woman he's no more than half-educated. And as for the missionaries, they seem to have forgotten how the Boss o' that there tuning fork of the weather up aloft, sent down word once about the outside of the cup and platter being of mighty little use."

When we asked him about his whaling experiences he made a gesture as if to brush the whole question aside, but we could see a reminiscent look in his blue eyes and then out came another of those anecdotes, lighting up the darkness of half-forgotten days.

"Danger in whaling? No," with a snort, "why, what chance has a man, blind drunk with rage, against a cool feller? That's what the whale is, blind drunk with rage. Oh, well, there was one little encounter I had. You see the wounded whale was jammed into ice like, just a nick in the ice and we thought there might be room to pass in the boat. Well, just as we were passing, up come the flukes of the whale and lashed out sideways on me and the feller in the starboard bow. If you can imagine several ton of good beef and muscle hurtling through the air and slashing at you, then you can guess what it was like. I took 14 years flying through the air, I did, and saw all that I'd ever seen over again; 20 feet I travelled before I reached the water. And I knew nothing till next day when I heard the fellers say: 'There's nothing to be done for old Cam. Only just make him comfortable.'"

"That was the first I knew and I said: 'If you think old Cam's stove in you're darned bigger fools than I took you for.' Then they said: 'How's your back?' And I said: 'Well, I guess my back's kind o' queer.' They hadn't got no doctor nor medicine, so they gave me the best physic in the world, a good tot of Jamaica rum and then they built me up in pretty good mason's work and plastered me in till I got to San Francisco. The man in the bows? Why he joined the silent majority within the week. I guess I was pretty near the bone-yard that time."

One day we discussed our journey with him. Was it true, as the old-timers assured us, that only lunatics and fish travelled by the Rat River route in summer? Was it true that the mosquitoes there were as thick as spruce needles on a branch? He took out his pipe and spat over the balcony with a thoughtful air.

"Them old-timers," he said, "they like to paint the country black, gives them a kind of reflected glory for having stuck it so long. But I never was that way myself. The north country is tough and cruel, you can't deny it. 'Tis no bed-o-roses, balmy, cradle life up here, nine months frozen hard and three months persecuted by them darned flies, but here we are for better or for worse and I believe if we stick by the country, why, the country will stick by us. The Rat River ain't no asphalt pavement laid for patent leathers but there it is, 'tis a trail same as any other and you'll get over all right."

There is no doubt that the captain had spent a life of unceasing action with very little time for anything else, ever since the day when he left the old folks and ran away to sea. Fishing, hunting, whaling, suffering shipwreck, seeking for gold and spending in three days what he had gathered in a year, that was his life. Judging by our all-too-easy standards he had been "up against it," all the time and everywhere from his sterner point of view he had got as good a fate as any other man. Even in that brief Arctic summer when the sun shone all night and all day, and bright wild flowers starred the ground between the spruces, there would be snow on the distant hills and lumps of frozen soil would fall from the concave banks into the river. Even in his palmy days he had neither butter, eggs nor milk. The grandest home he had ever called his own was a cabin of rough logs and the simplest one a sleeping bag of fur in the snow. He was a man of the North, tough and hardened by endurance. In his every word and comment you felt a keen edge, like the edge of the Arctic wind. No flotsam or jetsam of the North was our friend but a man tempered by circumstance and climate to the finest quality.

Yet the strangest thing was, that in the company of this man of action, we listened to his language spellbound, as if we had found in him a modern Demosthenes or Bossuet. Somehow he must have found, in his life of action, time for thought and speech, for these were closely knit, with never any hesitation or inconsistency. He had an unusual utterance, rather slow but never slurred. Often, he would roll his tongue with zest round a chosen epithet, some-times you could watch the deliberate movement and then the pride of ownership lighting up those cold blue eyes as he uttered some telling phrase. Yet there were never any adjectival, flowing periods, nor was there a superfluous word. His emphasis was gained by insight, not by labour or emotion or reiteration. His own hardness had shorn off flowery adjuncts but his cuteness had unearthed words that bit into the subject and lingered in the memory. Sometimes they were direct as a punch in the midriff, sometimes they sounded like a breaking wave with an echoing backwash. I doubt if either the Greek or the French orator could have added point to his favourite story, the yarn of the corpse and the missionary.

"There was a corpse frozen into the snow once when I was living at Herschel Island, unburied it was and the foxes came sniffing around. Best fox-bait in the world is a half-gone corpse, didn't you know that? Well, the missionary he set traps to protect the corpse until the thaw came. I soon had the yarn going that the sky-pilot was making a good job of trapping with corpse-bait. That yarn travel? Like hell-fire. Silent and happy like a clam in the ooze I was."

Curiously enough the day before we left Aklavik we heard him for the first time give expression to his reasoned philosophy of life. He was talking of the North, as a freeholder might show off his little property with pride, backing it against all other lands that the heart of a man could desire.

"A man comes in from outside once in a while and goes around asking for employment. Employment!" He uttered the word scornfully. "Give away one man's work to another when everyone has his own job. There's none of that here. We put it square to him. 'Now look here; if you've not a cent, pull out up the river, build yourself a cabin and set some traps.' Well, he takes mebbe a dozen traps and sets some deadfalls too. Deadfalls? Why, they are just timber propped up over a run; they hit the animal on the head—no expense—made right there in the country. Well, in a few days he gets four or five pelts, and there's a hundred dollars straight away. Good pay for a man's work and a man's his own boss too. That's the North. If you go outside and meet a pal in the city you accost him: 'Come and have a yarn.' He pulls out his watch and begins to reckon; he's got to catch a streetcar or get to bed at a certain time so as to be at the office bright and early, or else he'll lose his job. Up here a man don't reckon nor hurry, he's got all the time there is; time cuts no ice in the North. Then it may be he feels off colour and wants to lie around for a day or two. Well, there's nothing against that, a man is liable to fluctuations same as a river falls and rises. But outside you've no chance to follow the laws of nature, 'tis breakfast 7 sharp and off to work, or another man will get your job and then you'd have to move around quick and lively to catch something else, bowing with your hat in your hand and your heels together: 'Here's my papers, here's my credentials, please give me a job.' Regular as clocks you must be outside, and dull as a time-piece too. There's nothing like your independence and here in the North no man can deprive you of that."

We put the other side of the question to him and reminded him of some of the things that we had left behind but he did not change his tune.

"Oh yes, there's hard winters and long nights, and empty stomachs mebbe, and two bad seasons to one good mebbe and an off-shore wind with a leaking schooner. But you may as well keep smiling here. It's not much sunshine you'll get when you're put under."

And then, without a pause, the inevitable backwash.

"And put under we all must be, or at any rate if I'm not buried for love I guess I'll make a pretty fair plague spot for those around."

I4 Two Idle Weeks

Captain Cameron was not our only visitor at the convent and if I have dwelt at undue length on his life story it is because he seemed to be a very clear-cut type. Certain men are attracted to the North and, once inside that country, are moulded by its stern, uncompromising spirit into a strength which they betray in their beliefs and talk and actions; he was one of them. We had many other visitors and heard many stories but none of these tales were so well and truly seasoned as the tales of Captain Cameron, none had quite the same tang.

We had visits from some inmates of the convent. There were six nuns, some Indian children whom they were teaching, and the doctor's wife with her new-born baby. A priest was attached to the convent and two lay brothers lived in a nearby cabin, coming in daily to feed and to pray. Several of the kindly nuns came up to see us and we made friends with one of them, Sister Firmin, who worked in the kitchen and had hailed long ago from Ireland. Even these slight contacts with the nuns made us feel we were anchored to the place, that we were no longer mere spectators, travelling on from one picture show to another.

When the boat steamed away on its southward journey Aklavik seemed to shrink, all the life and movement died away, the Eskimos returned to the shore, the Indians to their camps, the white men to their cabins. Silence settled down on the settlement, a curiously starved and empty silence, without echoes from the past. Aklavik seemed to be a little colony wrapped up in itself, far from the sources of life, isolated in space like a fleck of thistledown drifting across a summer sky. Silence, loneliness, deprivation, monotony. When I try to describe this settlement I find myself adding one negative to another. I wonder what Lao-

*Church of England Mission
House, Aklavik, 1926;
Rev. Arthur Creighton
McCullum (left) and Rev.
Canon Edward Hester
(right). John F. Moran.
NAC PA100552.*

*All Saints Anglican
Hospital, Aklavik, 1926.
John F. Moran.
NAC PA167654.*

Grey Nuns' Mission de l'Immaculée Conception, Aklavik, 1925. Left to Right: M and Mme L. Mercier; Rév Sœur locale Elizabeth McQuillan; Dr A.L. McDonald; Mère Girouard; Sœur Ste Adelard; Miss Lyman (later, Mrs Kost); Sœur Obéline Pothier Firmin. AGNRC, Album no. 1, Aklavik, 1925-1954.

Tse's interpreter Kwang, of the 3rd century B.C., would have thought of life at Aklavik. "Vacancy," he said, "stillness, placidity, tastelessness, quietude, silence and doing nothing are the root of all things."

In Aklavik there were no eggs nor milk, for, even if hens and cows could endure the winter cold, the cost of freight for feeding-stuffs would be prohibitive. There were neither gardens nor fresh meat. There were no trees except innumerable spruces and these were stunted. There was never a stone underfoot, only soft earth bestrewn with chips of wood and empty tins. There were no roads, only one well-worn track of mud or sand, crossed by many a gutter. That road led from the English mission house, past the police barracks, the wireless station, the general store and the lined out cabins to the Catholic convent, a three-story building of fragrant wood. Each mission was guardian, as it were, to one end of the place and while the individuals in charge remained friendly, the silent tug-of-war for souls was never relaxed. The Catholics were probably on the winning side, for their priests and nuns, being celibate, stay in, whereas the Church of England missionaries come and go.

Day after day I would prowl along the banks, make friends with someone and bring him in to our upper room to entertain my imprisoned friend. There

HBC Store and Wireless
Station, Aklavik, 1926.
John F. Moran.
NAC PA102512.

would never be any awkward pauses in the conversation, every newcomer brought his own entertainment although what they gained from us I cannot imagine, except the interest of seeing Gwen's sketches.

One day, a Swiss visitor was quite absorbed in them and when, at last, we got him to talk about himself, he told us many things that he had learned, self-taught, about the cunning of foxes. "You must choose a windy spot for your traps, to blow away your scent," he said to us seriously, as if he thought we were going out then and there to trap foxes. Enthralled, we waited for more, as if our lives depended on catching a fox and then another and another. "You bait with fish or meat," he went on, "but stale muskrat is the best, and often a trampled-round site is the best, for the fox knows how to think and he has reckoned it out that a trampled place will most often have camp refuse, good for a meal."

The charm of all such talk lay in its first-hand quality. It had a freshness and closeness to life that one seldom meets in civilized circles. Everything the Swiss boy had learned about foxes and traps and the ways of the North, he had learned slowly, by his own experience and watchfulness.

Our next visitor was a bearded German, a lay brother who came in to call on us one evening; he had been in the North for 31 years and had forgotten how to speak his own language.

One of our visitors, a trader, told us a story of an Indian carrying the winter mail from Fort McPherson. He met bad weather and the dog-team was played

out. There was nothing for it but to lighten the mail, so he hung the bag of letters on a tree and took on the newspapers, thinking that as they were the heaviest item they must be the most important. The letters were brought in next season. At Aklavik they sometimes got a Christmas mail in February and then no more letters until July, and after September there was no more regular mail until the next year.

On one occasion we had a call from Archdeacon Whittaker and Captain Cameron at the same moment. It was not an easy situation to handle. There was Captain Cameron, full of polar bears and whaling stories and oaths and forceful language and quite at ease with us, for he had soon forgotten the Crown prosecutor's warning; and there was the archdeacon sitting opposite our delightful ruffian, looking, by comparison, rather proper and precise. Gwen and I each took on one of them by mutual silent agreement. Gwen had the captain and the archdeacon fell to my lot. I remember pricking my ears apprehensively, towards the end of some anti-missionary story, while I was engaged in hearty small-talk with the cleric.

In a later visit the archdeacon was extremely helpful when he suggested that we should persuade our guides to take us down as far as Sinclair's Point, near Shingle Rock, some 25 miles beyond La Pierre House, so that they might help us through the rapids in that stretch of the river. Our memorandum only told us that "some swift water may be encountered before the Porcupine is reached, but no rapids of dangerous proportions." Neither had our other two advisers mentioned these rapids as anything other than "swift water." However, we remembered the archdeacon's warning when we reached La Pierre House and our guides took us down to Shingle Rock.

I had hoped to give Gwen interest and occupation in pressing flowers for our collection but even wild flowers, like so many of life's luxuries, were scarce at Aklavik and I only found a few species. These were bog bean, marsh-marigold, bearberry, *Pyrola*, wild rose, yellow anemone, a small *Gypsophila*, a pink *Rubus* three inches high, and a dwarf form of grass-of-parnassus. For the rest vegetation consisted mainly of silver willows, alder and the stunted spruce that seemed to hem us in completely on either bank of the river.

One cold afternoon I walked for about three miles along the mud bank of the river, intent on the bird life of the country. The mosquitoes were very troublesome. At one point there were ten northern ravens together; I also saw terns, semi-palmated plover, sandpipers and yellowshanks and the nest of a whisky-jack with young birds. One day Canon Hester showed me a white-headed sparrow's nest on the ground, with four young. There were huge buzzards or eagles often to be seen, with very serrated wing-tips and once I penetrated to the swamp behind our convent and saw many grackles, and also had a close-up view of six yellowshanks standing in a bed of bog bean. It was seldom, however, that I left the river bank, for the undergrowth was impossible, with snags of fallen trees, grass tussocks between which one would stumble knee-deep, muskeg or spongy moss and clouds of mosquitoes.

The best afternoon of all was when, after four days of slow stalking of the bird's movements, I found a semi-palmated plover's nest with four eggs. It was on the ground among the willows, and the bird had given the most amazing performance of defensive tactics before my search met with success. Again and again it flopped on the ground to entice me away from the nest, feigning to have a broken wing, and fluttered within two yards of me. I went away hurriedly as soon as I had found the nest, and left that valiant mother bird in peace.

All this was but poor sport for Gwen who had to make the best of things by reading borrowed books, awaiting or enjoying visitors and, when it was warm enough, sketching from the balcony. But three superimposed parallel lines of muddy water, level forest and distant heights did not make inspiring subject-matter for a picture. Only on certain days, the blue colour of the Richardson range of mountains would glow with a most unearthly depth. It was like a promise of freedom to a prisoner. So Gwen ticked off the days, one by one, in her diary and exercised as much patience as possible.

Meanwhile I had been learning how to paddle a canoe. Finding on the shore an American just setting off to look at his fish nets, I enlisted his help and had my first lesson from him. Next morning I acquired an Irish friend named Tyrell who gave me daily lessons in his 17-foot canoe, when he went out to inspect his nets. He was a trapper and surveyor, married to an Indian squaw, discursive in talk like most Irishmen and incapable of being dull. We would paddle across the river to a beautiful green creek that led away into unknown country, and every time we entered that creek I felt the call of the unknown, insistent as a physical pain, but after taking out the white fish from the nets, we would always return by the way we had come. He had a theory that mosquitoes were sent by Providence to preserve ducks, which would otherwise be exterminated by the natives. In early June, he himself had been forced by mosquitoes to quit rat-trapping. Under his tuition I gained a certain amount of facility in handling a canoe with a single paddle and very soon the backward sweep of the paddle, with its after-thought twirl to keep a straight course, became automatic.

Sundays and weekdays alike we heard strange mournful chants issuing from the convent chapel opposite our room. It seemed as if the nuns spent many hours of each day chanting or groaning Gregorian tunes to the accompaniment of a wheezing harmonium. Once, when the chapel was unoccupied at midnight, I crept and Gwen hopped into it, and we saw from the window the sun resting on the far edge of the lake, and before it sank below the horizon it began to rise again. It was July 3rd. We had actually seen the Midnight Sun.

On our second Sunday we went to an Eskimo service in the Church of England chapel. Canon Hester literally squeezed out music from a harmonium. The women, dressed in bright cotton garments, all wore fur hoods above their greasy black hair and tattooed faces, the children were squealing and crawling about the floor. An Eskimo deacon read the lesson which sounded like a contin-

All Saints Anglican Church, Aklavik, winter. (The point of view of this photo compares well with that of Dorrien Smith's water-colour of the church [see below, 195].) n.d. Collection of Edward Zealley, courtesy Ruth Murray.

All Saints Anglican Church, Aklavik, and Rev. Canon Hester, c. 1925. O.S. Finnie. NAC PA100553.

Interior of All Saints Anglican Church, Aklavik. n.d. Alfred James Vale Collection, ACC/GSA P7559-151.

uous "Tik, Tak, Tok." Hymns were heartily sung in Eskimo. "Tusingait, tusingait," seemed to be the favourite refrain. Archdeacon Whittaker, with an interpreter, preached a short sermon on the duty of men, who should do hard work and leave light work to the women, taking the line of "When I want wood I don't send my wife, and, what I say to you, I say not only with my tongue but by what I do." We could not help thinking of that well-satisfied man who prayed with himself while he declared that he fasted twice in the week and gave tithes of all that he possessed.

Canon Hester took a very different attitude when face-to-face with the Eskimos. He had just come back from spending years among their tribes and was so unused to speaking English that, often he would stumble and hesitate before he could find the words he wanted. He had a simple, childlike faith and had identified himself completely with the Eskimo. I do not for a moment think that he ever felt he was their superior. He would try to enter into their minds, never would he attempt to impose on them an alien creed. For example, when he stayed with them and an Eskimo, as part of the usual hospitality, offered his wife to the missionary for the night, he would say: "No thank you. We white men don't." Then he would await questions and seize the chance to talk quietly of the white man's beliefs.

He had translated the hymn "Jerusalem the Golden" for them, because he thought certain lines would appeal to their imagination. "All jubilant with song … the daylight is serene … the shout of them that triumph, the song of them that feast." When he tried to describe hell fire he painted it as a very cold place.

He came to visit us several times, we had long talks with him and he bought some of Gwen's sketches. He was about to return, on leave, to England, where he was to meet his fiancée, who had been waiting many years for him, in London. He was sadly absentminded and seemed like a man bemused with too long solitude. Sometimes we wondered if he were on the verge of a nervous breakdown. I recall him as a small and rather insignificant looking man but he was a brave pioneer, completely selfless, led by his own vision into those northern lands. If ever there lived a true-hearted, wide-minded missionary, that man was Canon Hester. We always longed to know his subsequent history.

Looking back on our brief acquaintance with those two fine men, I seem to see the archdeacon occupying, by the very nature of his office and his mentality, a pedestal whereon he would remain for the "term of his natural life." But if Canon Hester had been placed upon a pedestal, he would, I am sure, at once have come down from it, such was the urgency of his need to mingle, with all humility and on equal terms, with his fellow man.

15 *Prelude to Adventure*

At last came the day when Gwen's patience was rewarded and the doctor cut the plaster from her leg. At once she donned her brother's knee-high boots, which were to prove a moral and physical support to her in the early stages of our subsequent journey. Then she hopped downstairs and out to see the *Pioneer*, a Northern Trading vessel that had come in during the night.

It had been a hideous night of noise, with the barking of huskies on the shore and the sound of Gregorian chants, sung to celebrate the mother superior's feast day, issuing from the chapel door opposite our bedroom. The words of that monotonous and melancholy music sound like "And all the afternoon" repeated again and again, until we longed for some variety in melody or words, as we tossed about helplessly on our pillows. However the dawn came at last, bringing silence and when we got up Gwen's foot seemed to be quite sound. We were to start on the morrow and it was a busy day for us. First of all, with the help of Sister Firmin, I baked slabs of bannock which were to serve us as bread for several days, at the end of which we should be reduced to hardtack biscuits. Then we paddled across the river with my friend Tyrell and took a couple of white fish from his nets. Later, after paying a farewell visit to the doctor, who bound up Gwen's foot, we repaired to the HBC store, where, with the help of our guide Lazarus and Mr Parsons, we packed our stores so that they could be easily handled in the canoe. We then attended a long and lavish tea-party at the mission house with Canon Hester and the missionaries, which was followed by a concert of old-fashioned gramophone records. We said good-bye, regretfully, to Canon Hester and then we went out to pay other farewell visits in the settlement and to exchange "nods and becks and wreathed smiles" with the Eskimos on the shore. Finally, we went back to our upper room and carefully checked over the list of stores we had packed, with the invoice of goods bought at Edmonton.

Our equipment consisted, first and foremost, of the two Loucheux Indian guides, Lazarus Sittichinli and the boy Jimmy Koe; then there was the 18-foot Peterborough canoe with tracking rope and three paddles; and 20 packages, ten of which were personal luggage, bedding, tent and cooking utensils. The other ten held food, packed in four boxes, and half a dozen sacks containing:

2 cartons prunes	I carton apples
I tin desiccated potatoes	I bag granulated sugar
I carton lump sugar	2 pounds Baker's Chocolate
2 pounds tea	10 lbs. white beans
5 lbs. rice	I tin baking powder
I tube Sifto Salt	I packet Pony Matches
I dozen tins pork and beans	I pail Harris Lard
4 tins Cambridge Sausage	4 tins boiled dinner
4 tins beef	3 tins cherries
3 tins sliced peaches	3 tins pears
15 tins reindeer milk	8 packets assorted biscuits
3 tins pineapple	9 tins Crown Syrup
10 tins assorted jam	2 tins strawberry jam
I case pilot bread	I case breakfast bacon and salt pork
I sack flour	

The first steps of an adventure are often over dull and level spaces. Perhaps there have been months of planning, with hopes and fears following each other in sickening fashion, when nervous expectation is only kept in control by recurrent moods of confidence. When at last the enterprise begins, Nature joins past and present with the strange continuity that she maintains beneath her diversity of forms and we are, it may be, hardly aware that the adventure has begun, for looking forward to it and playing our part in it have become merged like the drops of water in a river. There has been no jerk of transition.

So, at 8 on that morning of July 7th, when all Aklavik was asleep, we set off without noise, excitement or ceremony, in the gas boat, bound for the mouth of the Rat River. There were only the nuns, the reverend father and the two lay brothers to wave good-bye. A swarm of mosquitoes met us as we crossed the plank to the boat. There were six of us on board, Mr Parsons and a lad, our two guides and ourselves. For the next ten days or so we should be completely at the mercy of the two Indians. The success of our enterprise depended on their fidelity rather than on our own efforts and powers of endurance. Yet we were not troubled by any such thoughts when our boat steamed away from the mud banks of Aklavik and turned up the Peel River, churning the smooth, glassy water into foam and breaking up the rainbow-coloured reflections of the Richardson mountain range. On that still morning, our attention was riveted by every successive bend and forward reach of the river. We never looked back into our wake of water. We were moving forward, going up the current as steadily as a river flows down and the feeling of progress, after all those days of inactivity, was one of bliss. Every bird and tree and flower on the river banks, each reflection in the water, each new vista in our forward course, absorbed us as if we were under a spell.

There was forest on either side of the banks, bordered by the brilliant green of mare's-tails, with silver willows, green willows, alder, spruce, cottonwood trees and a few black poplars. Against all the greenery there were repeated splashes of blue lupin. We saw no animals except two red foxes, but there were many ducks, and once a couple of swans passed overhead and once we glimpsed a white-headed eagle.

At noon, when we went ashore to boil our kettle and have a meal the mosquitoes attacked us in hordes; it was the worst experience of them that we had as yet encountered. We lunched on black tea, pemmican and bannock but despite Sister Firmin's instructions I had rolled the bannock too thin. The pemmican was to prove a standby for the guides, eating it seemed to produce instantaneous energy, but Gwen and I, after eating a lump no larger than a greengage, felt we had devoured an enormous meal.

For 12 miles we steamed up the Peel River and then we came to the mouth of the Husky. All the way the water was more like a sluggish channel than a moving river and as we moved on in loops and circles we seemed to remain stationary beneath the same point of a mountain range which had barren summits and green ravines lit by patches of blue lupin. After a while we noticed that the river banks were a little higher, but always they were formed of mud, with one bank sloping smoothly into the water like the stone sides of an artificial reservoir, while the other was eaten away by melting ice and was overhanging the current. There was little sunshine and hardly any wind all day, and the mosquitoes came and went like an army attacking and retreating in mass formation. We met no gas boats on the sluggish river and throughout the day we had the world to ourselves. A feeling persisted that we were in a magic world where, round each bend of the current, we should find something new and more exciting than anything we had ever seen before. The sight of a hippogriff or a dinosaur would not have astonished us; in that mood miracles might seem to be a part of our birthright.

To follow a river, either up or down, will always bring to the traveller a sense of magic adventure, but I do not remember ever enjoying that sense so vividly as on that long day when we followed, without any personal effort, those seemingly endless coils of the Peel and the Husky rivers. The flowers that grew most abundantly on the banks were that beautiful lupin, a white valerian, a mauve vetch and a blue one, a yellow *Senecio* and *Pyrola*.

At last, after 12 hours spent circling round the base of the mountains, we came out of the Husky, in evening sunshine, to the mouth of the Rat. It looked like a little sluggish backwater, it was bordered by willows and seemed to be half asleep. For so many months we had read and talked about this river. For so many weeks, during our journey across Canada and down the Mackenzie, the old-timers' warnings had been echoing, like funeral dirges, in our ears. "You'll never make it. You'll never make it. You'll be eaten alive by mosquitoes. Yes, eaten alive. No sane person would choose to travel up the Rat for pleasure. It has a bad name and deserves it." And so on, and so on.

We landed there to boil our kettle and make tea and to refuel the boat with gasoline. There were clouds of mosquitoes about us but other things claimed our attention. We found, among the mare's-tails, a sandpiper's nest with four eggs and then Lazarus showed us tracks of geese and beaver in the mud. He could read these signs like a book and as the days went by we were filled with admiration for his knowledge of wild life which amounted to an almost mystical union with his own country.

As we steamed on again the spruce trees, reflected in the water, were gold in the evening light. We saw northern ravens, many ducks and sandpipers and various waders. The guides produced their rifles and after a fusillade, alas, they killed a white-fronted goose and then the young ones went waddling away up the bank, a forlorn little party. Like the Husky and the Peel, the Rat, in this part of its course was a succession of loops and bends and we remained tense with expectation, mistaking every snag of a broken tree for a caribou or a moose, every fallen

Beginning of swift water on the Rat River and probable location of Destruction City. 1994. Michael Peake. Collection of the photographer.

log for a bear. We did, however, see three muskrats on the water's edge and one of them was swimming; they were yellow, serious-looking, rabbit-nosed creatures.

We had travelled about 70 miles from Aklavik to the point where the Rat enters the Husky. "We shall leave you," Mr Parsons had said, "25 miles up the Rat, at Destruction City." Throughout that 25 miles we felt like the Ancient Mariner; surely "we were the first that ever burst" into that silent water. Surely our puffing engine was the first mechanical sound that had ever broken the age-long silence of the river.

It was after midnight when we came out from the narrow channel into a wide space where we could see, ahead, a mountain barrier suffused with a light of the strangest quality. The mountains were a deep amethyst turning slowly to pink, then to a fainter shade as if they were veiled in rose-coloured dew; yet the outline remained clear-cut as if defined by some light that came from beyond the range. In the immediate space about us there were only mud banks and a desolate tract of land overgrown with spongy moss.

"Here," said Mr Parsons, "we are at Destruction City."

We looked about us in surprise. There was no sign that any human being had ever passed that way, not a charred log of a dead fire nor any broken timber that might once have been part of a hut. As we helped the others to dump our bundles and boxes ashore on this melancholy tract of waste land, we tried to look as happy as if we had been landed for the night in a hospitable home. We had not learned that the Arctic shows little hospitality to intruders. We thanked Mr Parsons and the lad and they steamed away down the river. Feeling hungry and sleepy, we pitched our tent, sprayed the inside with Flit, laid our bags on a bed of moss and *Ledum* and set up our nets. We felt like Shadrach, Meshach and Abednego clad in "their hosen, their tunics and their mantles, and their other garments," when, fully dressed, we crawled in under our mosquito bars. Only after tucking in the walls of the net did we, by a gymnastic effort, remove our hats and shoes. Then we wriggled into our bags.

16 *Check to our Progress*

That night was a very short one, for we had not settled down to sleep until 2 and at 8 we crawled out, into a busy world of mosquitoes, to waken our guides. It had rained heavily during the night, the sky was an unrelieved gray and at intervals it was still raining as we breakfasted on fried bacon, bread and jam, and black tea. We ate standing in the smoke of the bonfire. A green range of mountains seemed to slope up from a point immediately ahead into the melancholy sky, but in reality it was only the precursor of that height of land which held the source of the Rat River. As we munched our bacon, scraping away with forks the mosquitoes that had settled on the fat and become embedded in it, we looked around for some sign of the tragic event that gave Destruction City its name.

In the 1898 gold rush, certain pioneers tried to reach the Klondike via the Rat River. Most of them failed and then, exhausted by their struggles with the current, retraced their steps to this place where they camped in despair and sat down to face their ruined hopes. They were broken men, having staked their all on the Klondike venture. There was no stone monument set up to commemorate this tragedy; all that misery, disappointment and despair had vanished. Sooner or later, nature will always cover up the traces of broken human hearts and human lives.

It took us a couple of hours to breakfast, strike camp and get away from that sad place and then, for a few hundred yards only, we had the exhilarating experience of being paddled upriver by our guides. Our easeful moments, however, were numbered and after the third or fourth bend Lazarus told us in his broken English that he must put us ashore. We soon discovered why. From now onwards the guides could seldom move upstream by paddling the canoe, they had to push or pull it up, yard by yard, sometimes even inch by inch, in order to keep moving onward up the muddy current. There could be no question of our adding to their labour by remaining in the canoe. Our part henceforward was to keep the guides in sight as we struggled along the shore, now stumbling over stones, now squelching through mud, but most of the time forcing our way through undergrowth of willows and alders, with arms curled round our heads to protect the mosquito veils which were, as we had already realised, our life-lines. They came at us in one wave after another, like Napoleon's inexhaustible attacking armies. Once, when walking behind Gwen, I noticed that they had massed on her shoulder blades, where the cloth was drawn tightly over the skin and the putty-coloured material was hardly visible through their wings and bodies.

Meanwhile, slowly but surely, Lazarus and Jimmy pulled the canoe through shallows and rapids. Sometimes Lazarus would shout and beckon us to get into the canoe, then they would ferry across to the opposite shore where there was a more open stretch of land for us and an easier reach of water for them. In these rare spells of easy going we were able to collect wild flowers and the highlights of that day were a pink *Oenothera* and a very showy, large-petalled willow-herb.

At some hour well after noon we stopped on a stony spit of land and the guides made a huge bonfire to roast the goose, while we sat on flat stones, trying to write up our notes and press our flowers. We were a muddy, unwashed, unbrushed, beveiled couple, wet to the knees from contact with dripping undergrowth, and we laughed at each other's appearance. The sun shone for a while and then came a puff of wind that scattered the mosquitoes for a short spell, during which we raised our veils and stepped into the river with sponges and toothbrushes. It was a blissful half-hour.

Meanwhile the guides were in their own seventh heaven with the goose. Lazarus plucked it, opened it out like a wafer and spitting it on a sharpened stick he toasted it fore and aft. It was a tough bird, but we all enjoyed it and both of us tried to forget those tragic orphan waddlers of yesterday.

Before lunch we had been moving up the river at about a mile an hour, but afterwards conditions became worse and progress was slower. More than once we came to what the guides termed "swift water" and we regarded as rapids, and several times, in order to reach an easier shore, we were ferried across one of these rapids on a diagonal course, swiftly losing ground as the current carried us downriver at a giddy pace.

Jim Koe dislodging canoe from a "Sweeper," Rat River, July 1926. Clara Coltman Rogers (Vyvyan). Collection of Edward Zealley.

During the afternoon we came to a new form of obstacle in the form of deep swift water below overhanging banks which were a tangle of fallen boughs and tree trunks, half in the water and half on the bank. The men could neither push nor paddle the canoe up any such reach of water, nor could they take to tracking the canoe until a pathway was cleared along the bank. They adopted a new form of progress. They would clear a track, with their axes, on the very edge of the bank. Then Lazarus would sit in the canoe, steering it outward from the snags at the water's edge which were too firmly wedged in the river bed to be destroyed.

Jimmy would pull like a barge-horse on the rope and haul it forward at a slanted angle. We were not much use in these emergencies, though we tried, with our own small axe, to help clear a pathway along the bank. Here, the river was much wider and its current was divided by many islands. Now and then it was joined by a tributary across which we would have to wade.

At 5 we came to deep, swift water and Lazarus said it was impossible to go on. We should have to camp and wait until the water level was lower. We began to make a camp. This was sited on mud and mare's-tail, but it had a beautiful outlook down the river and once again a little breeze had arisen, scattering the swarms of mosquitoes. I began to cut sweet-scented poplar tips for our bedding, according to Lazarus' instructions, while Gwen unpacked the tent and Jimmy brought the food ashore. Lazarus himself stood on the bank, quiet as a hunter frozen into immobility before he takes aim at his prey, but he was not looking at any animal, he was gazing down into the water. Then he turned to us, and by words and gestures made us understand that the level of the river was rising fast and that our chosen camp, being only a foot above water level, was unsafe. We must move at once. So we packed up again and paddled up a quietly flowing side-stream until a waterfall, with snags of trees on either side, made further progress impossible. It was a bad place to camp, situated as it was in stuffy air among the trees, and being only two feet above the water level of the tributary and very close to its edge. But there was no other possible place so there we stopped to camp for the night.

Things looked far from cheerful. The water was rising fast and Lazarus said it might take days to subside. From this point, it was impossible to proceed up the river by either bank. We might even be flooded out before the morning. All through supper Lazarus was sticking twigs into the muddy bank, watching each twig patiently and silently and then sticking in another when the last one was submerged. The mosquitoes were very bad and we went to bed directly after supper, tired and dirty but trying, as we always did when we encountered trouble, to encourage each other not to be down-hearted over the events of the moment. After all, we were in the wild and solitary country of our hearts' desire, we had seen fresh moose tracks in the mud and had supped well off potato and pork, rice and maple sugar. Also, even if in 12 hours we had not gained much in actual mileage, we had spent a glorious day, filled with personal endeavour, lit by intensity of purpose; we had gathered and pressed a certain number of flowers and had gained much experience in a completely new mode of travel. So, having "flitted" our sleeping bags and net walls generously, we turned to sleep, waking to reach for the tin of bicarbonate of soda whenever an intrusive mosquito bit us on the face, or on the bony part of the wrist. Gwen, being fair-haired, suffered more than I did from the little pests, although her skin had been toughened by exposure to all weathers and should not have been tempting to any insect. Though sallow-skinned and dark, I was on the whole less troubled by our enemies. Fortunately, the mosquito bites of the north country do not carry malaria.

We slept, on and off, for 12 hours, then Gwen crawled out of the tent to reconnoitre. There was no sign of life from the two guides. The water had risen and she put in another twig. A couple of hours later I went out and found that the water had fallen a little.

While we were breakfasting, late, the sky looked thundery, the Indians looked sleepy and were silent; there was no denying that our prospects were gloomy. We remembered all too vividly the story of the woman who had ventured alone to go up the Rat River with Indian guides and how they had taken her back when they had made less than half the journey, because she persisted in giving them orders to do this and that. Mindful of her fate, we adopted towards Lazarus a deferential manner that was almost cringing. I do not think that Gwen had ever cringed to anyone before.

After that breakfast of pork, bannock and pilot bread, we went back to our sleeping bags and I read aloud extracts from *Macbeth* while Gwen mended our mosquito veils. Later, after another heavy meal, it was obvious that there had been little change in the water level, and as there was no hope of moving on we set off up the river bank to hunt for flowers.

At the end of about a mile of level forest we came to a hill and clawed our way up it, through a perfect hell of mosquitoes, until we came to a paradise of flowers. There was *Linnaea borealis* and the *Oxycoccus* underfoot, in masses. There was pink *Menziesia*, a handsome yellow-flowered dock, a very showy pink *Pedicularis* about two feet high, mauve *Pinguicula*, larkspur, lupin, *Polemonim* and, on one high ridge, a whole sheet of yellow *Arnica*. All about us were many beautiful varieties of moss. We stood on that hilltop among scrubby willows that had soaked us to the knees, but we did not stay there for more than a few minutes. There were storm clouds overhead and a fine view of mountains, but we could not gaze at them, for the mosquitoes pursued us relentlessly. Even if they did not get inside our nets, the buzzing of the mosquitoes drove us into perpetual movement and we never could bear to stand still in a cloud of them. We had the incurable delusion that perpetual movement meant escape, therefore we never did any bird-watching on the Rat River and identified very few species. The stillness and patience needed for the study of birds was, we soon realised, impossible. With flowers it was different. We both had a quick eye for a new flower and we could pick one almost without stopping, even though we had to pick with leather gauntlets on our hands. On that hilltop we did, however, at last find a ridge blessed by a little breeze. We were learning to seek for wind as an Arab seeks for shade, and goes to sleep beside a telegraph pole when there is nothing better, so we sat down and each managed to smoke a cigarette through our veils. When we left that spot the mosquitoes renewed their attacks. They were wonderful crevice-finders; they would slip under the folds of our veils and bite us on the neck, they would slip through the holes of our lace up breeches, they would insert their probosces through tiny stitches on the back seams of our gloves.

At supper time the sun came out, and brought us hope of brighter prospects. Lazarus did not commit himself to any optimism, but he no longer gazed intently at the little sticks he placed in the mud. It was obvious now that the water was falling.

We went to bed early, agreeing that it was a blessed world, that we were leading a blissful life and that there was nothing to grumble about except mosquitoes and the swift water.

17 *Moods, Rapids and Islands*

The antics of memory are very strange. I realise as I re-read my Alaskan notes and diaries, trying to elicit from them a true and connected account of our journey, that memory will often distort or discolour truth and it is not easy, even with the help of jotted notes, to recapture from the past the story of any adventure, as it really happened. One thing strikes me forcibly and that is the enduring quality of spiritual experience as compared with factual events.

Were it not for the diary I should have completely lost the memory of so many details of our travels. This bird and that flower, some bend of the river, hills looming ahead, tributaries entering the main current, sand or pebbles on some island shore affording us flat ground for our tent and sleeping bags, the food we ate, our broken talks with the guides, the chunks of ice falling with a "plosh" from overhanging banks into the river. So many of these things are left behind in the immeasurably distant time of over 30 years ago, when we crawled slowly up the Rat River, and now only a shadowy outline of each experience remains in the jottings of a paper volume. Yet our moods and feelings we have never forgotten and, after all, what is a mood but a prolonged spiritual experience? Sometimes, it needs only a phrase or two in that shabby little volume to re-awaken our moods as if we suffered them, or were buoyed up by them only yesterday.

Once again we set out in a mood of high exultation, kindled by the explorer's inner light; hardship is to be welcomed, there shall be no limit to powers of endurance, we shall move in a world beyond the pin-pricks of daily life. In the early stages of the journey even hardtack is a delicacy, mosquitoes are a joke, wet feet and aching limbs a part of the game. Then the river rises, holding us prisoners and we feel weak as kittens in the hands of fate, our high hopes like fallen petals of a flower. All our strength and powers of endurance, are they to be snuffed out like a candle extinguished? Is the Rat a malignant enemy and are we unwelcome, fatally doomed intruders?

There were moods too of perfect confidence in Lazarus and Jimmy who were proving themselves bold, resourceful and tireless but there were also moods when, not understanding a word they said to each other, we found ourselves in the deadly grip of suspicion. But we were completely in their power and there was nothing we could do to escape. There were moods of fear too, from which I, being less courageous than Gwen, suffered much, especially the fear of rapids. Then there were moments of utter delight when we found some beautiful flower, or caught a glimpse of mountains ahead, or reckoned up our progress and agreed that even if it was slow it was surely and steadily forward. So, liable to such giddy alternations of hope and fear, happiness and suspicion, we crawled out each morning, taking it in turns to waken our guides at about 8. It was no easy matter to dress under a mosquito net, but we always emerged fully clothed; the only garments we discarded when we slept were boots and hats and puttees, but it required a gymnastic effort to struggle even into these from a half lying-down position and as for doing one's hair, it gave one a frightful crick in the neck. Gwen scored over me here, for after the first night she kept hers plaited, by night and by day, in a coronal.

On the third morning of our canoe journey, after a night when we were conscious of every bone in our bodies touching our mattress of spruce boughs, we woke early. The sun was shining and the river no longer gave out a loud roar, only a pleasant burble. Gwen got out and shook Lazarus, and in the usual two hours we had breakfasted, packed and loaded the canoe. The rapid that had checked our advance was now only swift water, but it was still unnavigable for a craft going upstream, so the men ferried themselves to the other side after Lazarus had directed us to walk on over the level land, until they could cross over and rejoin us.

We set off, happily confident that our guides would cross the river again before we reached our hill of the previous day, but we had not reckoned with the changeful Rat that now seemed capable of showing a new form of malice every day. We had to force our way along the bank, splashing in swamps or pushing through alder and willow, or climbing over fallen boughs. Moreover the river here was quite a quarter of a mile wide and was full of channels between islands

Jim Koe (bow) and Lazarus Sittichinli (stern), hauling canoe up Rat River, July 1926. Clara Coltman Rogers (Vyvyan). Collection of Edward Zealley.

that were overgrown with trees and shrubs, so that we were unable to watch the progress of our guides on the other bank. Only now and then could we glimpse them, tracking patiently or forcing the canoe up the current, one pulling the bows and the other pushing at the stern.

We came to the hill, began to climb and got so high that we could not make the guides hear our shouts. At last, however, we plunged down through undergrowth to water-level again and waded across a knee-deep channel to an island where we stood watching the struggles of the two men who were coming up slowly towards us.

Gwendolen Dorrien Smith, Lazarus Sittichinli, and Jim Koe (back to camera), encamped on Rat River, July 1926. Clara Coltman Rogers (Vyvyan). Collection of Edward Zealley.

Once, they were washed downstream like a cork, by a little stretch of rapids and were nearly capsized. They were unable to reach our island, so Lazarus waded half-way across the main channel, threw us over a carton of biscuits and told us to keep on going forward. He and Jimmy began tracking up the left bank and were soon hidden from us again by other islands. At last they rejoined us on our big island, having lost their axe in rough water. We set about making a fire with Jimmy and cooking our lunch of pork and beans while with our little axe, Lazarus began to chop down the overhanging willows ahead. It had been a tough morning for us all. We were streaming with perspiration beneath our veils and scarves as we stood by that fire in the sunshine, amid swarms of mosquitoes that were thicker than ever.

The afternoon was even more strenuous. We were all four of us still on the island, with deep water on either side when the guides put us ashore again on the right bank and returned to their tracking on the left one. We climbed again and were forced down by the obstacle of sheer rocks, to a ravine full of mud at the mouth of a tributary. The mud was spread out fan-wise and was fairly deep. Up till now Eddy's boots had saved the situation and Gwen's foot had stood up wonderfully to the rough going, but she found these muddy crossings difficult and when Lazarus saw her floundering along with painful steps, he and Jimmy came over and took her into the canoe for a short spell and then she travelled like Cleopatra in her barge, with Lazarus waist-deep in the water pushing her on and Jimmy ahead hauling on the rope. Her respite, however, was a short one, for we came to a shallow rapid boiling near the shore and the four of us had to haul and push until we got the canoe through. Then we went on again, with a spell of easier progress, but we were wet above the knees, there was thunder rolling round the green hills that enclosed us … and a shower of rain had fallen. Again we were filled with anxiety.

We stopped to make tea for half an hour and after that came the worst experience of the whole journey. I do not know to this day what Gwen's feelings were; she was always lion-hearted. For myself I never shall forget that hour when we stood alone on the muskeg, for the most part in silence, on a ten feet cliff above the river and I was face-to-face with naked fear. The guides had returned to the other bank, Lazarus saying that we would only do a short spell more that day and they would cross back very soon to rejoin us. At this point, many islands split the river and our guides were at once lost to view. We went on over an easy stretch of ground, keeping, as we knew, well ahead of the men, for, whether they were tracking or pushing and pulling, their progress through the water was bound to be slower than ours on land. After a while we came out into an open stretch of muskeg where the river was clear of islands. Here, the current was not more than a few hundred yards wide and although it was fairly swift we judged that the two would be able to cross over to us and then push up our bank until we found a level landing-place.

At first, we stood in that open place in the usual cloud of mosquitoes, happy and hopeful, feeling that it had been a grand though somewhat toilsome day and that we were appreciably nearer the height of land. Then a vague fear took hold of me; at first it was like that little cloud in the Bible, no bigger than a man's hand. Why were they so long in coming? If they had capsized and been swept downriver on the far side of one of those islands, how should we ever know? We began to pace up and down, nursing our thoughts, saying futile things. "Surely they'll be here soon. Perhaps they've met a lot of snags." "It may be the river is curved on the other side and they have further to go."

Our eyes were glued to the other bank, they ached with intensity of staring. Gwen kept on murmuring calculations and suggestions to explain their delay. My mind was fixed on our chances of survival, alone in this wilderness; there would be none I decided. Except for the biscuits that Lazarus had thrown across to us we had no food in our packs. Half a mile back we had seen a duck's nest with seven eggs, but the bird was sitting and those eggs would probably be uneatable. Fort McPherson might be only a few days march distant, on the map, but, alone, we could never cross the currents nor the mud shores of the many tributaries. Ahead of us was La Pierre House, an empty hut perhaps 150 miles away, and beyond that hut no human dwelling on this side of Old Crow which was another hundred or more miles down the river.

For the first time I realised how the mere size of a lone country may constitute a threat to the helpless creature whom we call man. Communications, communications, communications, I thought to myself. Trams, steamers, cars, waggons, horses, it is only by their bringing us food that we are kept alive. Here, on the Rat, there are none of these things. Only Lazarus and Jimmy stood between us and starvation. And what had become of them? At this point I ceased to think, for my whole being had become a white-hot point of fear. Nor had I any outlet for expression of this fear except to keep my eyes fixed on the other river bank. It was a rigid state for mind and body, and I imagine that it lasted for quite half an hour. Then suddenly we were aware of human movement, not on the far shore but close beside us and there was Lazarus walking along our bank to tell us that they had met swift water and had been forced to cross back again to our side and Jimmy was making camp a little lower down. We went back to a beautiful camp among spruces and now that our troubles were over, felt fresh and active although we had been travelling for about 14 hours. Drinking much tea and refreshing draughts of water from the river had kept us in good condition.

All fear was forgotten. The muddy crossings of that day, the steep climbs, the struggle with undergrowth, the bewildering maze of islands, all these were behind us. Lazarus had proved his worth in every possible way and we began to feel trust in him. We agreed that except for mosquitoes this was a paradise. After supper, we talked to Lazarus over the campfire, though this was difficult, for his English was limited. He had only once before negotiated the Rat in summer and that was about two years previously when he had taken a lawyer up, but after that trip he had sworn he would never go again. There were summers when nobody went up that river. How did he learn to navigate rough water, we asked, since the Peel and the Husky are smooth currents.

"Swift water Peel and Husky sometimes," he said.

I asked him if we should have died of hunger, had he and Jimmy been capsized and drowned.

"That feller no drown," he said, pointing to Jimmy as if to suggest that he was an unsinkable cork. I persisted that Jimmy *could* be drowned and Gwen asked him: "What you say Jimmy's father and mother if Jimmy drown and you go home alone?"

"I just say 'Jimmy he drown,' that's all," he answered, shrugging his shoulders.

Before going to sleep that night I said to myself severely: "You set out on this expedition with a craving to travel in wild country. Now you know what wild country can do to a man or woman and you should be satisfied."

Next day we pushed on upriver in a happy mood; our only care was to reach the head of the Rat and we knew now that Lazarus would take that care off our shoulders. As for the craving to reach wild country and yet more wild country, nothing, in over 30 years of subsequent travelling, has ever cured me of that and nothing ever will.

18 *To Barrier River*

After all the troubles of that day, troubles which had ranged from climbing steep hills to floundering across mud deltas, negotiating rapids and swift water, and finally fighting a battle with extreme fear, a new relationship formed itself between Lazarus and ourselves. No longer had we any fear that he would turn back with us, unless the Rat itself turned on him in one of its ungovernable rages and made further progress impossible. He had shown himself to be energetic, courageous and thoughtful and we began to rely on him with a happy confidence. Both guides, on their part, seemed now to be more at ease with us and we began to indulge in many small jokes together, which were for the most part centred on Jimmy and his goloshes. Lazarus had high boots but both guides wore wide-brimmed hats and mosquito veils all the time. They taught us one of nature's preventives against mosquitoes and every day we would rub wet moss into the seams and weak places of our gloves; this kept off their attacks so long as the moisture remained.

The Indians, like the white men in the North, were always telling us that we should come to the Arctic in the winter when there were no mosquitoes, and Lazarus would add: "Summer no good. Always hungry. Winter I hunt. Get fresh meat." Then he would rub his stomach mournfully, even while he was devouring large lumps of pemmican, which was the only item in our food supply that seemed to give any relief to the permanent hunger of our guides.

That next morning, I woke Lazarus at 6:30 and we began the day's journey by making a short portage, with the canoe and all our goods, across a patch of muskeg to a spot above the swift water where we could safely launch it again. As we

Lining canoe up Rat River,
July 1926. Clara Coltman
Rogers (Vyvyan).
Collection of Edward
Zealley.

struggled with the lighter packages I was sweating so much that I had to transfer
the dollar notes in a chamois leather bag from my bosom to an outside coat
pocket, for fear that they would get soaked through. Although lumps of melting
ice were continually dropping into the water from overhanging banks, the
temperature of the Rat valley was similar to that of a stuffy, English summer's day.
We lowered the canoe carefully into the water, loaded it and set off on another
strenuous day's journey. Hitherto our course had been south, now we turned
west and began to skirt the base of high hills with sheets of mud washing down
their sides. There were fossils in this loose soil and one slope was a beautiful
silver gray with *Artemisia* foliage. Usually there was enough flat foreshore to enable
us to skirt the base of the hills, but once or twice when these half-solid rivers of

mud dropped sheer from the hillside into the water, Lazarus would ferry us across. One such ferry journey across a rapid I shall never forget.

The two men took a paddle each and put all their strength into making for a point immediately opposite us on the other bank, but even so we were whirled downstream diagonally at a most terrifying pace. Gwen, an old sea-dog if ever there was one, fell into a mood of bliss at feeling herself rocked once again by rough water and kept on murmuring to herself "delicious, delicious," but I was in a state of what is known as "blue funk" and kept my eyes on the tree tops across the river.

Meanwhile, Lazarus and Jimmy were uttering to each other the most alarming cries that were like the sound of animals in pain, and we had no idea whether they were swearing, adjuring each other to pull harder, celebrating their progress across the river, or singing a death chant for the four of us. I had raised my eyes from the tree tops to a distant range of hills, so that I should not see the engulfing waters, when I suddenly realised that we had nearly reached the other shore. In another moment we were landing at a point some 200 yards below the spot that we were heading for. Here, so far as we could judge, the Rat was about a hundred yards across. Crossing rapids was, I thought, not only a fearful but an expensive form of progress, when we had to lose two yards down in order to gain one across.

The luncheon-hour that day was blissful, for we had crossed to an open stretch of shingle where the wind blew freely, scattering the mosquitoes. Usually at meals we employed a technique that we had acquired in desperation. We had found that while we took a plateful of pork or bacon from the cooking pot and made ready with knife and fork, quite a dozen mosquitoes would have become sizzled in the fat. There was always also the further delay of raising our veils in order to eat, and while we were doing this a fresh collection of fried corpses would appear on each plate. We just had to accept the corpses and deal with them, but we had to protect our faces, so we would take it in turns to stand ready with the bottle of oil of citronella. If I were on duty I would rub Gwen's face, taking care to avoid her eyes, and then my own face, a job at which I was clumsy, nearly always applying the oil too near my eyes and stinging them. We both ate standing up in the smudge of our bonfire smoke which gave us some protection.

In that most blessed open space we had freedom from our tormentors for one whole hour. We got out our sponge bags, repaired to the river and went through the customary morning ritual that we had been obliged to omit during the last few days. Then we sat down on boulders and ate our food slowly and happily. I was even able to put a film in my Kodak with ungloved hands and, finally, to smoke a cigarette in peace. Usually Gwen used her rubber mouthpiece, specially inserted in the veils for the purpose of smoking, but I had torn my rubber on a bough and, once the veil was mended, there was no more smoking for me. We had also evolved a technique for collecting and preserving flowers. Even during those hard days we would never pass a new one without adding it to our collection. We were skilful now in picking flowers with gloves, but when it came to pressing them we could not work in gloves and we had only a limited supply of oil of citronella. While I adjusted the little pieces of sticking paper that held our specimens fast on sheets of newspaper, Gwen would stand by and fan my hands vigorously.

Many that we found were old friends seen in different parts of the world, but quite a number were new to us. We agreed that among the best thrills life can offer is the sight of an unknown wild flower; but there is also the thrill of seeing our familiar garden ones growing wild in their own habitat, and last, but not least, there is the joyous excitement of seeing any wild flower, known or unknown, growing in masses of beautiful colour, as, on one memorable day, we saw lupins in a spruce wood. There is also special delight in seeing a well-known flower with a more than usually brilliant shade of colour and this is a common experience in far northern lands. Never, until that day on the Rat when we were nearing Barrier River, had we seen wild roses of such a brilliant pink.

We had a hard afternoon of travel after that outstanding luncheon-hour, but Lazarus and Jimmy were undefeated. Sometimes we were all four on the same bank, sometimes we had to follow one shore while the guides struggled up the other and then we would be anxiously watching their movements all the time. Throughout the day they pushed that canoe up the forceful torrent, gaining one yard after another by sheer perseverance. Often they were both waist-deep in the current, when Lazarus, being the heavier man, would usually allot himself the job of pushing at the stern, while Jimmy went ahead with the tracking rope and pulled or waded in the water at the bows. Sometimes, when they decided to track for a spell and the water was not too swift, Jimmy would sit in the canoe, fending it off from snags of fallen branches in the river, while Lazarus, with expert judgment, would pass the rope in front of all obstacles that were on the shore or in the water, often leaning his body out over the current in what seemed to us a most

*Lazarus Sittichinli,
Gwendolen Dorrien Smith,
and Jim Koe (foreground),
on a gravel bar lunch break,
Rat River, July 1926.
Clara Coltman Rogers
(Vyvyan). Collection of
Edward Zealley.*

perilous position. Sometimes they would repeat that terrifying performance of paddling diagonally across a rapid while we watched from the shore with our hearts in our mouths. More than once they were carried downriver for twice the distance they were trying to cover from shore to shore.

We came to a place that, obviously, we could not negotiate on foot, for rocky cliffs dropped sheer into the water. The current was deep and swift, although it was not actually a rapid. Lazarus stood quite still, thinking; he looked up the river and down, and then he looked at the other bank. There were wrinkles about his eyes as he looked all round again. Then he spoke.

"Water look bad," he said, "I guess we try it."

There followed a really nerve-wracking crossing of the Rat, in which the only part we could play was to obey orders and sit absolutely still in the canoe while the two men pushed us across. The water swirled about their waists, they slipped and slithered on stones at the bottom of the channel, but they kept the frail craft faithfully on her slanted course, with bows turned slightly upstream and we all reached the farther shore. The only casualty was the loss of one of Jimmy's goloshes and henceforward he had to wear moccasins.

The four and a half hours spell of that afternoon had been exhausting, we felt, when we stopped for tea and pork and pemmican after landing easily in shallow water on a beach full of stones and little pools. We had had almost enough, but Lazarus elected to go on for three hours more. He always gave the orders about stopping for a meal or for a night's camp and although he would get up most reluctantly each morning, it was by his own wish that we always called him early. In one matter we had a deep difference of opinion but, of course, we always deferred to him. Indians, he told us, always travel best if they do a short morning spell, then after a good dinner, they can face a long and strenuous afternoon. It is natural to a man, he said, to have a big meal in the middle of the day and it is natural to travel best with plenty of good pork and pemmican inside. We would have preferred to go "all out" in a longer morning and to lunch with a feeling that the worst part of the day was behind us, for we could never overcome a sense of slackness after lunch.

Now, on this occasion, after tea on such a gruelling day when Lazarus said: "I guess we go on three hours more," there was no question of our objecting. We had realised that to follow him without a murmur of dissent was our best chance of reaching the head of the Rat.

So we went wearily and doggedly ahead for three more hours, cheered a little by the view of a beautiful mountain range far ahead, plunging into soft muskeg, through woods with dead branches that threatened our veils, and dense alder thickets where the boughs continually tripped us up; and all the time the mosquitoes were quite devilish. At times, the whole world seemed to be a buzzing blackness, and we had a struggle to prevent panic seizing hold of our minds. At last we came to the point where Barrier River joins the Rat, and we camped on an island just above their junction. It had been a long day and an eventful one.

"Pretty tough going," I said to Gwen, as we Flitted ourselves and the tent. "Oh well," she said, "we are a tough couple. Got to be," she added and turned over to sleep.

19 *A Turning Point*

We slept on sand that night at Barrier River camp, and a very hard bed it was. Sand has no power of giving, whereas pebbles, as we proved to our own satisfaction, afford nestling pockets for the softer parts of the body. On some of the shorter days we slept on delicious beds of spruce tips or poplar twigs, but there were evenings on which neither we nor our guides could summon enough energy to cut and lay such luxurious bedding.

As I look back now on that camp, I see it as the turning point of our struggle with the Rat. The worst difficulties, though we did not realise this at the time, were behind us. The mosquitoes were still thick as ever and other torments awaited us in the nature of the ground over which we would have to walk or hop or jump, but battling at a slant across rapids and navigating swift water against the current, were things of the past and never again did we have to camp dangerously close to the level of a rising flood. On the other hand our reserves of energy were low. Continual struggle with undergrowth, continual wading through streams, long days and short nights, the unremitting persecution of mosquitoes, all these things were beginning to tell on us. We got up a little more reluctantly each morning, and each night went to bed more exhausted. A significant entry in my diary at this stage betrays the fact that we were flagging. "Short hours of sleep and long hours on the march, with hardly ever a sit-down in peace from mosquitoes, are beginning to make us feel a bit empty."

Remembering clearly, as I do, our evening feelings of exhaustion at that stage of the journey, I regard this entry as an understatement.

It was either at Barrier River or on the next evening, I cannot now remember which, that we had recourse to the brandy-flask, blessing, as we drank, our friends at Edmonton who had insisted on our filling it for any unexpected emergency. Remembering that we were two lone women with a couple of hundred pounds in our pouches, completely at the mercy of our guides, we thought it wiser not to let them know that we had any brandy with us so, putting the flask furtively into a rucksack, we strolled off into the willows while the guides were making a fire and in due course came back ostentatiously carrying bunches of wild flowers. It was a strange tippling-place, that thicket of willows in the wild country but never did any tavern-haunter enjoy his liquor more. It put new life into us both, we agreed, and thereafter it became, for the next few days, an evening habit. If there were no willows, there would be dense alders or secretive firs, and always there would be wild flowers to justify our absence and to grace our return.

We left Barrier River at our usual hour for striking camp and set off up the left bank towards a great flat space, but we soon found that level ground in the Arctic does not spell easy going. We were walking through a vast area of muskeg such as we had not yet encountered and it was like walking through a sea of sponges. The muscular effort needed for each single step was surprising, and we floundered on with some difficulty until we came to dense alder thickets. Unencumbered, we could have pushed through these like steam rollers, breaking the dead twigs without effort and parting the live boughs as a swimmer parts the water, but the need for protecting our veils was always uppermost in our minds and we had to stoop continually with both arms encircling our heads.

It was a day free from dangerous passages or startling events, but full of little things. The scenery was changing all the time and we looked about us with deep interest and a glowing sense of pride at the thought of all those miles of the Rat River behind us. It was one of those travel days when human powers of observation and enjoyment are fully awakened, when one offers mute thanksgiving to the Power that painted spots on a lady-bird and fashioned the peaks of the Matterhorn with the same artistry. It was dull and cloudy from dawn onwards. Once we had to climb a hill to avoid a sheer cliff or rock. After that the current was very winding and hills ahead were folded across our forward trail. Once we passed through a rocky canyon some 300 feet high. Bird life was more plentiful than on any previous day; we saw three loons, a robin, a gull, a few sparrows, a bird of the warbler type with black head and silver breast, and also yellowshanks.

More than once we saw moose tracks in the mud. All day the mosquitoes were vicious as ever, but the river no longer seemed like an enemy and we were now making a better pace, averaging perhaps a mile an hour.

After the ever welcome spell for lunch we came out from among those folded hills into beautiful open country. Already we were soaked up to the knees after wading through muskeg, willow and alder thickets, to say nothing of small creeks, and now there came a shower of rain that soaked us down to the knees. After another campfire and tea at 5, we went on again. Rain clouds were driving across the mountains ahead of us, but the nearer green slopes were sunlit and here and there through a break in the clouds we could see blue summits and patches of snow. Once again we felt that the country was a paradise save for the mosquitoes. Towards the end of the day we noticed that the river was much narrower.

Lazarus was unflagging as ever. He had been up until after midnight on the previous evening, mending his moccasins, but there had been no word of grumbling when we woke him at 6:30. At last we settled into bed on a stony spit of sand on the left bank. Through our mosquito bar and the tent opening we could see a wonderful mountain range. We had covered the stony ground with wet poplar shoots for our bed, and then outside our sleeping bags we laid our wringing wet coats and breeches, trusting that our body warmth would dry them. The highlights of that day had been the moment when we found a small Arctic rhododendron plant in seed, and another moment when we came suddenly on a beautiful yellow poppy, with finely cut glaucous blue leaves, growing on a stony flat.

It is not easy now to separate, in one's memory, our last three camps on the Rat River before we came out into open country. There was Barrier River camp with its bed of sand; there was the camp of wet poplar-shoots and sodden clothes on a stony spit of land; and there was an island camp on yet another bed of stones. The three are all telescoped in my mind, sharp details being lost in a certain feeling of relief from an oppression of which we had hardly been aware during our early step-by-step struggle up the river. There was not only the unspoken fear that we might never stay the course, there was also a physical oppression from being so shut in while following that river bed. The weather had been warm and we had always been enclosed, if not actually imprisoned, by thickets or trees or hills with mud rivers on their faces and day after day our efforts failed to bring us to an outlet. All this had only been sub-conscious, for actually we were happy as we struggled up the Rat, secure in the knowledge that our own efforts were helping us to reach our objective. Now, however, in the upper reaches of the river, we seemed to be coming out into open country and we were filled with an overbrimming sense of freedom. At the same time the burden of anxiety had somehow been lifted. Exactly how and where it was lifted I do not know, I only recall this part of the journey as giving us a sense that we had become almost light-winged, instead of being heavy-footed.

It was a dull and sunless morning when we woke in that stony camp and struggled into our still-moist coats and breeches. The river was now winding back on itself in one leisurely coil after another and we had an easy day's walking, often cutting across flat, stony stretches of country or being ferried across to a similar stretch on the opposite shore. The action of melting ice had evidently produced this form of alternating coils to the course of the current and we were to observe later, when paddling ourselves down the Porcupine, that whenever there was deep water underlying high banks on the left shore there would be shallow water and level stony spits on the right shore. Then, on rounding the next bend, the position of deeps and shallows would be reversed.

All that day the water was much easier for the guides and whenever we did come to rapids we found them shallow and easily negotiable. Now and then we had to resume our scramble through white poplars and undergrowth, but not for long. Even the mosquitoes had lessened their attacks, but whether this was due to the height of land or to the presence of a breeze, we could not tell. So weak had they become in their onslaught that after lunch, being careful to remain standing in the bonfire smoke, we were able to cut our nails and smoke a cigarette in comfort. Emboldened by this success we again took up our station in the bonfire smoke after tea and combed our neglected hair.

As we drew closer to those mountains we could see that some were very rocky, some were black, others reddish; a few had spruce growing half way up them, others were barren or covered with caribou moss. Once we saw three loons flying overhead and we heard their nostalgic, never-to-be-forgotten cry. Like the note of the bittern it can bring one the strangest perception, that must surely be a prenatal memory of worlds unfathomable or unattainable by our five senses. On that day, we saw tracks of bear and caribou. Truly, we felt, we had attained our hearts' desire and penetrated into wild country.

We had walked from 8 until about 8:30, stopping an hour for lunch and an hour for tea, when we pitched our camp on a spit of sand and stones. There were fine mountains all round us and a beautiful streak of red in the western sky. Near our tent, there grew several varieties of aster and there were masses of the beautiful yellow poppy among the gray stones. Indeed, throughout that day, the flora had been full of interest. After such a good day we felt that we had plenty of reserve energy, but we retired into the willows and took our nip of brandy as a precautionary measure.

"Just to keep our spirits up," said Gwen, who could always enjoy and hold her liquor. As for me, I detested brandy, but on that journey I looked on it as a means to an end and after all the end was not yet in sight.

There was the portage over the Divide ahead of us, then there would be the parting with our guides on the other side of La Pierre House, our lone journey down to Old Crow and, finally, the Ramparts and the rapids. Although we were beginning to feel a quiet confidence in ourselves, there was no question, when we took our nip of brandy among the willows, of premature rejoicing at success.

20 *Nearing the Divide*

The Divide. The Height of Land.

What romance and suggestiveness lie in those words, what a sense of continental vastness. They provoke thoughts of adventure and gold-seeking, of the Rocky Mountains and incredible feats of pioneers who were always driven by some nameless urge towards the sunset or the North. The height of land; the great Divide that separates Alaska from Canada.

I murmured the words over and over to myself in deep excitement, for we were actually nearing the Divide. All subsequent travels over cols and passes have been colourless by comparison with our crossing of the height of land which is like a dying effort of the Rocky Mountains to assert themselves in the North. The word "Pass" has a certain glamour, it is true, being suggestive of Tibetan Lamaseries, of the Khyber, of the Himalayas, of St Bernard dogs and their incomparable feats in snow. But what is a mere "col" in these modern days? A little something marked on the map in small letters, and when you come near you drive up to the top in your Jaguar or Austin or Riley by easy looping lines on a tarmac road that is smooth as glass, and when you have reached it you stop for five minutes to drink hot coffee in a restaurant and take a picture or two with your cine-camera, in the company of dozens of tourists like yourself. Then you drive down similar loops of a similar road on the other side and you have not the excitement of overcoming any difficulties or meeting with any dangers.

It may be that you traverse two or three such cols in a single day and that ever afterwards they remain confused in your memory.

We and our guides were nearing the Divide alone, having climbed thus far after days of muscular effort and there would not, of course, be company or comfort on our height of land. Nor were there any landmarks by which we could direct our course in this illimitable country. There was only the position of the sun and the direction of flowing water to help us in our journey to the Yukon. At the point where we found water flowing downhill away from the Rat, we should know how far we had come. When we did reach the top of the Divide it was, in fact, the loneliest place I have ever seen. On that day, when we were nearing the comparatively flat plateau, some of these thoughts were passing through my mind, but we had not yet finished with the difficulties and vagaries of the Rat.

We got away at our usual time from that stony spit which was, as we discovered to our surprise, an island, and when we discovered this we felt a heightened, perhaps rather childish, sense of adventure. It seemed a wonderful thing that twice we should camp on an island in the very middle of the Rat River. This heightened sense of adventure which comes and goes like gleams of sunshine in the traveller's overarching sky, was by no means often with us while we were pushing our way up the river. There were long spells when we thought only of how we could manage to put one foot before another, or extricate a boot from mud, or save our aching arms which had to be raised so often to protect our veils. The strange thing about those happy, sunlit moods is that they never may be summoned, nor commanded to stay. Such a mood may take possession of one for a whole plodding day, when there is nothing of spectacular beauty in earth or sky and it may desert one in the face of Niagara.

Progress was easy that morning for the river was flowing in pleasantly wide loops and much of the time we were walking across sterile spits of land where the only obstacles were stones of varying sizes. Among these pebbles and boulders we often found most beautiful flowers and the higher we got the richer was the flora. Several times Lazarus called us and said: "I guess you fellers chance go across," and then he and Jimmy would paddle us over to the other bank and deposit us on another stony spit where it was easy going. Lazarus was all the time as watchful and thoughtful over our progress as over his own. He would often point ahead to level ground where he could take a short cut and would say: "I guess you fellers make portage." ("Portage" seemed to be his only word for travel by land.)

The mosquitoes during that morning were very hungry as Lazarus said. After a while our easy progress came to an end and we had a wearisome spell walking over muskeg where, since it was a sultry day, we found it difficult to put one foot before another. Several times that day we were cheered by coming across the white carpets of the lovely little *Dryas octopetala*, so familiar to us both in the Alps and to Gwen in Norway. It seems to be one of the most adaptable plants in the world, with a very wide range. I have seen it flourishing in Italy, Switzerland and County Clare, and also crouching on the northern tip of Europe, at Nordkapp, where hardly any other vegetation survives and it is but a flat and miniature starveling.

The clouds had been low when we started, but after a while they cleared and we saw mountains on every side, some blue in the distance, others, the nearer ones, displaying their barrenness. They seemed to accentuate the silence of that upland world. Half-way through the day we passed, on our right, a big river flowing into the Rat—it was not marked on our inadequate little map. The country seemed to be gradually levelling itself out. We had left the poplars behind us and were now surrounded by spruce and willows. Over and over again we had to push our way through thickets of these scrubby willows or to wade across muddy side creeks which were now very frequent. How we managed to keep our feet in good condition I do not know, for they were nearly always wet and once we had crawled into bed there was no means of drying them. Perhaps their sodden condition prevented them from getting rubbed or sore; I only remember that one of my toes became so water-logged that, at a later stage of the journey, the whole skin peeled off like the sheath of an *Eschscholtzia* flower. Luckily, that was after the mosquitoes had left us and I could with impunity sit still in the canoe or walk about, shoeless, on sand or muskeg.

We lunched royally that day on the usual pemmican and pork, with Gwen's "puftaloonas" for dessert. It was several days since we had eaten the last of Sister Firmin's bannock and now, when we wanted to eat bread, we had to make the best of the hardtack biscuits which had the consistency of steel. Just as the Indians craved for fresh meat, so did we crave for sweet food. But neither of us had any aptitude for cooking. Gwen, however, made up her mind to produce doughnuts and she set to work with flour and sugar. There may have been other ingredients but I do not now remember the exact recipe for that memorable dish, yet I can see her at work on it, in my mind's eye, to this very day. Her method was simple and forceful. She would take the ingredients in the palm of a very horny hand that had been hardened by rowing sea-boats since infancy, she would then weld them as if they were pieces of metal and she herself a blacksmith. Sooner or later, by hard pommelling the mixture became homogeneous, and when satisfied that

Forks of the Rat River.
Sheep Creek flows in from
the left, Loon Creek (Rat
River) from the centre
(leading to McDougall
Pass), and Trout or Fish
Creek (Vyvyan's Fish River)
from the right. n.d.
Glenbow–Alberta Museum.

it was solid as a cricket ball, she would cast it into the frying pan with a determined gesture. The hot fat played its part and our sharp-set appetites did the rest.

The food chosen for us by our friends at Edmonton really made a good balanced diet but none the less we both craved at times for certain favourite dishes that now seemed like a dream. Sometimes in the middle of the night, while we were rubbing our wrists or knees with bicarbonate of soda, we would each in turn order our imaginary dinner. I would skip the fish and meat courses and order a double *Pêche Melba*, but Gwen would always murmur, in a sentimental, regretful tone: "And I would like a snipe just flown through the kitchen, all red and juicy." At any rate her "puftaloonas," cooked on one of our island camps, lasted us for several days and served to allay our epicurean longings for a change from camp food.

Later that day we came to Fish River, issuing from the mountains on our right. At this point, the water was not navigable and we had to make a short portage over muskeg and through willows in a shower of rain. Before launching the canoe again, we lit a fire and had strong tea and pemmican, standing as usual in the smoke of the fire while we ate and trying to get a little warmth to penetrate our wet clothes. Lazarus was a master-hand at kindling fires, however wet the day and however rain-soaked his material might be. He would pluck up a short piece of wood as thick as a man's thumb; this lighter would never be a crackling or brittle twig, it had to be old and weathered and hard. With his knife he would whittle one end, forming a beautiful pattern like a flower with turned-back petals, every petal being a fine shaving of wood still adhering to its stick. Then, having laid the fire in conical wigwam shape, he would put a match to his whittled stick and use it as a firelighter. This method never failed even when it was raining.

We lowered the canoe again into the current which was now a little winding stream about 25 feet wide, flowing with considerable strength and coiling in continuous loops. There was no chance of our seeing its blue line ahead of us in the open country, for it was lined by banks about 20 feet high. When we were left alone, standing on the spongy muskeg in open country, with our guides out of sight below us, we decided to keep in touch with them by following every bend of the stream, but we soon found that their pace was quicker than ours. Then observing that the fir trees, scattered thinly over that great open country, only grew on the edge of the river, we began to make for one group of trees after another, cutting across the river bends. Even so our progress was painful for we had now come to niggerheads.

These are a nightmare form of vegetation, bullet-headed tufts of grass, not wide enough to support the length of a human foot, with thigh-deep spaces between each tuft. When you step lightly as a ballet-dancer on a head, trying to balance on your toes or to grip with your heels, then the head will wobble and you will fall into the space between your tuft and the next one.

After a spell of this torment we heard the guides calling and found that they had come to more sluggish water, whereupon we got into the canoe and travelled forward, in the utmost ease, through peaceful green water bordered by willows. The banks were lower and we scanned the mountain slopes for a sight of wild mountain sheep, but in vain. All too soon we came again to swift water and had to return to the shore. Drenching rain fell and we camped, at last, on caribou moss beside a grove of trees, steaming ourselves out beside a fire of dead spruce before we got into our sleeping bags.

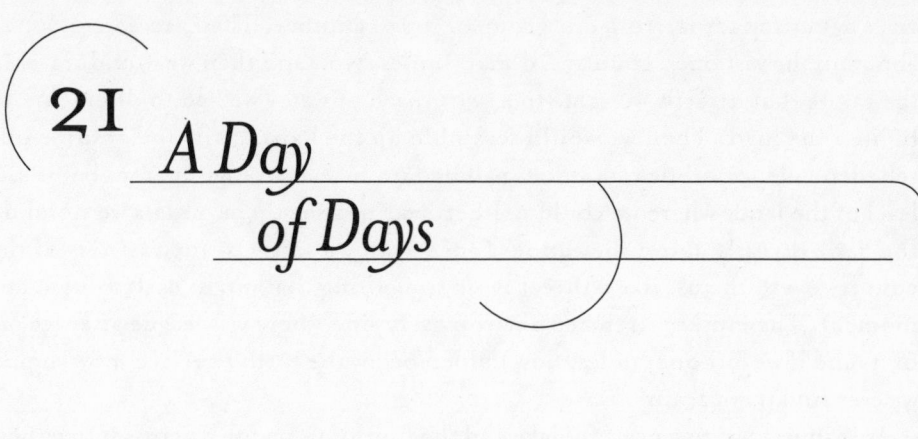

21 A Day of Days

"A most wonderful and full day."

Such is the entry in my diary at the head of the next day's chronicle. So much, or so little rapture did I allow myself to express over our triumphant arrival on the height of land. For it *was* triumphant, even though we were unwashed and unkempt and our upper garments were still wet and we had slept in our clothes for nine long nights.

"I do believe that you enjoyed pigging it," was the comment of our families when, eventually, we had returned home and were describing the scenery, the beauty, the difficulties and the conditions of our journey up the Rat. The outstanding fact to them was that we could not undress to sleep and how could we ever explain that, in our great enterprise, such discomforts were only a means to an end? We gave up the attempt. We would change the subject and describe the magnificent physique of Lazarus, the satisfying power of small lumps of pemmican, the aspect of the rapids or other such aspects of our journey that would appear to them strange without being squalid.

As a matter of fact we *were* beginning to feel extremely dirty and longed to resume our habitual morning and evening wash, but we had not hitherto found a mosquito-free camp where we could undress, step into the river and begin to remove what we felt was the dirt of ages.

On the morning of our arrival at the summit, clouds were low on the mountains, mosquitoes were more ferocious than ever and after a chilly, wakeful night we were not feeling, physically, at the top of our form. Mentally we were lords of the world, were conquerors, we were unconquerable, or so we felt as we began to repeat the manoeuvres of the previous day following the course of the sinuous river by cutting across from one group of firs to another. These trees were dotted about on the vast open country for many miles. Now and then we would travel in the canoe, but directly we came to a swift reach of water we had to disembark to lighten the load. Then we would scramble up the bank again and resume our self-dependence, while our guides paddled on in that strange current below the level of the land, where we could neither hear nor see them, unless we stood on the bank directly above the canoe. Once again, a sense of the vastness of the country overcame us, like a threat from something that might destroy us at any moment. The muskeg stretched away on every side, there was league after league of it, and if we lost our guides, now hidden below the earth's surface, how should we ever find them again?

We came at last to a peaceful lake and the four of us paddled across it together. Then the scenery began to repeat itself and something happened that increased our pride immeasurably.

Gwen had our wretched little map in her pocket, but it was of no practical use. The sun was shining and Lazarus had given us our general direction in case we got separated from the canoe. Actually, it was Lazarus himself who was nearly lost and when we saw him following a stream that seemed to come from the north-east instead of from the north-west, we shouted to him to come up into our world and reconnoitre. He scrambled up the bank, shinned up a fir tree, scanned the horizon and agreed that we were right. There was really not much credit due to us, since we on the bank had a wider general view than the guides below, but if we had not both felt the same pride in our own performance our conceit would have been unendurable to each other.

The flowers in this open country were very beautiful and every species that we had found on the way up from Destruction City seemed to be flourishing here together.

We made four portages, the first being a very short one from one lake to another. We did our best to help by man-handling the rucksacks and the lighter packages, but we felt weak as straws when we watched Lazarus and Jimmy carrying the heavy stuff. Jimmy's strength was nothing when compared to that of Lazarus but he was active and ever-ready for a job, with a disposition to laugh and smile. The next portage, again from one lake to another, was several hundred yards long. The third one, where we stopped to lunch, was half a mile and here it was that we saw a mountain sheep in the distance, hurrying up a rocky face. We

Above McDougall Pass, looking east (Summit or Loon Lake is in the lower left corner). 1994. Michael Peake. Collection of the photographer.

helped, as best we could, to drag the canoe over these longer portages, but it must be confessed that most of our energy was expended on keeping our balance, since the ground was carpeted with muskeg and niggerheads wherever it was not actual swamp. After that third portage we came to Loon Lake, ringed round by mountains and holding, in utter stillness, their reflections.

There are some feelings too deep for tears, some thoughts that may not endure the captivity of words, some memories that are set apart among life's enduring treasures. I can shut my eyes now, dismiss all that has happened in 35 years and recapture the silence of Loon Lake. We were two middle-aged women travelling for pleasure, dishevelled and unwashed, with tired feet and tired bodies but I think, as we stood on the shores of that lake, gazing down at the reflected mountains, listening to the silence that was almost audible, we must have experienced what the saints describe as ecstasy. Gwen said never a word. Nor did I.

We were now on the height of land, for Loon Lake marks the Divide between Canada and Alaska. The river at the far end of the lake was no more than a narrow brook hardly wider than the canoe and overhung by alders and willows. We teased rather than paddled our craft through this waterway until the boughs and leafage from either side met in the middle and then we had to carry it ashore for our last portage. Had it not been for those overhanging shrubs, we could have paddled across the Divide, moving through the water from Loon Lake to the Little Bell River which was now to become our highway during the next stage. We had begun the descent. Canada was behind us. We were going down, down, down into the Yukon.

At first the Little Bell was very like the Rat, sluggish and winding, with high banks on either side, but we had come into much wilder country and were now nearer the mountains. We sat in the canoe in utter lazy contentment, relaxing every muscle and at first it seemed as if we were going down at a terrific pace, so accustomed had we become to the inch-by-inch progress of toiling upstream. There were gleams of sunshine every now and then, lighting up the mountain peaks that towered above us; they were rocky peaks, some black, others reddish, others streaked with lines of gray and yellow where mosses seamed their slopes. One was snow-clad on the summit, reminding us, as those lumps of ice falling into the river had reminded us, that we really were in the Arctic world. Those high peaks seemed to be revolving round us, for as we followed the loops of the river a given peak would at one moment be on our right and then a few minutes later on our left. It made us feel quite giddy until we realised that we could, if we lost our way, steer a course by the mountains. Since we had discovered the right channel of the Rat when the guides had taken the wrong one, we had begun to look upon ourselves as Pathfinders.

After a while the nature of the small river changed completely. It became turbulent as it grew larger, the current ran more swiftly and was often broken into short rapids. We shot a succession of these, Gwen becoming on each occasion almost lyrical with delight while I was silent with fear. I found some comfort, however, in realising that these rapids were not nearly so deep as those that we had crossed obliquely on the Rat and that they were much shallower, so that we should probably escape death from drowning when the crash came. We had also to endure a new form of excitement. When we came to rough and very shallow water over stones, we went bumping downriver from one stone to another, expecting to capsize at any moment or to get caught in the branches of dead trees lying in mid-stream. It was almost a relief when the water again became so shallow that we had to get out to lighten the load, but our spirits fell when we found that during the next hour or so we had to negotiate about a mile of open country across niggerheads. Before we plunged into that miserable stretch of country, we took one last look at the sunlight falling on glorious mountain screes and a group of rocks to the southward which was like a man-made castle. Then, for a long spell, we could look at nothing in heaven or earth except the next niggerhead and the next, or at our unfortunately large feet.

There was no question of stopping to rest once we were among those giant grasses, we had to keep moving; it was our worst experience of walking on that journey or on any other. We are neither of us habitually fairy-like in our movements, but I would defy Ariel himself to trip across those wobbling heads with enjoyment or agility.

The Bell River, into which the Little Bell flows, was not far ahead now but, being below the level of the country, it was not yet visible. Lazarus pointed out the direction in which we were to go across those niggerheads, then he and Jimmy and the canoe disappeared as completely as if the earth had swallowed them up. "We must keep our heads," I said mournfully, as we started off with no landmarks to guide us, nor any sign ahead of the existence of a river. Each successive grass-head was wobbling under my feet. "We must keep our direction," returned Gwen shortly, as she tottered or lurched from one precarious foothold to another.

We were to await our guides at the confluence of the two rivers but how, we wondered, should we ever find it? We never did find it by our own efforts, for after a while we heard a shout ahead of us and there were the two men coming back to say they had not reached the Bell, but there was good water ahead and they could take us on in the canoe. Then we went skimming down through one long patch of broken water after another, while Gwen was, of course, crooning to herself "delicious, delicious" and I held on to the gunwale awaiting the final bump.

At last, when it was nearly 9, we came to the point where the Little Bell enters the Bell. A blessed cool breeze blew there and the place was free of mosquitoes and we camped on the left bank among willows and all ate an enormous supper to celebrate the day. We were too exhausted to wash ourselves thoroughly, the day had been over-full with physical efforts and changing moods, with upriver toil and portages and downriver dangers. The guides were in a most cheerful mood. All their troubles were behind them, not that they ever regarded rapids as troubles; they were more concerned with snags and boulders and the food supply. Risk and danger was all in the day's work, rapids were milestones on their natural highway.

After supper our energy revived enough for us to cook bannock and doughnuts. The old-timers had been false prophets. We had navigated the Rat. We had not been eaten by mosquitoes. We had crossed the Divide. Now there was only the downriver journey before us.

22 *A Grizzly Bear*

Our freedom from mosquitoes on that high land was like a release from prison. As usual we woke early, dressed ourselves standing up in the tent and agreed that dry, clean clothes were a luxury that we had never fully appreciated in our home life. All day we were in the canoe, taking turns at paddling or lying back and drowsing in the sunshine as we went down the sluggish current at about five miles an hour. The river was some 50 yards wide and the banks were fairly low. We had come again into the region of white poplars and some of the mountains above us were densely wooded. Jimmy shot at and missed some ducks. Lazarus was all the time straining his eyes for caribou and talking about fresh meat, while we spotted two enormous black eagles and beaver tracks in a patch of mud, and when we stopped to lunch there were wolf tracks on the shore. The day brought no anxiety and was filled with only small events, until in the late evening we came to the most exciting experience of the whole trip.

It was after 8 when we reached La Pierre House on our tenth day out from Aklavik. What we had been told about the place was only too true. There was no sign of a settlement nor of any human presence. There were only two deserted wooden shanties, one of them tied up with a dog chain.

"So much for our old atlas at home," said Gwen with a grunt when she saw that dog chain. "Our atlas is a liar."

We entered the other hut and found tinned food, three bunks, a stove, various old boots, an encyclopaedia, matches, rifle ammunition, fur coats, axes and, hanging outside, several tubs. All these things had been left there by the traders, Jackson Brothers, for travellers who should come over by land from Fort

"All That is Left of La Pierre House," c. 1921.
From Mason, The Arctic Forests *(1924),*
opp. [76].

McPherson. There was nothing that we wanted and nothing that we needed, so we paddled down towards the next bend to find level ground for a camp. As we opened up the next reach of the river we saw, on our left, the strangest object. It was creamy white, rather bulky and humped up in the middle so that it looked like a reduced but fattened camel. It had the curve of an archer's bow and it was quite still and it was like nothing that we had ever seen before, but we both knew, with a swift, intuitive knowledge, that it was something *alive.*

"Wolf," said Jimmy, in a low tone of excitement. Jimmy had been brought up in a mission school and he knew little about wildlife and Lazarus would often say scornfully: "Mission school no good, never teach Jimmy live off the country."

Now he answered Jimmy's question with a hoarse whisper. "Bear," he said, and we knew at once it was a grizzly.

He had come down to the water's edge to drink and his cream pallor in that green world was very beautiful. Lazarus and I each took a shot with our rifles and missed. I handed my rifle to Jimmy who shot twice and wounded it. The bear staggered away into the alders; we could hear it breathing heavily. The guides went ashore, after telling us to paddle across to the opposite bank and to hold on to some overhanging tree boughs. A wounded grizzly can be dangerous, Lazarus told us, and he refused to let us come ashore with him. As we watched these two men scramble up the bank with their rifles so as to stalk the bear from above, our excitement was intense. Every minute seemed like half an hour, but at last we heard two shots and then, after a pause filled with heavy silence, they appeared on a narrow shelf of land some 20 feet above the water, dragging the carcase of the grizzly. There was no other place for a camp. On that narrow and rather muddy terrace an orgy of butchering, cooking and eating now took place.

We began supper with bear steaks. Lazarus and Jimmy were nearly off their heads with excitement and when Lazarus had eaten two or three steaks he rubbed himself with a happy smile.

"By God," he said, "I've had a sore stomach all day, now I feel real good."

As we sat there, close to the reeking corpse, consuming fried bear steaks and rice and treacle, we tried to regard this revolting scene as a matter of course. Sometimes life catches you up and whirls you into the strangest experience from which there is no escape and you just bow your head and wait until it is over.

It was nearly midnight but still broad daylight when we settled into our sleeping bags; there were beautiful red streaks in the north-west sky; the corpse of the grizzly, only partially dismembered, lay some ten yards from our tent. As I look back on that incident now I feel shame rather than pride over the shooting of the bear. After all, he had only come down to drink from his own river in his own country; we were not only strangers but I rather think that on this occasion we were also butchers. I never have forgotten the strange beauty of that cream-coloured form, with curved back, standing at the water's edge as we came swiftly and quietly round the bend in the evening light.

I cannot now remember for how long we travelled in the land of midnight sun, but I know that one midnight at Aklavik I photographed the sun when it was just a ball of fire resting on the far end of a little lake behind the convent. Then, while travelling on the Rat, the Bell, the Porcupine and the Yukon, I cannot recall any hours of real darkness. At first, the continuous daylight had been very exhausting but we had now become used to it. The almost horizontal rays of sunlight now lit up the scene of the grizzly's murder, investing every object with uncanny beauty.

We were up early next morning, for on this day our guides were to start on their 90-mile walk back to Fort McPherson, across muskeg country. We had cold rice, treacle and boiled bear for breakfast, the guides enjoying that meal to the full although they had been feasting and cooking for most of the night. To us the bear's meat tasted like string; it certainly had the texture of string. The bear's skin lay beside us and all the meat had been neatly cut into joints and portions. After breakfast, Lazarus returned to the hut at La Pierre House to take a pair of boots for himself and to hang a large joint of bear's meat in a bag on an outside rafter, as payment to Jackson Brothers.

The guides put as much meat as possible into their own packs and then insisted that we should take a lump of meat with us in the canoe. At Shingle Rock, only 15 miles distant, our guides would leave us and we should negotiate a more or less clear course ahead as far as the settlement of Old Crow. We could only hope that Old Crow would not turn out to be a second La Pierre House, "a dumping ground for the old boots of Jackson Brothers," as Gwen described that honourable trading depot, in tones of contempt. Lazarus, like everyone else, assured us that Old Crow had a settled population of Indians and that we would certainly be able to obtain a guide there who would take us through the rapids and the Ramparts down to Fort Yukon.

We landed on a spit full of boulders just below Shingle Rock for a farewell dinner. Again we feasted on bear. Then we paid our guides $210 each, at the rate of $14 per day, reckoning ten days pushing up the Rat and five days walking back to Fort McPherson.

If ever two men had earned their wage by faithfulness and labour, those two were Lazarus and Jimmy, but we still felt that we owed a grudge to Stefansson for having set the natives' standard wage so high. Three pounds a day meant no more to the Indians than one pound a day; the three pounds would bring them no more luxury, no more happiness. The only luxury they craved for was fresh meat, and always more fresh meat. From this point of view, we felt glad that our last evening had been celebrated beside the reeking carcase of the grizzly. Lazarus was a fine fellow; he had never failed us in any particular, being gifted with muscles of iron, a cool head and a sure judgment. By comparison, Jimmy was a pale shadow, but where Lazarus led he would always follow, and it was with real regret that we said good-bye to these two faithful companions.

We were absolutely alone now in this wilderness. If we wanted help, there would be none forthcoming except from our own resourcefulness. If we met with an accident, no one would be any the wiser. If we should encounter rapids, snags or swift water, we should have to call on our own reserves of initiative and skill. I do not think that all these things were clearly in our minds as our guides walked away, but we did feel, as we looked about us, a queer depth and breadth of solitude that we had never known before. However, instead of dwelling on unknown difficulties ahead, we decided to look upon our solitude as complete freedom and to celebrate this freedom we undressed completely, stepped into the water, each with a cake of soap, and washed thoroughly from head to toe. While we were soaping ourselves in such a fervour of cleanliness as we had never known before, we discussed the next lap of the journey. We decided that we would do away with early rising and pushful travel, we would get up when we felt like it and not a moment earlier, we would savour leisure to the full, and drift down on the current, or if we did paddle, we would paddle gently, without making any effort. This was our first reaction to release from strenuous travelling but of course in 24 hours the mood had passed and we began making for Old Crow, if not in feverish haste, at any rate like travellers with minds set steadily on reaching their goal.

When we had dried ourselves we dressed again, packed, loaded, pushed off the canoe and had a glorious, effortless, peaceful, slow-moving day with never a mosquito to torment us. We were moving through wooded country. Every now and then we came to a bend in the river and then we would be looking down a long, straight reach ahead, where the water, sloping very gently downwards, was like a sheet of molten glass. We saw several black eagles, a white-headed one, and a squirrel. Also, a small flock of Canada geese went overhead, their notes echoing and re-echoing among the quiet trees.

In the early afternoon we came into the Porcupine River and paddled on quietly, taking an hour ashore to build a fire and make tea and then at 7 we found a perfect site for a camp, on a spit of land with a beautiful view of mountains. There, we unpacked all our personal belongings to find that everything in the canvas bags was soaked and mildewed, so we hung up each article one by one on a willow tree to dry. Our camp was on mud and mare's-tails but we cut and laid out willow shoots to keep out the damp. Gwen cooked "puftaloonas" and we turned in under that strange northern light which had kindled the water and all the trees and their reflections to a dull gold.

We slept and slept again as we had not done for many nights and when at last we woke, to find ourselves in broiling sunshine, in a world still free of mosquitoes, we decided to have a washing-day.

We washed ourselves and our clothes in the river and dried the garments on stones and willow boughs. Then, ignoring that lump of bear's meat in the bows, we lunched happily on chocolate, tinned beef and doughnuts and finally, when noon was already long past, we loaded and launched the canoe and pushed off down the river again.

As a matter of fact we continued to ignore the lump of bear's meat which Lazarus had insisted on our taking with us, until a time came when we could ignore it no longer, and then we dropped it overboard into the Porcupine.

23 Down the Porcupine

It is difficult, at this point, to maintain coherence and continuity in
the story of our travels, although the entries in my diary suddenly became discursive, whereas during our Rat River struggles they had been extremely brief; but all
at once the rhythm had completely changed. Then we had been forcing our way
up against the current, now we were moving swiftly downriver. Then we had been
confined in one narrow river bed, now we were moving across the roof of a whole
continent. Moreover on the Rat we had seen no living soul other than our two
guides whereas, between La Pierre House and Fort Yukon, encounters with
human beings became ever more frequent.

On the height of land the vastness of the unpeopled country was apparent and
at first it was terrifying, it seemed to be a menace to security, but after a while the
open spaces filled us with exhilaration. This was the country that we had come to
see, the land beyond the bounds of civilization, the wild land that had lured us
from our homes to cross the Atlantic, to journey across Canada and down the
Mackenzie River. There were even moments, each evening, when this new world
was bathed in golden light and we would feel that it was our real home, for it held
a hitherto unimagined beauty that had always been missing in our lives.

If the true story of our Arctic journey could be recaptured, its main concern
would be with enlightened moments when we were face to face with absolute
beauty and the tale would be told in winged new words, free from cumbersome
associations; but I have no such words at my command. The name of some flower
that we found, some bird that we saw, details about camps and bedding and speed
of water and weather conditions, such things as these occupy too much space in

Gwendolen Dorrien Smith in camp on a rest day, July 1926. Clara Coltman Rogers (Vyvyan). Collection of Edward Zealley.

my diary, but when I write about crossing the rapids and Gwen murmuring "delicious, delicious" and when I note how the evening sunlight would gild all natural objects from a spruce bough to a wide river, then I am getting near the truth. The truth was that despite a few tremors over snags and currents, during our four and a half days of paddling or drifting from Shingle Rock to Old Crow we were living an enchanted life. We moved in a golden light down a golden river, free as butterflies, forgetful of all yesterdays, without care for any morrow. That is how I see the journey now, although I know, of course, that we did stop to wash and to eat hearty meals of pork and doughnuts and that we had to watch out for troubled water and for snags.

Realising that we had to depend on our own exertions had steadied my nerves. Whenever there were frequent bends in the river, one of us would always be on the lookout for snags and boulders while the other paddled. Sometimes there were rough patches of water to negotiate, swift or swirling currents, and some-times, when we saw sand-bars ahead, one of us would land and scan the obstructions through field glasses and plot our forward course. Once when I was paddling, we passed under a bank hollowed out by fallen lumps of frozen soil and were suddenly confronted with a dead tree branch sticking up in the deep water. "Backwater," shouted Gwen and I failed to respond, for it seemed to me that we were back-watering all the time, with our single paddle stroke, and my mind did not work quickly enough. However, we went swirling down and missed the tree by inches. "Landlubber!" was all that Gwen said and indeed I was surprised that she said nothing worse until I remembered that, to her seafaring mind, there could be nothing worse than a landlubber.

Soon after that incident the river straightened out and everything around us seemed to have become immeasurably vast. The forest stretched away to the North Pole, the hills were interfolded endlessly and the straight reaches of the river must, in some places, have been six or eight miles long. Sometimes, when looking ahead down one of these reaches that were green in the morning, gold under noonday sun and burnished gold in the evening, we felt that the current must be taking us down to bottomless gorges or to cataracts like Niagara. It was like a dream in which everything had begun to swell, to extend and to deepen in all directions.

It was very difficult to judge our speed when travelling downstream. The current seemed to be running at about two or three miles an hour and often we just steered and drifted instead of paddling. We had short hours of travel, we slept long nights, we lingered over meals and sometimes went ashore between meals for Gwen to sketch while I prowled about and collected flowers. Often that glassy water seemed so still that we did not appear to be moving, and only when we looked at the banks did we realise that the current was alive. So we went down, down, on that green or golden river into unknown country. Sometimes there were echoes. A swan would go honking overhead and the trees would echo the sound back again. Or a northern raven would fly croaking into the forest and once we passed some fine rocky bluffs where peregrine falcons and eagles were screaming overhead but always, when those echoes had died away, the unearthly silence of that country would come flooding back to fill our world. We paddled softly, trying not to break that silence.

We had been told that there was neither a settlement nor even an inhabited hut between La Pierre House and Old Crow, so when one day at noon, we came round a bend and heard children's voices, we thought we were having hallucinations, until we saw two tents and a white man with an Indian family.

"My name is David Low," he said, after tying our canoe to his scow and helping us to scramble ashore. Half a dozen half-breed children were clustering round us and then his flat-faced Indian wife came forward. We shook hands and went into one of the tents and sat there chatting for some time. The husband was a French Canadian who had come in from Quebec during the Klondike gold rush and had never made enough money to go out. When we left, he gave us a present of some king salmon he had caught and it proved to be a most welcome change in our diet.

It was strange, we agreed, after we had waved good-bye and had paddled on again, that neither of us wanted to meet any more strangers in huts. Were we becoming queer in the head like those solitary trappers who could not bear to have another hut within a hundred miles of their own, we wondered?

Actually, we did meet more strangers before reaching Old Crow, for a day or so later we found a couple of old Indians encamped on the right bank. They were living alone in a tent beside four empty huts and they spoke very little English, so, having pulled in and landed to exchange a few courtesies by dumb show, we went on our way.

There was one night when we decided to sleep in the open; I was glad to be saved the trouble of helping to pitch the tent, for I was hobbling about in a single shoe, being unable to get a shoe on to the other foot until my sodden toe had finished peeling. We chose a place about 20 yards from the river. We had given up wearing veils, but there were still a few mosquitoes out, so we put up our mosquito bars and then went to sleep in great contentment under the open sky. Something, possibly an unusual sound or movement close at hand, woke me early and there, within ten yards of the tent, standing as still as if it were posing for a picture, stood a single caribou. I nudged Gwen in the ribs and she sat up just in time to see him plunge into the river and that was the only caribou we saw in all our 600 miles of travel through wild country. Later, when we met the

Gwendolen Dorrien Smith, Porcupine River above Old Crow, July 1926. Clara Coltman Rogers (Vyvyan). Collection of Edward Zealley.

tourists who had flocked up by steamer from Seattle to the Yukon, and had sat comfortably on deck day after day watching the country pass by them, we heard that they had seen, from their deck chairs, a whole herd of caribou on migration. Such is the chancy luck of the traveller.

We stayed in bed for a couple of hours after that sudden awakening, just in order to enjoy the delicious scent of the muskeg and *Ledum* on which we lay. We had seen wolf tracks on the beach below but no wolf had come near us.

On the whole those were days of calm and leisure, with some anxious moments over snags and swirling water, but no need for strenuous effort and no call on our powers of endurance, so we enjoyed them to the full. After lunch we would take shifts of work and rest, while one steered the canoe with the paddle the other would curl up in the stern to enjoy a nap. It was hard to keep awake in the afternoon sunshine, half blinded by the glare from the water and suffering from the sense of having eaten too much lunch, for we fed on tinned meat or Canadian boiled dinner ready mixed in the tin, and rice or treacle and doughnuts. Once, when a pleasant little breeze was blowing, we rigged up one of our groundsheets on a stick and sailed for a while, Gwen steering while I held the sail rope and obeyed orders.

On the morning of the fourth day we began to keep an anxious lookout for Old Crow. The river had become very wide and the current extremely strong and we felt that in our little canoe we were like a cork borne down on the water and completely in its power. I began to visualize, all too vividly, the moment when we should sight Old Crow and have to turn and head the canoe upriver before attempting to land and to wonder how we should ever perform this manoeuvre without getting swept away, broadside-on, and capsized. To add to our worries the river was now full of large islands and of those backwaters that in the North are always known as "sloughs," the word being pronounced "slews." We could not always hug the right bank on which Old Crow was situated, for in passing islands we had to take whichever side offered the safest water and it would be quite possible to pass down on the left side of one of them and miss Old Crow altogether. We had tried to keep a rough reckoning of the distance that we had come from Shingle Rock, but we never knew exactly how fast we were travelling. David Low's reckoning of our mileage coincided more or less with our own; when we questioned her, the old Indian woman had pointed to Gwen's wrist watch and said that we should reach Old Crow on this day when the sun was overhead. Also, we had checked the time of our passing by a certain Willow Island described by Lazarus. I went through all these reckonings again and again, it was past 12 and our spirits sank to zero. Clouds rolled up and we lunched on the left bank, hoping to see Old Crow round the next bend, yet fearing disappointment and almost afraid to put the matter to the proof. After lunch, we paddled on and on through a maze of islands and then we passed one slough after another. Could it be that Old Crow was set back from the main river, out of sight in a backwater? Had we missed it? We became more and more desperate. Even Gwen had no grunting words of optimism with which to face the situation. The hours went by. Once more, we looked at our wretched map. Once more we counted the miles and days and hours. Then we began to make up our minds to the worst: 70 miles more, alone, before we came to Rampart House which was inhabited. Dangerous rapids between us and Rampart House. Only the remotest chance of our passing some trapper's cabin or of meeting a trader coming up in a gas boat. Our friends at Aklavik had said, with conviction, that it would not be possible for two women to negotiate those rapids alone. The wind had risen now and, for the first time, we had to battle with waves on the river. We passed a wide backwater, paddled round a bend and then, at 5, after seven or eight hours paddling, we saw as if we were in a dream and had to rub our eyes to see clearly, a long row of huts lined out on the river bank.

We had arrived at Old Crow.

24 *Friendly Faces*

The Indians came crowding down the bank to meet us. Gwen made a good landing, turning in gradually towards the shore, then paddling furiously for a few strokes against the current before making in to the beach. The Indian chief came first, wearing a dark blue yachting-cap and dark European clothes. He shook hands warmly and the others followed suit.

"Is Harry Anthony the trader here?" we asked, following the instructions given to us by Mr Parsons.

"No," said the chief.

"Is there any white man here?" we said.

"One," answered the chief, as he beached the canoe and led us up the earthen path, shaking hands again as we went. The only white man proved to be a youngish trader named Frost, partner to Harry Anthony. He at once welcomed us into his spotlessly clean and tidy two-roomed cabin, and set to work to produce a meal. Then we sat down to a supper of salmon, figs and fresh coffee feeling that we never wished to see pork and beans or pemmican again.

While Mr Frost was asking us about our journey, the Indian chief and another Indian had been sitting quite still in a corner of the room. They spoke never a word, but their eyes were gleaming in the dim light. When we talked of our future plans and the business of getting a guide to take us to Fort Yukon, the chief said as he rose and stepped out of the room:

"See if catch im feller, perhaps catch im feller, perhaps no."

Two minutes later he reappeared, having caught "David" who followed at his heels. David was a sturdy looking young Indian and Mr Frost arranged then and

Left to right: Jack Frost,
Frank Jackson, and Charlie
Young of Jackson Bros. and
Co. Ltd., Old Crow,
1940s. Collection of
Edward Zealley, courtesy
Clara Frost.

there that he should take us to Fort Yukon for $5 a day with food, the days to include, of course, his own return journey. When we talked about pitching our tent, our host firmly insisted on our sleeping in his living room for the night; one of us could have the bed and the other must camp on the floor.

"As a matter of fact," he said, "I don't want to go to bed tonight. I have been asleep all day for we were dancing all last night."

In these latitudes, where there is hardly any twilight demarcation between night and day, it is apparently quite usual to take no notice of which is which. After we had finished our meal, Mr Frost took us round the settlement where we visited the church and then we called on Martha, an Indian woman who agreed to produce two pairs of moccasins for us by the morning. Then we returned to that hospitable cabin and spent the evening pressing our flowers, with the luxury of a table to help us, looking at Mr Frost's photographs of the country and having a long chat with him. He had been in the North-West Mounted Police, but after leaving the force had discovered that he could not bear to leave the north country; he liked his independence too much.

In that room we had the joy of sleeping in partial darkness, but there was no open window and we found it very stuffy. So we got up at 4, and our host appeared at once and cooked us a superb breakfast and then took us along to Martha, who had spent the night making our moccasins. We traded some of our beads and silks for one pair and some pork and biscuits for the other, Mr Frost arranging the exchange to the satisfaction of all parties. He told us that the whole settlement was agog over our unexpected arrival. They had never seen women come over the Divide like that before and they were all saying to each other, in tones of awed surprise, "Those two women they came down the river paddling their canoe like a couple of squaws." Then he added his own opinion of our journey: "Gee-whiz," he said, "but I guess it was fierce, your trip up the Rat."

We would gladly have listened to him and his tales of the North for many days but some travel urge was pushing us on and regretfully we said good-bye to him, knowing that we would never have a chance to make any return for his thoughtful kindness. So we set off with David, using two paddles, each of us in turn taking a two hours spell with our guide. All day we studied the river shores with the greatest interest, for the last few days the banks had been continually changing their form and direction. Sometimes there would be overhanging banks some 12 feet high, with chunks of ice, like tree stumps, embedded in the earth and the water below would be swirling round at a tremendous pace on the concave shore. On the opposite side of the river, there would always be a flat spit of ground covered with stones. Sometimes, as we looked ahead, we would see these stony spits of land jutting out into the current now from the right bank and now from the left and apparently meeting, or even overlapping in the middle. In the same way, when walking down a narrow valley in mountain country, one sees the peaks ahead on either side. They seem to be interlocked, barring all exit, yet day after day one walks on, finding a road between those peaks and then yet more mountains ahead, still apparently interlocked and standing as prison walls to the valley.

On the Porcupine River these tongues of shingle seemed, in perspective, to form a pathway of stone in mid-current, yet always we found a way through. After a time we became accustomed to this rhythm of the river, whereby it maintains its

Buildings as I found them - Aug./26 - Old Crow.

Mission House   Church   New Church started

"Buildings as I found them." Anglican Mission House and Church, and new Church under Construction, Old Crow, August 1926. Rev Arthur Creighton McCullum. Collection of Edward Zealley, courtesy Jean McCullum.

perennial existence and even conquers new territory. Now and then we passed rocky cliffs, backed by forest. These outcrops of rock occurred only beside the river, so that after a while whenever we saw a cliff face reared up ahead among the trees, we knew that it marked our course. At one point, while Gwen and David were paddling together, we passed high mud cliffs grooved by melting ice. Reverberating echoes accompanied each falling chunk of ice from this cliff, chunks that would at once disintegrate into mud and splay out fanwise on the edge of the water. So the river's work goes on, ever eating into the heart of the land and widening itself.

The sloughs or backwaters also interested us deeply, they were so very deceptive. We could have sworn that the Old Crow River flowing into the Porcupine was a backwater flowing out of it and then, later, there was a backwater leading out of our river that we mistook for a new tributary coming in. We passed one cabin that day which was perched on the edge of the river, within a yard of the bank, it was doomed at any moment to slip into the water. Needless to say, it was not inhabited. David told us that he could remember when, some 16 years ago, that cabin stood a hundred yards back from the river. There was nothing unusual about this, he said.

Old Crow was a landmark in our journey, not only geographically but mentally, for it marked the end of our solitude. From there onwards we were to meet, at intervals, one friendly face after another, and every one we met was deeply interesting. We did not, of course, at once shift our whole attention to people; on the contrary our allegiance to the vast country in which we travelled was whole-hearted and enduring and some of the river scenery between Old Crow and Fort Yukon was magnificent. But every man of the North who began to tell us even a fragment of his own life story was like the Ancient Mariner. He would hold us spellbound. The people whom we met, like the people on the *Athabasca* and the *Distributor*, were unlike anyone we had ever encountered before. There may have been some rogues and some rapscallions but there was never a dull dog among them. Of course the hospitality of men in unpeopled places is proverbial but there was something more than hospitality in the welcomes that we met, something that spoke directly to our own hidden feelings. Perhaps it was that we understood and admired their passionate love of wild country and of independence.

We soon realised that we were making good headway and should meet the dreaded Ramparts that evening, but there was no need to indulge our fears now that we had a guide. Our friend Mr Frost had assured us that we should find a welcome there from the North-West Mounted Police. We did reach the Ramparts

after ten hours paddling and on entering that gorge were carried down by swift water and a sinister cold wind that blew from behind us. Magnificent cliffs towered overhead on either side, the rocks were red, black, white, gray and yellow. Rampart House was perched on a little gap in this gorge and there we landed. It could hardly be called a settlement for it consisted of the police barracks, the church, the solitary cabin of a trader named Cadzow and three other houses, but it was the international boundary of Canada and Alaska. The two police living in the barracks at once welcomed us, and cooked us a supper of eggs and potatoes. Those eggs tasted like caviare. "Of course we'll give you our two beds for the night," they said, "we've got a tent." The names of these two memorable hosts were Thornthwaite and Allington. The first thing that I remember about Mr Thornthwaite is that when I offered him one of the last of our English cigarettes he exclaimed with delight: "Hullo, a tailor-made, haven't seen one for years." He then proceeded to roll one for each of us and to give us a lesson in rolling our own, but it was an art that we never could learn.

Mr Allington decided that he would like to come down with us next morning for a short holiday at Fort Yukon. It was a wet, cold night and when they had settled us into their room and left us, we were glad of the warmth from four shel-

Bishop Isaac O. Stringer and Sarah Ann Alexander (Sadie) Stringer, camped on Peel River Portage, 1924. Isaac O. Stringer Collection, ACC/GSA P7517-86.

tering walls and partial darkness once again. We were also thankful that a small pane of glass was broken, for, like Mr Frost, these two men lived with sealed windows. Our hosts came in early from their tent and cooked us a mammoth breakfast. When we started off in the canoe Mr Allington rigged up a mast and sail and we began to work across the current diagonally. I watched Gwen's face of horror. The roar of the rapids in the next reach of the gorge was audible and she knew too much about sailing to approve of this rather amateur effort. Providentially the wind still blew in icy gusts and before we were in mid-current the mast snapped. David then took charge and we cleared the Ramparts without mishap.

Our new guide was quite efficient, but we missed in him something that we had revered in Lazarus. Idealism perhaps? If Lazarus had understood what an ideal was, he would, no doubt, have laughed at the idea of his possessing any such thing. Yet he had one, at least, although he never came near to expressing it in words. His ideal man was one who, unlike Jimmy, knew how to live off the country. There was, however, more than that one streak of idealism in the character of Lazarus: there was fidelity to whatever he had undertaken, ability to think and feel for others, courage, and indifference to bodily exhaustion. We had never expected to find another Lazarus, but we missed him, and we missed his laughter, for, once we had learned how to kindle it, at the end of a long day, that laughter would often prove a blessing to the whole party.

In the middle of that morning, we heard and then saw a gas boat coming towards us and there was the *Moose*, puffing up the river to La Pierre House, with one of the Jackson Brothers on board and also Bishop Stringer, the Bishop of the Yukon. We all went ashore to exchange greetings and news and have a friendly chat. The only unfortunate thing about this meeting was that Mr Allington had to forego his trip and return upriver in the *Moose*, for he had hoped to come back in that steamboat from Fort Yukon, on this very trip, and he could not now prolong his absence until she made her second summer journey.

We could not help noticing that the bishop had not shaved. I do not know that I have ever, before or since, consorted with an unshaven bishop, but then we met with many strange things and persons in the Yukon and after a while we began to realise that none of them were really strange, it was we ourselves who were the strangers.

The party had tied up to the shore during the previous night, on account of the head wind. We told Mr Jackson about Lazarus and the boots and the bear, and we longed to have further talk with the bishop who was a most interesting man, but our little morning party on the beach came to an end all too soon. They gave us, as a parting gift, a bag of potatoes and a tin of tomatoes. In those days the tinning of tomatoes had not yet become a fine art, but even so, they were wonderful, they tasted as if they were fresh from a garden.

Then those friendly people steamed upriver in the *Moose* and we went paddling down in our canoe.

25 *To Fort Yukon*

So we went paddling down towards Fort Yukon, overcome by drowsiness when the sun shone, huddled in many coats when the wind blew. Our guide was a stolid and rather silent individual, but he did his job. We had no major adventures after we had passed the Ramparts in safety, but each day was marked by different incidents and we fought our drowsiness because we did not want to miss any part of the beautiful river. Never, we decided, could travelling by canoe in such country be monotonous. It took us five days to paddle from Old Crow to Fort Yukon.

A few hours after parting from the *Moose*, we went ashore at Old Rampart where there was a settlement of Indians, but the men had little English and all the women had gone out to pick berries. Then we passed a lone cabin, inhabited, so David told us, by a man named Martin who had been in the country for 20 years, and had only gone out once for a few weeks, in all that time. Realising that we had ample supplies of food, we put ashore to ask him if he had need of anything that we could give him, but we found a morose person, guarded by three or four huskies, and our talk did not last five minutes. He made it clear that he did not want any food nor any visits from fellow-creatures. He saw plenty of company, he assured us; there was a scow or gas boat passing by every month or so in the summer. We heard later that he was well-known as a type of recluse frequently found in the Yukon, a man grown queer in the head from too much living alone.

We guessed that we travelled about 60 or 70 miles that day, but the speed of water is always an elusive thing to reckon when travelling in a canoe. In fact running water has many other elusive characteristics. Often, when in mid-stream, we paddled steadily downward with a fair wind behind us, we seemed to be drifting or even merely floating in one spot on the face of the water, but when we looked at the banks, there they were apparently rushing past us. Also, when paddling down we would often mistake a rock or snag for some animal swimming up towards us.

One day we sailed for some distance, with a moderate and pleasant breeze, using the sail from the police barracks and wrapping ourselves in warm garments until the sun came out, hot and burning. The river side was rich in wild life and on one rocky bluff there were martins' nests, clustered as thickly as a swarm of bees. We saw loons too, and peregrines, ravens, gulls and ducks. Once, we saw a young black bear on the shore and we were entranced in watching his movements, but all too soon he went gambolling away into the bushes, with his strange playful walk that seemed to be crying aloud for a companion. Later we saw a prehistoric-looking porcupine, with wind-blown spinal fringe of fur, ambling about on an island, but when he spotted us he shuffled away, moving with a graceless amble and showing all his quills behind.

One day at lunchtime we climbed a rocky cliff and found that the top was covered with low-growing alpine flowers, most of them familiar to us both. Then we came to a camp of Indians who were catching king salmon in nets, and we went ashore and talked to the men, but the women were too shy to come near us. The river had now become tortuous again and was filled with islands and channels and many snags. It was not at all easy to follow its course and once we took a wrong channel, but David soon discovered his mistake and then we had a hard battle against the current before we got back to the main river again. We camped soon after that adventure and slept on a bed of stones and spruce boughs, watching, behind the pointed firs, a beautiful sunset glow.

On the fourth day out from Old Crow we had brilliant sunshine, but what with the heat, and the glare from the water, we had great difficulty in keeping awake, even when we were paddling, but we managed to keep going, turn and turn about, for we felt that it would be bad for David's morale if we both slept at the same time. As a matter of fact, there was only one comfortable place where we could sleep and that was in the stern where one person, and one only, could curl up comfortably like a hedgehog.

The river was running in great curves now, with never a long straight reach and never a hairpin bend, but always with generous, gigantic loops. The banks were lined with spruce and poplar and here and there with birches. In the evening we saw a gas boat towing a scow coming towards us and we all pulled ashore to exchange news. The men were traders, David told us, going up to Old Rampart.

"My name is Hely," said the man who had been steering the gas boat. "And mine Dorrien Smith and mine Rogers," we echoed in turn. We asked him many questions, after we had answered his; and then we checked our muddled estimates of mileage. It seemed that we had travelled faster than we had thought and that we were now not far from the Sheenjek River and only about 50 miles from Fort Yukon.

During the last week or two, we had realised that we should just miss the steamer at Fort Yukon, bound for Dawson and Tanana, but what did that matter? There would be another steamer sometime. We decided that there was no need to hustle and we paddled on in glassy still water, passing the Sheenjek River about 8. Then we made camp without the tent, covering the hard sand with a pile of willow and poplar boughs. There were wonderful echoes in that part of the river and when we spoke the trees would give us back our own voices. No wonder that many of the lone dwellers in Alaska become spook-haunted and queer.

The next day, which we knew would be the last in our canoe, the sun was scorching and we took one hour shifts at paddling with David and found these more than long enough. Soon after lunch, he announced that we had come to the portage where we must leave the canoe and walk across a point of land for two miles to Fort Yukon. We looked about us and we could see neither landing place, nor track leading up the bank to the trees, nor any sign that this portage had ever been made before. David explained that five miles further down the Porcupine River, it was joined by the Yukon and that Fort Yukon stood two miles upriver from the meeting of the two currents. A man could not paddle a canoe single-handed up those two miles. We should have to walk across to Fort Yukon and hire a gas boat. Having beached the canoe we left it there with all our belongings in it and set out to follow David across the shortcut from one river to the other. We should never have found it alone, for it seemed to us that we were walking in trackless country. It took even David some time to discover the beginning of this old trail and how he found and kept to it remains a mystery to us, for we could see neither marks on trees, nor footprints on the ground, nor any other sign that man had ever passed that way. It was a very long two miles, we felt, as we followed our guide through close-grown spruce trees and through scrubby growth of bushes. Then we had to push our way through grass, which in some places was knee-high or even head-high, and then at last we came to a beaten trail leading

*St Stephen's Mission
(Episcopal), Fort Yukon,
Alaska. n.d. Walter Phillips
Collection, Archives, Alaska
and Polar Regions Dept,
Elmer E. Rasmuson
Library, University of
Alaska Fairbanks,
85-072-33.*

*Harry Anthony. n.d.
From Mason,* The Arctic
Forests *(1924),
opp. 96.*

The Burke Family at Fort Yukon. Left to right: Grafton Burke Jr, Clara Heintz Burke, Hudson Burke, and Dr Grafton Russ Burke. c. 1924. Frederick B. Drane Collection, Archives, Alaska and Polar Regions Dept, Elmer E. Rasmuson Library, University of Alaska Fairbanks, 91-046-53N.

into the settlement. The highlight of that portage was our discovery of a lovely scarlet *Chenopodium*.

So often had that happened in our travels. Some beautiful flower would appear as if on purpose to cheer us over a difficult stretch of land or water. When we talked about this, we sometimes felt, in our nasty, superior English fashion perhaps, a genuine pity for those who travel in a country without noticing its wild flowers.

On our arrival at Fort Yukon, we went straight to Harry Anthony the trader, and he sent his gas boat off, with our guide on board, to bring in the canoe. We looked about us and felt like insects dazzled in lamplight. Fort Yukon was so very large. It was more like a town than a village, but one does not speak of towns and villages in the North, every inhabited place is either a settlement, or a camp, or in the case of a solitary hut, a cabin. Fort Yukon had a much more settled atmosphere and seemed to be more prosperous than any of the Mackenzie River ports. Yet actually, as we found out in due course, it had a large proportion of floating population, for in the summer months many lone trappers would come in to repair their boats and to take in stores for the winter. There were neat palings, a big wireless station, a hospital, a church and many other signs of permanent habitation, whereas the other settlements had seemed like swallows' nests, as they stood precariously clustered together or lined out, on the banks of the Mackenzie which was their life-line.

We went to call on Dr and Mrs Burke at the English mission and there, without any delay, we found a "home from home." We shall never forget their large comfortable living room nor the lavish kindness of that couple. After a few minutes talk they asked us to stay there until the steamer was due. We decided, however, that we must not tax their hospitality nor lose our independence, so we camped beside the river, about half a mile above the old fort, and found that we were constantly in and out of their home, for they provided us with everything that we most needed. Not only did we enjoy many cheerful tea-parties and supper-parties there but we were made free of their bathroom and their books.

After we had made our plans and had heard that the steamer was due to arrive in about seven days, we went back to Harry Anthony, to await the arrival of David and the canoe and while waiting there fell in with an old-timer called Willoughby Mason, who entertained us with many stories. He had just been married, and was taking his new wife up the Porcupine for the winter in a gas boat.

Later, when we were having supper at the mission, we heard more about him and his new wife.

"They won't see a soul till next June," said Mrs Burke.

"He has been trapping for 21 years," said Dr Burke. "Will she ever get that man out?"

"She is taking napkins this time," added one of the guests.

While we were listening to this old-timer, the gas boat returned with the canoe. We found it was partly water-logged so we hurriedly baled it out and went off to pitch our tent. There was little time to be lost for we were due at the mission house for supper. We shuffled out of our breeches and into our skirts and then went off to the Burkes, as happy as if we were to see old friends.

It was a wonderful meal in a happy atmosphere. There was Dr Burke with his fine, sensitive, overwrought-looking face; and Mrs Burke, the happy home-maker; and a pecking kind of woman from Los Angeles, in silk stockings, whose speech was sharp and quick like the movements of a bird, and who seemed to get on Dr Burke's nerves. We could never remember her name so we always called her, between ourselves, Mrs Pecker. There were also three men from the geological survey on the Sheenjek River.

There was fish, lettuce, asparagus, pineapple pie and coffee and then talk that was full of life and vigour and excitement. Finally, we had hot baths in a palatial bathroom.

That was our first evening in Fort Yukon. We had travelled nearly 600 miles by water in our own canoe.

26 *At Fort Yukon*

During the next seven days our life took on a completely different aspect. We lived in a social whirl, but mercifully free from the finery, feathers and conventions of society, for our clothes were not looking their best after being in a wet suitcase for many days.

However, we were happily encamped in a lonely spot beyond the settlement and its empty tins and we celebrated our first morning by lying in bed late and breakfasting on our usual fare at 10. The number of "Breakfasted on pork and tea and biscuits" entries in my diary is remarkable, we must have had the digestion of ostriches. It was blowing a hot gale, but we found the water very cold when we bathed in the river, each with a cake of soap in hand. After we had sorted our clothes, cleaned our pots and pans and eaten lunch we paddled the canoe along to Harry Anthony and left the Rampart House sail in his care. In due course we sold the canoe for $20, having bought it for $97.

The heat was terrific and we spent a cool and blissful afternoon at the mission, having tea with the Burkes and various neighbours; in that hospitable home people were always dropping in for a meal, or to borrow something, or to ask for help. As soon as Mrs Burke offered to lend us books, I left Gwen who was at work on the wild flowers and began browsing on the books and papers that were scattered generously about the room.

Never, in a long, book-loving life, have I experienced such delight in the printed word as I experienced at Fort Yukon. We had cut down personal baggage to the minimum and travelled with a single volume of Shakespeare's tragedies. Gwen had soon wearied of *Macbeth* and the others, nor had I found them suitable

for tired moments and our borrowed books at Aklavik had been of the lightest kind. Now, after eight weeks separation from real writers, I fell on some back numbers of the *Atlantic Monthly*; in those days it gave the reader a wide outlook over European literature. I read them eagerly, as a thirsty man drinks water.

In the following days, whenever Gwen was occupied in sketching I would bury myself in a book or magazine. The bird-like woman, Mrs Pecker, would look on at us in surprise, for she was not one of those who love to bury themselves in an occupation, she liked to flit and skim and her talk was always full of exclamations. She had a sharp eye and mind and tongue and loved to see life from every angle, but she changed her angles frequently.

The Burkes' home became the centre of our lives, but we made many friends outside and would spend hours listening to their yarns. There were so many new faces, that trying to recall any one of them is like trying to remember some portrait seen in a crowded picture gallery.

Hudson Stuck Memorial Hospital, Fort Yukon, c. 1922. From Mason, The Arctic Forests *(1924), opp. 192.*

There was Harry Anthony. While he looked over Gwen's sketches with interest he told us of a trip that he made with Michael Mason (author of *The Arctic Forests*) to cope with a man who had stolen their oil claim. They had started in a hurry, taking rations for eight days. They had to travel for 19 days. They had found a cache of food and had taken some, but they were true to Arctic traditions and did not leave it empty, so they went on with their needs half satisfied and then, for the last five days, they were without food.

Many such stories as these were related in an almost casual tone and we had to use our imagination to realise the toughness of the men who could endure such hardships. Even the most casual encounter was fraught with interest; there was no perfunctory nor commonplace talk with our fellow-creatures at Fort Yukon. One day when I was outside our tent oiling the rifle, two American students came along the beach. They were spending their summer vacation in the North, travelling on a gunboat and selling a medical book to help them pay their college expenses. One was a medical student, the other a Seventh Day Adventist. As they came down the Yukon they had seen, from the deck of their boat, herds of caribou.

At Mrs Burke's suggestion we called one day on the matron of the hospital and asked her to show us round. There were 22 beds and two nurses. She told us much about her work and the life of the place and how the Indians would come in for Christmas with dog-teams and would dance every night for a fortnight.

SS Yukon, leaving Fort Yukon, Alaska. n.d. A.L. Washburn Collection, Archives, Alaska and Polar Regions Dept, Elmer E. Rasmuson Library, University of Alaska Fairbanks, 82–58–218N.

"It is gay here in winter," she said, "but just now Fort Yukon is emptying for the fall."

We had watched the trappers pulling out one by one, each with his scow lashed to a gas boat, his goods, dogs and families all piled together on the scow. They would go up the Porcupine, the Black or the Salmon rivers, spend six weeks getting their cabins ready and after a solitary winter would come down again next year after the melting of the ice.

We lingered talking to a grand old man of 90 with a gangrenous leg. One foot had got frostbitten and he had been for weeks alone with his dogs and now it was too late to operate.

"You should be here in the winter to see it all," he said. "It's a good life." And the matron echoed him.

We heard that on all sides and we longed to stay on and see the winter through.

One afternoon Dr Burke took us through the forest by well-worn trails to the old HB Company's burial-ground. We stood beside each grave as he told us stories of the men below. We went into the church and saw Indian bead-work on the altar and he told us how an Indian chief had wanted to "put up a fence" as a memorial to his wife, and there it was, the fence, inside the church, a $100 altar rail of oak. The doctor lingered by the grave of Archdeacon Hudson Stuck and told us much about his life and work and mountain climbing.

"A fine man," he said. "You couldn't hand him anything. He did his own thinking."

Later, when I came to possess and treasure the archdeacon's books, I realised that he was not only a fine man but also a fine writer.

Among the new faces, I remember one man as a kindred spirit: Frank Foster, an old-timer and a rich man as riches go in Alaska. He was busy building a boat. "He traps a little," Dr Burke told us, "and he loafs around and cannot leave the North."

He had come in by our route during the gold rush of 1898, leaving Edmonton in April and reaching the Klondike in September. He had spent six weeks travelling up the Rat and had brought with him to Fort Yukon 1,300 pounds of food and stores, only to find that there was plenty of everything there. The sand-flies on the Rat had been awful and the water very low.

One evening when we were having supper at the Burkes, doing our best with a colossal joint of moose, I sat next to Frank Foster and we had a long talk. He was a Yorkshireman, a great reader and also a thinker; he had a passion for the Brontës and we discussed books with fervour. He was going off next week to the upper Porcupine; he hated the summer weeks spent outfitting in Fort Yukon and longed to get back to his cabin, his books and his solitude.

Another evening, I left Gwen precariously perched on an old shanty that was built on sand, while she sketched the church and I wandered off to have a yarn with him. He was on the shore, with a man named Tony who hailed from the Azores, working on his boat but he dropped his tools and led us into his cabin where we sat talking about life in Alaska. I could have listened for days.

Tony's story of the rapids is the one that I remember best. He and Buffalo Jim of Crow River had rescued three men from the jaws of death in some canyon where a boat will shoot forward between two walls of rock, borne along like a feather on the foaming current. Way up the river you can hear that water roaring and once you are in it you know it is just mad, boiling over, but if you keep your bows straight, balanced on the top of the combed-up crest of foam in the middle of the current, then your scow won't swing in to those "darned black rocks" and in five minutes it is all over.

"My God that water is swift," Tony went on. "We was half-way through where the rock on the left kinda opens out sideways and there's a back eddy. I saw three men clinging to the rock in that eddy, just hanging by their finger tips that they'd hooked into crevices. 'Back in,' I sez to my partner sharp as a flash and I gave one big stroke and Joe hearing me holler leaned hard on his paddle and we swept right around off the crest of that combed-up water. We had some job getting those three water-logged men aboard, we went for them first of course, then we picked up some of their grub, cases and sacks floating around. Their boat had got broad-side on, shipped water and capsized them. Yes, they found the boat again, way down beyond the canyon. Once you're right there in swift water there's no looking back, you go on like a blast of wind and that wall of rock on each side shutting out the blessed sunlight. Gee-whiz! but they was lucky to get out."

There was an afternoon when Mrs Pecker came wandering along the beach and found us making tea over a fire outside our tent. She was in town clothes, silk stockings and all. We gave her a mug of tea and a "puftaloona" and a box to sit on and then drew her on about life in Los Angeles where she worked in an office. She was quick to argue, to seize a point and to move on to the next one; in her company I always felt that we had very sluggish minds. She was like a figure moving through life over niggerheads that always wobbled under her, never giving her rest nor stability. She seemed rather out of place as she sat there drinking tea. However we did our best to be hearty, for which we were thankful in due course when Mrs Burke invited us to sleep at the overcrowded mission on our last night, for Mrs Pecker said at once: "I'd be tickled to death to move out of my double bed for you, I could have the small room." And tickled to death she was.

As for Mrs Burke, she had been the first woman missionary to go up to the Kobuk country and she had inside knowledge about the Eskimos and Indians. She had seen the Indians perform their Beaver dance. An Indian lies face downward on the ground, balanced on his toes and elbows, imitating a beaver as he wriggles round and round a post until the onlookers are giddy. There is also the Crow dance of the Indians when a corpse, covered by a shawl, lies on the floor and the dancers come round and peck at it. She had watched the witch doctor, Meesuk, mesmerizing an Eskimo. Dr Burke was a missionary and medical doctor in one and a friend to every soul in Fort Yukon.

Our last evening came. The steamer was due next day. We packed up our tent, clothes and bedding and repaired to the Burkes for supper which proved to be an impromptu party swelled by various unexpected guests, two geological surveyors, a gold-prospector and a trapper, all full of reminiscences and stories.

It was after midnight when we repaired to Mrs Pecker's bed. We slept on a spring mattress but the huskies howled all night and nearly all the time the sun shone relentlessly.

Next morning we were strolling restlessly up and down the bank having last words with friends when we heard an unfamiliar sound, the hooting of a steamer and suddenly a great vessel swung round the bend of the river and turned in towards our bank. There she tied up and anchored, towering above the shore like some white leviathan that was full of eyes and openings. She looked immensely large and strange, looming there above the settlement, dwarfing the cabins into pancake forms.

The Burkes were there to see us off. It was a sad moment when we said good-bye to them; I shall always think of those two as standing like beacon-lights in the lonely northland, keeping alive and shining the spirit of true Christianity. We shook hands warmly with Mrs Pecker and then we left them at the foot of the gangway and went on board, out of their lives for ever.

We stood on the deck among our miscellaneous bags and bundles, two shabby, tanned and embarrassed women, as the steamer moved off down the Yukon and the silence of the forest was still echoing in our ears, louder than the chorus of the tourists who were milling about us, thick as ants in an ant-heap. They were all talking at once and talking in a hurry.

"Gee-whiz! but I guess this is the dandiest little city I ever saw."

"See those little cabins right there?"

"I reckon they must be for pygmies."

"But ain't they just cute?"

"I guess this is the real North."

"My, but it's fierce."

We suddenly felt very cold as we turned our backs on the warmth of those Fort Yukon homes and welcomes to settle in among this crowd of strangers.

27 Travellers, Rivers and Mountains

While that steamer turned out from the bank and then went swiftly down the Yukon River, we stood on the deck alone, feeling as if the Fates, in angry mood, had dropped us heavily there to face a life of captivity and noise.

How those tourists did stare at us and how they did chatter! We were attacked from every side at once as they began firing questions at us like bullets. Only later did we learn that the Hudson's Bay Company had spread far and wide the news that two English women would be crossing the Divide by the Rat River route and coming out on the Yukon steamer. The officers on board had, it appeared, been expecting us since April. No doubt they had found it impossible to believe that we would be so daft as to travel by the mosquito-haunted Rat in summer, but they kept such thoughts to themselves and were extremely kind and friendly during our short cruise. Our journey by this unusual route had been a source of endless gossip among the passengers, hence their curiosity when we actually did arrive in their midst. We only learned this later and in those first moments we felt as if we were rare migrant birds, caught and caged and surrounded by faces peering in between the bars.

No doubt our appearance encouraged them to stare, for Gwen's face was peeling and mine had become the colour of mahogany, and our water-logged clothes had lost any freshness that they had ever had, but the curiosity of those tourists was blatant. We felt inclined to turn and run for the shelter of our cabin, so humiliating was our feeling of "What-are-we-among-so many?" Had it been so many trees, so many birds or flowers, or even waves, we would not have minded, but these pop-eyed, siren-voiced human beings were a menace to our peace of mind. Pride, however, stiffened our attitude, so we turned slowly and went off to find our cabin, not in the manner of persons beating a retreat but with a deliberate sauntering air, as if we owned the ship.

"Must keep our end up," muttered Gwen, who disliked crowds even more than I did. In the solitude of our cabin she expressed herself more freely. "If those inquisitive Yanks go on staring at us," she said, "I shall take strong measures."

I could guess only too well what those strong measures would be. Heavy boots and shoes in a rucksack and the pack whirled round her head with increasing momentum until she could stand alone and free in the middle of a crowd. I remembered our arrival at Belgrade railway station and how, while I went off to make enquiries, she had cleared off the clamorous touts and porters in this manner until, when I returned, there was not a fez-crowned head to be seen within three yards of her. "The blighters came too close," she said.

After supper on that first evening we leaned on the rail and watched the murky brown current of the river beneath a blue-black sky as we swirled down past cottonwood, spruce and poplar forest, noting each bend and level spit and cut-bank intently, as if we were still navigating the river alone, but now our pace seemed terrific and we missed the rhythm of paddling our own canoe. An onlooker's life is no life at all, we thought. In due course, we made a few friends among the passengers and some of these would act as spies, retailing, in order to make us laugh, some of the things that the tourists said about us as they measured us with their eyes.

"It's a wonder," said one, "that those ladies haven't lost their manners being away so long from civilization."

Some thought we would have forgotten how to use a knife and fork and waited eagerly for us to hold our meat in both hands and gnaw it. Others felt sure that we had lost all memory of the King's English, after hearing only heathen tongues for so long a time. A few were inclined to use gestures and pidgin English when they spoke to us, but we did not respond very heartily to these, so the rumour got around that, from constant association with Alaskan bears, we had become sore-headed and morose.

Our first friend was a lad of the geological survey party, who had injured his leg when working on the Porcupine and we had long talks with him about that river. Soon the passengers began to question him. "How did you penetrate the reserve of those two?" they asked.

"Humph!" said Gwen when he told us this, "only themselves to blame if we *are* like bears with sore heads, they make too much noise."

"I suppose," I said reluctantly, "we must try to be more genial."

But when we did try we learned that geniality is nature's own gift and is not to be acquired by art or effort.

After a while we invented several techniques for dealing with their questions and their staring curiosity. We would stare back at them, or assume an air of dumb stupidity as if we really had lost the use of our language, or question them about themselves, both speaking at once in order to confuse them. When these tactics failed I would produce Gwen's sketches which they would admire immensely, until they understood that they were for sale. I nearly effected good sales to a rich Jew, but he decided in the end that picture postcards would be just as good for souvenirs, and would be far cheaper. However, a few sketches were bought by the more discerning passengers.

Among the strangely mixed crowd on board we made several friends. The boy with the injured leg could not move about so we used to settle down beside him to have nostalgic talks about the Porcupine River. Then there was an interesting, much-travelled nurse who had been in Labrador with the Grenfell mission, and a delightful self-made couple from Seattle, reputed to be extremely rich but quite unspoilt by riches and endowed with simple tastes and manners; there were two attractive and breezy American girls; an old-timer from Fiume who came in 40 years ago and had never been out since and was now keeping a general store; and another old-timer, with a Swedish wife, returning to his mink farm near Anchorage.

There was also one lasting friendship we formed on that journey. Soon after coming on board we noticed two men whose clothes were almost as shabby as our own. In fact, what caught our eye first were the boots of the very tall one, for both his soles were nearly detached from the uppers and were flapping as he walked about the deck. He was Professor Harold Innis of Toronto University, and his companion was an undergraduate named Gibbs. They had been exploring the border country between Canada and Alaska, and had crossed the Divide at a point considerably south of the Rat River. We soon made a habit of going ashore with these two and a very happy quartet we were, enjoying freedom from the tourist world in which we found ourselves so ill-at-ease. We always kept up with Harold Innis and some years later when he came over to England for a Royal

Geographical Society's meeting, he came down to Cornwall to stay with me. He was a fine fellow, with a great mind and a wide outlook on life.

The most exciting tales that we heard came from a prospector who had been seeking, and sometimes finding, gold for 22 years. Once he had made as much as $135,000, but it was soon lost in a futile venture. He told us of a volcanic basin in Alaska that was three and a half miles wide by seven miles long. It was so hot there that the soil was cooked into a kind of crust and each year the melting of the snow would form a river in that valley and the river, rushing down to open country, would throw up, to right and left, sandbanks that nearly smothered the treetops. He had been in an unexplored part of the Chugach Range with no maps and only the coast line to give him bearings. Once he came to a mountain that had in its side a white line, perhaps half a mile long, which looked like a quartz reef.

"I just had to climb that mountain and see that reef," he said.

When he got up there he found only the white bones of birds that had been killed by volcanic fumes escaping through a rift in the mountain.

As we listened to such stories we could hardly bear to remind ourselves that we were now homeward bound and would have to leave behind us all that wild untravelled country. We felt a great longing to turn back and spend the rest of our days wandering about the unknown, cruel, magnificent land. If destiny had ordered our sex, our background and our characters differently, we might have indulged such longings and become, in due course, old-timers. However, as we adapted ourselves to the change from camp life to a crowded ship's routine, we soon realised that the Fates had really been kind to us for among our fellow-travellers we discovered many congenial persons. Moreover, during that journey by river and rail through Alaska to the coast, and then by ocean-going steamer through the Pacific fjords to Seattle, there was beauty all the way and very often it was spectacular on a scale that we had never yet imagined.

Of course the pace and the noise of the Yukon steamer were such that we never could regain the deep sense of intimacy with a river that we had enjoyed on the Porcupine, when, alone with the Arctic silence, we had drifted down a golden waterway to an unknown land.

When you walk beside a river, following its course from mountain cradle to the sea, or dip your paddle in the water, keeping on the middle downward course, after a while you are carried out of yourself, becoming subject to all the moods of your mighty companion, becoming also aware of a power that is self-sufficient and independent of your friendship, beneficent to the land through which it flows, tyrannical and ruthless in the face of obstacles, subservient to nothing in the world save wind and frost. A little river is often, in moods of calmness, faithful mirror to the sky but the great rivers of the world are changeful as any chameleon, being now as smooth as glass and now broken into a myriad ripples, and then, with the melting of the snows that feed its perennial current, like an unchained demon in a rage. One thing in Alaska that we longed to see above all others was the river Yukon in the spring, for then, with the coming of the thaw, it hurtles downwards gigantic floes in a chaos of ice and water, moving with irresistible power. Of course we could never gain any sense of intimacy with the Yukon but during those few days when we travelled down to its junction with the Tanana River at Tanana, the outlook from the steamer decks was magnificent. The current was wider than that of the Porcupine, broken into larger sloughs and longer islands and it was more turbulent than any river we had ever seen. We felt as Noah must have felt on the top of Mount Ararat, when he looked about him and saw on every side unpopulated country.

One evening the captain sent and summoned us from our bunks to come on deck and see the Northern Lights. The sky was broken up into sinuous waving bands of colour with straight edges like a crystal, but half transparent like wispy clouds and long tentacles that shimmered and trembled across the starlit sky, becoming now and then great sheets of milky light. The heavens seemed to emit a crackling sound; it seemed as if an earthquake were taking place above us and those rainbow-coloured streamers filled all our overhead world from one horizon to the other. I remembered the poet's line: "When earth's foundations fled away," and wondered if the sky really was disintegrating and leaving us at the mercy of—What? Of nothingness? Never before had I realised that day after day and year after year the sky is like a protective presence that keeps us anchored in this world of ours.

More important, however, than even the Northern Lights or the Yukon River were the glimpses that we had of Mt McKinley. The sight of this mountain, even in the far distance, had an almost stupefying effect on the mind. Each time we saw the peak it was as if our hearts stopped beating and our brains ceased to function under a sudden onrush of awe and admiration. Mt McKinley, or, to use the more beautiful native name, Mt Denali, is the highest of the three Alaskan giants, for it is over 20,000 feet, while Mt St Elias is only 18,000 feet and Mt Logan only about 19,500 feet. We never had a close sight of Denali, indeed the view we enjoyed for the better part of a whole day was from a distance of 100 miles. The first time we saw it was one evening about sunset. The clouds had lifted from the summit of that gigantic, nugget-shaped peak. It was partly lit up to an ethereal shade of pink and partly in shadow, while lower down one cloud-bar cut across the mountain and below that again was a repetition of the ethereal pink colour produced by sunlight on snow.

Next morning the two breezy American girls came to our cabin at 4, with a message from the pilot asking us to come on deck at once. There was Denali, still very far away, bathed in the dawn light, outlined in perfect clarity from roots to summit, the most beautiful mountain we had ever seen. No modern flood-lighting of an ancient building was ever so spectacular.

Later, after steaming up the Tanana River, we left the steamer at Nenana and had to wait there 24 hours for the train to Seward. We breakfasted, took rooms at the hotel, bought sandwiches and hurried to a ridge overlooking the town, in order to spend the whole day up there looking at Denali. It dominated our thoughts just as it dominated its own semi-circular range of peaks and the whole landscape, although it was about a hundred miles distant. The vast intervening flattish country was aflame with rosebay willow-herb, then in its seeding time, with all the purple flowers turned into red seed-pods.

We remained on that ridge all day, Gwen sketching while I lay stretched out beside some trees, gazing at the mountain.

That peak was regal, dominant, or, to use the jargon of today, it was something "out of this world." Our whole day spent in its presence was a privilege that we never could forget. As we turned away to come down the hill for supper, we met two men carrying the meat of a bear that they had just shot. One of them was a Swiss who had been 22 years in the country and was now living on a lake a little way down the river. Whenever he wanted food he would go out and shoot a deer. Somehow this encounter seemed to be a fitting end to our day spent gazing at Denali, the monarch of that wild country.

One more view we had of the mountain during our railway journey from Nenana to Seward. This was from Broad Pass on the height of land. The mountain still dominated every other object, dwarfing each peak of the range from which it was reared up towards the sky.

28 The Journey Home

Even when we had left Alaska, embarking on the steamer for Seattle, there was nothing formal nor familiar about the pattern of our homeward journey. Our experience was rich and varied and we had never a moment for looking back, so that many weeks elapsed before we realised that we had come "out" for good and that the North, which had made so profound an impression on us, was now far behind in time and space.

During our eight days voyage to the south we went in and out of fjords that were beautiful beyond description; we called at settlements with great factories for canning salmon, halibut and herring and we never missed a chance of going ashore; we spent hours sitting on deck gazing at the mainland scenery of glaciers and mountains and hours leaning on the ship's rail bemused by the utter calmness of the ocean and the beauty of reflected islands; or we listened to the widely-ranging talk of some of our fellow-passengers who, like Ulysses, had known many men and many cities. There was never a dull moment and we had no time to remember or regret what we had left behind.

On the second morning of the cruise we woke at 7:30 to find ourselves at anchor beside Columbia Glacier; we were somewhere between Latouche and Valdez. The glacier was a marvellous creature, and must surely, we thought, be alive and semi-conscious for no inanimate thing could be so beautiful. It was a mile long and its great lip was curled over into the sea and the waves were washing it all the time, forth and back, forth and back, making no diminution of its immensity. It rose 280 feet from the water and was full of pale and dark blue rifts and crevices, some of which emitted a soft pink light. The sky was gray and the

Left to right: Clara Coltman Rogers (Vyvyan), Gwendolen Dorrien Smith, Dorothy Dashwood; Picnic on Vancouver Island, Aug.-Sept. 1926. Collection of Edward Zealley.

edge of the glacier was muddy and serrated. Every now and then a chunk of ice fell into the sea. The sound of these falling ice-blocks was tremendous and we waited for each one in tense excitement. For a whole hour we stood on deck, only half dressed beneath our overcoats, mute as pillars, watching that glacier. It was a sad moment when we turned back from that apparently land-locked sea towards the Pacific.

It was during this voyage that Gwen and I had our first and last quarrel. It was about each other's hats. I told Gwen that her mustard-yellow felt hat was a foul colour and was getting on my nerves; she retorted that mine was a misshapen disgrace. We exchanged hats to ease the situation and all was well, but when we got to Seattle we went to a hat shop. Funds were running low, so we bought an electric blue hat for one dollar and wore it in turns to give ourselves a kind of cachet.

We found Seattle most bewildering, the general hustle was like a cold wind blowing in our faces, the cafeteria where we fed could seat 800 persons. "All this country is on wheels," someone said to us and indeed we had the impression that everyone was trying to move faster than their own steps could take them. Near one beauty spot, we observed the notice: "Picture ahead. Kodak as you pass." Everywhere we felt the tyranny of the unforgiving minute. No one stopped still for quiet enjoyment of a scene and anyone who wanted to express admiration could only say: "Gee-whiz but it's fierce!"

We arrived at Parksville on Vancouver Island after a day of rain and it seemed as if the whole island were scented, so delicious was the resinous breath of the big trees. Later we saw trees 225 feet high and after a while we felt as if the island were one great forest. Gwen's old friend D.D. welcomed us to her little home set in four acres of rough land and for nearly a month she put up with our comings and goings, often sharing them. She was a large, middle-aged, cheerful person who had solved the problem of adapting a small income to a love of travel by taking jobs in other people's kitchens or gardens, or by growing her own sweet-peas for market. Whenever she was solvent she would travel; when she was "broke" she would find another job.

We spent two days reading our letters, the first for 13 weeks, washing our clothes and making plans and meeting friendly neighbours and then we all set off for Howe Inlet in British Columbia, with the mountain camping-ground of Garibaldi Park as our objective. We spent another two days at Daisy Lake where Gwen and I slept out on the river bank beside the little inn, joining D.D. for meals. The last stage we made with pack-horses through 13 miles of silent green forest, where pendulous lichens hung from the trees. D.D. bestrode a powerful nag and Gwen and I took turns to ride our horse. The undergrowth was full of whortleberries and others, waist-high berries, knee-high ones and crouching ones, some blue, others red, but all delicious. We never met a poisonous berry in the North.

The mountain-climbers' season was over and at Garibaldi we had the world to ourselves, such a world! We were over five thousand feet up, camped by a dell with running water, in an amphitheatre of peaks and glaciers, with the pale green water of Garibaldi Lake plumb below us and two great glaciers sweeping into it. In the west there was a whole snow-clad range, tipped with flame and gold by the setting sun. We had supper in the dark over a bonfire, intensely aware of the deep silence that was like a living presence all about us. In that place we lost all count of time, each day we explored some new peak or glacier or waterfall, and each day we bathed in a lake or stream. All the time we had green and white waterfalls for companions and every evening a flaming sunset sky. We soon discovered that D.D. found our standards of living rather austere and always held aloof when we chose to sleep beneath the stars or to bathe in glacier water. "Bit too civilized for

Clara Coltman Rogers (Vyvyan) at Mount Arrowsmith, Vancouver Island, Aug.–Sept. 1926. Collection of Edward Zealley.

us," said Gwen and that was her only comment on her friend. However D.D. would always be happy with her sketch book and we might have gone further to find a third companion, and fared much worse. What she thought of us, I really do not like to think. She must have realised, on several occasions, that we were two to one.

On the way down we slept at Rainbow Lodge, a tourist hotel complete with beds of nasturtiums, annexes in the garden and rustic bridges over streams. There, in a nasturtium bed, I saw one of the few miracles that have indelibly marked my life. It was the sight of a hummingbird, brown and iridescent red. I stood looking down on this little miracle trying to convince myself that it really was a bird and not a moth.

On our return to Parksville we were caught in a social whirl among neighbours who were mostly retired English people: tea-parties, picnics, joy-rides filled the days. Three things only remain in my memory: certain sunsets seen from Qualicum Beach, bathing in the shallow Pacific bay with never a soul overlooking us and visiting a shy Scotsman. Gwen would sit in his verandah sketching the bay, while he and I browsed in his cosmopolitan library; his books were his best friends.

Our next small excursion was the climbing of Mt Arrowsmith, 5,400 feet high. Standing on the summit, we felt as if we held Vancouver Island in the palm of one hand; the clearings in the great forest below were no larger than a pocket handkerchief. We could see the mainland beyond the sound as we stood there on equal terms with clouds and snowclad peaks. Far below us was a deep, green lake and to northward there were other lakes below the main range of Arrowsmith. That world was like an opal.

We soon set off on another camping expedition, making for Great Central Lake in the heart of the island, travelling by "stage" motor bus through raw country and magnificent forest to Alberni. We slept in the Ark, a tiny hotel floating on a lake, built on logs and anchored. Next day we went by gas boat, three hours' journey up the lake to our camp, a dirty cabin with a boat, clean linen and firewood all let out to us for a dollar a day. Our solitude was complete. Gwen and I pitched our sleeping bags on a rocky knoll above the lake, with pointed firs all round and brilliant stars over head.

Next morning, we all set out early to walk 12 miles to Dalla Falls, but after three miles D.D. returned to her sketching. This country was like the North, it was outsize, immeasurable, untamed. We walked beneath enormous trees, past huge boulders embedded in turbulent rivers and had to cross them by rough bridges of felled trees and at last we came to the thundering waterfall. After a 24-mile walk, we had early supper on the knoll and again slept out under the stars. Two days later we were travelling back by the "stage" to Parksville, with a blood-red sunset in the west and Mt Arrowsmith, now deep purple, looming overhead.

When we left Parksville we made the CPR journey in stages, so as to pass through the Rocky Mountains by day. Trees were beginning to colour up for the fall; maples were red, dogwood deep crimson, poplars gold and green and some-

Gwendolen Dorrien Smith (left) and Clara Coltman Rogers (Vyvyan) at a railway station, 1926. Collection of Edward Zealley.

times soft pink or russet. When we tipped our heads back to look at the snow peaks above, they seemed, with their uniform white austerity to belong to another world.

We slept a night at Sicamous and a night at Field and spent a long day at Banff and then we took to sleeping-berths on the train, waking next morning to find ourselves in the golden-brown spaces of the prairie, desolate and lonely, stretching away without hope or incident to the distant sky's horizon. In Vancouver Island we had met a woman suffering from "prairie fever," a particular kind of melancholia. Her friends had at last brought her away, but she had never really recovered.

The next, and in fact the last, event of importance on our homeward journey was our stay in Winnipeg. Our friends received us as if we were heroines and we felt extremely embarrassed. We had four long social days there, during which we were lunched and dined and fêted and shown off to our friends' friends. We very soon suspected that we were being paraded not only to their friends but also to their acquaintances, for the circle grew and grew. However, it was good to feel the warmth of welcome that we received from Gordon Mactavish, Mr Christie and Lady Tupper. The cocktails were a menace to me and how Gwen steered me through one particular dinner-party, after four cocktails each, I do not now remember, for faces were revolving about me in a fog, disappearing and reappearing and whether they were the same faces or new ones I could not decide. They gave an enormous party for us, with Gwen's sketches on show and she sold $172 worth.

On the second day a reporter came to our hotel with Gordon and questioned us, and then he took us to the *Free Press* photographer. We went like sheep to the slaughter and were photographed under a purple light. I enjoyed watching Gwen's reluctance and began to enter into the spirit of the thing and decided to encourage her. "We may as well enjoy all this nonsense and admiration." I said, "Never again shall we be baby lions." The best interview was with Sheriff Inkster, a fine upright old-timer aged 83, who loved talking about the Rat River. At one point he threatened to kiss Gwen. It was the only time I ever saw fear in her eyes.

Those days in Winnipeg were the end of our adventure. The rest of the journey was anticlimax and when we got home no one, except Mr Cunliffe, was really interested in the Rat River. Our friends and families were far more interested in the fact that we had spent nine days and nights without changing our clothes. "Well," they would say, "some people take their pleasures sadly," and they would give a sympathetic sigh over our folly and that would be their final comment on our Arctic journey.

The net result in outward and visible signs was threefold: 267 kinds of pressed wild flowers were sent to Kew Herbarium; $600 worth of Gwen's sketches were sold. We both, in our respective home areas, had many invitations from Women's Institutes to come and talk to them about our travels.

But what of the inward and spiritual grace? For myself, I keep certain pictures indelibly imprinted on my memory. Those pelicans above Fort Smith, ranging to and fro over the troubled waters. The crackling of the Northern Lights. The kindness and hospitality that we received from strangers. Columbia Glacier. The hummingbird. The strange clarity of near and far objects and the golden colour of lake and river when lit by Arctic sunlight. Paramount among all these is the memory of those days when we paddled alone down the Porcupine, having achieved absolute freedom in a world of absolute beauty.

Watercolour Sketches by
Gwendolen Dorrien Smith

Edmonton 1926.
Gwendolen Dorrien Smith.
Watercolour over pencil on
paper, 25.3 x 35.4 cm.
Collection of Susan Lea.
This watercolour was made
from the window of the
women's room at the
Macdonald Hotel.

Athabasca River, Fort
MacMurray *[sic]*,
1926. *Gwendolen*
Dorrien Smith.
Watercolour over pencil on
paper, 35.5 x 25.4 cm.
Collection of Susan Lea.

Fort Smith 1926.
Gwendolen Dorrien Smith.
Watercolour over pencil on
paper, 25.4 x 35.4 cm.
Collection of Susan Lea.

Mission Is[land] Gt
Slave Lake, June 15th
1926. *Gwendolen*
Dorrien Smith.
Watercolour over pencil on
paper, 17.8 x 25.4 cm.
Collection of Susan Lea.

Burnt I. June 16
1926. *Gwendolen
Dorrien Smith.
Watercolour over pencil on
paper, 25.4 x 17.8 cm.
Collection of Susan Lea.
Vyvyan's field notes for 7,
11, 14, 16, and 28 June
record the trip of two
schooners to Aklavik, to be
sold to Inuit there.*

Fort Norman, June 20-1926, Mackenzie R. Bear Rock. *Gwendolen Dorrien Smith. Watercolour over pencil on paper, 17.8 x 25.4 cm. Collection of Susan Lea.*

Inuit Schooners, Aklavik. *Gwendolen Dorrien Smith. Watercolour over pencil on paper, 25.4 x 35.6 cm. Collection of Joan M. Boucaud.*

Atlavik *[sic]*. 1926.
Gwendolen Dorrien Smith.
Watercolour over pencil on
paper, 17.8 x 25.4 cm.
Collection of Susan Lea.

Atlavik *[sic]*,
Mackenzie River,
The Wood Pile.
1926. *Gwendolen*
Dorrien Smith.
Watercolour over pencil on
paper, 25.4 x 35.6 cm.
Collection of Susan Lea.

All Saints Anglican
Church, Aklavik
1926. *Gwendolen
Dorrien Smith.
Watercolour over pencil on
paper, 17.8 x 25.4 cm.
Collection of Joan M.
Boucaud.*

Eskimo at Atlavik
[sic]. 1926. Gwendolen
Dorrien Smith.
Watercolour over pencil on
paper, 9.8 x 17.8 cm.
Collection of Susan Lea.

Porcupine R 1926.
Gwendolen Dorrien Smith.
Watercolour over pencil on
paper, 25.4 x 35.2 cm.
Collection of Susan Lea.

Appendix 1

Vyvyan's Field Notes
15 May—15 August 1926

The field notes of C.C. Vyvyan (Clara Coltman Rogers when she wrote them) are held in a private collection in England. They occupy one beige notebook, with "Alaska" and "1926" written in black fountain pen ink on the front cover. The notebook measures 17.8 cm x 11.5 cm, and contains 72 leaves (144 pages) of lined paper, and two leaves—one at each end—of unlined paper. The inside back cover bears the names "Lazarus Sittichili" and "Jimmy Koe" in blue ink on two lines. A short-form mark favoured by the author is the use of the letter X to denote "cross," as in aX, Xed, and Xing. The writing bears one other interesting feature: because, as is clear from a remark in the field note for 9 July, Vyvyan found her pen useless for "uphill" writing in a tent, most field notes during the canoe trip were written in pencil. These were overwritten in ink at a later date. It is possible that the overwriting occurred around the time of the preparation of the book, for the overwriting is shaky—the handwriting in pencil is firm—and resembles that seen in letters written by Vyvyan in the 1970s.

As one would expect of field notes, nearly all the writing in the notebook comes under dated headings, beginning at 15 May and extending through 15 August 1926. (Some additional material follows the last dated entry. It includes a report of the trial at Aklavik, a list of expenses as well as sales of some of Dorrien Smith's sketches, two recipes, a list of books read during the journey, and various names and addresses[225-29].) Each note is written in the context of the day's experience—in the cities of the Canadian west, among the old-timers of the North, or in the mosquito-infested valley of the Rat River. The abbreviated style (parataxis) and concrete details of travel create a vivid sense of immediacy as, with the author, the reader journeys across Canada in 1926. The excitement and bustle of Winnipeg, the newer, growing city of Edmonton, the small northern communities—all appear as Vyvyan encountered them with eyes accustomed to the grand historic buildings of English cities and the different scale of the Cornish landscape. Since she was already a published writer, Vyvyan doubtless had some idea of writing about this trip; thus, the field notes form not only a record of expenses and activities but also a repository of description and anecdote, impression and detail, fuel for future writing. As such, they offer a vivid first impression of Canada through the eyes of the professional writer.

Any material that occurs in the field notes but not in the published narrative has been printed in italics in this appendix (however, see note at the bottom of p.226). While some of the italicized material merely highlights weather observations or incidents of travel that Vyvyan repeated or emphasized in her daily entries, other passages are more significant. Personal details, and many people mentioned in the field notes, were also omitted when Vyvyan wrote her book. A few personal names were also altered in the published version ("Harris of Simpson" becomes "Murphy" in the narrative, and Capt McIntyre becomes Capt Cameron), and many more were left out, their owners described only as "the judge" or "the doctor." Vyvyan attempted to standardize and correct place names in writing her book, and left out some of the stories recorded in the field notes. Descriptions of communities are often condensed, perhaps because, after so long, Vyvyan was more interested in character and wilderness than in the settlements, or was unable to distinguish among them any longer. The published narrative also had to balance local colour with the geographical movement of the narrative in order to avoid having the travel overburdened by anecdote and incident.

When she wrote her book, Vyvyan seems to have had little interest in updating her material historically. More important to her than the facts and details recorded in the field notes were the impressions evoked by the wilderness; accordingly, the book is structured in terms of geography and event rather than in terms of daily entry. This restructuring means that material appears differently in the narrative. Of a fairly incidental significance is the attribution of information to different characters in the narrative than in the field notes, such as when Vyvyan attributes the description of Hudson Stuck to Dr Burke (above, 171), whereas it was Harry Anthony who told her that Stuck was "a man who did all his own thinking. You could hand him nothing" (25 July). Diction becomes more formal in the transition to publication: the six "scally-wags" on the jury in Aklavik (24 June) become "a collection of the toughest ruffians imaginable" (60), and the "comic opera" of steamer landings in the field notes becomes "some scene in a ballet" (48). Details of travel are also moved, simplified, or combined to tighten the story; thus, on the trip across Great Slave Lake, the SS *Distributor* ties up at both Mission Island (14-15 July) and Green Island (16 July) in the field notes, but only one unnamed island is described in the book, and it draws on elements from both field note entries. Similarly, the caribou sighted the morning of 19 July and the wolf tracks recorded on 21 July are conflated in the book into one night's observations (148-49). In another example, the "King William land Eskimo long haired man of the woods" who performs the seal dance with Ikagena in Aklavik after the murder trial (24 June) disappears from the book, and Ikagena himself, who, "with his long hair and strange face, seemed to us like a wild man of the woods" (58), performs the dance alone.

Of more significance, and perhaps in the service of propriety when entering the public arena, Vyvyan's indictments of the HBC's exploitation of its northern customers (27 June) do not appear in the published narrative, and her nega-

tive descriptions of the northern churches and their appeal to the indigenous peoples are tempered. As well, many of the strong female figures met by Vyvyan and Dorrien Smith play no part in the published narrative, which portrays the north more conventionally as a place for male adventure in the wilderness. Miss Ross, the nurse at Fort McMurray (3 June), and Mrs Burgland, who is raising a family in a one-room Alaskan cabin (28 July), seem to have inspired the women with admiration, but cannot be found in the book. Mrs Laura Frazeur survives in the book as a previous traveller, but is not connected with the anonymous woman who was abandoned by her guides and who so haunts Vyvyan's relations with Sittichinli and Koe.

Creating a story, where tension and doubt are overcome by the women's steadfast resolve, thus produces changes in the material. The playful question, on 9 July, "Has the Rat a spite against us?" is heightened in the narrative to musings about the "malignant" Rat (39, 108). The field notes underplay the women's doubts as they prepare for the journey; the narrative uses their doubts for aesthetic purposes, to engage the reader in their undertaking. In the field note entry recording Sgt Anderton's encouragement for their endeavour, Vyvyan celebrates his knowledge and judgement as being "So different from Winnipeg + SS. Distributor croakers," and notes that, in the context of other northern exploits, their own adventure appears "smaller," less risky (27 June); with the adventure still ahead of them, Vyvyan considers it a reasonable, manageable undertaking for two inexperienced travellers. In the book, where their adventure is the centre of the story, Vyvyan's perspective emphasizes how significant it actually was in relation to their inexperience, which she suggests Anderton underrated (74-5). It is not that one version or the other is more "true," but that, having accomplished the journey, looking back from a lifetime of travel, Vyvyan sees the experience differently from that earlier self, who was preparing, psychologically and physically, to face the Rat River.

Editorial notes concerning the field notes will be found collated with the notes to the chapters of the book; they come after the last note to each chapter and are arranged so that they appear under whichever chapter covers the events of their respective dates.

In this presentation of the field notes, the form of the dated headings has been standardized, but spelling and punctuation remain as they are in the original. Where they vary substantively from Vyvyan's field notes, Dorrien Smith's are quoted in notes.

SATURDAY 15 MAY 1926
Left Southampton Empress of Scotland 1:30 PM May 15 About 7 heard the engines stop + going up on deck found ourselves inside Cherbourg harbour: in the embrace of 2 long stony piers. Grey town grey evening white-gray cliffs. Cold wind. Acquitania at harbour mouth silhouetted on orange sky. Gigantic, 4 tunnelled, raised up out of the water as if she wd. assert her independence: funnels sloping backward made her look like some monster about to spring: a wonderful *evening silhouette* was that ship against the orange sky. *Man's power outlined on God's beauty.*

On the other side of us the tender was landing (bringing on) emigrants: shawled women children in striped garments, men carrying little wooden chests or bundles Czecho-Slavs + *heaven knows what medley* of E. European nations. They berth forward: under the name of "continental emigrants" *(but the French are not included as a rule).* We have 2nd class cabin but 3rd class meals + deck

SUNDAY 16 MAY
Sunday. Church in 1st class. Hot sunshine basked on upper deck

MONDAY 17 MAY
Cold + calm saw a whale + his tail came right out before he sounded

TUESDAY 18 MAY
Cold enough *head wind* Wretched

WEDNESDAY 19 MAY
Cold + less rough How the hours drag.

THURSDAY 20 MAY
Engines stopped dead last night from 2-6 + every now + then a bell tolled mysteriously in the silence. So weird without throb of engines after these throbbing days. Went up on deck after b'fast a gray-brown sea + a gray fog all round us + a strange briny smell w. a tang to it as if some sea monster were breathing out *ice + frost.* Engines stopped again + we drifted or wallowed in

that *mysterious* gray silent world. Presently a little iceberg came drifting snow white + blue w. a spout like a teapot rolling in the waves Every now + then nearly submerged + looking then like a line of foam. *Later, on our port side,* the air grew deadly chill + the fog denser + as we tried to pierce the fog we cd see (or 1/2 see) a line of foam on the horizon or was it a low cloud, (then it seemed) like 2 spouts of steam changing (now + then) to a darker patch. *Mysterious + the longer we looked the less clear it seemed.* Drifting nearer + nearer it took form + at last came quickly even with us: it was like a monstrous island in ice like a huge bit of mainland cut off + drifting: the most sinister thing of snow white peaks + edges with dark caves in the face of it + breakers rolling up against it + clouds of fog smoking w. foggy steam rising from the breakers. Never thought any cold thing cd. be so diabolic + sinister + all that day we were looking out for those evil white wisps on the gray (+ clouded) horizon. We drifted more or less till stewardess calls us "In cabin a little ice box most refreshing". we being only ones w. open chink Gwen's fists mercifully strong enough to open any porthole. Eve + it seemed as if we had been drifting for centuries. Then the fog cleared a bit + we went ahead. All day the cold was penetrating + we cd. not sit still for long even w. 3 layers of clothes. Talked a good bit to a *1/2 mad* Irishman Digby Hussey de Burgh.

FRIDAY 21 MAY
Cold but sun shone *now + then. We have seen gulls with white spots on wings these last 3 days* We passed Cape Race 2 hrs after midnight *thence 46 hours to Quebec so we get in tomorrow night.* About 7.45 to 8.45 when it got darkish we saw the whole island of Anti Costi a wonderful gray outline with much snow on flattish high top + the gray face of it streaked with snow + a gray sea + a gray. sky. Most impressive. *We have put back clock 40 mins. each day 60 mins.* 1st day Passengers more sociable *came up in sun like butterflies.* Long chat with red-hot Irishman Digby Hussey de Burgh + others. island Pacific ideal emigrants

SATURDAY 22 MAY
Cold but sunny all day we steamed along the gulf of St. Lawrence *a wide Calm sea* R. bank hidden almost in haze or distance L. shore a dismal country patches of snow among brown trees + on brown grass + lines of huts or dwellings along the shore: *a brown repellent land with even line of hills cutting the sky.* Saw a large whale some way off + 11 Eider ducks in flight. *Passengers swarmed on deck in crowds strange freaks we had never seen before like spawn upon the decks.* At sundown

another medical farce when Dr. came on board + all 3rd Class passengers herded in dining room for over 1/2 an hour till you cd. cut the air stewards guarding every gangway + nothing done in the end. *A glassy sea all day with blue or greenish colour after those brown seas off Newfoundland.*

Sunday 23 May

Quebec at 6 o'c dismal brown rainy deserted wharves. *Up at 6 ashore at 8* for four hours we were penned herded + kept waiting for train in huge waiting rooms where YMCA, Red + + every organization had little side rooms. About 6 hours run to Montreal *2nd class.* Lovely yellow Erythroniums, sheets of white Trillium + a claret Herb Paris. Woods just breaking into green: country flat + raw untidy shacks for dwellings. Copses full of poplar (faint gold leaves) birch, spruce + a maple with red bunches of flowers. Took train at Montreal *to Mt Stephen Avenue friend of Gwen's* then back + supped *at Government Hostel Drummond St.* for 1/6 each. (35C.). So into our sleeper *+ on at 10 o'c:* Tourist sleepers

Monday 24 May

Infernal night heat turned on till we nearly stewed 28 bunks in 1 coach: windows shut we had a fly trap wh. let in a little air. Dressed somehow b'fast 7.30 in dining car 1.50 between us. *Sunny day:* lakes rivers dark firs green-yellow Poplars just breaking into leaf. Untidy shacks, *lumber camps:* monotonous country *but the trees are fascinating.* Miles + miles of a low growing shrub Cassiope? of whortleberry habit. *Gulls on a lake a brown heron? a blue king-fisher? with white below—crows. Dined in dining car + to bed again a cool night. 20 mins. stops at North Bay + Sudbury.*

> Gordon Mactavish
> 200 Trust + Loan Bloc

Tuesday 25 May

Dull day at 1st country much greener white poplars now in leaf + birches just breaking: midday 1st tunnel (by daylight) since Quebec. Many lakes + ponds few birds evening flatter land almost prairie better soil (black) lovely evening light. Winnipeg *8.15* + walked to St Charles Hotel off Main St. Mr Mactavish came round + had a long chat. *he brought literature + much advice + is thrilled.*

Wednesday 26 May

B'fast 8.30. Mr Mactavish came at 9 o'c for us + we had such a day. 1st to Canada Bank of Commerce + Bank of Montreal *fine*

buildings then to Hudson's Bay *(Mr Brooks)* + *Mr Harman who gave us maps + introductions.* Then to Hudson's Bay stores + *bought a copper kettle + saw the Museum with interesting Indian relics bead work goose skin + beadwork +c +c* Then to Fort Garry gate. Then to Mactavish's flat to see his books + taste pemmican + borrow his rifle + flower books. Then to book shop for bird + flower books. Then to Mr Christie in his office a fine old face.

W.J. Christie 300 Paris Buildings

Then to an A 1 lunch at Fort Garry Hotel with Mr Mactavish Mr Christie + Lady Tupper. *All day Mr M. talking of Hudson's Bay + explorer's history his heart in it all + he is thrilled over our journey : a charmer.* Mr C then motored us round Parliament Bldgs + parks *a few animals confined a gopher wild + a palm house well kept.* Then a lovely run *20 miles* along Assiniboine + Red River to Lower Fort Garry. *Hot day + everywhere lovely fresh green of Manitoba maples.* Most exciting birds: yellow canary flicker, oriole, ducks terns grackles robins. Tea in delightful Fort Garry Club 100 Year old fort *on the river with woodpeckers in garden.* Then back to Mr Christie's house to dinner Mrs. C + a son: cool room overlooking river such a dinner. *Winnipeg a finely laid out town with long wide streets one—Portage Avenue running away to Rockies—Mr C* motored us to station at 10.30 + he + Mr McT put us into our Tourist Section. *Winnipeg looked fine lit up at night. A full + well spent day:* we begin to realise the bigness of our undertaking: everyone filled with envy + wonder *but still more because of Mr McT's hints about our outfit. Left Winnipeg about 11.30.*

Thursday 27 May

Woke up 6 to find ourselves in lovely fresh valley with rolling slopes + a river teeming with bird life + birds singing + a spring feeling in the air. Heaps of ducks. *A yellow lupin.* All day the ponds were teeming with ducks + waders unlike the waters of eastern Canada. Rolling plains + ridges + richer looking land. *Spring is here in the W.* strange contrast to the brownness bleakness + snow of Quebec. *Dull + thundery evening.* Slept our 2nd night on train + to Edmonton at 6.50 AM Friday 28th May. *To Macdonald Hotel very swagger 5 $ for double room.* After breakfast to Hudson's Bay Co. with our letter. A long chat with Mr Brabant *+ then poked round Woolworth's + the H Co. Stores + fixed up to meet Mr Warner. Lunched low haunt for 35 cents.* Mr Warner came to see us at 3 o'c + we got several points cleared up (1) Our Indians walk back in 4 days from La Pierre House the road we track up in 9 days. (2) We buy our paddles + Tump line with canoe. (3)

Indians will bring their rifles + fishing lines. (4) we walk those 6 days while they tow (5) 3 lbs food a day on average. (6) La Pierre possibly + old Crow certainly can reprovision us so we need only start with 12 days provisions. (7) More warnings about our guides *Mrs Laura Fraseur was simply left by them + had to return + do a long trek with a party fr. fort Macpherson.* At 3.45 we went round to store + the Manager Mr Dynes took us a run round Edmonton in circles in his Bewick car. Material prosperity greenness in towns every little house has water telephone electric light. Fine buildings with fine spaces round them. Edmonton stands well on the R. Saskatchewan wooded country all round. All things cleaner + more comfortable than ours but how much energy goes to that? Pretty well all + then what else is there for the energy. "This country is just full of optimism" said Mr Dynes. Tremendously proud of their own achievements. Evening sat out on Terrace + Gwen sketched river + *wooded country* from upper window. *So hot: lovely evening where lights twinkled aX river.*

SATURDAY 29 MAY

Out to Hudson's Bay Co. for rifle ammunition mosquito bar brandy +c +c . Then to Mr Brabant's office to pay for our tickets + kept them to 1st arrangement tho' they tried to have our berths + meals unpaid for on daily reckoning + as ice is likely + delay we stood firm.

Macdonald Hotel. Edmonton

Also to Bank of Montreal + Canadian Bank of Commerce to cash £160 and £180 more than we like to carry but there are no banks or posts up north. *Then back to lunch + spent aft. writing + washing.* Mr Warner to tea <u>H.A.O. Warner 21 Credit Foncier Building Edmonton</u> with photographs papers food list for us + many hints. A curious type loves the wilderness went in as a teacher + failed: teeming with ideas *sort of man who would fail:* unusual + interesting has done things: idealistic: has built his own house + boat. *In a confidential pamphlet* he lent us a report for *W. W. Cory Deputy Minister of* Dept. of the Interior he discusses fur trade Eskimos, Missions + Police with insight + ability. He says of the church: "After 1900 years the church remains today the most impractical of all our institutions. If a missionary is a zealot he is short on practicality + if he is not a zealot he generally fails as a missionary."…"Bishop Stringer of Yukon Territory…said it had taken 30 years to Christianize those same Eskimo" (Mackenzie delta Eskimo). "30 years. what a lot of energy + thought has been expended to attain this result. And such a

result. For the Christianity of the Eskimo is but the incorporation of white man's medicine with his own, taboo added to taboo." He told us much about Indians their greed + fawning ways + how the white man has ruined the dignity they had. Told us also of a grizzly Bear that came into their camp smelling fried bacon 15 yards away red mouth in huge head. Indian rifle against tree but Indian did not shoot "him got no shell in it"—they ran aX the stream + Warner followed feeling bear's hot breath behind him. The bear burnt his foot in cinders + retired. Grizzlies will hardly ever attack. *Pouring wet evening we did some repacking. Reporters have put us in to papers in crudest form.* Everyone says *with a drawl* "My but I guess you're making some trip."

SUNDAY 30 MAY

To church at Pro- Cathedral + after Miss Ferguson Bishop Gray's governess came to lunch with us. Then we took trams to Capital Hill where we found dwarf Polygonum leaf of Linnaea borealis + leaves of Pyrola + many other treasures. *Cold + windy day. So few trees in this country black poplar white poplar, birch, spruce. Music evening in hotel wh. is a fine spacious panelled imitation of old English home.*

MONDAY 31 MAY

Another nightmare day of shopping *in Hudson Bay Stores + Woolworths:* Beads silks bicarb. Viscol—Bandage—Axe—Tin Basin—Pillow—Soap—*Cloths*—Forks Matches Cold Cream +c +c After lunch shopped. *Gwen's pictures in Pub. but none sold.* We are fed up with hot air of Pub *confinement among houses +c +c. Dashing over to Hudson's Bay to pay for our Food stores 50$ for 4 people for 14 days, to say Goodbye to Mr Dynes, to get note from Mr Warner for Pursers + Gwen to call on Bishop's wife Mrs Gray. Mr + Mrs McDonald to tea friends of McTavish. Sat out on terrace after lovely lights aX river. Nightmare packing.* Despatched 4 boxes to Vancouver + took on 3 canvas rolls rifle small despatch case suitcase + ruck sack. Why so much stuff when our 1 aim is simplicity?

TUESDAY 1 JUNE

Away at 9 o'c w. our 7 packages in taxi *5 miles* to Dunvegan. Crowd to see off immensely long train going N. the 1st one to catch N steamer this spring. Mounted Police. an Archdeacon. Judge. female missionaries—Brabant +c +c. Train moved off in leisurely fashion quite a send off. *We are getting full of warnings + information about difficulties of handling Indian guides. Thank heaven we are 1 step nearer the wilds. Yet the wilds recede in a curious fashion + tho we begin now to meet 1st hand stories of them we are little nearer. Now we hear that we may* have 2 or 3 days to wait at Waterways. *It all depends on where the steamer lies as regards "the end of steel". A Mr Macn. Inspector for Dept. of Interiors inundates us with stories + information no doubt having read that awful puff in papers thinks we're journalists but tis all interesting. Here in the train to Waterways we are at last 1 step nearer the unknown north.* To begin with our fellow passengers are a queer mixed lot hardly like a mixed lot belonging to the ordinary world + all the talk is of men who have "gone in" or "come out" as if the North were some prison. *Yet they do not speak of it with fear but admiration as if it were some possession of their own full of a stern value.* Many go there to fly from drink because once there they cannot get it. *Provisions more expensive as you go farther "in" saw a Tommy at Boyle buying bananas in July for last time. At supper (we split the 1.25 cent meals but "no plates has" says the waiter when we ask for 2!) we sat opp.* a rough looking youngish man we took for a trader or prospector then found he was going N with the French Canadian Judge on these Eskimo murder trials: he goes for the defence knowing no Eskimo + having never seen his client + the Policeman will be his interpreter. It seems the accused shot a neighbours dog: neighbour walked off to get "shells" for his gun: accused shot the neighbour in self defense once, twice + killed him. It was certain death to wait for the neighbours "shell" for when an Eskimo stops smiling he is dangerous. The defence is all for lenient sentence + discussed the Eskimo outlook on death: how they kill their old folk ("Dear old Ma she's 69 tomorrow fetch your gun) + their female babies ("*This baby is 8 1/2 oz too big* drop it in the lake) till there are 3 men to one woman + of course that leads to fighting specially as the men have several wives sometimes, 1 good sewer 1 good cook, 1 good hunter +c. At Lac La Biche 7 PM we had an hour ashore. Smooth water beautiful lake untidy tents with half breeds: we walked along lake to E sooty (?) terns, cowbells, still water. Scent of poplars: wonderful. *A friendly crowd to see off the Judge + others as we got back to station:* "Don't wait for introductions in the North" says the Judge. *We went + had a smoke with him + the "Defence" in his "stateroom." + so to bed each in a lower bunk with mounted Police on top of us.*

WEDNESDAY 2 JUNE
Woke in wooded country poplars +c + saw Ledum + Kalmia from window. About 10.30 or so we arrived at the new Waterways *2 miles or so beyond the old one + 4 miles short of McMurray.* W. consists of one huge new shed + some slides for luggage + a scow or barge lying alongside. We all—ie. about 40 passengers—sat about on piles of wood or our luggage or wandered among poplars + willows for more than an

hour when a tug came up the river with another scow + away we went 8 miles down stream *manoeuvring awkwardly now tugging, now pushing, now in double harness with the scow.* River so lovely: green water wooded slopes above thickly clothed with pale poplars among dark firs: the silver stems of poplars wonderful very tall + slim. *Lunch 2 o'c in middle of our river boat cabins opening out from dining room all mosquito proof doors + windows. After G + I out along bank had to keep moving when we plunged into woods for mosquitos: Found Prim farinosa + blue Sisyrinchium on bank. Sat on beach + watched clouds + wind among the poplars coming suddenly out of some great space + stirring every leaf to delirium. Coming down in tug we saw tarsands sloping to river supposed to be valuable for asphalt here + different soil crumbling whitish gray ledges. Green woods sand bars + a great stretch of river beyond + behind + its good to be out in it all even with 40 fellow creatures round us.* We had some chat w. Archd Whitaker a fine man the 1st we have met who has actually done the Rat in a canoe Mr. Warner did the portage in winter: he says he did it with 4 or 5 guides his wife + baby being in Eskimo skin boat + he himself often chest high in water. However we will not get the wind up the only ? that worries us now being will 2 guides only undertake the job. *Fine Sunset*

THURSDAY 3 JUNE
Bell woke us at 7 + up we got reluctantly. Scow + tug going up at 8 o'c we head to Waterways + McMurray. But we are already learning the unhurried ways of the north *so we pressed our flowers + about 10 o'c away we went up stream strong current. hot day. these lovely white poplar stems among fresh green. Notices everywhere "Help us to prevent Forest Fires". One shack en route where a German lives trapping + fishing. These timbered solitudes are lovely. At* McMurray *we got out + walked 1\2 a mile to the settlement about 200 people + walked in + introduced ourselves to a Miss Ross (a Public Health Nurse) who had been mentioned to us by the French Canadian Judge Le Beur. She gave us cool drinks + her friend a fat Mr Bennett accompanied us by asphalt smelling tarsand cliffs along river to saltmines now idle. Some trouble shaking him off but we did so + climbed the hill + ate our last Bath Olivers among trees + Pyrola leaves + Trientalis +c Mosquitos not too bad if we smoked. Down to Miss Ross again who gave us a good tea in a cool lean to with sacking behind the rough log hut filled in with mortar which is her home + hospital (2 beds). Fine type of woman trained in Montreal: no church in McMurray: rough lot + a good many seem to drink: optimism again in her one meets it everywhere: her sympathy with drunkards make the best of them. An old lady who came w. us is going to Fond du Lac to see her son she a millionaire from Pittsburg: he a hopeless drunkard. We begin to know our passengers: 9 women + about 30 men: the Judge very pleasant: the prosecutor (Howatt) in Eskimo trial: the Defence (O'Connor) ditto. A Yankee trapper rough looking: 10 CMP 3 or 4 RCCS*

the MP many from old country fine types. Archdeacon Whitaker + wife. A *giggling nurse, teacher + missionary.* 2 French Canadian seamen old Brabant +c +c. *Sand pipers about but otherwise not much bird life on river.* Time tables exist not. We got ashore McMurray 1 o'c Capt said might leave 3 o'c. We strolled down to wooden floating barge about 4 o'c. Our Tug *the Canadusa* came along about 4.30 with no loading at all from Waterways because it was King's birthday so trip was useless today. *Then we waited an hour or so while ramshackle car came + went with sacks + lumps of ice + the engineer who was having his hair cut (like a convict blue of course). Then we transferred all the sacks + ice 1/2 way down to another smaller barge to save towing up large one next trip + left large one above the quasi rapid moored to a poplar tree! No dovetailing here + no hurry: "it's the North" says everyone + laughs. Much heartiness handshaking + introductions seems to be also part + parcel of the north including introductions to store keeper who sells you a p.c.*

FRIDAY 4 JUNE

Hot + steamy. Still moored. Walked after b'fast about 1 1/2 miles up river along limestone ridge full of fossil shells: flocks of lovely yellow swallow-tail Butterflies. The barge returned from Waterways noon but we were not yet off for the Sergeant Major of M.P had left a box of tools at Waterways *so back they went in a little tug after lunch + we i.e. S.S. Athabasca River moved slowly down to a spot on L. river bank where we tied up + took on a pile of new cut wood: 1 1/2 hours there perhaps. G + I wandered ashore + had to put on mosquito veils for 1st time. Then 4 o'c we moved down + tied up to R. bank till Tug + tool box overtook us.* Long chat w. C.M.P. man who has been 2 years in Ellesmere Land + is now ordered N to Bernard Inlet it may be: he showed us interesting snow photos. *About sunset time 9 o'c we passed Fort McKay + an Indian settlement with shanties + dusky figures + tents on the banks.* And then came the after-glow: bluest light against the firs, river opening out wide before us purple reflections in it + one molten bar of cloud: *peace + distance wonderfully beautiful.* So in that evening light we came to sandbanks 2 1/2-breeds on the biggest loaded barge that we shove before us take soundings with poles + silently raising each pole slide one hand along to show the depth. Thus the Capt. watching from wheel house sees the pole + hand silhouetted on the sunset sky + takes his bearings. Once we nearly stuck + they hastily shoved out in a canoe to take soundings the mate standing up + a 1/2-breed paddling. *Poplars swaying + swishing close to us clouds + water growing more purple: a cool wind blowing—Good world. Gramophone only false note.*

SATURDAY 5 JUNE

Lost all count of days. Furious wind blowing + quite a sand storm but still proceeding slowly through shoals + sand banks. *We tied up for wood in the morning + went ashore into spruce wood + found 2 green orchids: no mosquitos in this wind. Wrote + had a washing day.* We are leaving the white Poplars behind + now have come to cotton woods. Evening came to deeper water river full of corkscrew bends + ducks: flat wooded banks. We went up to the Captain's wheel house + there sat enjoying every bend of the river as in a dream without beginning or end: afterglow + sunset only faint but the wind had died down *+ the peace + loneliness was beautiful: only a trapper's hut here + there.* The Captain a silent man hailed from Switzerland 45 years ago.

SUNDAY 6 JUNE

Notice how everyone talks of the North as of some enclosed place. "He has not been out for 40." "I went in in the nineties." +c +c. Indeed the N.W. Territory is not even represented in Parliament the candidate for this part ranges from McMurray to Fort Smith where Alberta ends. Mr Moran + old Brabant were telling yarns of old Hudson Bay C. employees + others. One *Harris* of Simpson + how he missed the priesthood. "We chaps went up to seminary at Montreal + the Priest he looked us over + says "All right you come back June 24th" So I went away + off I goes on the toot. One day I comes to myself + looks about + finds it's 27" All right I says to meself only 4 days late," So I goes up to the seminary + sits down for a chat with the Priest. Presently he says to me "Do you know what day of the month it is Mr Harris?" "Why sez I tis the 27th" "And do you know what month it is Mr Harris ?" sez he. "Yes" sez oi "tis the month of June." "If my eyes serve me right sez he Mr Harris tis the month of August on this calendar." "God bless me" sez oi I've been blind drunk for 2 months then" + I picks up me hat + out I goes + that is how I never joined the priesthood"...*A very cold rainy windy day. At 6 AM we went ashore at Chipewyan for 10 mins. rocks + quite a settlement of whitewood houses: rocky land for 1st time with little hills covered with firs. Early this morning about 3 AM we came through Lake Athabasca luckily before the wind rose or we would not have got through. After b'fast passed along a waste of mud flats. Country very flat but more open + low. Spring Cottonwood + firs. Very cold rainy day: we spent our best hours in the wheel house with the slow-spoken Swiss Captain. Service after lunch Archdeacon Whitaker. We passed the Echo at 3 o'c. Great rejoicing as she had started 24 hours ahead of us but her barges would not stand the rough water. This navigation from Waterways to Fitzgerald is a tricky affair: to begin with the water is rather low everywhere + the channel very* winding: then winds are prevalent + barges will not stand any sea without bumping each other. We came thro' Athabasca Lake in the nick of time at midnight when the wind had dropped for an hour or two: otherwise we'd have been held up all day. Then there are one or two hours of semi-darkness when it is not safe to travel + then frequent tyings up to take on firewood. Altogether as different from any ordinary scheduled steamer trip as one could imagine. We got into Fitzgerald about 8 o'c after supper: it looked quite a township after the only settlements seen since Waterways: the larger stores with square ended false wooden fronts over gables to make them look more imposing. Chilly brown evening. We at once darted off + got one or 2 flowers + then wandered on to where we saw the rapids 1 mile below Fitzgerald a great brown river spread out into combed + crested ripples roaring wickedly. An old timer whom we knocked up in a wooden house took us out to where he had cleared a wind path for mosquitoes + cd. look down on rapids: Been through Klondike rush like so many others we meet. An old party w. white beard came in to the steamer about 9.30 + sang impassioned old doggerel songs to a guitar: a strange scene with all the strong rough faces gathered round. At 10 Judge Dubuc took us ashore (I in my nightgown) to do the Social at Mrs Leggo the Factors wife + a very wearing performance it was. From 10 till 1.30 we sat in a heated airless room making conversation to our fellow passengers (for our hostess had none) I to Judge Dubuc G. to O'Connor (the defence for Eskimo) + to Price the gold seeker who nodded irresistibly. At last mine host came in + talked about the country moose buffalo trappers a dotty one who lives in Barren Grounds + eats raw rabbits fur + all for want of fuel or meat + does not even get a living Hornby by name. At long last came toast + coffee. All this time the talk dribbled on of steamers, delays, Indians, wind, trappers, Eskimo trials, furs, wireless (which they had in the house) +c +c quite another world to the one we have left behind. At 1.30 we staggered out into what was nearly daylight sunset or dawn—weary + giddy

MONDAY 7 JUNE

Got up at 7.55 feeling like 0 in Earth + staggered into breakfast which is not served after sinking so low as to breakfast in hat +c not dressed! Cold dismal day spent in waiting about for news of Distributor which was lying below Fort Smith 16 miles away down the rapids getting ready for 1st summer trip. I nipped out + found Pyrola + a few flowers. Cold has sent in mosquitoes but Fitzgerald gloomy + the soil a horrid slippery clay. At 3 o'c the Capt. pushed us off the boat + we hung about for cars in Warehouse full of freight + Buffalo skins +c. We were lucky enough to get a "little Roadster" for 2 + away we went over black soil like a ploughed field bump bump bump. Twisty road among poplars cotton

wood firs +c This is the 16 miles portage but what a history under that 1 word. Our driver a Swede + Eskimo mixed called McNeil told us he had driven buffalo teams over it as late as 1911. Only last week a tractor towed two ten ton schooners destined for the Arctic over the 16 miles not mounted on anything they were too heavy but just sailing along the road. 4 days they took in the "old days" driving through unfelled saplings the 16 miles. Now several cars 20 horse teams or more plod along + transfer the 250 tons we brought up. The road is awful but towards Fort Smith it changes to pure sand. We met Mr Brabant who turned us back to the "Hotel" + told us to take his room + until nearly 9 PM. it seemed doubtful if the Distributor would turn up. We had supper at the Hotel with a very rough assembly at the other table "old-timers" no doubt. Then we went with Judge Dubuc, Mr Brabant + Mr Howatt the Prosecutor a great talker + laugher to call on the RC Mounted Police a Mr Fletcher (English) from the old country as they say in a very pleasant but overheated room. We escaped after awhile + walked along the ridge above the river + saw 12 pelicans on a rock in mid-stream. Fine view wilderness of brown rapids rocks + fir woods aX such an expanse of river. Some Pelicans floating about in mid stream serene among those cruel rapids. Then we sighted the Distributor coming up from her winter quarter she had been pushed off the bank yesterday. We scuttled back to Pub retrieved our things + went down to our boat more luxurious than the last + so to bed a cold gray night. Mr Fletcher's talk interesting. These North country men are very slow of speech they take 5 puffs at a pipe + then make one remark. All their talk is of skins + state of the water + movements of the steamers: Mr Fletcher lived a month on Pork + Beans lately stores having run out.

TUESDAY 8 JUNE

Up to this painful 7.30 breakfast. Cold. Away with a snack in our pockets at 9.30. Walked 8 miles on road back to Fitzgerald tried X country tracks once but got bushed so came back. Road laid flat in ridges by tractor like a Tank so pleasant walking on flattened sand. Jack Pines Cotton wood poplar. Turned back to neck of Peninsula + along ridge to end where we got close down to Mountain Falls : a desolate scene + wonderful. Turbid waters + troubled for ever + ever flowing in all directions at once tossed whirling: one long straight sweep like a smooth pavement set in motion then a cauldron seething with foam + brown water their waves tossing their crest backward Falling up stream all such a vast rocky sewn river no sign of house or man only firs + poplars aX the river + Pelicans in mid stream. We went down close to the water on flat rocks. Cool day so few mosquitoes luckily. Rough going on peninsula stooping over brushwood +

through dog wood + the shrub with a leaf like Korrea. River sown with fir covered
islands + rocks. Back along another track shorter to road + last 3 miles got a lift
on top of a loaded lorry on a wet tarpaulin + very glad we were to bump pitch +
sway along the deep ruts. So back at 6 o'c. Saw waxwing + American 3
toed wood pecker with yellow crest. *Pressed flowers + turned in early.*

WEDNESDAY 9 JUNE

After shoe cleaning w. Viscol we set out 9.30 up stream track along ridge +
climbed down on to pink granite rocks smooth as marble which push out into
Rapids. Left Gwen sketching there + rambled on + found a flower or two: Jack
pine + moss below where mosquitoes in clouds. On the ridge cooler poplars
growing + every now + then a view of the troubled brown + gray waters. Sunny but
cold wind. After lunching on sandy beach we sauntered up about 3 miles feeling v.
slack then back to call on Mr McDougall administrator for Dept. of Interior: he
lent us books + will fix our trip to see Pelicans. After dinner a poor exhibition of
shooting clay pigeons oranges tins +c by an advertising man from Montreal.
Introduced by the Judge to the Old Dr: fine old face: but he also drinks or has
drunk. ""Prescription" Dry Store" = Drink sold here. "He has a
permit" = means drink permit. The old Dr ranges from here to
McMurray + Resolution: 100s of miles: "How don't patients
die before you get there?" "They do" he said "or sometimes
they wait for me. "I came in" (that mysterious "in" again
meaning the North) 16 years ago + for 2 years I didn't much
like it but afterwards I kinder got used to it + now I like the
quiet life here." *Mr McDougall has wireless + told us how his son spoke to*
him from Edmonton. Wireless must revolutionize the N more than any other 1/4
of the world + has already done so to certain extent. Quite a number of the army
men going N with us are bent on wireless jobs—establishing wireless stations.

THURSDAY 10 JUNE

Cold + very wet + the Boiler being inspected! so we washed our clothes in cold
water coffee coloured mud + had out Alaskan maps +c. After lunch we set out on
trail to Bell Rock cart track among firs besprinkled with little spots of lichen like a
frosted wood. After 2 or 3 miles we turned R handed down disused cart trail + on
+ on through firs + poplars always enclosed + always hoping to
come out, always imagining the light of the river bed + sky
above just ahead as we glimpsed sky thro' poplar crests + always
deceived. Can well imagine one going mad walking among trees
on + on + on + hoping to come out into space: a frantic futile
struggle. Lovely open spaces here + there like a pasture or swamp only it was
neither then again avenues of poplar + at last a blue line of opposite
river bank from a ridge: down into sphagnum moss among firs where
mosquitoes greeted us + on through swamps nearly knee deep to the long sought

river only a mud bank willows debris + tree trunks + wood chips + hardly any
view. Soaked to the knees but the rain had stopped. Met no living creature or
beast. Along the main trails are white canvas notices nailed to trees in Indian
characters: + one notice we met today ran:
Menu
1. Beans + Bacon
2. More Beans + Bacon
3. Coffee + a Smoke
4. Water 6 Pails + Elbow grease to put out the fire

The country is full of notices about camp fires + preserving the
forest. This new country very alert to conserve its natural
resources: bird protection too seems well advanced though it
may be rather late in the day. Back to dinner after a 12 mile
walk.

FRIDAY 11 JUNE

Cold on board + cold outside. Boiler Inspection so our clothes still wet. Only 2
small stoves we sat + read books borrowed fr. Mr McDougall on Alaska +
Conservation of Wild Animals in Canada + strolled out to P.O. + store. After
lunch attended by Judge + Mr Harris we went to a store + had soft drinks: rough
place with Billiard Room attached: "No Treaty Indians allowed in." "No minors
allowed." "No bad language." Then to Hospital run by RC French
Canadian sisters real pioneers *One wizened little Nut has been "in"*
32 years with only 1 trip out to Montreal. About 13 beds which
we saw: a 3 story building + *operating theatre:* saw Indian patients
strange looking people. RC missions stick where C of E don't:
they pioneer in growing potatoes +c + do much out Patient
work. *We visited the 2 schooners alongside 10 tons each + saw Mr Carel who is*
taking them down to the Arctic to sell them to Eskimo: he has done the Rat R. in
summer + gave us figures re. the distances +c: only Archdeacon Whitaker + himself
so far have done the Rat in summer. G + I left the Judge + on to tea with Mr + Mrs
Hasting he the wireless man: but they get no News Bulletin. She has only been "in"
11 months + was telling us her domestic troubles. He + Mr Fletcher talked of
Buffalo Bear + Eskimo. Mr Fletcher has only seen 1 Bear + 1 Moose in 31 River
trips on the Bank. All seem to agree that these trials of Eskimo for murder are a
farce + are trying to impose on them standards beyond their ken but they don't
suggest what should be done when an Eskimo murders a white man. Meanwhile
the Judge, Defence Prosecutor + Clerk look on the thing as cause of a joy ride.
Judge D. described the North as "the Harbour of wrecked
men" mentally + physically. *After a long sit at the Hastings came 5 o'c tea*
+ then scurry home to dinner at 6. After watched the schooners steam out N each
with a gas boat lashed alongside. Finer looking sky + a streak of bronze above the
darkened firs aX the river. Cold still + Mosquitoes about.

SATURDAY 12 JUNE

Sunny day at last. Set out 10 o'c in *Hubaco* motor launch *rented by Mr. Boa the shooting man from Hudson B. Co.* Also *Mr Hastings + Mr Moran with his Movie Kodak. A 1/2 breed Pilot 1/2 breed Canoeman + English mechanic.* We steamed right aX river anchored + all 7 got into a cockle shell canoe and paddled close under a rapid in an Eddy + felt about grounding on rocks till we landed on a flat granite (pink) island. No Pelicans to be seen + *only then they told us that Pelican Island is above Mt Rapid + can only be approached from Fitzgerald: duds everyone of them muttered Gwen.* However we enjoyed it much: great experience standing on that polished island with a waste of rapids + debris all round us: scene of loneliness + desolation: only some wooden frames on shores + islands where Indians had dried fish + by a pink island a line of floats of a fishing net. *Back + landed on farther shore + followed track aX a mile or so all 7 of us + saw notched trees where gold seekers had staked claims.* Tis hard to realise the vastness of the country just here for the trees are so monotonous + *forest line so low against the sky that the wildness of it does not "sauter aux yeux":* but we realised it today: the debris brings it home as much as anything where a chip of wood + a tree trunk share the same fate + are tossed by the Rapids with equal facility. *Back at 3: G sketched + I sauntered by RC Cathedral along swamp back to Mrs Hasting's to borrow books. Mosquitoes bad.*

SUNDAY 13 JUNE

Hot. To RC Church with Mr Brabant + the Judge. *Strange scene:* we stood outside as the Indians came along + they shook hands w. Mr B + we were introduced to several including Chief Squirrel ancient fires in his look now in yachting cap + slouch blue serge suit with longish gray black hair. Mr B remembers him in full war paint with feathers +c. *Long service.* Bearded priest preached in French then Chipewyan (Jesus vous aime) in a rapid voice. Thin female voices chanted mass. Tinsel + paper + gold lilies adorned the wooden building. *The Indian faces were a study. High cheek bones chin running forward head running back: medium physique: one big fellow with shock head + rolling eyes like a bull.* The chief with patient not interested expression + a glazed look in his eye that spoke of ancient fires, *of strength diluted to resignation.* Some faces were bored some puzzled some absent not one thrilled or inspired. Thought of rough old Turks at Mohammedan service + the differences. *After we walked a mile or 2 up river bank + were tormented by mosquitoes: had to hold veil in one hand + eat bun inside with the other.* 7.30 came the settlement folk to dinner *Mr Mrs Master + Miss McDougall Mr + Mrs Hastings. Mr Fletcher Mr Murphy the Post master +c +c*

About 20 or more of us: the Judge + Mr Brabant leading hosts dispensing much prized whisky + liqueur. *Speeches: Hudsons Bay, wireless, Dept. Interior, Police +c +c : old Brabant in merry mood.* The HBCo gets much chat: "It was founded in 1602" *O'Connor is always saying.* Sometimes called "Half breed Curse" or "Here before Christ". Walked back to the Hastings' where we danced to a gramophone but were recalled by telephone to S.S. Distributor. So back in cool night air accompanied again by the Hastings + finally at 1.30 pushed off: yells + screams + whoops of 1/2 breeds raising anchor + cutting capers on piled boxes below, pale faces quite distinct on shore even at that hour still night new moon + one star: the roar of the rapids now grown such a friendly sound + slowly slowly we started off—off on our long long journey to the north last goodbyes + greetings being called from shore. *So to bed bung-eyed. 2 good yarns we have heard: Irishman in New York where all police are Irish: he in a Ford Car behind a Rolls Royce or what not which pulled up rather suddenly + he ran straight into it RR beckons policeman to take Fords No. +c: "What is yr. number? Name? Oh where from? Limerick? On me soul? And do ya know Pat? + Mick +c Then at last "So the damned son of a bitch backed into your car did he? I'll take his number." All this told by the Judge with inimitable French flicks of eyebrows + forefinger.* The other yarn was of a 1/2 breed marriage: agreement 1/2 children to be RCs 1/2 Ch. E. 27 children born + it became a yearly race whether RC Bishop or Ch.E got down river 1st, RC nearly always won + he was getting a big majority: regular annual Event. Ch. E consulted Police Inspector: who replied that he must not only get down on 1st Boat each year but bring a fire hose + baptise the infant from the steamer while the Bishop was stepping ashore.

MONDAY 14 JUNE

Delightful day. Sunshine cool breeze. We breakfasted bung-eyed at 7 after pretty well sleepless night what w. 5 huskies howling on lower gunwale, pause at woodpile + *noise of dumping wood on board* + mosquitoes singing in our ears *so to bed again till 10 o'c. Mackenzie River wider here but still low shores many duck + about 10 Canada geese: more frequent bends of marshy land + patches where Resolution Mission from 20 miles aX country reaps its hay. Delightful progress on + on in winding river green + fresh. In this 24 hours run to Resolution we steam 17 + spend 7 at woodpiles.* Talked a bit to a surveyor who has been in Barren Ground: often walked 5 miles to gather enough fuel of willow roots to boil a cup of tea in evening: has seen Caribou on autumn migration between 2 lakes passing perhaps 15 to the acre for 6 continuous days: has seen 8 inches of snow on the ground on August 1st. *Every other*

*person has these tales or such like at 1st hand. Sat all aft. in wheel house. Evening
wandered out at woodpile + found dwarf Arum: mosquitoes very thick.* At 9 o'c
we came out into a great space Great Slave Lake dotted with
islands + sandbars *the 2 schooners + the Hubaco lying in the delta* then we
turned L. into a green bordered channel at the end of which we
tied up by a flat little island not venturing out into Lake
because of wind. Wonderful sunset: orange + blue line that
looked like Mts but was only cloud or distance. Middle of night
we touched at Resolution but did not get up. Huskies howled
passengers stumped hell of a night + little sleep. *We put out into
Lake but came back encountering too much sea* + tied up under *Mission*
Island

TUESDAY 15 JUNE
*Wind still blowing. We went ashore at 1.30 in ship's motor boat + started walking
round the stony shore. Came on 2 halfbreeds in a bark + canvas shanty living
there to fish. They put us on a track so we walked on + on round 1 point after
another now on the track now on the shore over boulders + piles of driftwood +
soft 1/2 mouldy fibre.* Saw Resolution prosperous red roofed settlement. Found
Pink Orchis. *After awhile plunged into thick bush to cut corners nightmareish
going + always imagining daylight ahead where there was none however we got
back 6 o'c having completely circled the island about 7 or 9 miles. Dwarf Juniper
spruce + the Korrea leaved shrub everywhere. Mosquitoes in bush but none on
shore.* Anchored all night by Mission Island.

WEDNESDAY 16 JUNE
*Steamed on at 8.30 till 10 when wind changed + we anchored in shelter under
Green Island:* the Distributor is no more than a barge + needs
nearly a dead calm to X the Lake. *After lunch a party of us went
ashore: delightful island easier walking no mosquitoes or very
few hot scent of spruce fresh wind sunshine masses of little
pink Orchis. Walked all round in a couple of hours or so. Talked a bit with
Bishop Brenner R.C. who inspects missions in all this district.* He built a steamer
at one time opposition to Hudson Bay now it is wrecked on one of the islands.
Wind fell at sunset. The 2 schooners came up + anchored alongside. Calm sunset.

THURSDAY 17 JUNE
4.30 came round a bend + in misty morning saw <u>Hay River
Settlement</u>. Went ashore. Very Indian tepees + tents: Ch. E
Mission + RC church + the usual store all on a *peaceful river.
Attractive place: an hour or two ashore + then after a 7 o'c
breakfast a dream journey through the Great Slave Lake to
Beaver Lake: glassy sea clear sky myriads of ducks: thin green
line: great space. Icy cold wind wandered round ducks seeking shelter + put*

on all our coats. Long talk with Gray Nun the Mother Superior
who goes "out" to Montreal + keeps touch with the world.
Bumped over some sand bars + so to <u>Providence</u> *about 3 o'c. Several false
attempts to land in shallow water under the high bank where* school children
Nuns priests + population were silhouetted also the church.
Like a comic opera scene: Indian children of the mission boys
in blue corduroy with large white ties girls in scarlet skirts white
blouses + black boots. *Went ashore to RC Mission Grand Meeting of our 6
Sisters on board with the 6 or 7 other: they fluttered like birds + twittered in the
mission passage: Then the Rose of the North a fat sweating sister took us over the
school an attractive 50 year old building. Then all wandered down the
settlement: very hot. Back to dinner on steamer. Some interesting yarns:
Conybeare an old timer now 2nd engineer was talking of Indians + their
inevitable disappearance before white men. Course of nature might just as well let
it go its own pace he says—all this Gray Nun Mission work + others no good they
relapse at once on leaving school—girls quicker than boys. Told story of himself +
Indian: Sunday morning: "Going to church?" "No." "Suppose you're waiting for
R.C. Mission." Just then an MP passed by 1/2 drunk Indian, "Now what have
you to teach us." Conybeare* walked 900 miles *from Smith to Simpson to*
stake for gold + ditto back in about 3 winter months: river
being the only highway winter as in summer. Next chat we had
was w. a bearded priest from Rome who has lived 20 years in
Colombo + is now inspecting the N after U.S.A. *The Bolshevist
Yankee tripper says few people in U.S.A. know anything of this Mackenzie R. trip
+ some one else added that many people at Edmonton are quite ignorant of it.*
Gwen took up with a gold toothed nugget of a trapper wearing
breeches high boots + an old womans coat jumper + bringing 5
huskies up on the boat. He invited us to his shanty a biggish
wood room ceiled neatly with brown paper a stove rough table 1
chair + little else but the stink of martens in it. He had caught 4
alive for breeding purposes but unluckily the male died + only
3 females survive. He will now get a Govt. permit to catch
another alive this breeding being an experiment. He got 100
skins last season: worth about 20 dollars cash. *He is off next season
trapping in hill country about 50 miles away.* A big party of Indians +
half breeds on board now a lot of attractive sly-eyed slit eyed
smiling girls going home from school +c +c. A most interesting
+ mixed crowd.

FRIDAY 18 JUNE
G awoke with sprained or strained foot all night very painful.
Everyone buzzed offering advice + remedies or tales of their
wife's mother-in-laws sprained ankle knee or wrist. Salt + cold
water seemed best of remedies applied *Wide river banks rather higher:*

wood pile at breakfast time. Many mosquitos also bull dog flies: *as a rule mosquitoes don't follow us on the boat. At 12.30* reached Fort Simpson: fine situation on island at mouth of Liard river stands on a high bank some big buildings. Wandered out alone twice: thundershower. After supper to wireless station + India. Agency w. *Judge Dubuc. Mr Harris the Indian agent hero of the priest tale came on—All this "life" unreal:* + the landings each time like a comic opera. *One scene particularly seemed unreal:* I stood in RC church entrance: from R + L of altar a gray Nun came slowly through doors with candlestick each mounted small stool + slowly solemnly placed them on altar: old white bearded priest saying his rosary. Paper streamers adorned roof. All this seemed somehow pathetically out of place w. the June sunshine pouring down outside on a raw settlement where 1/2 the necessities of life are missing + leagues of virgin forest stretch away on either river bank. Thought of Italy + old R.C. churches with century old associations—*Judge Dubuc introduced me w. the same polite ceremony he uses to one + all to an unshorn wood cutter who cut 200 cords of wood one season: a cord is a pile 8 ft. long by 4 high of 4 ft logs + contains about 150 or 200 pieces. When not cutting he traps sleeps out even in winter does not care about sleeping in towns. Also introduced to Mr Harris Indian Agent who has a fine library* ~~Greek~~ *(for these parts) Greek–Latin RLS–Dickens–Thackeray +c: but drinks like a fish + has married a 1/2 breed.* So many come North drink driven + when here eke out a life of struggle + poverty. *Glamour of the North yes but also the seamy side.*

Nahanni=Fort Simpson
SATURDAY 19 JUNE
Woke at 4:30 to see a lovely range of barren hills bathed in sunshine: 1st hills seen since *Dartmoor May 13th: think of it* 5 weeks travel all flat. Quite a thrill. Gwen rather troubled night with ankle + ditto all day: 2 very anxious days these are: we dare not think too much about the Rat but just carry on. *Lovely scenery all day.* Passed a lump of ice 9 AM the steamer stopped + men brought in huge blocks: vetch growing alongside. Wrigley at noon. Small post with lovely views forward + back. Saw 2 story building of *Tim* the H B Co Manager with upstairs kitchen + balcony: his own work. *Fine rock opposite "La roche qui trempe dans l'eau."* Whisky bottle buried at top. Watched Mr. Harris bury old cove paying treaty money in a shanty to servile rather flat faced Indians: the 3rd race we have seen. *Chipewyans at Smith hooknosed + handsome: Slaves at Hay river flatnosed + Mongolian.* Found Cipripedium in bud at evening wood pile took on wood at 10 AM and 9 PM: *2 hours stop at* Wrigley. Evening river spread out more wider + flats + hills in turn: lovely blue lights + turns all

day + some steepish cliffs *like the tar sands again.* Talked to Yukon MP about his gravel River trip in search of 2 lost oil prospectors: winter travel: no tent: *cut fir wood + clear snow.* He also has met Steffannsons' men + has no good word for him: says he is a self advertiser who grudges credit to fellow-explorers. Gwen stuck fast all day + 100 arms to help her when she hopped: buzzing like bees with advice + enquiry.

SUNDAY 20 JUNE
Arrived Fort Norman 2 AM. I got up 5:30 + went for walk along beach + up Bear River 1/2 a mile: lovely fresh morning. Ice on edge of river. Bear Rock towering aX the river *barren with 3 pink patches of rock on it (Beaver skins Indian Legend) The RC church is much painted by a priest.* Fine chains of snowy capped mountains all round. G hopping round with less pain. *Left* Norman about 9 o'c. Very fine scenery all day snow capped Rockies wide river a treat. open world. Late in evening *about 10:30* it seemed as if our ship were charging a wall of rock + then the Ramparts opened + we slid into a narrow channel between these 100–200 ft straight walls of limestone rock for 2 or 3 miles. a most amazing show. Sans Sault rapids about an hour before that. *And so to bed with* Fort Good Hope *in sight as we left the Ramparts. These night landings at settlements are very trying: noise all night + most people Sisters Mr Moran +c +c have to go ashore + do their business middle of the night but that doesn't seem to matter up here. Left Good Hope AM sometime + then had to stop again + cut up drift wood being short.*

MONDAY 21 JUNE
Cold + windy. About 10:30 came to a wood-pile with a shanty where a Swede + a Luxumbourg man live: log cutting trapping fishing. The Flemish man took me in his canoe to fishing nets where he had Corny Jack Fish Blue Fish: *They had cut about 120 cord of wood in the winter 6 dollars a cord say £125 between them. It costs 2 men 1000 to 1500 dollars to live on beans + bacon in the year say £100 to £150 each.* Summer slack time only fish + drying fish for dogs. *The Flemish man a V. good trapper caught 50 foxes one season. He says "too many people up here,:" meaning Indians + fellow trappers. And yet he ranges over 60 miles of country + there is no sign of a human or a dwelling for miles and miles. Does not pretend to like the life but has been here 20 years + has no use for jobs in cities: "Man is too much like a dog." Supposes he'll go "out" when he's taken.* Grateful for some Edmonton May 31st daily papers we'd brought for pressing flowers + says they'll read them 4 times. Wind + sandstorms. *G still hobbling + not setting foot to ground. Aft. very windy sandstorms wide river stunted spruce very thin + scraggy*

great sand banks. Had some difficulty getting in to wood pile 5:30 tied the boat with iron ropes to saplings which were uprooted once or twice. Fine sandy beach: M Police had sports. Found a semi-palmated Plover's Nest with 4 eggs.

TUESDAY 22 JUNE
Cold *+ sunless*. Reached Arctic Red River 4:30 AM + went ashore for an hour at 5:30. Squalid place: Indians in tents: *looks out on Lesser Ramparts from the Arctic Red River*. Great lumps of dirty ice on beach an acre or two. *RC Mission + PO in one. Indian women's faces. Bishop. conversion!!* by About 11 o'c turned up the Peel River after passing Indian Houses. Peel R. very attractive: narrow with deeply working black mud banks where ice action hollowed out soil + great bits dropped in with a splash every now + then: *leaving the poplars + firs with roots exposed growing on bank top or bending over when completely undermined to their last fall*. Young Poplars fresh green: *blue Delphinium in woods*. Tied up at noon at woodpile: *impossibly steep crumbling place so slept from 1-2. Then we went on up the winding Peel every now + then green swampy bits opened out* + the land of our dreams the Rat divide + snow touched Mts. in sight. *This at end of a long straight reach* after passing Husky R. on our R. was Fort Macpherson: on top of high bank facing fine range of mountains. *Behind the settlement a swamp + a lake. Yellow anemone*. G putting foot to ground.

Eskimo names
murderer = Ikagena
witness = Panuyak
dead man = Ulukshuk
wife = Nalugiak
wife = Hanergak

WEDNESDAY 23 JUNE
Woke at 7 to see a range of mts. on our L. + we corkscrewed round till it was on our R. + came to Aklavik at 8. Prosperous looking settlement (comparative—how our standards have altered in 3 weeks). Astonishing crowd of Eskimos on mud beach: tents schooners over 100 tethered huskies. Eskimo woman incarnate broad smiles fur lined hoods long cotton shapeless dresses *+ shupacks of fur or skin*: babies tightly bound on backs in hoods women waddle toes turned in stooping forward. Men in parkies trousers + high shupacks. Spent AM seeing RC Convent English mission + Hudson's Bay manager Mr Parsons after securing the Doctor who prescribed 2 weeks delay for Gwen's foot (tendons) + rest: accommodation? rather difficult

RC best but more cut off + 4$ a day. *Cold wind + evening shower. A drunken fighting lot of traders. Sold my 38/- boots for 15 dollars (62/6) + We* were introduced *gaily* to the murderer. *The lawyers seeking information: O'Connor (defence) says to Eskimo: "Why did you kill him"? Eskimo. "He was mad with me." O'C "Why was he mad?" E. "I stole his wife." Simple smiling people shaking hands all the time*. Our guide Lazarus came on board + had a talk: looks a good fellow. Arranged for canoe 90$. Evening to Eskimo service very deep voices tuneful hearty Eskimo service.

Aklavik

THURSDAY 24 JUNE
Cold. Eskimo trial. Extraordinary show. Murder. O'Connor defended: *Howatt crown Counsel*. Jury of 6 scally-wags. Eskimo crowd: Accused Ikagena came from ~~Fall~~ Fairy River Coppermine way fine face. Interpreter very dark + handsome. Not guilty verdict after guilty of manslaughter: quite apparent. *A farce: our verbiage + their simplicity. Sat from 10-12: then 2-5.30 then 7.30-9*. We attended all day *in dining room*. Dr. plastered up Gwen's foot. I saw Eskimo dance at Mission House ending about 2 o'c: weirdest thing ever seen + honest to primitive man. *A King William land Eskimo long haired man of the woods* + Ikagena did a seal dance with drums I sided flat with a handle + wooden stick. They bend forward + shuffle legs sideways moving every muscle like elastic: curious groans hisses roars: very near borderland of man + animal: imitation of seal's flipping movements. Took one back to cave men. *Women also danced one with her baby unconcerned strapped in on her back*. Saw one old Eskimo with 2 Labrets. Saw Stefannson's wife an old *hag. Their smiles + greetings + handshakes are too attractive*. Home in chill daylight with Mr. Howatt at 2 AM *afterglow in sky + they say its gets no darker now: most uncanny*.

Aklavik

FRIDAY 25 JUNE
Chilly but some sunshine. Packed + wandered round *+ got a photo or two*. Lunch all our party deserted to feast at convent. I was solo with a U.S.A. trapper who is taking home an Eskimo wife for a jaunt. He has been 14 years in the country: says its very hard to find 2 men even 2 good men who can spend a winter together without quarrelling. *Last job he was alone nearest neighbour 40 miles*. Mr Howatt introduced me to Capt. *Macintyre a rough sort of loose morals*. He warned Capt. *M*. that we were ladies + he was to remember it. I said: "What a pity you told him that it may

cramp his style + I want him to come up to the convent + amuse my friend." He said: "You can easily take the lid off that!" About 2:30 Gwen was carried ashore on a mattress + stretcher by 4 men + taken straight up to convent balcony + S.S. Distributor backed out from the bank + steamed slowly away leaving us with the queerest sense of isolation: Eskimos cheering from the banks + a mixed crowd. Here we are now fairly marooned no communication with the outside world till the next boat comes in August maybe. We have a fine view of mountains + big clean room and wooden building put up in a year by a carpenter who has *just* gone "out." To our horror Mission time 2 hours slow + Mission supper 6.30 which meant that we lunched at 12 on boat + had to wait 8 hours for next meal: after which to bed for 12 hours.

Aklavik

SATURDAY 26 JUNE
The lethargy of the North is stealing on us both. Went out at 10 AM + found Aklavik like a city of the dead. Called Wireless station *for books: Mr Young* "under the covers." Called on my trader to look for him dead asleep. Called on missionaries busy washing + sewing. Walked down mud river bank: met Ellesmere M.P. walked back w. him to MP hut: some typing or reading or cooking others sleeping: good library of novels borrowed 5. Aft. came Capt. MacIntyre to our balcony for a yarn: a hardened old sinner with a most pictorial tongue. *Cold wind all day no mosquitoes. Dr. syringed my ear: beastly painful.*

SUNDAY 27 JUNE
Sunny + cold wind. Mass in our little chapel. Swiss boy came along for a yarn + to see sketches: talked of trapping + of cunning of foxes. Choose a windy spot to blow away traces: bait with fish or meat or stale musk-rat: often a trampled round trap more enticing than solitary because fox thinks it likely to have camp refuse—walked down or rather up river + found another semi-palmated Plover's nest 4 eggs. Aft. in high boots pottered round swamp at back of convent saw 6 yellowshanks in bed of buckbean + many grackles + a canary like bird. Sergeant Anderton walked in to see us + had a chat about Eskimo + about our Rat R. tour. Perfectly all right he says for us to do those 3 days from LaPierre House to Old Crow alone. *So different from Winnipeg + SS. Distributor croakers.* The Rat adventure grows smaller as we approach it. Now we plan hiring a motor boat to tow us right up to the slack water of the Rat, save 3 or 4 days. Sergeant

Anderton talked much of Eskimos + of handling them + of utter uselessness of the evidence got from them. Facial expression the only evidence + their minds like those of children of 12. He took a year bringing in the murderer who was acquitted + says M.P. go with lives in their hand + control Eskimo by bluff about numbers of Police. This trial a farce of course + only impression made on Eskimo was when 2 criminals were taken out to Edmonton + imprisoned for murder: they came home immensely impressed with our numbers + *kept their tribes in check. Sad stories of H B Co's rapacity on freights +c: for instance flour 6 dollars higher at Norman than here because here a trader beats it down coming in from San Francisco. Also they still trade a tin cup for a fox skin. Govt insist on sending in fork spoon + cup +c as bonus to stop infanticide in spite of MP's requests for objects the natives would really welcome.* He is going for ~~winter~~ summer to Bernard Harbour + then away to O'Reilly Island to range round K. William ~~Is~~ Land Victoria Island +c in winter. *He says MP prevent Eskimos exterminating each other + the fauna of the country. Not much good words for missionaries.* Archdeacon Whitaker exposed Steffannson + his old hag in pulpit in Toronto + Stefansson's fiancée went + married a Yank but what of Archdeacon Whitaker?

Aklavik

MONDAY 28 JUNE
Woke to find snow on the ground + the range of mountains covered with snow catching a rare gleam of sunlight. Wandered out for an hour + found a Yank in a canoe going to his fish nets + tried my hand at paddling aX the river and back. *Met Mr. Brabant + Capt. MacIntyre + Mr Karel just came in w. the 2 schooners after a rough trip + dropped in at English mission. Aft.* Canon Hester *called:* vague overworked but a simple childlike man who can enter the Eskimo mind + work on those lines not enforce missionary morality from without: e.g. offer of another man's wife (part of their hospitality) "No thank you we white men don't?" "Why what do you do?" And there's my chance. *Story of blood feud + 3 men 2 discussing whether they should kill the other: decided to do so on which No 3 went under the bed to fetch the sinew to be strangled with*—translated "Jerusalem the Golden" fine hymn to appeal to Eskimo imagination: Hellfire no use: paint cold place. He bought *95 dollars worth of* sketches.

TUESDAY 29 JUNE
Washing day. Sunny but rather cold. Sisters all in gt. excitement over unpacking candelabra cotton bales +c their summer stores. One sister missed her last year's mail so is anxiously awaiting the Northern Trader. We sat out on balcony for

lunch. I walked down mud flats some way: saw 10 Northern Ravens together, Terns, SemiPalmated Plover, Yellowshank, Sandpipers. *Reading Galsworthy + Service's "Ballads of a Bohemian" aloud.*

WEDNESDAY 30 JUNE

Very cold: *horrid in the morning.* After lunch walked down mud flats: 3 miles slow going + heavy up river. Saw huge Buzzard or Eagle very serrated wing tips: saw nest of white headed sparrow (?) on ground with 4 young that Canon Hester shewed me. Mosquitoes bad in bush. Only silver willows mud + a few spruce along river: good sized lake. *No visitors today.* Eskimos mostly gone. *Looked in on the patient in the convent Mrs Cook: cheerful + enjoys the N but owns to a feeling of loneliness when the September boat pulls out + none will come for 9 months. Squally evening.*

THURSDAY 1 JULY

Cold very autumn wind blowing. Walked down to M.P. barracks to change books. Made assignations with Mr. West (H B Co inspector) + Capt. *McIntyre* to come + see us. Aft. explored bush behind wireless rough paths more or less cut down. Found Whisky jacks. nest with young. Saw many marsh marigolds—Pyrolas—Bearberries + longed to go on + on for ever: scrub of spruce + alders + bogs. Back at 3. Visitors dropped in *Mr Bonnycastle + West latter bought 105 dollars worth pictures.* This Capt McIntyre full of Polar Bear + Whaling stories + oaths + pictorial language + at the same overlapping *Mrs. Whitaker pale* proper *washed out.* He anti-missionary: however we each towed one + all went well.

FRIDAY 2 JULY

Still overcast but warmer. Walked down river seeking semi-Palmated Plover nest cd not find it. Called on Wireless re: cost of telegrams home 30 cts. a word. Called on Parsons + fixed to go with his motorboat to Destruction City. *Aft. up stream behind the lake but mosquitoes unpleasant. Archd Whitaker called: pity he's so narrow + against R Cs.* Told us of rapids at Sinclairs Pt in 1st 25 miles beyond La P. House.

SATURDAY 3 JULY

Found an Irishman called Tyrell who took me aX river in his canoe lesson in paddling. We took out white fish from nets: lovely green creek winding up + away into the unknown that is always beckoning: *a whisky-jack flitted aX.* Tyrell is Irish: surveyor + trapper: married to squaw. *Then to Canon Hester for stamps + a cup of tea w. Mr. Coghlin a man w. sprained ankle + Blake a Galway man + ex- H B C. All very down on HBC's methods in last years surly to own customers + keep free*

Traders out. Talking of Shingle Point white whales + Eskimos: makes one long to go there. Mountains a lovely soft blue these days. Aft. down river + found semiPalmated Plover's Nest 4 eggs on ground among willows after 4 days stalking: bird flopped + feigned broken wing within 2 yards of me. Canon Hester came after supper to talk + look at sketches: *sadly absent minded time he went out.* We saw midnight sun from chapel window it never touched horizon.

Aklavik

SUNDAY 4 JULY

Mass began at 8 with its melancholy drone. I went out with Tyrell to fish nets in 17 ft. canoe: *only 2 fish.* He has a theory mosquitoes are sent to preserve ducks which wd otherwise be exterminated by natives. As it is mosquitoes on June 10th made him knock off rat trapping. *Lovely sunny day X breeze to drive away mosquitoes. Canon Hester + Archdeacon W. to call after lunch.* To Eskimo service in C of E. Curious show: Canon Hester squeezing tunes from small harmonium: women in bright cotton garments + hoods. greasy black hair tattooed faces children squealing + crawling about: men in white + an Eskimo deacon read lesson Tik tak tok it sounded like: we sing hearty hymns in Eskimo—Tasingait Tasingait—Archd. Whitaker preached short + rather useless sermon with interpreter on men doing hard work + women light work. "When I want wood I don't send my wife. Mr Fry ditto. Mr Geddes ditto. What I say to you I say not only with my tongue but by what I do." NOT quite the missionary spirit somehow. *Pharisee.* Canon Hester has it nearer than anyone: simple childlike identifies himself with them. Evening the 2 lay brothers called: bearded one a German been in N 31 years nearly forgotten German.

MONDAY 5 JULY

Freedom. Dr. cut Gwen out at 10.30 + away she hopped down to see the Pioneer (Northern Trader) wh. had come in in the night. A hideous night of Gregorian chants + barking huskies + *heavy booted Priest coming in for Dr. Mother Superiors' feast day* they seemed to be chanting all night in melancholy tone "and all the afternoon. and all the afternoon." Aft. unpacked new stores in HB warehouse + *saw the Whitakers set off in gas boat + scow with huskies Indians a tent a stove mosquitoes sluggish progress. Evening down to Mission house hot sultry day.* Gwen's foot seems sound as a bell.

TUESDAY 6 JULY

I baked bannock with Sister Firmin's help. *Gwen sketched church.* At 11 we both paddled over to creek with Tyrell 2 fish *crooked back* + white fish. *Saw brown eagle. Overcast day but sun came out* Aft. packed our food w. Lazarus, Mr. Parsons +c and then to a tea-[light?] such a meal at English Mission with *Miss Catt + Hackett + Mr. Geddes* + Mr. Hester. Gramophone music. Then to Dr. final binding up of Gwen's ankle. *Mosquitoes bad fine cloudy sky.* Mr. Geddes told us tale of an Indian taking winter mail to Macpherson: dogteam played out Indian had to lighten mail so took on newspapers thinking they wd. be most important being heavier: hung up letters on tree they were brought on next year. Here they got their Xmas mail in February + no mail from Sept. to February. *If we write from Vancouver to tell them of our arrival in Yukon they will not hear till Feb. Makes one realise the loneliness a bit.*

WEDNESDAY 7 JULY

The Start

Goodbye to the sisters Father + Brothers + many at last at 8 o'c!! Left in a swarm of mosquitoes: no one awake. Our 2 guides Lazarus + Jimmy: Mr. Parsons + Aberdeen boy in H.B.Co gas boat with our 20 packages 6 sack food 4 boxes food 10 of baggage + bedding. Rainbow reflections of Richardson Mts in glassy still water. Sultry day. Away 12 miles up Peel R + then into mouth of Husky R. Banks flat brilliant green of mare's tail silver willows, green willows + alder + spruce: a few black poplar + cottonwood after a while + all the while splashes of blue lupin among the pale green. Saw 2 red foxes: many ducks: 2 swans: white headed eagle. Stopped ashore at 12 to boil kettle. Mosquitoes fairly charged us among the willows: worst experience we've had a thick cloud. All the day we wound about the sluggish channel at the foot of that Mt range: barren tops lovely green sides with blue patches (lupin) + green ravines. *After passing Black Mt.* banks a little higher: mud: one side sloping smoothly like sides of swimming bath the other eaten away + crumbling the silent action of ice + flood chiselling these banks *on a more colossal scale than the works of man.* Mosquitoes came + went but very little wind + little sun. Lunched on Pemmican bannock (which I'd rolled too thin + jam) Wonderful day every bend full of thrill. No gas boats come up this sluggish river: we have the world to ourselves. Flowers commonest all day the blue lupin, white valerian, mauve vetch, Pyrola, yellow senecio. Blue vetch. At 8 PM after 12 hours running + circling round + round *Black* Mt. we came in sunshine to the mouth of the Rat: a

little sluggish river bordered by willows: we have dreamed of it for months. Landed to boil kettle + refill boat with gasoline: mosquitoes in plenty. Sandpipers nest there in mare's tail 4 eggs. *Then up an enchanted river. Very narrow + felt it was a fine world all our own after weeks of vast Mackenzie R.* Sunny evening + spruce reflections golden in water banks being too high for sun to fall directly. Tracks of beaver + geese on mud banks Lazarus watching keenly + reading them like a book. In this land we begin to seek a handful of wind with the fervour of an Arab seeking a handful of shade. Comes a puff and mosquitoes are gone. Saw Ravens many ducks gulls various waders very many sandpipers. They had a fusillade + alas! Killed a white fronted goose while the young ones went waddling away up the bank. The Rat winds also so that we still have that wondrous thrill round every bend. Expecting moose + caribou in every snag + bear in every leg. Saw 3 musk rats: serious, rabbit-nosed, yellow, on water's edge, 1 of them swimming. Glorious untrodden feeling as we steamed up Rat as if our own puffing engine were 1st thing to break in on its lifelong silence. 70 miles we reckon Aklavik to where Rat enters Huskie R. So on 25 miles to Destruction City at 12.30. *Saw big owl.* Just before we got there came in sight of mt. barrier a wonderful mixture of sunrise + sunset light we came out from deep channel spruce silhouetted on yellow sky to mountains seen from a wider space: one range was a wonderful colour amethyst turning to pink + washed in faint rose-coloured dew as it turned so wonderful you expected it to melt away + yet all the time very clear cut. Destruction City has few remains of the old Klondiker's settlement: a green range slopes up skywards + at last we see the land from which the Rat takes rise. Gas boat went straight on to Macpherson + we shuffled hungry + sleepy into our tent on S. side of river. Mosquitoes too awful: we cd. only rig our mosquito bar + crawl in fully dressed: took off hat + shoes sprayed ourselves with Flit + so to sleep on a bed of Indian moss + cranberry. Poured with rain in the night wh. was a short one.

THURSDAY 8 JULY

The Rat River

Woke our guides at 8 + we crawled out to a world full of mosquitoes + had breakfast of fried bacon + bread + jam + black tea. Got away at 10 gray unrelieved sky + rain on + off. We landed a good 100 yards up river + then began our jaunt. We were put ashore to plunge through willows + alders or along muddy or stony shore while our guides pushed the canoe often waist deep through shallows + rapids. Mosquitoes swarm. Sky gray. Progress 1 mile per hour? *Green folds of hills hem us in sparsely wooded.* Every now + then the canoe ferries us aX to where it is possible to walk in the open. Unwashed unbrushed beveiled we begin our journey up the Rat. Several new flowers: a lovely willow Herb + pink Oenothera. As I write now in 2 veils wet ankles + knees Lazarus + Jimmy are making huge bonfire to roast the goose + we sit on flat stones in the smoke to protect ourselves from the little enemy. The sun came out on that stony spit + a puff of wind came + we had a happy hour with the goose wh. Lazarus plucked opened out like a wafer + toasted fore and aft by spiking it on a spit which he sharpened to a fine white point *for balancing the other end on stones.* Tough bird but a happy meal veils up + we even had a sponge + cleaned our teeth in the river. We made I suppose 4 miles in 3 hours lunched from 1 to 2.30 + then went on. Conditions became worse + *in the next 2 1/2 hours we made hardly 2 miles.* We Xed one or 2 very swift places rapids in fact, diagonally getting carried down at a giddy rate. Then there came deep + swift water + we took to tracking with the rope now + then, Lazarus in canoe close to bank Jimmy pulling on rope ahead: this was slow work as they had to clear track 1st on edge with axe—River wide + sub-divided: we scrambled along banks all day except when they ferried us aX + every now + then we waded aX a shallow arm. At 5 o'c we came to deep impossible swift water + camped on mud + mare's tail passing back a lovely spot with a little breeze: we cut young poplar tops for bedding + partly unloaded canoe + fixed up mosquito bar. At this point L. announced the river was rising fast + our camp being only 1 ft. above water we must move so we packed up + they canoed up a still side stream we scrambled on till a fall among snags stopped us. *Unloaded again carried canoe + goods 20 yards* to a spruce grove + camped in a bad place but the only possible allowing ourselves say 2 ft. above ~~of~~ water level on a tributary. Things don't look cheerful. Water rising fast + Lazarus says it may take days to go down. Progress impossible. flooding out possible mosquitoes very bad: dirty sleepy. However 'tis wild country and solitary we saw fresh moose tracks in mud. Supper on pork + potato + rice + maple sugar. L. kindles bonfire by peeling bark of old willow. So to bed at 9 "Flitting" ourselves.

FRIDAY 9 JULY
Wrote all this under difficulties can't sit up under bar couldn't make f. pen ink run. We slept on + off 12 hours. Gwen got up + reconnoitred: water risen: got up again in 2 hours + it was falling a little. We all had breakfast about 10 the Indians very sleepy + silent: sky thundery prospects gloomy. We ate pork + bannock + Pilot bread (ship's biscuits) + then retired to our bags with boots on + I read Macbeth aloud while Gwen mended our veils *killing mosquitoes often inside our bar.* For meals we stand inside our bonfire smoke till our eyes are weeping + anoint our chins with Citronella oil. All night we rub on Bicarb. of soda + spray with flit. After lunch *at about 2 (Canadian Boiled dinner + beans cooked yesterday + a tin of cherries)* Gwen + I set out up the river. We were anxiously watching the river all day placing little sticks in the mud: It is neither rising nor falling—*Has the Rat a spite against us? We do not like this marking time.* Showers + thunder but no heavy rain. About 1 mile up the river we struck the hill + up we went in a hell of mosquitoes to a paradise of flowers. Linnaea borealis + the little Oxycoccus a pink Menziesia a handsome yellowish dock, a very showy 2 ft. pink Pedicularis, mauve Pinguicula. Larkspur, lupin + Polemonium + up in the ridge a whole sheet of yellow Arnica, lovely mosses on soft bed of them—Fine view ahead + behind of mountains. Stormy clouds. Up on hill scrubby willows which soaked one above the knee. How lovely but mosquitoes pursued us still though in one place on the ridge they were not so thick + we sat + smoked a cigarette through our veil (I burnt a hole + mended it with plaster later). Mosquitoes tortured our necks slipping through + also our hands biting through a seam + stitching of gloves. *Back to a meal at 6.30 or so. Sun came out prospects brighter + the pests thinned enough for us to wash our teeth + brush our hair by the river one fanning the other.* A good life this bar mosquitoes + swift water. Happier to bed q à c.

SATURDAY 10 JULY
Woke at 5 after rather bony night on spruce boughs. Sun shining river sounded less of a roar. Gwen shook Lazarus. Away at 7. Lazarus + Jimmy canoed over to the other side in swift water + told us to keep on level till they came over. We gaily expected to be picked up where the hills of yesterday began about 1 mile up through alders spruce + swamp. But we had not reckoned with the Rat who seems to shew a new form of malignity every day. It is about 1/4 mile wide cut up into endless channels + islands overgrown with spruce + willows. We nipped or rather scrambled up the hill *very bad going along the side but lovely*

flowers beds of Linnaea + Oxycoccus: Every now + then we could see them struggling up the other side tracking or pushing + pulling in the water. *Then we saw them stop for a long time* + we were so far up on the hillside we cd. only just make them hear our voices. *We did at last* plunged down waded a knee deep branch of the river Xed through a wood (island) + came to main river where we cd. see them. They got aX *2 channels* towards us, one bit of rapid water they were swept down like a cork + nearly capsized. The last bit they cd. not X but Lazarus waded 1/2 way, threw us a carton of biscuits + shouted to us to go on. We continued up stream being now on an island + losing touch again with canoe. Very soon the canoe came along our side + *tracked for a bit* they had lost their axe. We came to thick overhanging willows wh. wd. take some chopping with our little axe so L. chopped while Jimmy made fire (dead stick peeled out like many-tongued torch of bark) + we cooked pork + beans +c. *It had been a pretty stiff climb all morning up among the spruce like Switzerland or Norway. Only stopped 11.30–12.30 for lunch having done 4 miles?* streaming with perspiration we were. Hot veils + silk chokers sunshine swarms of mosquitoes. After a bit of tracking left canoe again Xed from our island to main N bank. Climbed again very rough going indeed *alders, long grass, muskeg,* ravines of soft mud. *Delicious drinks (river) all day. Once got very high up among firs mosquitoes seemed to be worse high up.* We plunged sheer down ending in a stream + *thence forward along shore of alders + willows* + great silted mud heaps where streams had poured a mud path through soft hills spread out fan wise as they touched the river. Some of these pretty hard to X. Then a sheer bit of hill *into water with a 3 ft wide path or less of stones + soft earth along which we scrambled.* Canoe came over again + took Gwen in for a short spell Lazarus pushing + wading + Jimmy pulling rope. Then came to a 2 ft. rapid boiling near shore Lazarus + we 3 hauled it up *a fine show.* Then on again easier going but wet above knees for thunder rolling round the green hills that enclose us + a shower had fallen. We stopped to make tea for 1/2 an hour then over they went once more leaving us. We walked on to muskeg where mosquitoes swarmed around us *in sunshine* swift water below + there we waited *an hour or more* very long no sign of canoe. They had said they would not go much further wondered what wd. happen if they'd upset. Macpherson only 1 days walk away but no chance of Xing river: + in other directions? La Pierre House! All very well but the size of this country constitutes life + death problem. We had seen a ducks nest with 7 eggs but they were set. *At nearly 9 o'c* Lazarus came walking up our side our eyes still glued aX the

river. They had met swift water + had to come back to our side. Back we went *5 minutes* to a lovely camp in spruce wood. *Started settling in at 9 fresh after 14 hour day thanks to much tea + drinks of water.* A really good day + but for mosquitoes what a paradise of a life. *Very birdless country.* Talked to Lazarus over camp fire. He had only been up Rat once before 2 summers ago + then swore he'd never go again. Took up a lawyer. Some summers nobody goes up at all. Where did he learn how to canoe in such rough water? On Peel + Huskie both smooth but Peel sometimes swift. *He screamed with laughter* at idea of us dying of hunger if he upset + at idea of Jimmy drowning. I said "What you say to Jimmy's mother + father if Jimmy drown?" "Oh I just say Jimmy drown that's all."

SUNDAY 11 JULY
Woke Lazarus 6.30. *2 hours striking camp* + I doing short portage of all our goods + canoe aX muskeg. Sunny + *muskeg just soft moss with masses of dwarf Ledum whortleberry +c:* perspiration streamed off me + I had to shift my dollars +c in bag to outside pocket. Off we went *at 9.30 lowering canoe into river. We kept on up R bank soon got into alder thicket +* then turned from our S direction due west + skirted the base of high hills with great sheets of mud washed down the sides: fossils in this crumbling soil + up one slope a silver gray Artemesia foliage. *We kept the canoe in sight* + hills rose sheer + steep when the banks of mud hills were too sheer Lazarus came over + ferried us aX a rapid Gwen murmuring "delicious" as we were whirled downstream in spite of their battling aX. I looking away fr. the water at the mountains. For lunch we Xed again to shingle + enjoyed our glorious hour mosquito-free: washed our faces + I even put a film in my Kodak with both gloves off—also smoked a cigarette instead of having whiffs at Gwen's through my veil! She has a rubber mouthpiece in veil but mine is mended with plaster! After lunch we kept on up R. bank. Lazarus + Jimmy are undefeated. All day they shoved the canoe on, both waist deep in water pushing + pulling: or ditto Lazarus pushing + Jimmy pulling on a rope: or tracking along shore Lazarus passing rope behind trees + snags + Jimmy shoving canoe off with paddle: or both paddling like the devil against current + getting swept down say 100 yards in efforts to X 50 yards. One place looked nasty that we had to X: Lazarus wrinkled his eyes + looked up + down + said: "Water looks bad: I guess we try it." We 2 got in canoe + they shoved us aX a swift armlet of the river both waist deep. From 12.30 till 5 they toiled on then a cup of tea + pork on a

beach of pools + stones. After that exhausting walk on 6-9 through muskeg *firs* alders lovely. Mountains ahead still *due west high hills aX river*: mosquitoes quite devilish all the world buzzing + black with them till one got almost panicky. At 9 we came at last to Barrier R. on L. bank + camped on island just above the junction pretty tired. *Mosquitoes a little better than among the stones + willows we slept on sand. Men saw a beaver. A tiny bright yellow warbler we saw but a very birdless country. Masses of blue Lupin in a spruce wood. Wild roses lovely brilliant pink. Linnaea also lovely.* Fine mountains ahead of us. We have broken back of journey now we feel. Discovered one of Natives' remedies rub in sphagnum moss to seams + weak places of gloves keeps off mosquitoes so long as moisture remains.

MONDAY 12 JULY

Left Barrier River camp at 8 o'c not a bad night on hard sand. We set off up the L bank muskeg + very spongy going: then alder swamps with broken twigs aX our faces devilish hard work stooping. *Dull cloudy day.* One climb up a hill-side to dodge a face of rock. River very winding + hills enclosing it folded in on each other one a regular canyon rocky perhaps 300 ft. high. Mosquitoes very bad all day. Some very brilliant terracotta-red stones. *Walked from 8-11.30* making better pace say 1 mile an hour. At 12.30 on again + at last out from the folded hills to view of open country + *a fine mountain range.* A shower fell enough to wet us + the walking through muskeg willows + alders + wading small creeks soaked us above the knees. Saw more birds today: 3 Loons: 1 Gull: yellowshanks: robin: a warbler like bird silver breast + black head + a sparrow or so. We have seen tracks of moose in the mud more than once. Found a most beautiful yellow poppy with finely cut blue leaf growing on stony shore. Another campfire 5-6 + then on again till 8.30. Brandy at tea to binge us up. Short nights + continuous going with never a sit down in peace for the mosquitoes are making us feel a bit empty. Rain clouds driving aX mountains lovely green slopes catching the light blue summits + here + there a little patch of snow. Found small rhododendron in seed. *Lonely + satisfying* country a paradise but for the little devils—Easier water all day. *2nd half of day we Xed over R bank.* River much narrower now + towards end of day *stones smaller.* Lazarus a wonder. He was up till 10 o'c mending mocassins last night + quite cheerful when we woke him at 6 AM. Settled in to bed by 10.30 with wonderful mountain view on stony spit on L bank. We covered stones with wet poplar shoots + ourselves with our soaking wet breeches + coats.

TUESDAY 13 JULY

To Island Camp

A dull sunless morning. *We got up at 6 + left at 8.* River winding back on itself in coils all the time + we had a very easy day's walking cutting aX flat stony bits of ground + often being ferried across. Water much better too. few rapids + mostly shallow. Now + then we had a scramble through white poplars + *jagged* undergrowth whose dead sticks threatened our veils + puttees, *2 things dear as life just now.* On the whole mosquitoes better all day. We were pretty well surrounded by fine mountains now a *wonderful solitary bit of country.* So good (!) were the mosquitoes that we were able to cut our nails + smoke after lunch + after tea comb our hair—*we have to snatch at such moments.* The mountains are very rocky red + black many barren others with moss to summits + spruce fir growing 1/2 way up. Saw 2 red-throated Loons flying down, heard the Loon's note, *saw 5 or 6 common gulls,* tracks of bear + caribou. We walked from 8 till 8.30 or so: stopping an hour for lunch ditto for tea. Camped on a stony spit on sand. Fine mountains + sunset looking-sky. Plenty of reserve energy after such a good day. Several Asters on stony ground + quantities of that lovely pale yellow poppy on gray stones. Flowers up here full of interest. *Made Dough Nuts (Pufftalunas) for supper. Sun came out after tea but except in muskeg where mosquitoes were thick as ever a pleasant breeze kept them down a bit.*

WEDNESDAY 14 JULY

Got away at 8 o'c from our stony camping ground which we found was an island. At 1st we had some easy walking + pleasant loops being canoed aX from one stony flat to another. *Dull day clouds down over the mountains* + mosquitoes very hungry as Lazarus says. Whenever he stops to ferry us he says "I guess you fellers chance go across": + points out where we can short cut a river bend by saying "I guess you fellers make portage." We had some very tiresome walking through muskeg + it being a sultry day it was as much as we could do to put one foot before another. Came on sheets of the white Dryas (octopetala?) in muskeg: a lovely show. Clouds cleared up + we were still ringed in by the silent mountains some deep blue some barren. In an hour or two it seemed as if we were on a plateau on top of the divide so level was the winding river after the rapids of the last few days Soon after breakfast we passed on our R. a big river coming in not marked on the map. We have left behind the poplars mostly + see little but willow + spruce now. We had a lot of walking among scrubby willows + Xing of tiresome muddy creeks. *saw 2 more Red throated Loons. Walked from 8-11 and again from 12-3 when* we came to Fish river <u>going away into</u> (<u>coming away from</u>) Mts. on our right. We made a short portage over muskeg + willow in a shower of rain + made a fire for tea + Pemmican. After that the Rat became a little winding river some 20-25 ft. wide *bordered by willows* + scattered spruce firs winding back + back on itself ~~up up into~~ *as it issued from a great barren mossy slope* completely hidden by 20 ft. banks. We walked at 1st could only cut straight corners from loop to many loops ahead by watching the tree line + plunging feverishly from one niggerhead to another: nightmareish form of vegetation hard heads of grass sunk knee deep or thigh deep in bog + when you step on them they wobble + you sink into clefts between. After awhile we went in the canoe so peaceful green willow-bordered + sluggish current. Mountains enclose us still we scan them in vain for mountain sheep *A lovely wild place.* Drenching shower just after we left the canoe on coming to swifter water + at last at 8.30 we camped on Caribou moss after steaming ourselves dry standing by bonfire of dead spruce.

THURSDAY 15 JULY

A most wonderful + full day. Clouds low on the mountains, mosquitoes more ferocious than ever after a chilly + rather wakeful night. We set off at 8.15 up that curious winding river *hidden away in the muskeg under 25 foot banks* its course discernible only by spruce firs wh. looked like dotted lines up the slope. We canoed + walked in turn + came out to a most peaceful lake. Took a wrong turn soon after turning left up a burn instead of straight up the now sluggish Rat. We were walking + guessed Lazarus was wrong so *ran* + intercepted him + he nipped up a spruce to scan the horizon. *Mountains green + very fine clouds cleared off.* A land of flowers. All *the treasures* we have found seem to be in bloom at once here. We did 4 portages the 1st a 15 yard one from one peaceful lake to another: the next a few hundred yard one ditto: the next where we had dinner a 1/2 mile one. We helped to drag the canoe along these portages over muskeg niggerheads + swamps. Last of all we came to Loon Lake ringed by mountains with most beautiful reflections *a solitary Loon there.* At the End of Loon L. wh: is the divide between Alaska + NWT we made another portage of 2 or 3 hundred yards: the canoe teased its way along a channel just its own breadth overhung by alders + willow completely + but for these shrubs we could have paddled right into the Little Bell. A wonderful feeling of triumph. During the 3rd portage, the long one, we saw a mountain sheep hurrying up the rocky face. Then we began the

descent wh. seemed wonderfully fast after the toil of many days. At 1st very sluggish + winding like the Rat with high banks. There we sat + lazily went down wonderful mt. peaks towering above us. (Sun came out in gleams). They were rocky black + reddish patches of snow + great lines of gray + yellow where mosses seamed their sides. We cd. only keep our sense of direction by looking at these peaks: now one wd. be on our left + the next moment on our right. Presently the current was more swift + we shot a succession of little rapids: almost too exciting + rough water over stones which we bumped expecting to capsize any moment or catch in the branches—swirling down with the deep water. Then it became too shallow + we got out to walk again + had a mile *or 2* of open country aX niggerheads with sun on glorious mts screes + rocks like a castle to our left. We lost all sight of our guides + made for a point more or less where Lazarus pointed out Bell R. wd. come in: Knee deep or deeper often between the tussocks, + they got there 1st + came up the bank + holloed to us. Got in canoe again + shot a succession of *worse* rapids Gwen murmuring "Delicious delicious" each time I holding on to edge awaiting final bump. *Found on top near Loon Lake Draba, a white pond weed, a new yellow Flower +c +c.* Came at last at 8.45 to where the Bell joins the Little Bell + far from mosquitoes at last camped in a cold wind on L. bank among the willows such a good supper. A wash of sorts + *a change of clothes after 9 dirty days* ~~+ nights~~! Our guides are more + more cheerful at feeling their troubles behind them. It is a fine feeling going down stream after so much toiling up. Cooked bannock + Dough Nuts.

FRIDAY 16 JULY

Woke up 6 o'c to find no mosquitoes. Took down net + dressed standing up in tent + got into dry clothes a welcome change. *Away at 7.30.* Lovely day of sunshine in canoe all day. We took turns at paddling or lay back in canoe + drowsed in blazing sun as we went downstream about 5 miles an hour. *Fine mountains still:* river perhaps 50 yards wide + sluggish, banks Fairly low. White-stemmed poplars again now, + the hills more densely wooded. Saw *a loon* + 2 black eagles *with white wing spots fine huge birds with very serrated wing feathers.* Saw fresh beaver tracks in mud + *all got out + climbed bank to a little lake but no beaver!* Jimmy had a shot at some ducks. These Indians *live for fresh meat* + are straining their eyes for caribou all the time. *"My God says Lazarus "but I feel strong when I get fresh meat." and he stretches his arms as if to feel his muscles.* The world is mosquito-free + we enjoy every minute of this rest + sunshine.

Stopped on muddy beaches for lunch + tea saw wolf tracks. Paddled on till we came to La Pierre House 8.30: 2 deserted wooden shanties one tied up with dog chain. We looked in + found food, 3 beds, a stove, old boots, Encyclopaedia, matches, ammunition, Fur coats, axes + tubs hanging outside: all left by the Trader Jackson Bros. for people coming over the portage. We went on round the corner for a camp + saw a grizzly bear at the water's edge come down to drink, so pale in the evening light. Paddled on very silently Lazarus + I had a shot + missed I handed rifle to Jimmy who shot it once or twice. It staggered up into alders. We paddled on heard it breathing heavily. The 2 guides went ashore + up to top of rise + stalked it from above + put in 2 more bullets while we stayed in canoe. Then ashore + cooked bear steak. Lazarus + Jimmy off their heads with excitement. "By God I've had a sore stomach all day," said Lazarus "but now I'm all right." We dined close to the reeking corpse on fried bear + pork rice + treacle + so to bed 11 o'c *on a ridge with alders + willows* + a lovely sunset sky + *no mosquitoes.*

SATURDAY 17 JULY

Awoke at 4:30 up at 6 + all 4 away at 7 after eating boiled bear for b'fast cold rice + treacle sitting by the skin + meat Lazarus had hung up for Jackson Bros. in payment for his boots. The 2 took us down to Shingle Rock 15 miles, beyond a little patch of swift water where we landed on a spit of stones had a farewell dinner paid them 210 dollars each (14 per day) primed them with food + utensils for their 90 mile march aX muskeg back to Macpherson + said good-bye to them. Fine fellows + Lazarus especially never failed us in any particular Then we went forward on our own very slowly + lazily on our solitary 100 odd miles journey down the river to Old Crow. Heavenly day no mosquitoes brilliant sunshine. Wooded country with sudden turns when the river looked like a sheet of glass sloping gently downwards. We saw several *big* Eagles, the black + the white-headed, a squirrel, + several parties of Canadian geese *with their young* their note echoing + re-echoing into the still wooded country. *Passed some lovely bits of Delphinium a fine bedstraw, the white Asphodel: + the very handsome yellow-flowered eatable dock we have seen in quantities on the river bank ever since Fish River. A quite wonderful day.* We left our guides *at 11* + paddled till 7 with an hour for tea. Then found a camp on a spit with lovely view of mountains + took out our luggage all soaked + mildewed through the canvas bag + stuck it up on willow sticks to air. Cooked Puftalunas + weary to

bed at 10.30 with a *quite lovely* light over the river golden reflections. Our camp was on mud + marestails with willow boughs for bedding *+ above us the white asphodel + all about us a very fine blue mauve garlic.* Passed Porcupine R. mid-day.

SUNDAY 18 JULY

Such a sleep + did not get up till 8 o'c. Broiling sun no mosquitoes went straight into river + had a good soap from head to toe. Washed + dried our clothes + set off at 12.30 after early lunch on chocolate beef + doughnuts. Paddled slowly. *River wider now perhaps 200 or 300 yards. Still glorious hot day:* River winds among hilly wooded country on immense scale: hills vast + all folded into each other: river less + less twisting + looking down its long straight reaches with water smooth as glass it seems to be running down down into bottomless gorges where there must be cataracts. Yet the water is so still one hardly seems to be moving only when one looks at the banks one realises the current alone carries the canoe down at 2 or 3 miles an hour. A most exhilarating feeling sliding down down that green river into vast unknown country the silence of 100 miles ahead of us + the same behind. Echoing sound of a swan honking. Trees on the hills give back echoes. *Paddled for 4 hours then tea quite exhausted with heat then paddled 6-8 quite lovely in evening light: unearthly stillness great bends of the river beds of blue lupin sharp turns into those unknown gorges which only prove long stretches of unbroken water.*

MONDAY 19 JULY

Woke at 6 + saw a Caribou within 10 yards of our mosquito bar antlers outlined on river I woke Gwen + he plunged into river. We were lazy + lay in till 8 + got off at 9.45. *Another lovely day river widening + reaches being longer.* At noon we heard high children's voices + came on 2 tents *+ some Indians* + a white man French-Canadian "My name is David Low" he said as we stepped ashore into his scow with 5 1/2-breed brats round us + his flat faced Indian wife. He came in from Quebec with the Klondike rush + has never made enough money to go out. We stayed + chatted sitting in his tent. *Pushed on + spent 3 hours ashore some 4 miles below Salmon Cache lunching sketching baking bannock + bathing.* Puffy wind we sailed a bit with ground sheet on a stick. *Paddled only 6 1/2 hours. Camped on stony beach in vetch plot golden light on rocky mossy hills opposite quite wonderful. Several ducks red-throated divers eagles Clouds rolling up for rain sun not so hot.*

TUESDAY 20 JULY

I write under mosquito bar on muskeg 8.30 PM sun not yet down record early bed but we were up at 6.15 away at 8.15 + have paddled about 8 hours in all. Had some nasty bits of water to negotiate swift + swirling + the wide river intersected with sand-bars so that we had to land + scan ahead with glasses—current very swift too + we went whirling down. *Passed fine rocky bluffs eagles screaming + peregrine falcons. Rather anxious work now the river is so big. Sun hot but pleasant. We lunched on R bank behind us a lovely group of dark blue delphinium. Glimpses of mountains behind* Very long reaches 6 or 8 miles. Vast country. *Saw a few geese, scoter ducks, loons. Some strong puffy head winds* other bits smooth as glass with that wonderful downhill glide.

WEDNESDAY 21 JULY

Delicious scent of Ledum + muskeg on which we lay *last night. Gleams in the sky all night:* wolf tracks on beach but no wolf came. We slept without tent. *Up at 6.30 threw our bedding down cliff + away at 9.30* About 10 met a tent + 4 empty huts on R. bank stopped + talked to 2 old Indians who knew little English. On + on river very wide now *perhaps nearly 1/2 a mile in parts* Passed a slough wh. we guessed to be Old Crow R. David Low's reckoning of time coincided: ditto old Indian woman's who said we'd reach it 12 o'c: ditto our own reckoning of time: ditto Lazarus account of Willow Island. *One or 2 spasms about spits + swift water.* Clouds rolling up heavy shower. Lunched on L. bank expecting to see Old Crow next corner. Went on 1 o'c + after an hour concluded we'd missed Old Crow looked at map felt sure of it + floating down down with Rampart-like rocks on left made up our minds to the worst i.e. 70 miles more on to Rampart House alone with chance of gasboat + a cabin or so. One tremendous battle with waves + wind. Passed what looked like a backwater + at 5 o'c came suddenly as those who dream on Old Crow a long line of huts!! Indians crowded out to meet us. Swift current as we pulled in *after 7 1/2 hours paddling.* Indian Chief came down + shook hands: ditto others We said "Is Harry Anthony ~~here~~ trader here?" "No." "Any white man here?" "One." And he pulled up canoe + led us to him shaking hands as we went. The trader a youngish man (Frost) welcomed us in a spotless 2 roomed log cabin + gave us such a meal of salmon (fresh) coffee figs. Indian chief sat there + another, eyes gleaming in dark corner still + silent. A 3rd slipped in. Discussed guides. Chief slipped out "See if catch im feller perhaps catch im perhaps no." 2 mins. later appeared, caught David 5 dollars a day food + return fare (days) David came in, a fine fellow. We went up

village bartered beads + silk for mocassins with Martha saw church, pressed flowers, had a long chat with host saw photos of wild life. He was in M.P. but got out + cannot leave the country now, likes his independence. To bed *at 9 o'c* "Gee-whiz but it's fierce"—Came down the river like 2 squaws

THURSDAY 22 JULY

Porcupine R. *I write peacefully in the canoe: water glassy still: sun 1/2 veiled wonderful soft clouds + shadows on green + gray mountains that face us. River must be 1/2 a mile wide now: spruce: willow: eagles.* The river bank most interesting last 2 days: sometimes deeply overhung banks 12 ft. high *of black soil* where the water swirls round quickly on concave shore. Sometimes rocky ramparts high cliffs topped + backed by forest in fact just a rocky face showing through leagues of forest + marking far ahead the winding course of the river. Great chunks of dirty ice embedded like tree trunks in black soil. On shallow bank of river endless stony spits + shoals which are seen so far off down these long reaches that they appear to intersect + one can hardly guess where to steer. Sloughs + back-waters very deceptive too: we cd. have sworn y'day Old Crow River flowing in was a backwater flowing down: + vice versa the backwater we mistook for the river. Just now while Gwen + our *stalwart* guide David are paddling we are passing high mud cliffs channelled by melting ice + every now + then a dull reverberating sound rolls about + echoes thinly over the wooded country as chunks of ice roll or shoot down *looking like bits of black soil* The cliff face is furrowed with these channels + mud splayed out fanwise at bottom : so the river's work goes on river ever widening its banks eating into land: we had a happy though stuffy night in darkened room no windows open. Woke at 4. Mr Frost cooked us such a good breakfast. All the village sleeping turning day into night after night of dance. We got 2 pairs moccasins, from Martha who sat up all night making them + we gave her beads + silks; also another pair for pork + biscuits. Mr ~~Foster~~ full of interest tales of North. Away at 6.45 we passed one cabin just on edge of bank next yard's fall it will slip in: David says in 1910 it was 100 yards in: river banks eaten away. *Very hot sun middle day:* we paddled turn + turn about 2 hours *in a 12 hour day* 10 hours going *2 hours meals Some wind.* Evening came to Ramparts fine scenery red black white yellow + gray cliffs enclosing swift water in icy cold wind blew us onward + such a sinister wind blowing down all the little gorges. *Every sound intensified in this silent land.* Came at 7 to Rampart House in a little break of this double barrier: MP barracks Trader Cadzow

+ 3 other houses + church. The MPs made us welcome Thornthwaite + Allington cooked us such a supper eggs + potatoes + gave us their 2 beds. Wet cold night + we were glad of a fag: glad also a small pane of glass was broken as no window open. Nights still all daylight.

Friday 23 July

Our hosts came in from their tent + got busy about 6 over such a breakfast + at last we got off *at 8.30.* Icy cold. Mr Allington came down with us for this trip. We rigged a sail of the Police + sailed down till the mast snapped. The Ramparts *like a vault* full of cold wind. About 10 o'c we met Jackson Bros. + Bishop Stringer puffing up in the Moose. They had tied up all night owing to wind. We landed + had a chat w. J. Bros: gave us a bag of potatoes + some tinned stuff most welcome. *Sailed on down the Ramparts with my ground sheet + walking stick.* The MP went back with the Moose, done out of his trip to Yukon as he dared not go down + wait for next boat. too long. *Mystery of Maccullum unsolved. Cold day much wind.* We went ashore after 38 miles (?) at Old Rampart only a few Indians + women gone out to pick berries. *Salmon River comes in there a picture of French Willow Herb + Delphinium blue. Many Bank Swallows. Lunched on stony beach below Old Rampart at 2.30 + then went on till 8.30. Came out into open country a little head wind + sun came out.* Called at a solitary trapper called Martin who wanted 0 of us: been in this country 20 years got out once came back again. He sees quite enough people. Some one passes up every 2 weeks or so. *Wonderful sunset deep blue water stony banks all gold.* We camped late + had a spruce bed on mud floor. The mileage here is very puzzling + uncertain + maps don't seem accurate. We seem to have come 70 y'day + 60 today but landmarks are few + rough reckoning by strength of current + so many miles per hour is nearest we can get Current too very elusive in fact travel on water plays havoc with imagination: often in mid-stream we seem to be drifting or even floating if we look at water only but if we look at banks we see them tearing by. Also paddling quickly down we have mistaken a rock or snag for some animal swimming upstream.

Saturday 24 July

Up at 6 away 7.30 Rigged the MPs sail + sailed quite a lot with a moderate fair wind Overcome with sleepiness. Very cold 2 jumpers 2 coats later sun was hot + burning. Passed lower rocky bluffs *like miniature Ramparts.* Saw clusters of martens nests in rocks thick together as swarm of bees *mud nests:* loons *with grey*

heads: peregrines: ravens, seagulls + ducks: we lunched on R. bank + climbed the rocky bluff + full of Alpines all over: Dryas Linnea, Campanula, Saxifraga, Androsace +c+c *Then we left the rocks + came out among stony spits + willows.* Saw a young Black Bear on shore a 1 year old *a little dear* went gambolling up the bank: Later saw an ambling prehistoric porcupine with light wind-blown spinal fringe of fur ambling on an island shore: he fled from us *"doing his best" as David said,* that best being a most graceless shuffle showing his quills behind. *Passed the Sucker River about 9.30 (Colen on map?) + a camp of Indians. Went ashore for 10 mins. Lovely timber black poplars no mosquitoes.* Indians catching King Salmon in nets women too shy to come out. *We journeyed on from 7.30-12 + from 1-5 + from 6-9.* Took a wrong turn after tea + had quite a little battle *poling* up stream. River bed very confusing. *Lovely hot sunshine all day + the moderate wind all in our favour.* Had a camp on stones + spruce with such a lovely sunset behind the pointed spruce. River very tortuous now + full of islands + the channels filled with snags of fallen trees *+ the eaten-away banks a scene of desolation with uprooted trees. Mosquito free + a blessed world.*

Sunday 25 July

Up at 6 + away by 7.30. Hardly any wind + what there was contrary. Sun hot. We are finding it rather strenuous + the longing to sleep in hot sunshine is torture. *We paddled on 7.30-12 + 1-5.* River always flat + taking great curves. Poplar spruce + a few birch. *Saw Gulls + one or two Terns + a speckled Hawk size of Buzzard. Lunched on Pork again + Mr Jackson's present of delicious tinned tomatoes: also Potatoes.* David *a sleepy individual* not up to Lazarus. About 6.15 saw a gas boat + scow coming up + pulled in to shore. Traders going up to Old Rampart: "My name is Hely." "And mine Rogers." "Mine Dorrien-Smith." We ?ed him + checked our muddled mileage he says we are only 10 miles from *Salmon R. which is the same as Siheneck:* + 50 from Fort Yukon *+ should do it in 7 hours.* We have come better than we thought then, *averaging 6 miles an hour.* We shall miss the steamer for Dawson + Tanana but what matter? Made up our minds not to sprint + paddled on in a glassy still evening passing *Salmon R.* about 8 o'c + camping without a tent on baked sand willows + poplar boughs about 9. There are wonderful echoes all down the reaches of the River: the trees give you back your own voice. *Fine sunset.*

Monday 26 July

Away at 7.30. A scorching hot day we paddled in 1 hour shifts + quite enough it was. *terrific* glare from the water. *The silence of these spruce trees grows on one + they begin to have a human feeling. Lunched in shade + leisurely no longer any hustle +* at 2 o'c David announced we had come to portage *or shortcut* to Fort Yukon wh. he found after some search. 2 miles but a long hot 2 miles it was. We'd never have found it alone. Spruce trees undergrowth *a boggy stretch* with dry grass knee high + hay head-high + then at last a mile or so of beaten trail. A lovely scarlet chenopodium. *And so in great heat to Fort Yukon.* Straight to Mr Anthony who sent his gas boat up with David for canoe, *down river 2 miles + up 5.* Fort Yukon a bigger settlement than we have seen + more prosperous neat palings + sidewalks big wireless station. We called on Mrs Burke at English Mission a *luxurious* house with big room. Had a chat + were asked to stay but decided to camp on site 1/2 a mile above Fort. Back to await canoe + had a talk with Willoughby Mason old-timer 52 just married taking his *New York* wife up Porcupine 10 days up in gas boat. They won't see a soul till next June. *His brother goes too.* "She is taking napkins this time!" He has been trapping 21 years. *They plan retiring to Los Angeles but* "will she ever get that man out?" the Mission ask themselves. Canoe came waterlogged we unpacked hurriedly on bank shuffled into skirts + to Mission *at 7* to dine. Such a dinner + such a home. Dr. Burke fine sensitive overwrought face: Mrs. Burke happy home-maker: a pecking woman from Los Angeles in silk stockings who gets on Dr Burke's nerves: 3 men from geological survey down from Scheneck river. Such a meal of fish + lettuce + asparagus + pineapple pie + coffee + then talk + hot baths in palatial bathroom! *both the Burkes steeped in North Country +* a home full of books + comfort. *Home at 10.30 sending wireless to England sunset + moon rising over Yukon River.*

TUESDAY 27 JULY

Up lazily + breakfast of Pork + *Rice Balls* at 10. We cleaned up pots + pans + sorted clothes + had another meal + then paddled our canoe along to settlement + dropped the MP's sail at Anthony's + spent a cool aft. at Mission fixing up our pressed flowers + having tea. *Miss Butler +* another woman in to tea. Heat terrific. *We paddled up a lovely green + gold backwater.* After supper Gwen sketched the pink sky + *I strolled along* + had a V. interesting talk with Harry Anthony who *is steeped in the lure of the North:* Came up the Rat to Klondike talked of *lonely trappers +* Michael Mason + Hudson Stuck—"a man who did all his own thinking You could hand him nothing." *Such a sky, pink, + smooth water.* We are happily camped nearly a mile from the settlement + the empty Tins.

WEDNESDAY 28 JULY

B'fast 10 or so Pork again. Rain last night. Blowing a hot gale. Mr Hunter came along + had picnic lunch with us Marshal (M.P.) Butler to see canoe also a Mr. Macgregor. Aft. Gwen + I to Lake 7 mins: behind hospital very large crescent shape once more size of country strikes one anew for we had to take bearings to run canoe back (Dr lent us his) into same groove of mare's-tails. Stopped + chatted in house of a swede Burgland woman + 6 kids. They trap. She is happy as a Queen in her 1 room cabin + says life in the N is all sport + adventure meals so easy no social ties +c. One of her children at least born when away trapping with no woman at hand. Every soul you meet full of tales of the North. Bought tinned stuff cold supper made fast our tent rising wind + then to call on Mr. Anthony. Enjoyed a chat with him as he looked at Gwen's sketches. He told us of a trip *to Norman* with Michael Mason staking oil claims rations for 8 days + they travelled 19: last 4 or 5 days without Food: *shortcutted on face of Bear Rock to save 12 miles + got into Norman. An Imperial Oil Co.* man pinched their claim + delayed them, hence the trouble + they had scrupled to take much of another man's cache. *These tales thrill one + the lure of the North grows. He talked of Northern Lights too + how sound travels in frosty air + of the superstitions of Indians.*

THURSDAY 29 JULY

B'fast at 10 in leisurely fashion. Wind gone down. Cooked Puftalunas + then strolled up to the Fort: to the Marshal who had bought another canoe: to Mission for drinking water the river being brown as coffee: saw Mr Mertie + his collection of wild flowers. Back to cold lunch. Dr. Burke called for us + we went with him by *delightful trails thro' spruce forest (orange + red berries on ground)* to old Hudson Bay Co. burial ground. He was full of stories about each graveyard. Then to the church with Indian beadwork altar + Indian memorials (Indian chief wanted to put up "a fence" in memory of his wife 100$ oak altar rail). Then to Cemetery Archdeacon Stuck's grave + he talked much of him, a fine man. *Then on to further end of settlement + called on Joe Ward a fine blue-eyed trapper w. Indian Squaw. Discussed marriages with Dr. Burke he was full of yarns of decent women throwing themselves away on ne'er do wells: + then the reverse side, these fine men who are content with squaws.* Then to see Frank Foster who was building a boat a rich old-timer who "loafs around" traps a little + cannot leave the country. He talked of the Rat R. as he came up it in the Klondike rush of 98 leaving Edmonton April 28 + reaching Klondike Sept: 6 weeks on Rat. Brought 1300 lbs food +c as far as Fort Yukon + then found there was plenty in the country: sandflies were awful. Rat River water low. All these people full of interest. *Called on Mr Mertie + Hunter to get them to auction our canoe tomorrow. Back to supper +*

then it being a cold + colourless unsketchable evening to call on Linklater fine old-timer. H.B. servant, with a heart in bed. Indian wife Catherine—as good a hunter as he. He says its wonderful how a man appreciates his wife in the woods she hunts with him, paddles her own canoe, they win thro' difficulties together + he gets so as he can't leave her. When she lived at Old Crow she went 250 miles in winter dog team to Herschel Is: to get tea + tobacco for her father there being only girls in family: no timber: they had to dig in snow for willow for fuel. They lost one boy who moved from snow where they'd left him, crawled into igloo + died his dog stuck in igloo door + died. She saved the lives of 2 men with her who were unable even to light a fire of willow shoots. Full of praise of this life in the North: "give a man a pinch of tea + a gun + he can live." Longing to get back to Old Rampart. His sister wrote + tried to decoy him to Winnipeg Lake a plot + house for him own automobiles—seaside resort—aeroplanes. he wrote "I've a jack-plane that's enough for me."

Friday 30 July

Very cold we huddled in our flea bags while it rained + at last sprang out hopped straight into the muddy river with our soap. Paddled the canoe downstream against the wind quite a choppy sea + beached her by the N.C. store. Then to the Mission for water + back paying our debts en route for a cold lunch. After to the sale which we found was all over + our canoe unsold 20$ highest bid. Found Anemone Pulsatilla, went over the Hospital 22 beds 2 nurses the matron describing the life + work also the life of the place in winter how all the Indians come in with dog-teams for Xmas + dance every night for a fortnight. The place is emptying already for the fall: the trappers are pulling out every day by gas boat lashed to barge with goods + families + dogs piled round them. They go up the Porcupine the Black + Salmon Rivers +c + spend 6 weeks getting ready their cabin for the winter's work. Saw one patient old man of 90 with gangrenous leg got frost-bitten foot + was months alone with his dogs + now too late to operate. Just longing to stay here a winter + see it all. Not only is it a good life but everyone is conscious of it: you hear it on all sides: "Pecker" Mrs Heinz ie. Mrs Burke's M in law wandered down the beach as we were making tea + joined us + sat in the tent in the rain after: a typical American sharp of tongue + eye + mind. office work in Los Angeles: sees life from more angles + has more firm grasp of it so it seems then we sluggish English but not the attractive type quick to love + argue. We had a great clean up with hot water + put on skirts after 3 weeks freedom + called on Linklater to show him Gwen's sketches + so to supper at the Mission with Dr + Mrs Burke Mrs Heinz Mr Mertie of the Geographical + the old timer from Bradford Yorkshire Frank Foster: colossal supper off moose joint +c. Enjoyed the evening much. Had a long talk with Foster who is a great reader: he is off next

week for his 10 months solitude up the Porcupine he hates his 2 months in Fort Yukon nothing to do but loaf around + is happy when he gets back to his routine + work: very keen about the Brontes. Mrs Burke told story of a school teacher weight 240 lbs travelling by dog-sleigh: driver swore freely. She rated him: "Guinness if you swear I'll not pay you a cent." Next day no swearing. Then they came to thin ice + seemed like sticking in the in the middle—mushy— + the teacher cd. only get out of the sleigh by having it rolled over sideways. She urged him on. "If I swear you no pay me wages." "Swear Guinness swear + I'll pay you double." This became a mocking chorus "Swear Guinness swear." Home 11.15 getting dim lights now.

Saturday 31 July

Up at 8 or so + straight into the cold river for an all-over soap. G to Mission to copy a sketch. I to McGregor to sell our canoe: finally he gave us 20 dollars for it on Dr Burke's estimate we muddled the deal having paid 97 for it. 2 USA students came along beach as I was oiling rifle they are selling a medical book travelling on gas boat, to pay their college expenses one a medical student one 7th Day Adventist they saw herds of Caribou in R. Yukon this week. Aft. G. sketching Mission + church from roof of a shanty perched on sand: I to call on F Foster who was building his boat + went into his cabin + had a long yarn with him + Tony a man from the Azores: mostly on the freedom +c of the North. Back to camp to fetch cold supper in canvas basket + then G + I in canoe on Lake fine sunset she did 2 sketches. More sunshine today but cool + summer already waning.

Sunday 1 August

Hot sunshine: G did a sketch before breakfast + we had a muddy bath + after walked down town + paddled our canoe back + she copied a sunset sketch in tent while I wandered off to bush. After lunch packed cleaned our pots + paddled baggage down in canoe + visited Linklater. He very interesting on Indian (Crees) sun dances, initiation of young men + women at age of 17 or 18 in Saskatchewan in 1893. They carve sun moon + stars in bark of tree arena opposite: young people stand up in baskets or cages + dance to sound of drums 3 days + nights with no bite nor drop. Allowed 1 hour sleep each night + every now + then the music stops + they stop for 10 minutes. He has seen a groove in ground 8 inches deep worn by dancing feet. An old man leader of dance takes a 6 inch long sharpened bone picks up skin of his breast on each side pierces it ties string to bone + attaches end to bleached buffalo head on ground which he drags round after him. Linklater says infidel Indians far more honest to deal with than those who have associated with white traders: also generous will share their last bite with you. He married a French Canadian 1st who spoke no English + he never spoke English for a year. That man has had a rich life: such a quiet dignified way of expressing himself as he *lies in bed. deep pleasant voice + old hawk nose.* To stay at mission. *Church 8 o'c Dr Burke read a sermon of Fosdicks.* Mrs. Burke very interesting on Eskimo dances she was 1st white woman up near Kobuk R. *She teaches the other missionary:* full of Indian Beaver dances: they lie on ground on toes + elbows + wriggle round a post till you are giddy imitating a beaver: also crow dance of Indians a corpse lies on floor covered by shawl the others pick: Witch doctor Meesuk mesmerizing Eskimo. *Talked to Mr Macgregor who is off prospecting up Sucker (Colen) R. with a tent + stove flour beans sugar tea choco-late dried fruit in cartons rice + a few books for 8 months or so. does a little trapping.* He dropped in + was made welcome as all are here the 4 geological survey men came also + supper came round *on a trolley* + we got to bed some time after midnight. The talk of every person you meet is full of interest.

MONDAY 2 AUGUST

Slept in a *double* bed on a spring mattress but the huskies howled + the sun seemed to shine all night. *Breakfast at 10 + then we sat about* waiting for the boat *S.S. Yukon* which hove in quite dwarfing the cabins *about 1 o'c + left about 5.* Quite sorry to say goodbye to the Burkes who have been good friends to us *+ to Pecker who is a very perfect type of a sharp tongue. No meal till 6.30* dinner + then we sat + watched the murky brown water of the Yukon against a blue black sky + we swirled down past cotton wood spruce + poplar same river as ever. Stony spits + many bends + cut away banks some crowd of tourists on board + how they all stare: *2 young Bear cubs.* A friendly set of officers, they have been looking out for us since April.

TUESDAY 3 AUGUST

Passed Beaver late last night. Up at 8 passing through Ramparts well-wooded hills Cold wind. Inquisitive tourists stare unblushing and ? us about our trip. *At noon went ashore at Rampart + saw a Fox farm silver foxes caged in but allowed natural burrows kept by a Norwegian: about 75 foxes. He gets about 200$ a pelt.* Sunny later + at 7 we stopped at Tanana a pleasant place long drawn-out on R bank decaying now. Went ashore + found a few flowers + chatted to storekeeper an old-timer came in 40 years ago from Fiume never been back since. *Then for several hours feeling our way about the channel among sand-banks like some giant blind monster. men sounding with poles to port + starboard. Fascinating swirls in water + a most beautiful clear sunset.* Baited tourists with Gwen's sketches. Talked to an interesting much-travelled nurse Miss Williams been with Grenfell Mission in Labrador. *Many birch trees.*

WEDNESDAY 4 AUGUST

Went ashore twice at wood piles berries most lovely: cornel shrub + herb raspber-ries + delicious dwarf rubus. Hilly country wide river delicious sunny day. Evening we sighted Mt McKinley + just before sunset the cloud line cleared off top + we saw him wonderfully: a nuggetty shaped giant about 100 miles away lit up one side to ethereal pink by sunlight other side in shadow then a cloud bar aX + lower down that ethereal pink again of the sun on snow. *Fine purple + red sunset.* Trippers ubiquitous but we sorted out one or 2 interesting ones a self made couple *at 11 o'c supper + others.*

THURSDAY 5 AUGUST

2 breezy young American girls woke us at 4 by Pilots' request + we went up to Pilot House + saw Mt McKinley bathed in rosy sunlight right down to the roots. *Got in to Nenana about 5.30 + got up 8.30* + after breakfast left the steamer we got a room at Southern Hotel + took tickets + checked our luggage. Then bought *ham + cheese* sandwiches *for 25 cents each + away aX the great bridge + up the hill beyond the river. Very hot had a sleep + lunch +* Gwen sketched + then up to ridge with magnificent views all day of Mt McKinley + a great range about 100 miles long or more with snow peaks. Met 2 men carrying back bear's meat just shot: one a Swiss came over 20 years ago: *more praise of the North "you go out + make your own track + no man asks you where you are going."* He *traps down river* + lives on lake + shoots a *fat duck* whenever he wants food. Nenana has railway + *frame houses + but lovely surroundings. Back to supper at café + out after along lovely road with* pink willow herb seed. *Sun sets about 8.30.*

FRIDAY 6 AUGUST

Out to Japanese Restaurant for breakfast: 1 dollar a breakfast between us + 3 dollars a double room + 1 dollar a telegram to Seward for reservations on S.S. Yukon. Met an old timer who said Lloyd climbed McKinley year before Hudson Stuck + he'd photographed it with flag on top. We mooched about + train left an hour late 10.30. *A delightful journey soon ran into mountains + gorges + glimpses all the time of River Hely. At 1.30 all turned out at Hely + the whole train poured into a Restaurant for a 1 dollar lunch.* When we came to the divide Broad Pass we had fine view of Mt McKinley *but shaded by direct sunlight so snow was not apparent: it dwarfs every other moun-tain: circular range all round it 1 fine glacier. Saw Blue Cranesbill + some new berried plants from train + a big leaved thing in seed like Swiss yellow gentians. Ran down alongside Shoesilver River fine gorges + great sweeps of wooded country.* Talked a bit to Russell the boy who hurt his knee on geographical survey: he says the trippers asked him how he had "penetrated our reserve!!!" So we must be more genial. Struck a Rat R. old timer at supper with a Swedish wife years in Fairbanks: they have a Mink farm SW of Anchorage. *Not being trippers we opened out to them. Her hat was a corker + taught us once more not to judge by appearances. Some very fine pictures in the big luxurious hotel by S. Lawrence English artist Mt McKinley Northern lights starlight +c. After supper out aX shaky Suspension Bridge over wide swift river + up to a waterfall. Dusk at 9.30*

SATURDAY 7 AUGUST

Called at 6 + at 7.30 the whole hotel full stepped into train + away through lovely mt. + river scenery French willow herb flower + seed blazing over miles of country At Anchorage 12.45 + stopped for an hour + saw in Anchorage Hotel very fine picture by S. Lawrence of Mt. McKinley. After that followed Turnagain arm a lovely find snow mts. looking down vast extent of water sand + mud + the gateways of the Pacific. Then up + up among glaciers + Mts train stopping every now + then for trippers to hop out + photograph glaciers! And at Lawing to see stuffed heads. Scarlet + alder Berry + orange rowan a sight. At 7 arrived Seward + failed to get any agent for S.S. Yukon so to Hotel Seward for night + then to Restaurant + Cinema for show. Dark at 11 when we got in + the Mt towering above the shoddy town.

SUNDAY 8 AUGUST

To Agents at 9 + got berths to Seattle upper deck so our trust in Providence justified. Then to b'fast at Restaurant sitting on high stools. Surprising system you order say Eggs or fish + they throw in all manner of things. Bought a sandwich got luggage checked + away up a gorge. Ice snow baby glaciers masses of both willow herbs + a yellow willow herb. Alder + large black poplar: up + up crossing the torrent again + again. Had a glorious bathe in ice water + lunched in willow herb under snow peaks. Back + on board SS Yukon 4 o'c. Such a horde of trippers— sailed at last about 10 after luxurious dinner + pleasant evening chatting + reading Rex Beach.

MONDAY 9 AUGUST

Looked out at 2 AM hardly light little islands with fir trees down to level of smooth water. towering hills above us hardly yet light + morning mist. During the night we stopped + we called at Port Ashton Port Benny + Crab Bay to take on cases of frozen fish Halibut Salmon Herring from the canneries + at La Touche at 8.30. We steamed on through a maze of fir covered islands + promon- tories clouds low + a fine rain (2nd biggest rainfall in the world here) + a range of snow Mts. At 11 o'c went ashore on Knight's island + found almost tropical vege- tation. Water deep deep green: a cannery + 0 else: no tracks: hills rose sheer up. I scrambled up through moss ferns fallen trees rocks to a bluff + looked down on it all wet to the waist: many berries a whortleberry shrub waist high + in the bogs

several new flowers including a giant leaved skunk weed in seed. Had most interesting yarn with a prospector called Beed: has gold fever here in country 22 years. Been on Alaska range described a volcanic basin surrounded by mountains: basin 3 1/2 + 7 miles hot enough to cook soil like crust it melts snow + starts a river in summer where 20 ft sand banks nearly smother tree tops. He has been in Chugach range quite unexplored + no maps except for coast line. Described *Mt Redoubt volcanic* + a great quartz reef in side perhaps a mile long. He set out: felt he must climb it: came to reef where a split occurred in volcanic basin of summit + found the apparent quartz reef was a heap of birds bones they had been killed by fumes that escaped by that rift. *He is to be married next year + longs to travel.* He has made as much as 135 000 dollars but always lost it again in some new venture. *These are good days bewitching green water + peaceful travel: books: good meals full of variety: + interesting characters whenever you like to sort them from among the Tow Rows. saw a lovely Blue Jay black crested on Knights Island. Read Rex Beach's "The Silver Horde" all day + steamed on from one stinking cannery to another through lovely inland lakes apparently with deepest green water + fir clad rising sheer from water + golden fringe of seaweed. About 6 o'c an ethereal range snow Mts (Chugach) caught the only gleam of sunlight for the day—"those Halls of Sion" tinged with pink + full of glaciers. Stopped at Nellie Wans about 9 o'c.*

TUESDAY 10 AUGUST

Woke 7.30 to find ourselves close to Columbia glacier a most marvellous creature 280 ft. rising from the sea over a mile long: full of pale blue + deep blue chinks soft, pink light + serrated muddy edges against a gray sky. Chunks fell in every now + then with far resounding plash. Stayed an hour + gazed at it 1/2 dressed. *On thro' more apparently landlocked seas with mountains tipped with snow + fir clad hills + deep blue water + glaciers among the Mts. At 11 to Valdes quite a town + a long straight road 4 miles to a dirty glacier: we went out on the Moraine but found no flowers only young poplars + the 2 Epilobiums. On at 1 o'c + a lazy warmer afternoon on upper deck reading Victor Hugo + watching the deep blue water + blue hills. At 7 o'c to Cordova a more prosperous town 1/2 a mile from dock with wooden roads to it + a railway to Kennecott Copper Mine + a young bear in captivity. Went to Dr Tutt's Christian Science Lecture + came out again: he is a fellow passenger: nothing to hold one: A silver sunset + away at 10.30. Getting more used to fellow passengers + more tolerant but they think of places only in terms of food + hotels + measure scenery by inches + it's hard to switch on to them suddenly after the wilds.*

WEDNESDAY 11 AUGUST

Overcast day we passed Cape St. Elias a weird detached rock like a pillar + saw before + after fine snow ranges + glaciers but only in glimpses + the clouds were too low to see Mt Logan + Mt St. Elias. Open sea but not rough. No incidents we read all day + turned in early noise of gramophone + Tourists being too much for us.

THURSDAY 12 AUGUST

Thick fog + we went dead slow then stopped. At noon it lifted suddenly + we found ourselves under wooded mountains with a hundred yards or so of Port Althorp. There we went ashore with Innes the young Toronto professor + saw the huge cannery of salmon + astonishing machinery for cutting up tinning lidding + labelling fish: Philippine labour. Then for a scramble up a gorge behind. Fog at sea still + at 5 o'c we steamed back into it. It lifted about 7 just before sunset behind snow mountains wonderful reflects of Gold rim on snow + rolling cloud banks + little drifting icebergs + pink clouds. Talked to a Botanist Professor Harshberger from Philadelphia who named our plants for us. Gwen showed her pictures to the tourists in the morning + sold 47.50 + we got some fun out of it. Luri said his p.p.cs were better souvenirs because they only cost 2 cents each! At midnight we heard *a tripper shriek* "Northern Lights". *Gwen cursed them: then we hopped out in case it was not a tripper's joke + there they were.* Wavy in straight ~~streaks~~ edges like a crystal yet waved about sinuous + 1/2 transparent like wispy clouds or search lights. They waved + shimmered + were full of trembling movement in great sheets of milky light aX the starlit sky: now + then faint rainbow hues apparent. *We stayed out on deck 20 mins. or so in coats + nightgowns + then they faded. The dark forms of trippers + their exclamations were a queer setting.*

FRIDAY 13 AUGUST

Got up at 5.30 + out to see Juneau for an hour: we had stopped there at 3 + left at 7. It is built on piles largely has wooden streets + is squeezed between sea +

mountains: great mine works on hill side. Biggest town we've seen since Edmonton Lovely day hot sun cool breeze: all morning steamed past beautiful Mts + glaciers on our left but not very close to us. Islands every side + spruce (Sitka spruce) clad hills. At 2.45 passed Petersburg + entered Wrangell narrows then 3 hours of very narrow winding channel. Clouds of black headed gulls at Petersburg like snowflakes never saw so many. At 6 o'c came to Wrangell: + went ashore for 1 hour after dinner. Full of Totem poles + Curio shops. scrambled up hill a little way saw huge strawberry plants + masses of mountain ash berries. Away at 8 in a beautiful sunset.

SATURDAY 14 AUGUST

Got in to Ketchikan early up 6.30 + after breakfast ashore we 2 + the 2 men from Toronto Innes + Gibb. *Attractive town partly on piles + wooden streets. Walked 2 or 3 miles Innes + I had a delightful scramble up a gorge. Then on to tropical looking forest Thupa placata Hemlock spruce Tsuga hedaeriphia one 18 ft. round + Jack Pine Pinus Murrayana. Saw some salmon in pools. Then back to town + saw saw. Mill fascinating machinery carving great trees just hauled up from the water like slices of ham. Away at 2 + thereafter a dullish gray day down among islands. Fancy dress masque ye gods!!!*

SUNDAY 15 AUGUST

Wrote in desultory fashion smooth water dark islands + lovely hills + a lovely sunset. The high hills veiled last day or 2 but today was bright + sunny again. Went thro Queen Charlotte Sound in morning open sea on 1 side + evening thro very narrow passages. Wonderful sea journey this 7 days in smooth water + such scenery. Passengers sang hymns + danced. We have only hobnobbed with the Reynolds family from near Los Angeles + the 2 Toronto men Innes + Gibb.

Notes on Eskimo Trial Aklavik June 25. 1926

Scene S.S. Distributor Union Jacks against pantry

Judge Debuc white tie black coat.

Accused of murder = Ikagena

dead man = Ulukshuk

wives (of both) = Nalugiak + Hanugak (Khaki shirt + trousers
leather belt

witness = Panigiak (muklocks coloured tops: small

(eyes narrowed forehead

<u>Sergeant Baker</u>

I declare this court open in the name of the King

<u>Interpreter</u> reindeer parkie pointed in white high wolverine
collar mocassins blue trousers aristocratic dark face forward tilt
of chin *hair upwards* alert dark eyes gold ring on black fingers: 1/2
Kanaka 1/2 Eskimo. intent. moistens lips with tongue: *handsome
face made to kill hearts + be gay but today v. serious* looks earnestly from
?er to witness

<u>Judge to Witness</u>. "White men's religion on that book see? *When
you want tell Truth in court* kiss that book + speak. When Not speak
Truth very bad. *Do you know difference bet. Truth + Lie. You know, not tell
Truth—bad. Will you promise tell Truth?* Tell him he must tell only
what he knows. *(lucidity of French mind apparent + admirable even in this
pidgeon English)*

How many wives has Ulukshuk? Kooktenna. *Cookylooky.*
Naloonga.

<u>Woman</u> Naloonga *(?) arched mouth: lower lips droop:* slit eyes, *only
open with sudden sly look + eyebrows raised intelligently. 8 Tattooed lines
nostrils to ears chin to lips eyebrows to sleek black hair. Slit eyes almost disappear
upward sometimes with* a look of fright or anger that lights up face
strangely.

O'C. (defence) Ulukshuk bad man make plenty trouble for
people?

Int.   Yes: medicine man.

O'C.   He in touch with spirits to make better?

Int.   (puzzled)

O'C.   When Eskimo get mad what that mean?
            And he took his rifle with him?

Int.   *Yes said must "do something" bout that Dog*

O'C.   *Was Ilukshuk a (sharmen?) Witch Doctor*

Int.   *Yes.*

O'C   *Did he come sneaking up round tent + was he mad?*

Int   *Int. Yes <u>he never sing</u> no laugh.*

KC.   Did she (wife) ever see Ikagena watch Ilukshuk when
            Ilukshuk was mad?
            Fighting spirit + manner seize on lawyers +

O'C.   Now I protest my Lord how can such a woman know
            a man's mental condition?

*Further ??s on I's 3 wives + how he treated them Strest fact that he hunted + fed
them w. white man's food. I. good hunter not much good for people (titter)*

Int.   *Lots more boys good hunters like Ilukshuk (he seems to see wave of
            feeling going to prove I. a (villain so adds this on his own as it were*

Books read May–Oct. 1926

Lost Endeavour   Masefield

The Alhambra   Washington Irving

Astoria

Mendel   G. Cannan

Captives   Galsworthy

The Gray Nuns in the Far North   P. Duchaussois

Odyssey   12 books

Down the Mackenzie + up the Yukon in 1906   Elihu Stewart

The Toilers of the Sea   Victor Hugo

Maria Chapdelaine   L. Hemon

Romance   J. Conrad

Moby Dick   H. Melvill

Journal   Mackenzie

Bannock

1 teaspoon B. powder

1 cup flour

1/2 tablespoonful lard   Prick

Dough Nuts

1 cup sugar

1 pinch salt

1 cup diluted milk

2 cups flour

2 teaspoons B. powder

fry in lard flat pieces

Mukluk

Parkie

C.C.R. received 15$ for Boots

Received for Pictures

Mrs Hastings	Sea Pinks in June		10.00
Mr O'Connor	Woodpile in Oil Well		10.00
Mr. Howatt	Sunset + Bonfire not paid 15.00		15.00
Canon Hester	Chartres	15.00	
	Santa Margherita	15.00	
	Scilly S. Helen's	10.00	
10.00	Fort Macpherson		
10.00	Schooners Aklavik		95.00
5.00	Schooners Fort Smith		
10.00	Sunset Mission Island		
20.00	Mackenzie River calm water		
Mr. West 12.50	Sunset Gt. Slave Lake		
15.00	La Roche		
7.50	Mackenzie R		
12.50	Fort Smith Rapids		
12.50	Bear Rock		105.00
15.00	Aklavik		
5.00	Mackenzie R.		
5.00	Brabant R.		
20.00	Mackenzie R.		
Canon Hester	Herefordshire Garden		17.50
Dr Burke	Mackenzie R 20 Yukon 10 Drier Bay 5.00) 30.00		
SS Yukon (Drier Bay 10.00 Nenana 20 Bear Rock 12.50)			
			47.50
Mrs Lefevre Norway			12.50
			————
			342.50

Note to pages 226–229: *Vyvyan did not reproduce in her book any of the material that follows the account of the murder trial at the end of her field notes; however, for the sake of readability, these pages have not been set in italics.*

Mr Carel Eskimo Schooner
Fort Smith
June 11

_____

	miles
Macpherson down stream (canoe) to Rat R.	75
Rat R. to Destruction City dead water (canoe)	20
To Top of Rapids (walk)	35
Top of Rapids to Loon Lake ⎤ Summit ⎦ walk?	15
Summit to Bell R. Portage	1/4
Little Bell to La Pierre House 5 days	
2 days La Pierre House to Rampart	

Carel did this in 1913 in 11 days in scow with 1 ton stuff: 5 people.

Paid for both

	£ – s – d
R. Tkts Quebec Calgary	49 – 6
Berths Winnipeg	2 – 12 – 6
Berths Edmonton	1 – 10 –
Daily Expenses 7 days Quebec–Edmonton including shoppings +c	9 – 10 –
Hudson's Bay Co. 2 Tkts Aklavik 339$	71 – – –
Outfit odds + ends about	6 – – –
4 days Edmonton ~~Hotel~~ food +c+c	5 – – –
Macdonald Hotel 4 days	5 – 5 –
Hudson's Bay Co Food for 4 for 14 days	10 – 10 –
Freight for same Waterways–Aklavik $39	8 – 2 – 6
Parsons 90$ canoe 7$ paddles + rope 30$ gas boat	26 – 9 – 4
127 Convent	17 – – –
Doctor 15$ Wireless 2.70	3 – 10 – 0
Two Guides Rat River 420$ 14$@15 days	88 – – – –
David 5 days	10 – 10 – –
Yukon Wireless Washingtn	2 – 10 – –
Tkts Nenana	20 –

_____

£ 336 – 9 – 10

Baggage Taken
Luggage 175 lbs 40-40-30-65 = 175)
Groceries 295 lbs   = 295)   470 lbs

	£ - s - d
R'way Tickets Seward	10 - -
⎰ Nenana Pub	
⎱ Curry Pub +c $7.95	4 - 10 -
⎰ Anchorage + Meals Pub	
⎱ Seward Luggage +c	2 - -
⎰ Ship Tip's Luggage Hats	
⎱ Seattle Victoria Tkts	12 - -
Tkts Calgary $52	
Sleeping berth 4 nights 20$	15 - -
Photos Shoes Cable +c	2 - -
Garibaldi	17 - -
Great Central	12 - -

74 - 10 - -
336 - 9 - 10
_____
410 - 19 - 1

Tkts Seward–Seattle   30 - - -

440 - 19 - 10

D Dashwood   7 - 10 - -

448 - 9 - 10

Recommended by D. Dashwood
S. Francis Hotel
Vancouver
(nr Station + Pier)
(cheap + clean)

James Bay or Strathcona
Victoria

BIRDS OF EASTERN CANADA   P.A. Taverner
recommends
COLOUR KEY NORTH AMERICAN BIRDS
F.M. Chapman + CK Reid
$2.50
KEY TO THE BIRDS OF N. AMERICA
Elliot Coues 1903 2 vols.

General
HOW TO STUDY BIRDS
THE SPORT OF BIRD STUDY ⎤— H.K. Job
WILD WINGS   ⎦

BIRD CRAFT   M.O. Wright
RAMBLES OF A CANADIAN NATURALIST   S.T. Wood

May 15th Inland   GDS £281
"   "   CCR £273   £3 Aklavik Boots

Estimated cost of Trip for each
_____

	£ - s - d
Southampton–Quebec Return	33 - - -
Quebec to Edmonton Return	24 - 5 - 8
Standard or Tourist sleeper	8 - 0 - 0
Food + Inns Quebec–Edmonton	10
Ticket Parksville–Edmonton	15

£90 - 5 - 8

	£ - s - d
Edmonton to Aklavik	40 - - - -
Aklavik to Fort Yukon	50 - - - -
Fort Yukon to Seward	15 - - - -
Seward to Seattle	16 - - - -
Seattle to Parksville	5

£126 - 0 - 0

	£ - s - d
Vancouver Island	50 - 0 - 0

Details of Aklavik - Fort Yukon

2 guides 13 days	364	
@14.00		
1 guide Porcupine	50	= £130
Canoe	100	
Grub for 3 @ 20 days	115	
" " @ 13 = 1 1/2 {629		

W.J. Christie	300	Paris Buildings - Winnipeg
Gordon McTavish	200	Trust + Loan Bld "
H.A.O. Warner	21	Credit Foncier - Edmonton

Dr + Mrs Burke   Fort Yukon Mission

John F. Moran   Constable A.B. Thornthwaite
N.W.T. Branch   R.N.W.M. Police
Dept. of Interior   Rampart House Y.T.
Ottawa   via Fort Yukon
                              Alaska

Irving B. Howatt   Dr R.W. Reynolds
728 Tegler Buildings   237 S. Hill Avenue
Edmonton   Pasadena California

L. Romanet
H.B. Co.
Edmonton

Archdeacon Whittaker
Penetang Rectory
Ontario

Total Expenditure
£278 - 3 - 0

Guides-   Lazarus Sittichili
          Jimmy Koe
          ——————
          David Elias   (alias)

Appendix 2

*List of North American plants
collected by Gwendolen Dorrien Smith and Clara Coltman Rogers
May to July 1926*

Written in Vyvyan's hand and reproduced here in the original order and numbering, this list represents plants found by the women on their route, extending from the prairies to the Pacific Coast. Added to botanical names are brackets containing, in order of appearance, the following:

- common names;
- references to sources in which descriptions and, in the case of Trelawny, colour photographs of the species occur; and,
- in the case of first appearances of genera in this list, the numbers, if any, of additional species of the same genus, or duplicates of a particular species.

Authorities are cited (with a few exceptions) as Vyvyan originally recorded them—these do not in all cases conform to current nomenclature.

May 26 Wynyard, Saskatchewan

1   *Comandra pallida* A. DC. [bastard toadflax—SCOGGAN 610]
2   *Astragalus hypoglottis* L. [milk vetch, locoweed, rattlepod—SCOGGAN 983; also, see below, nos. 67, 167]
3   *Thermopsis rhombifolia* Richards. [prairie bean—SCOGGAN 1027]

May 26 [sic: 30] Capital Hill, Edmonton, Alberta

4   *Smilacina stellata* Desf. [star-flowered Solomon's-seal—TRELAWNY 5, also false Solomon's-seal—SCOGGAN 504]
5   *Cornus stolonifera* Michx. [red osier dogwood, western dogwood—TRELAWNY 100, SCOGGAN 1184; also, see below, no. 28]
6   *Lonicera involucrata* Banks [black twinberry—SCOGGAN 1419; also, see below, no. 8]
7   *Prunus demissa* Walp. [choke-cherry—SCOGGAN 942; also, see below, nos. 15, 76]
8   *Lonicera glauca* Hill [limber honeysuckle—SCOGGAN 1418]
9   *Ribes irrigum* Dougl. [Idaho gooseberry—SCOGGAN 877; also, see below, nos. 38, 41, 72, 75, 86]
10 *Anemone canadensis* L. [Canada anemone—SCOGGAN 722; also, see below, nos. 66, 85, 88, 105, 150, 237]
11 *Aralia nudicaulis* L. [wild sarsaparilla—SCOGGAN 1149]
12 *Actaea spicata* L. [red baneberry—SCOGGAN 720]
13 *Streptopus amplexifolius* DC. [twisted stalk—TRELAWNY 4, SCOGGAN 505]
14 *Nasturtium palustre* var. *hispidum* Fisch et Mey. [yellow cress-SCOGGAN 844]
15 *Prunus* — [one or another species of plum or cherry]
16 *Valeriana sylvatica* Banks [marsh valerian—SCOGGAN 1428; also, see below, no. 103]
17 *Vicia americana* Muhl. [vetch, tare—SCOGGAN 1035]
18 *Viola canadensis* L. [Canada violet, tall white violet—SCOGGAN 1109; also, see below, nos. 47, 127]

19   *Thalictrum dioicum* L. [meadow-rue—SCOGGAN 757]

20   *Mertensia paniculata* Don [tall lungwort, bluebells—
TRELAWNY 136, SCOGGAN 1290]

21   *Lathyrus ochroleucus* Hook. [vetchling, wild pea—SCOGGAN
1001]

22   *Maianthemum canadense* Greene [wild lily-of-the-valley—
SCOGGAN 501]

23   *Cerastium arvense* L. [mouse-ear chickweed—TRELAWNY 22;
field chickweed—SCOGGAN 685; also, see below, nos. 36,
63]

24   *Fragaria virginiana* Duchesne [wild strawberry-TRELAWNY 69;
strawberry—SCOGGAN 919; also, see below, no. 56]

25   *Mitella nuda* L. [stoloniferous mitrewort—TRELAWNY 53;
also bishop's-cap—SCOGGAN 869]

26   *Arenaria lateriflora* L. [grove-sandwort—SCOGGAN 679; also,
see below, nos. 64, 124, 137, 163, 175]

27   *Rubus arcticus* L. [dwarf raspberry, nagoon berry—
TRELAWNY 80; also blackberry, bramble—SCOGGAN 956;
also, see below, nos. 31, 249, 251]

28   *Cornus canadensis* L. [dwarf dogwood, bunchberry—
TRELAWNY 101; also dwarf cornel—SCOGGAN 1182]

29   *Corydalis aurea* Willd. [yellow corydalis, golden corydalis—
TRELAWNY 41, SCOGGAN 774]

Anzac, Alberta

30   *Ledum latifolium* Ait. [Labrador tea—SCOGGAN 1203; also,
see below, no. 174]

31   *Rubus chamaemorus* L. [cloudberry—TRELAWNY 81; baked-
apple berry—SCOGGAN 956]

32   *Draba nemorosa* L. [draba—SCOGGAN 825; also, see below,
nos. 53, 125]

33   *Ranunculus fascicularis* L. [early buttercup or crowfoot—
SCOGGAN 747; also, see below, nos. 79, 94, 95, 183, 207,
241]

34   *Corallorhiza innata* R. Br. [early or pale coral-root—HULTÉN
492, SCOGGAN 528]

June 2 Waterways, Alberta

35   *Salix sessifolia* Nutt. [river willow—SCOGGAN 569; also, see
below, no. 77]

36   *Cerastium viscosum* L.? [mouse-ear chickweed—SCOGGAN
687]

37   *Arabis* [one or another species of rock-cress; also, see
below, nos. 80, 90, 231, 243]

June 2 Fort McMurray Athabasca River, Alberta

38   *Ribes hudsonianum* Richards. [northern black currant—
TRELAWNY 56, SCOGGAN 877]

39   *Primula farinosa* L. [bird's-eye-primrose—SCOGGAN 1224]

40   *Trientalis americana* Pursh [American star-flower—SCOGGAN
1227]

41   *Ribes americanum* Mill. [wild black currant—SCOGGAN 876]

42   *Potentilla anserina* L. [silver leaf—BLACK 29; silverweed—
TRELAWNY 74, SCOGGAN 929; also, see below, nos. 54,
69, 70, 81, 159, 178, 219]

43   —

44   *Elaeagnus argentea* Pursh [buffalo-berry—SCOGGAN 1123;
also, see below, no. 71]

45   *Erigeron philadelphicus* L. [fleabane—SCOGGAN 1544; also, see
below, nos. 157, 168, 173, 187, 194]

46   *Hedysarum mackenzii* Richards. [northern sweet-vetch, wild
sweet pea—TRELAWNY 87, SCOGGAN 997]

47   *Viola* [one or another species of violet]

48   *Sisyrinchium angustifolium* Mill. [blue-eyed grass—SCOGGAN
522]

49   *Vaccinium* — [one or another species of blueberry, bilberry;
also, see below, nos. 55, 262]

50   *Echinospermum redowskii* Lehm. [stickseed—SCOGGAN 1286;
also, see below, no. 208]

51   *Saxifraga tricuspidata* Rete. [three-toothed saxifrage, prickly
saxifrage—TRELAWNY 66, SCOGGAN 893; also, see below,
nos. 121, 130, 149, 151, 169, 234]

52   *Androsace septentrionalis* L. [pygmy flower, fairy candelabra—
TRELAWNY 120, SCOGGAN 1217]

53   *Draba nemorosa* L. [as above, no. 32]

54   *Potentilla* [one or another species of cinquefoil]

—   *Woodsia ilvensis* R. Br. [rusty or fragrant woodsia—SCOGGAN
172]

Fort Fitzgerald, Alberta

55   *Vaccinium* [one or another species of blueberry, bilberry]

56   *Fragaria virginiana* Duchesne [as above, no. 24]

57   *Habenaria* [one or another species of bog orchid; also, see
below, nos. 84, 254, 258, 260]

58   *Ophrys auriculata* (Wiegand) House [auricled twayblade—
SCOGGAN 540]

59   *Antennaria canadensis* Greene [pussy-toes, everlasting,
ladies'-tobacco—SCOGGAN 1467]

60   *Pyrola* [one or another species of wintergreen; also, see below, no. 61]

61   *Pyrola elliptica* Nutt. [shinleaf—SCOGGAN 1191]

62   *Rosa acicularis* Lindl. [prickly rose—TRELAWNY 80, SCOGGAN 947]

63   *Cerastium arvense* L. [as above, no. 23]

64   *Arenaria* [one or another species of sandwort]

65   *Chrysosplenium* [one or another species of golden carpet, golden saxifrage; also, see below, no. 138]

June 10 Fort Smith, NWT

66   *Anemone patens* var. *nuttalliana* A. Gray [pasque-flower, wild crocus—TRELAWNY 31; also prairie-smoke, prairie-crocus, lion's-beard—SCOGGAN 724]

67   *Astragalus alpinus* L. [alpine milk-vetch, mountain locoweed—TRELAWNY 84, SCOGGAN 983]

68   —

69   *Potentilla* [one or another species of cinquefoil]

70   *Potentilla* [one or another species of cinquefoil]

71   *Elaeagnus* ? [perhaps silverberry—TRELAWNY 95, or another species of oleaster—SCOGGAN 1122]

72   *Ribes petiolare* Dougl. [gooseberry, currant—SCOGGAN 877]

73   *Shepherdia canadensis* Nutt. [soopolallie, buffalo-berry, soap-berry—TRELAWNY 95; bear-berry—BLACK 45, SCOGGAN 1123]

74   *Viburnum pauciflorum* Pylaie [squashberry, mooseberry—SCOGGAN 1424]

75   *Ribes hudsonianum* Richards. [as above, no. 38]

76   *Prunus americana* Marsh. [American plum—SCOGGAN 939]

77   *Salix* [perhaps arctic willow (*Salix arctica*)—TRELAWNY 15, SCOGGAN 563]

78   *Orchis rotundifolia* Pursh [one-leaf orchid, round-leaf orchid, fly-speckled orchid—TRELAWNY 8, SCOGGAN 543; also, see below, no. 126]

79   *Ranunculus lapponicus* L. [Lapland buttercup—SCOGGAN 750]

80   *Arabis holboellii* Hornem. [rock-cress—SCOGGAN 796]

81   *Potentilla fruticosa* L. [shrubby cinquefoil—TRELAWNY 75, SCOGGAN 932]

82   *Petasites sagittatus* (Pursh) A. Gray [arrow-leaved sweet colts-foot—TRELAWNY 173, SCOGGAN 1584; also, see below, no. 236]

83   *Taraxacum officinale* Weber [common dandelion—TRELAWNY 182, SCOGGAN 1619; also, see below, no. 155]

84   *Habenaria bracteata* R. Br. [frog-orchis—SCOGGAN 538]

85   *Anemone multifida* Poir. [red windflower—BLACK 17; cut-leaf anemone—TRELAWNY 30, SCOGGAN 723]

Great Slave Lake, Mission Is., NWT

86   *Ribes lacustre* Poir. [swamp gooseberry, bristly black currant, prickly currant—TRELAWNY 57, SCOGGAN 877]

87   *Senecio cymbalarioides* Nutt. [few-leaved groundsel, alpine meadow butterweed—TRELAWNY 177, SCOGGAN 1599; also, see below, nos. 118, 156, 186, 188(B), 195, 199, 247(B)]

88   *Anemone multifida* DC. [as above, no. 85; SCOGGAN makes a distinction]

89   *Geranium carolinianum* L. [cranesbill, wild geranium—SCOGGAN 1045]

90   *Arabis* [one or another species of rock-cress]

91   *Calla palustris* L. [wild calla lily—A-Y 3, SCOGGAN 454; water arum—BLACK 38, SCOGGAN 454; also, see below, no. 102]

92   *Calypso borealis* Salisb. [likely *C. bulbosa* (L.) Oakes: calypso, fairy slipper, lady's-slipper, false lady's-slipper—TRELAWNY 9, SCOGGAN 527]

Fort Simpson, NWT

93   *Stellaria borealis* Bigel. [chickweed, starwort—SCOGGAN 707; also, see below, nos. 133, 146, 226]

94   *Ranunculus* [one or another species of buttercup]

95   *Ranunculus lapponicus* L. [as above, no. 79]

96   *Empetrum nigrum* L. [crowberry—TRELAWNY 93, SCOGGAN 1062]

Wrigley, NWT

97   *Chenopodium capitatum* Benth. and Hook. [goosefoot—BLACK 91; strawberry blite—TRELAWNY 21, and Indian paint—SCOGGAN 650; also, see below, no. 206]

98   *Plantago criopoda* Torr. [plantain, ribgrass, ribwort—HULTÉN 1070]

Arctic Red River, NWT

99   *Dryas integrifolia* Vahl [mountain avens, white dryas—TRELAWNY 68, SCOGGAN 915; also, see below, no. 123]

100   *Arnica alpina* Olin and Ladau [alpine arnica—TRELAWNY 160, SCOGGAN 1473-74; also, see below, no. 165]

North of Fort Norman (woodpile)

101 *Cypripedium parviflorum* Salisb. [yellow lady's-slipper, yellow moccasin flower—TRELAWNY 10, SCOGGAN 530]

Great Slave Delta, NWT

102 *Calla palustris* L. [as above, no. 91]

July 22 Fort McPherson, NWT

103 *Valeriana capitata* Willd. [capitate valerian, mountain heliotrope—TRELAWNY 153, SCOGGAN 1428]

104 *Caltha palustris* L. [marsh marigold, yellow marsh marigold—TRELAWNY 34; king-Cup, cowslip—SCOGGAN 728]

105 *Anemone canadensis* L. [as above, no. 10]

106 *Cardamine pratensis* L. [cuckoo flower—TRELAWNY 44; also lady's smock—SCOGGAN 809; also, see below, no. 162]

Arctic Red River, NWT

107 *Lupinus* [one or another species of lupine]

108 *Eriophorum vaginatum* L. [sheathed swamp grass, cotton grass—BLACK 93; SCOGGAN 441; also, see below, no. 116]

Aklavik, NWT

109 *Polygonum polymorphum* Ledeb. [knotweed, smartweed—SCOGGAN 631; also, see below, nos. 152, 164, 192, 204, 210]

110 *Silene* [one or another species of campion, catchfly; also, see below, nos. 122, 172]

111 *Menyanthes trifoliata* L. [buckbean—TRELAWNY 130; also bogbean—SCOGGAN 1245-46; also, see below, no. 253]

112 *Parnassia kotzebuei* Cham. & Schlecht. [Kotzebue grass-of-Parnassus—TRELAWNY 55; also bog-stars—SCOGGAN 870]

113 *Lycopodium annotinum* L. [stiff club-moss—SCOGGAN 134]

114 *Pedicularis* [one or another species of lousewort, wood-bettony; also, see below, nos. 158, 166, 182]

115 *Equisetum* [one or another species of horsetail]

116 *Eriophorum angustifolium* Roth. [cotton-grass—SCOGGAN 438]

117 *Ericaceae* — ? [one or another species of heath]

118 *Senecio palustris* var. *congestus* Hook. [perhaps mastodon flower, marsh fleabane (*Senecio congestus* R. Br. DC.)—TRELAWNY 175; groundsel, ragwort, squaw-Weed—SCOGGAN 1596]

119 *Sisymbrium canescens* Nutt. [tansy-mustard—SCOGGAN 814-15]

120 —

Loon Lake and McDougall Pass, NWT.

121 *Saxifraga hirculus* L. [yellow marsh saxifrage, bog saxifrage—TRELAWNY 62, SCOGGAN 888-89]

122 *Silene acaulis* L. [moss campion—TRELAWNY 25, SCOGGAN 700]

123 *Dryas octopetala* L. [mountain avens, eight-petalled dryas—TRELAWNY 68, SCOGGAN 916]

124 *Arenaria* [one or another species of sandwort]

125 *Draba alpina* L. [alpine draba—TRELAWNY 46, SCOGGAN 820]

126 *Orchis rotundifolia* Pursh [as above, no. 78]

127 *Viola palustris* L. [alpine marsh-violet—SCOGGAN 1113]

Rat River, NWT

128 *Polemonium humile* Willd. [see below, no. 129]

129 *Polemonium humile* var. *pulchellum* A. Gray [Greek valerian, Jacob's-ladder—SCOGGAN 1267]

130 *Saxifraga integrifolia* Hook. [white saxifrage—SCOGGAN 889]

131 *Oxycoccus macrocarpus* Pursh [large or American cranberry—SCOGGAN 1204]

132 *Pinguicula villosa* L. [hairy butterwort—TRELAWNY 150, SCOGGAN 1395]

133 *Stellaria* — [one or another species of starwort, chickweed]

134 *Andromeda polifolia* L. [bog rosemary, wild rosemary—TRELAWNY 106, SCOGGAN 1196]

135 *Gentiana acuta* Michx. [felwort, northern gentian—TRELAWNY 126, SCOGGAN 1242; also, see below, nos. 215, 248]

136 *Linnaea borealis* L. [twin-flower—TRELAWNY 152, SCOGGAN 1415-16]

137 *Arenaria* [one or another species of sandwort]

138 *Chrysosplenium tetrandum* Th. [northern water-carpet—TRELAWNY 52; golden carpet, golden saxifrage—SCOGGAN 864]

139 *Cheiranthus pygmaeus* DC. [wallflower, treacle-mustard—SCOGGAN 831]

140 *Papaver nudicaule* L. [Iceland poppy—TRELAWNY 41, SCOGGAN 770]

141 *Aconitum delphinifolium* DC. [northern monkshood—TRELAWNY 28; also wolfbane—SCOGGAN 719; also, see below, no. 214]

142 *Delphinium* [perhaps tall delphinium (*Delphinium glaucum* Wats.)—TRELAWNY 35, SCOGGAN 731-34]

143   *Castillcia* [likely a misspelling of *Castilleja*, one or another species of paintbrush]

144   *Crepis nana* Richards. [dwarf hawk's-beard—TRELAWNY 168, SCOGGAN 1532]

145   *Aster montanus* Rich. [aster—SCOGGAN 1504; also, see below, no. 154]

146   *Stellaria* [one or another species of chickweed, starwort]

147   *Erysimum* [one or another species of wallflower, treacle-mustard]

148   *Tofieldia calyculata* Wahl. [false asphodel; species lacking in TRELAWNY, SCOGGAN, HULTÉN, AND PORSILD AND CODY; also, see below, no. 263]

149   *Saxifraga punctata* L. [heart-leaved saxifrage—TRELAWNY 63, SCOGGAN 891-92]

150   *Anemone richardsonii* Hook. [yellow anemone—TRELAWNY 32, SCOGGAN 725]

151   *Saxifraga* [one or another species of saxifrage]

152   *Polygonum* [one or another species of knotweed, smartweed]

153   *Haplopappus* [one or another species of golden-weed]

154   *Aster* [one or another species of aster]

155   *Taraxacum ceratophorum* (Ledeb.) DC. [dandelion—SCOGGAN 1617]

156   *Senecio frigidus* L. [groundsel—TRELAWNY 175, SCOGGAN 1594]

157   *Erigeron uniflorus* L. [fleabane—SCOGGAN 1546]

158   *Pedicularis* [one or another species of lousewort, wood-bettony]

159   *Potentilla nivea* L. [snow cinquefoil—TRELAWNY 76, SCOGGAN 934]

160   *Epilobium latifolium* L. [broad-leaved fireweed, dwarf fireweed, river beauty—TRELAWNY 98, SCOGGAN 1134; also, see below, nos. 202, 221, 232, 246]

161   *Spiraea betulifolia* Pallas [spiraea—SCOGGAN 966; also, see below, no. 244]

162   *Cardamine* [one or another species of bitter cress]

163   *Arenaria lateriflora* L. [as above, no. 26]

164   *Polygonum viviparum* L. [alpine bistort—TRELAWNY 19, SCOGGAN 633]

165   *Arnica alpina* Olin and Ladau [as above, no. 100]

166   *Pedicularis* [one or another species of lousewort, wood-bettony]

167   *Astragalus eucosmus* Robinson [alpine milk-vetch, mountain locoweed—SCOGGAN 985]

168   *Erigeron uniflorus* L. [as above, no. 157]

169   *Saxifraga reflexa* Hook. [Yukon saxifrage—TRELAWNY 65, SCOGGAN 892]

170   —

171   *Saussurea monticola* Rich. [saussurea—SCOGGAN 1589]

172   *Silene douglasii* Hook. [campion—SCOGGAN 701]

173   *Erigeron compositus* Pursh [cutleaf fleabane—TRELAWNY 170, SCOGGAN 1541]

174   *Ledum palustre* L. [northern Labrador tea—TRELAWNY 110, SCOGGAN 1203]

175   *Arenaria* [one or another species of sandwort]

176   *Moneses uniflora* A. Gray [single delight—TRELAWNY 102; one-flowered pyrola—SCOGGAN 1189]

177   *Cassiope tetragona* Don [white mountain heather, arctic white heather—TRELAWNY 109, SCOGGAN 1199]

178   *Potentilla anserina* L. [as above, no. 42]

179   *Achillea millefolium* L. [common yarrow, milfoil—TRELAWNY 157, SCOGGAN 1458; also, see below, no. 205]

180   *Solidago multiradiata* Ait. [northern goldernrod, mountain goldenrod—TRELAWNY 181, SCOGGAN 1609]

181   *Oxytropis campestris* L. [late yellow locoweed, northern yellow oxytrope, field oxytrope—TRELAWNY 89; stemless locoweed—SCOGGAN 1018; also, see below, no. 188b]

182   *Pedicularis verticillata* L. [whorled lousewort—TRELAWNY 146, SCOGGAN 1370]

Loon Lake, Yukon

183   *Ranunculus pallasii* Schlecht. [buttercup, crowfoot—SCOGGAN 752]

186   *Senecio hookeri* Torr. and Gray [groundsel, ragwort, squaw-weed—SCOGGAN 1597]

Bell River, Yukon

185   *Sanguisorba media* L. [burnet; species lacking in TRELAWNY, SCOGGAN, HULTÉN, AND PORSILD AND CODY; also, see below, nos. 247, 261]

Porcupine River, Yukon and Alaska

184   *Allium schoenoprasum* [wild onion, wild chives—TRELAWNY 2, SCOGGAN 492]

187   *Erigeron glabellus* var. *asperus* T. and G. [fringed fleabane—A-Y 169, SCOGGAN 1542]

188(b)   *Senecio lugens* Richards. [morning groundsel—BLACK 46; black-tipped groundsel—TRELAWNY 177, SCOGGAN 1597]

188b *Oxytropis lambertii* Pursh [stemless locoweed—SCOGGAN 1020]

189 *Ligusticum* [one or another species of lovage; also, see below, no. 211]

190 *Linum lewisii* Pursh [perennial flax—SCOGGAN 1039]

191 *Matricaria discoidea* M. [pineapple-weed—SCOGGAN 1581-82]

192 *Polygonum aviculare* L. [prostrate knotweed—SCOGGAN 626]

193 *Campanula scouleri* Hook. [harebell, bellflower—SCOGGAN 1437; also, see below, no. 225]

194 *Erigeron glabellus* Nutt. var. *asperus* T. and G. [as above, no. 187]

195 *Senecio resedæfolius* Less. [dwarf arctic butterweed—TRELAWNY 179, SCOGGAN 1599]

196 *Rumex* [one or another species of dock, sorrel; also, see below, nos. 230, 245]

197 *Bupleurum ranunculoides* [thoroughwax—SCOGGAN 1161]

198 *Ornithogalum* [star-of-Bethlehem—SCOGGAN 502]

199 *Senecio frigidus* L. [as above, no. 156]

200 *Tanacetum huronense* Nutt. [tansy—SCOGGAN 1615]

201 *Galium boreale* L. [northern bedstraw—TRELAWNY 151, SCOGGAN 1410]

202 *Epilobium angustifolium* Scop. [fireweed, willow-herb—TRELAWNY 97; also great willow-herb—SCOGGAN 1133]

203 *Galega hicinalis* L. [goat's rue; species lacking in TRELAWNY, SCOGGAN, HULTÉN, AND PORSILD AND CODY]

204 *Polygonum polymorphum* Ledeb. [as above, no. 109]

Fort Yukon, Alaska

205 *Achillea multiflora* Hook. [yarrow—SCOGGAN 1459]

206 *Chenopodium capitatum* Benth. and Hook. [as above, no. 97]

207 *Ranunculus circinatus* Sibth. [white water-crowfoot—SCOGGAN 746]

208 *Echinospermum* [one or another species of stickseed, beggar's lice]

209 *Potamogeton perfoliatus* L. [pondweed—SCOGGAN 203]

210 *Polygonum amphibium* L. [water smartweed—TRELAWNY 18, SCOGGAN 625]

211 *Ligusticum* [as above, no. 189]

212 *Sagina* [one or another species of pearlwort; also, see below, no. 233]

[Because the leaf of the page is torn along the lower edge, item 213 is illegible.]

214 *Aconitum columbianum* Nutt. [aconite, monkswood, wolf-bane—SCOGGAN 719]

215 *Gentiana* [one or another species of gentian]

216 *Cicuta vagans* Greene [water-hemlock—SCOGGAN 1162]

Rampart River, Yukon

217 *Lithospermum angustifolium* Michx [stoneseed, gromwell, puccoon—SCOGGAN 1288]

218 *Trifolium hybridum* L. [alsike clover—SCOGGAN 1031; also, see below, no. 220]

219 *Potentilla hippiana* Lehm. [a species of cinquefoil lacking a common name—SCOGGAN 933]

220 *Trifolium macrocephalum* Poir. [a species of clover lacking a common name—SCOGGAN 1032]

221 *Epilobium horemanni* Reichenb. [alpine willow-herb—SCOGGAN 1133]

Tanana, Alaska

222 *Prenanthes alata* A. Gray [rattlesnake-root—SCOGGAN 1585]

Cordova, Alaska

223 *Apargidium boreale* Torr. and Gray [apargidium—SCOGGAN 147]

Seward, Alaska

224 *Geum macrophyllum* Willd. [large-leaved avens—TRELAWNY 71, SCOGGAN 922]

225 *Campanula lasiocarpa* Cham. [alpine harebell—TRELAWNY 154, SCOGGAN 1436]

226 *Stellaria* [one or another species of starwort, chickweed]

227 *Mimulus luteus* Linn. [monkey-flower—SCOGGAN 1360]

228 *Tiarella* [one or another species of laceflower, sugar-scoop; also, see below, no. 259]

229 *Medicago lupulina* L. [black medick—SCOGGAN 1014]

230 *Rumex acetosella* L. [sheep-sorrel, common sorrel—SCOGGAN 637]

231 *Arabis lyrata* L. [rock-cress—SCOGGAN 797]

232 *Epilobium* [one or another species of fireweed]

233 *Sagina saginoides* (L.) Britton [arctic pearlwort—SCOGGAN 696]

234 *Saxifraga* [one or another species of saxifrage]

235 *Oxyria ligyna* Hill [sorrel; species lacking in TRELAWNY, SCOGGAN, HULTÉN, AND PORSILD AND CODY]

236 *Petasites frigidus* Fr. [arctic sweet coltsfoot—TRELAWNY 173, SCOGGAN 1584]

237 *Anemone* [one or another species of anemone]

Tanana, Alaska

238 *Artemisia vulgaris* L. [common mugwort—SCOGGAN 1486; also, see below, no. 242]

Curry, Alaska

239 *Veratrum viride* Ait. [white hellebore, Indian poke—SCOGGAN 511]

Seward, Alaska

240 *Eriogynia pectinata* Hook. [partridge-foot—SCOGGAN 924]

241 *Ranunculus eschscholtzii* Schlecht. [mountain buttercup, Eschscholtz buttercup—TRELAWNY 36, SCOGGAN 747]

242 *Artemisia norvegica* Fr. [sagebrush, wormwood—SCOGGAN 1481]

243 *Arabis lyrata* L. [as above, no. 231]

244 *Spiraea silvester* Kost. [spiraea; species lacking in TRELAWNY, SCOGGAN, HULTÉN, AND PORSILD AND CODY]

245 *Rumex britannica* L. [water-dock—SCOGGAN 639]

246 *Epilobium luteum* Pursh [fireweed—SCOGGAN 1135]

247 *Sanguisorba sitchensis* Wate. [Sitka burnet—TRELAWNY 82; Canada burnet—SCOGGAN 962]

247(B) *Senecio triangularis* Hook. [spear-head senecio, arrowleaf senecio—TRELAWNY 179, SCOGGAN 1600]

Drier Bay, Knight Island, Alaska

248 *Gentiana douglasiana* Bong. [Douglas gentian—SCOGGAN 1240]

249 *Rubus pedatus* Smith [raspberry, blackberry, bramble—SCOGGAN 959]

250 *Drosera rotundifolia* L. [round-leaved sundew—TRELAWNY 50, SCOGGAN 852]

251 *Rubus spectabilis* Pursh [salmonberry—SCOGGAN 960]

Juneau, Alaska

252 *Impatiens œurea* Muhl. [perhaps a misspelling of *Impatiens aurella*: touch-me-not, balsam, jewelweed—SCOGGAN 1080]

Drier Bay, Knight Island, Alaska

253 *Menyanthes crista-galli* Menzies [deer-cabbage—SCOGGAN 1236]

Ketchikan, Alaska

254 *Habenaria* [one or another species of bog orchid]

255 *Kalmia glauca* Ait. [pale laurel, bog-laurel, swamp-laurel—SCOGGAN 1202]

256 *Romanzoffia sitchensis* Bong. [romanzoffia-SCOGGAN 1275]

257 *Menziesia* [fool's-huckleberry, false azalea—SCOGGAN 1204]

258 *Habenaria graminifolia* L. [bog-candle, scent-bottle—SCOGGAN 536]

259 *Tiarella trifoliata* L. [laceflower, sugar-scoop—SCOGGAN 895]

260 *Habenaria* [one or another species of bog orchid]

261 *Sanguisorba media* L. [as above, no. 185]

262 *Vaccinium parvifolium* Smith [tail huckleberry—SCOGGAN 1212]

263 *Tofieldia glutinosa* Willd. [western false asphodel—TRELAWNY 6, SCOGGAN 507]

Wrangell, Alaska

264 *Veronica americana* Schwein [brooklime, American speed-well—TRELAWNY 148, SCOGGAN 1385]

265 *Harrimanella hypnoides* Coville [moss-heather—SCOGGAN 1198]

Ketchikan, Alaska

266 *Gaultheria shallon* Pursh [salal, wintergreen—SCOGGAN 1201]

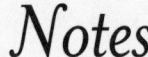

Notes

to Chapters of the Book
and to Vyvyan's Field Notes

ABBREVIATIONS:

AATC	Alberta and Arctic Transportation Company
ACC/GSA	Anglican Church of Canada/General Synod Archives
AGNRC	Archives of the Grey Nuns Regional Centre, Edmonton
CPR	Canadian Pacific Railway
GSCI	Gwich'in Social and Cultural Institute, Yellowknife
HBC	Hudson's Bay Company
PAM, HBCA	Provincial Archives of Manitoba, Hudson's Bay Company Archives
NAC	National Archives of Canada, Ottawa
NWMP	North-West Mounted Police
NWT	Northwest Territories
NWC	North West Company
RNWMP	Royal North-West Mounted Police
RCMP	Royal Canadian Mounted Police
RGS	Royal Geographical Society, London

CHAPTER 1: DREAMING OF THE JOURNEY

Henry van Dyke
American Presbyterian minister, professor of English
Literature at Princeton University, editor, and author of forty-
four books between 1884 and 1927, Henry Van Dyke

(1852-1933) wrote moralistic essays and sermons, romances
and short stories, poetry, literary criticism, and travel sketches,
including *Camp Fires and Guide Posts* (1921). They were "distinguished for their graceful style, but representative of the
Victorian standards of taste" (*Who* 2:1445-46; James Hart
879). Those standards were upheld through Van Dyke's
membership in the last American generation to champion
Ideality. Through many publications, including the magazine,
Outlook, this group aimed to "prolong the tradition of
American Idealism by presenting a unified front to the materi-
alism of the late nineteenth century, resentful of the claims of
the realists" (Spiller *et. al.* 1:809). His first book, *The Reality of
Religion* (1884), "presages his lifelong attempt to fuse religion
and practical, everyday living in a keen personal enjoyment of
life" (Herzberg *et. al.*, 1174). (Although in Chpt 24 Vyvyan uses
the term "Idealism" to describe a quality in Lazarus Sittichinli
which she cannot otherwise identify, she does not seem to have
this tradition in mind.)

CHAPTER 2: WE PLAN THE JOURNEY

**Mr A. Brabant, the managing director of the Alberta and
Arctic Transportation Company Limited**
Angus Brabant (1866-1928) joined the HBC as an apprentice
clerk in 1886. After serving at Manitoba House, Cumberland
House, and Fort Smith, he became inspector of the Athabasca
district in 1905. He was manager of the Mackenzie River

district 1908-20, during which period posts on the Arctic coast were established. On his first trip north as manager, he travelled with Agnes Deans Cameron, who mentioned him in her book (26; rev. ed. 20). In 1920 he became Fur Trade Commissioner ("Brabant"). Following the advice of senior traders, Brabant led the HBC on an aggressive campaign against its competition, Lamson and Hubbard, which ended with that company's ceasing operation in March 1923 and the HBC's acquisition of its assets in 1924, including a three-year-old subsidiary, AATC (Ray 159). Thereafter, it "was operated as a part of the HBC's Mackenzie River Transport. Its legal existence as a separate company continued until 1941" (Morton). Brabant retired in January 1927 and died at Vancouver 8 November 1928 ("Brabant").

Mrs Laura Frazeur

Laura Frazeur (1871-1933) was born Ann Laura Renshaw; she married Jesse Frazeur in 1890. She studied classics at the University of Chicago, completed her M.A. in 1908, and began work on a Ph.D. in 1910. She earned her teaching certificate at the Illinois State Normal University in 1890, and taught at various schools in the Chicago area and at Crane College until her death in 1933. She was a member of both the American Alpine Club and the Cordon Club of Chicago; she was a Mountaineer of Seattle, and she served as secretary of the Geographical Society of Chicago (Rayfield). She was an "ardent mountain climber," and had climbed in Greece and in the Canadian Rockies ("Mrs. Frazeur"). Although the book does not identify the Laura Frazeur of Romanet's letter as the woman who failed to treat her guides with respect and "had to return and take another route with another party" when they refused to guide her farther, the field note for 27 May clarifies that they are the same person. If Frazeur wrote an account of her own northern journey, it has not yet come to light.

L. Romanet

Louis Auguste Romanet (1880-1964) was born in France and, at age twenty-three, resigned a commission in the French infantry to join the French fur-trading company Revillon Frères. He served in Ungava 1903-16, then joined the HBC at Moose Factory as general inspector. He served in the French army during the First World War, then returned to the HBC. From 1923 until he left the HBC, he was district manager of the Mackenzie and Athabasca districts, and general manager of

the AATC (Romanet). In 1927, he oversaw a loss of $40,000; his employment with the HBC ceased in 1930 (Bonnycastle, *Gentleman* 15, 134). After leaving the HBC, he was employed as Mackenzie River agent for several oil companies (Romanet). The story of his Ungava years was written by Lowell Thomas and published under the title *Kabluk of the Eskimo* in 1932.

The memorandum by Mr Warner

Copies of two different memoranda by Harry Warner remain in the Vyvyan Papers: one, "From the Mackenzie to the Yukon," is fifteen single-spaced, typewritten pages; the other, "Re. Mackenzie River — Yukon Trip," is seven single-spaced, typewritten pages. It bears a thematic resemblance to "A Summer Trip to the Arctic," a tourism promotion by Robert Watson, editor of *The Beaver* from 1923 to 1933, which had appeared in the magazine's issue for June 1925. The March and June 1926 issues contained the first page-length advertisements by the AATC. The second of these quotes verse by "R.W." (probably Watson) in the manner of Robert Service, which enjoins its reader to "forget awhile the city's noise and seethe" and to spend thirty-five days seeking "the freedom of God's Northern open spaces" ("To the Arctic"). Written in a similar vein to encourage tourist traffic, the longer of Warner's two articles deviates from factual into purple prose, such as the following:

> any person in moderate health who can afford a two months' summer vacation and a thousand dollars, may experience the thrill of travel and adventure well beyond the edge of things. Can stand on arctic shores, rub noses with eskimos, barter with the Indians and, by slight deviations from the beaten track, can pitch his tent in solitudes where no white man has ever before been. Fur traders and missionaries, trappers and whalemen, prospectors, sourdoughs and squaws; colour that is strictly local and not imported and where a traveller is a man and a friend and not a mere tourist. And all this is without leaving the American continent and without being more than two months out of touch with the outside world, office or business. ...
>
> It is the journey across the arctic mountains between the MacKenzie and the Yukon that constitutes the piece de resistance of the trip from the adventurer's point of view ... [It] is not particularly arduous to anyone at all experienced

in the out-of-doors, even though such experience may have been gained no further afield than the Adirondacks or the woods of Maine and it has been accomplished winter and summer by hundreds of travellers since the country was first opened up by white men. Many white women have made the journey and more than one sick person has been carried across the mountains to where, in earlier days, the nearest succour could be obtained. The trails followed may almost be called commercial highways, for they have been used by traders, prospectors and explorers for a century past. With the establishment of steamboat transportation on the Yukon and Mackenzie Rivers and the decline of the gold-mining industry with its constant drift of prospectors to and fro, the trail has ceased to be an essential commercial link and the amount of travel passing over it today is but a fraction of that of former years. Nevertheless, there is still sufficient movement back and forth of natives and occasional white men to keep the memory of the trail alive and no difficulty will be found in obtaining Indians perfectly competent to conduct a party across the divide on any route. Indeed, the landmarks and trail signs are such that any experienced traveller could dispense with guides, though such a course is not recommended. And as not the least important function of so-called guides is that of doing all the manual work of the trip, the paddling, tracking, camp-making, etc., in such capacity alone their services are desirable and they are worthy of their hire. (Warner, "From the Mackenzie" 1, 2)

CHAPTER 3: SOUTHAMPTON TO EDMONTON (15–27 MAY)

Vyvyan's field notes commence with the entry starting this chapter, slightly edited for publication. The chapter emphasizes the women's strong characters more than the field notes do at this point: Dorrien Smith's indignation at the shipboard medical inspection and Gordon Mactavish's tale of missing the women at the Winnipeg train station because their apparent certainty belied the possibility that they could be strangers to the city do not appear in the field notes, nor do the field notes emphasize the women's public notoriety to the same extent as the book.

"without form and void"
This is a quotation of Genesis 1:2.

CHAPTER 4: OUTFITTING IN EDMONTON (27 MAY–1 JUNE)

The reference to the prospect of eating goose during the canoe trip has no corresponding entry in the field notes and seems designed only to foreshadow the dinner described in Chpt 15. Generally, this chapter follows the field notes' depiction of Edmonton—rather unimpressive in comparison to Winnipeg, where the women had enjoyed a guided whirlwind tour while the transcontinental train paused for twenty-four hours. This contrast might be accounted for by the women's knowing no one in Edmonton, in their having to spend time shopping for supplies and attending to the logistics of a northern itinerary (activities that evidently appealed to neither woman), and simply coming to another prairie city still without beginning to head north—after all, they had no "wilderness" experience to show for their eighteen days (14-31 May) of travel. Included in American Fullerton Waldo's six articles and one book about his travels north and down the Mackenzie in 1922 is a very different view of Edmonton, one that includes, if fulsomely, a high regard rather than rebuke for its citizens' optimism (*Down* 1-22).

Edmonton
By 1926, Edmonton had been known for three decades as the Gateway to the North, thanks largely to those who travelled to the Klondike by way of the city during the gold rush in the last years of the nineteenth century. According to the Dominion Census of 1926, the city's population was 65,163 that year, having shot up from only a fifth of that just two decades earlier. It was a burgeoning regional centre for agriculture, but also had served the entire near North and western Arctic from as early as the last decade of the eighteenth century. Then, the HBC, as part of its foray into the Eldorado of the Athabasca district, established posts on the North Saskatchewan River in the vicinity of the present-day location of the city. The more southern post was to provide reliable supplies of pemmican (made from pounded, dried buffalo meat, unobtainable in large quantities farther north) to permit brigades of voyageurs to complete long-distance return trips by canoe to Hudson Bay

before freeze-up each year. Edmonton's ambitions mounted when it became the provincial capital in 1906, a year after the Province of Alberta was created; in 1908, it gained approval as the site of the provincial university. However, the choice of the southern prairies, rather than the Yellowhead Pass, for the transcontinental route of the Canadian Pacific Railway (CPR) had given Calgary, Edmonton's provincial rival to the south, an economic advantage and consequently greater growth in population from 1883 onward. In 1891, Strathcona, on the south bank of the North Saskatchewan, obtained rail service from the Calgary and Edmonton Railway, but only in 1905, when the Canadian Northern Railway completed a bridge across the North Saskatchewan River downriver from Edmonton, did the north side of the city receive train service. Thus, Vyvyan and Dorrien Smith arrived on a route little more than two decades old. (See MacGregor, *Edmonton*, and Stelter.)

Edmonton, now a suburb of London, England, was the birth place of John Peter Pruden, an early HBC clerk. The name itself derives "from the Anglo-Saxon Christian name *Eadhelm* and *Tun* or *ton*, which means 'field' or 'enclosure'" (Harrison 81).

a large expensive hotel
According to Vyvyan's field note for 27 May, the women stayed at the Macdonald Hotel. Restored and re-opened in 1991 after being shut since 1983, this hotel now operates in as elegant a style as here concerned Vyvyan. Opened in 1915 as a Grand Trunk Pacific hotel, it was designed in what became known as the Canadian national château style (sixteenth-century French Renaissance) by architects Ross and MacFarlane of Montreal, creators of the Château Laurier in Ottawa (1912) and the Fort Garry in Winnipeg (1913; White and Baxter 14). Hotel Macdonald, as it is now known, perches atop the north bank of the North Saskatchewan River valley, at the corner of Jasper Avenue and 100 Street, and perpetuates the name of Sir John A. Macdonald (1815-91), Canada's first prime minister (1867-73, 1878-91). At least one of Dorrien Smith's watercolours was made of the river valley as viewed from the women's hotel room (see above, 190). As to its being "a large expensive hotel," Vyvyan's accounts, which occur in the field notes following the last dated entry (227), show that the ladies' bill came to £5 5s, or about $25.00. (Vyvyan's calculations throughout show a conversion rate of about $4.70-$4.80 per pound sterling.)

A reporter, a woman, asking questions about our trip.
Neither "Miss Moon" nor the newspaper that employed her have been identified; moreover, no field note mentions her. However, it is clear that the women's arctic journey attracted attention from newspapers in Winnipeg ("Two Englishwomen," "Social and Personal," "Return," "Englishwomen Brave"), Edmonton ("Women," "Two Women"), and London, England ("Englishwomen"), both before and after their trip and with varying degrees of accuracy. The novelty of women who travelled, particularly to the North, created public interest. Miss Moon was spurned by Dorrien Smith, not because the reporter showed interest in the journey itself, but because her interest fastened on the fact that it was two *women* who were about to undertake the arduous trip. Perhaps the denial of an interview can help both to identify Miss Moon as the editor of the "Women's Activities" page of the *Edmonton Journal*, and to explain the inaccuracy in the article that appeared on that page: it reported that the women "will travel into the north alone on a fishing and hunting trip" ("Women").

All the newspaper coverage emphasized the adventure of the women's journey. "Two Women on Arctic Jaunt to Use Canoe" was featured on the front page of the *Edmonton Journal* on the day of their arrival in the city, and included three sub-headlines: "Clara C. Rogers and Gwendolyn Darien-Smith [*sic*] Seek Adventure," "Both Hail from South of England," and "Both Went through War as Nurses with the British Army." But the most sensational report appeared in England. Under the title "Englishwomen in the Arctic," *The Daily Express* carried an empurpled account featuring photos of the two women and secondary headlines: "Nightmare Journey through Alaska," and "Mosquito Plague." Embarked on a "perilous adventure," the two are described as having survived terrible conditions: Vyvyan is quoted as saying that, "'Most of the days we walked in blazing sunshine, and at night we slept in a perishing Arctic cold'." The women returned home scarred by "a memory of mosquitoes that it will take months of cold weather to dim." The theme of the mosquitoes as the dark adversary is one of two that persists in the article: "They found ... on most of the journey wonderful masses of gorgeous coloured plants and flowers, but not once did they pause to admire [*sic*]. Always the mosquitoes drove them on." As well, the women, whose guides are not mentioned, are credited with killing a "grisly" bear; thus, the theme of pure adventure is established, then heightened by the implication that the women were keen to consume the bear meat, "their first fresh meat meal."

Historically, interest in women's travels *because* of gender was a mixed blessing: if a woman's narrative had the appeal of novelty and the titillation of a woman's "adventure" outside the safe space of domestic propriety, its authority as serious literature was often also discredited for those same reasons.

Mr Warner

It is unclear what relation Henry A.O. ("Harry") Warner had with the AATC and for how long. What is known is that in 1921 (presumably after he "had gone north as a teacher and had failed"), due to his extensive previous experience, he was working as superintendent and chief engineer for both the Alberta and Great Waterways Railway and the Lacombe and Northwestern Railway (Schneider 113). However, he was replaced by the end of that year and must have taken a position with the AATC after the HBC acquired it in 1924. In that year, he was photographed with Judge Lucien Dubuc on the SS *Distributor* sailing north down the Mackenzie River (Dubuc, Photo Scrapbook 21 recto). In the judge's scrapbook, as well, Warner is photographed as a member of the six-man jury panel (the custom at the time in Alberta, and so in the Northwest Territories) for the Inuit trials presided over by Dubuc on 7 July 1924 aboard the *Distributor* while it was at Akalvik. In his caption to the photograph, Dubuc lists Warner as an independent trader at Aklavik and Edmonton (Photo Scrapbook 42 verso; see also PAA A3698).

the manager of the great HB Company's store, Mr Dynes, drove us round Edmonton

F.E. Dynes had been appointed the store manager at Edmonton in the previous autumn. A photo of him illustrated the announcement of his promotion in the December 1925 issue of *The Beaver*, which described him as "a local man with eight years' merchandising experience in Chicago, two and a half years in Minneapolis and eight years in Edmonton" ("Introducing").

wild flowers … the beginning of a collection … for … the Kew Gardens Museum

The travellers' ignorance of their surroundings may be gauged from the implication that any specimens collected on Capital Hill (the site today of the Provincial Museum of Alberta and of the residence of the lieutenant-governor of the Province of Alberta) would be new to the Kew Herbarium. This need, if it had not already, would have been met by the Faculty of Science at the University of Alberta, established in 1908 across the river from the ladies' collecting grounds.

Dunvegan

Dunvegan Yards remains on the east side of St Albert Trail, north of the Yellowhead Trail, now well within Edmonton's city limits. It was the departure point for trains travelling the 480-km (300-mi) route to Waterways on the Alberta and Great Waterways Railway line (Kitto, *North West* 56). This train, which had earned the nickname of "Muskeg Limited" by 1920, when Philip Godsell rode it, was one of four Government of Alberta lines. Construction of it began in December 1913 and was completed as far as Lac la Biche in February 1915 (Schneider 75, 79; Hatcher, *Northern Alberta* 1).

Godsell's description of it in 1920, when contrasted with Vyvyan's, suggests that the train had both improved greatly but also lost some of its colourful character by 1926:

… a conglomeration of dirty red box-cars, flat-cars, and one very rickety old-fashioned coach with a caboose tacked on to the rear ….

The lucky ones got hard plush-covered berths in the coach but the majority were forced to make the best of the open flat-cars. As the engine gave her last wheezy whistle the nondescript train, with much bumping and a good deal of noise and ostentation, commenced her swaying journey through prairie land and muskeg.

Twice a day there would be a brief stop for meals, then the passengers would all pile out onto the track with frying pans and tea kettles in their hands, build hurried campfires, sling on the kettles, warm up a tin of pork and beans and snatch a hasty meal.

After the first fire every one knew everybody else and the artificial barriers which civilization imposes were very soon let down. …

A truly remarkable railroad was the A. & G. W., as the rotting box-cars, which had fallen from the crazy track into the ditch, so amply testified. Straight ahead it went, up hill, down dale, through the woods and into the deepest muskegs where, for hours at a time, the rails would be invisible beneath the watery slime. Once or twice, after frenzied efforts to reach the top of some ridge, the engine would stop with a loud despairing snort, then the conductor would apologetically ask all passengers to please jump off and walk in order to reduce the load.

    After backing up a couple of miles the engine would come swaying along, puffing and wheezing mightily, and finally top the hill. "All aboard" some overalled trainman would yell and we would jump on once again. Ere long the train would come to another stop—a clay-cut—and each passenger would have to take hold of the business end of a shovel and help remove a few tons of clay and earth which had fallen in upon the track. (*Arctic* 179–80).

At the railway station there was quite a crowd
According to Dorrien Smith's field note for 1 June, Richard Bonnycastle and John F. Moran numbered among those who boarded the train with them, while the well-wishers included Bishop Gray, his family, and Miss Ferguson. Arriving in the city in 1895, Henry Allen Gray served as the first Anglican bishop of Edmonton from 1914 to 1931. Dorrien Smith's field note for 31 May mentions visiting Mrs Gray at their home, 10049–103 Street.

the immensely long train
The size of the train is perhaps attributable to the fact that 1926 marked the first year the HBC decided to "re-route their 'West Arctic Trade Goods' via Waterways … instead of sending them via Bering Strait" (Hatcher, *Volume 2* 7). Sherwood Platt counted fifty-two cars when he boarded the train on 6 July 1926 (6). Waterways was the terminus of the railway line about three kilometres southeast of Fort McMurray. It was the transshipment point at which goods going north in the summer season were transferred from rail to steamer and barges on the Athabasca River (Mardon 204). Although she does not mention it in her book, Vyvyan did visit Fort McMurray while waiting at Waterways. Originally a NWC post abandoned some time after 1821 due to a smallpox epidemic, Fort McMurray was rebuilt by the HBC in 1870 and named after HBC factor William McMurray. It functioned as a fur trade post and transportation centre connecting Edmonton and the Athabasca district. Before the railway, travellers and freight travelled by wagon road from Edmonton to Athabasca Landing, and thence by barge down dangerous sets of rapids on the Athabasca River to Fort McMurray. Once the railway arrived, the town relied

for its existence on the Lake Athabasca fishery, salt extraction from the nearby salt plains, and its location near the Waterways transportation point (Cooke 99–102).

Field Note for Saturday 29 May
W.W. Cory Deputy Minister of Dept. of the Interior
William Wallace Cory assumed the office of commissioner of the NWT in 1918 (Fumoleau 155). (The territorial commissioner's role resembled that of provincial lieutenants-governor.)

Field Note for Sunday 30 May
Miss Ferguson Bishop Gray's governess came to lunch with us
Dorrien Smith's field note for this date identifies Miss Ferguson as a friend of Dorothy Dashwood, their hostess on Vancouver Island at the end of the trip.

CHAPTER 5: LURE OF THE NORTH (1–5 JUNE)

The book takes on a different style in this chapter's use of the present tense, creating a sense of timelessness lacking in both women's field note entries, which are full of concrete details about people and places, and daily information, such as the steamer's navigation of the river's varying course by having the "1/2 breed" mate take soundings from a canoe (4 June). At the end of the chapter, this information is embellished with physical description and transformed into the image of the mate silhouetted against the water, frozen in Vyvyan's memory and embodying the significance and triumph of the (white) pioneers of the North. Generally, the movement from field notes to book follows this pattern during the steamer journey, omitting some of the facts and information, and imbuing the book with an impressionistic sense of the timeless and endless space of the northern wilderness. Also evident throughout the book (and not the field notes) is Vyvyan's retrospective evaluation of herself and Gwen as tourists, "fair game to those men of the North who love to spin a yarn to the ignorant" (23).

the French-Canadian judge, going to Aklavik to preside at an Eskimo murder trial
Vyvyan's field notes clarify that this judge was Lucien Dubuc (1877–1956; "Chief"), the stipendiary magistrate for the NWT

at the time. The fourth of ten children born to Chief Justice of Manitoba Sir Joseph and Marie-Ann (*née* Henault) Dubuc, Lucien studied at the Jesuit College of St Boniface and the University of Manitoba, where he received his law degree in 1900. Marrying Marguerite Richard, he then moved to Edmonton (Dubuc, "Généalogie"), where he played an active part in the Francophone community, serving as secretary of the Separate School Board from 1901 to 1905 (E.J. Hart 33), as a member of the Saint-Jean-Baptiste Association and the Société du parler français (52), and as president of the Association canadienne-français de l'Alberta in the late 1920s (107). Dubuc ranked among the most prominent French-speaking lawyers in Edmonton. He was called to the Alberta Bench in 1920 (111) and became the chief justice of the Regional Court of Northern Alberta in 1944. In May 1924, he became the first judge in Alberta's history to hear a case entirely in French (112). In 1937, Dubuc received an honorary Doctor of Laws degree from Laval University ("News").

Dubuc's trip in 1926 with the Englishwomen was not the first he made to hear a trial in the Arctic. In 1920, Franklin Hugo Kitto had reported to the Department of the Interior that "the need for stipendiary magistrates being appointed was impressed on [him] at every post. An appeal from a decision of a local Justice of the Peace is practically an impossibility now" ("Report" 29). Likely in response to this situation, in 1921 Dubuc travelled to Fort Providence and Fort McPherson. He heard many cases, and, for the first time, sentenced a man, Albert Lebeau, to death (Philip Godsell, *Vanishing* 183-90). The trial at Fort Providence, held on 29 June, was the first trial by jury in the NWT (Fumoleau 172). In 1923, Dubuc travelled to Herschel Island, Yukon to hear the case against two Inuit: Tatamagana (also transcribed as Tatamigina, Tatamageena, and Tatamerana) and Aligoomiak (also transcribed as Alik Omiak, Alikomaik, and Alekamiaq). They were accused of killing RCMP Corp W.A. Doak and Otto Binder, a white trader, in April 1922 near Tree River (67°41'00" N, 111°53'00" W), east of Coppermine River in the central Arctic. (A photograph of the accused men is reproduced in the papers of Knud Rasmussen, the explorer from Greenland/Denmark [*Intellectual* facing 268].)

Extending from 16 to 20 July, the trial ended with the jury finding the men guilty of murder in the first degree and Dubuc sentencing them to death. This verdict and sentence kept Dubuc's name in the press for some time. James Richard

Lucas, the Anglican bishop of Mackenzie River 1913-26, attended the trial and denounced the verdict, citing such improprieties as having the two men testify against one another, rendering a verdict on evidence that would not have been sufficient to convict white men, bringing the wood needed to build the gallows with the trial party in advance of the proceedings, and delaying the sentencing until just before the judge's departure from Herschel Island. Lucas' complaints stirred a hot debate, especially in eastern Canada, where a reprieve was sought on the grounds that the Inuit were insufficiently familiar with "the laws of civilization." In the end, it was left to the federal cabinet to review the sentence. It was confirmed and the men were executed at Herschel Island 1 February 1924, the first Inuit executed for murder under Canadian law ("Eskimo Murder"; Philip Godsell, *Arctic* 234-39, 255, 263, 295; Mason 245-49; Morrison 160-61; Frank Peake, *The Bishop* 145).

However, the trial brought to public awareness both an image of Inuit as other than smiling, lovable children and the reliance on a policy of policing them in the absence of any policy for governing them. So sensational did the English press find the story that one newspaper reported the executions more than a month before they took place ("Eskimos Executed"). Rasmussen told the world that he had been "informed that this execution had cost Canada something like $100,000; among other expensive items being the cost of the executioner, who had to be brought up and kept there all the winter, as none of the Police themselves would have any hand in this part of the work" (*Across* 280).

Certainly, the observation made by Vyvyan in her field note for 11 June, but less forcefully in her book, is provocative. Even more telling is a remark made in her letter to her mother, dated 3 June, when she was still at Waterways, about the trial at Aklavik three weeks later: "they only hang Eskimos when they murder white men, and this case was a fellow Eskimo."

We reached Waterways in 24 hours

Two years later, in 1928, under the impressive name of the Northern Alberta Railway Arctic Express, the train still took 23 1/2 hours to complete the trip; the "two passenger cars were both so antiquated that by night they were lighted by coal-oil lamps that hung precariously from the ceiling" (Fleming 282).

Waterways was located three kilometres southeast of Fort McMurray, at the mouth of Hangingstone River. It, and not

Fort McMurray, was established as the railhead because its location, higher above the river, left it less susceptible to flooding (Aubrey, *Place* 76).

poplars that were very tall and slender with silver stems
It seems unusual that Vyvyan does not mention aspen, the dominant deciduous tree in the region; given this description, it may be that she does not distinguish one species of poplar from another.

SS *Athabasca*
In 1883, when it built and launched the *Grahame* at Fort Chipewyan, the HBC began substituting steamers for its big wooden supply boats, which had to be tracked upstream (Innis 344 n8). Two years later, a steamer named *Wrigley* was built and launched at Fort Smith, and commenced service on the Slave-Mackenzie waterway all the way to the Mackenzie Delta and Arctic Ocean. Thereafter, once northern travellers reached the Athabasca River watershed, their travel by steamer was relatively unencumbered. The major obstacle never overcome, however, was twenty-five kilometres of the Slave River between forts Fitzgerald and Smith, where the river falls thirty metres over a rocky projection of the Canadian Shield, causing a series of rapids, named Cassette, Pelican, Mountain, and Rapids of the Drowned (the correct order is seldom agreed upon [Back 67]). By the time of Vyvyan and Dorrien Smith's trip, the Mackenzie River steamer could usually make three return trips between Fort Smith and Aklavik each season. Steamboats plied the Athabasca and Mackenzie routes for six decades before they were replaced by diesel tugs in 1947 (Ethel Stewart, "Early" 41). The SS *Athabasca River*, which was retired that year, measured 146 feet in length; with a beam of 36 feet, it drew 3 feet of water. It could carry 150 tons of freight, handle a 200-ton barge, travel at a speed of 13 knots, and provide saloon accommodations for 58 passengers (Chalmers 70-3).

The archdeacon ... had towed his wife and baby upriver in an Eskimo skin boat
Charles Edward Whittaker (1864-1947), who was born near Burford, Ontario, was educated at Wycliffe College, Toronto and St John's College, Winnipeg ("Whittaker"). Ordained in 1896 and married in 1898 to Emma Hatley, sister to the wife of Bishop Lucas, he served as missionary to the Inuvialuit from 1895 to 1917 ("Whittaker"), spending 1902-06 at St Patrick's

Mission on Herschel Island (Saxberg 9). He later became archdeacon (Boon 232, 451), and from 1918 to 1921 was rector of Christ Church, Whitehorse. In 1921, he and his wife left the Yukon for Ontario, where he was rector of St John's, Cookstown (1921-23) and St James and All Saints, Penetanguishene (1923-30), although he periodically visited the Yukon ("Whittaker"). He published one book, *Arctic Eskimo* (1937). On 28 March 1911, he officiated at the Fort McPherson burial service for Francis Fitzgerald and the other mounties of the lost patrol of 1911 (Steele 157).

Portions of Whittaker's field notes from his trip up the Rat River in 1900 are quoted in his memoir as follows:

"Through the Company I bought an Eskimo skinboat, and engaged five men to take us over the Divide, arranging for the men's pay to be given them on their return. Laid in provisions for twenty days for eight persons, with tent and other necessary camp gear. Also a large bag of moccasins, and store of tobacco, as these must be furnished the men, in addition to wages. ...

"Reached the first rapids early. A jagged stone cut a hole in the boat, which I plugged with my handkerchief. When through the rapid, we hauled out and patched the boat, smearing the rent with tallow. We have sixty miles of this stream ahead of us, passing an average of forty to fifty rapids a day. We cook and eat morning, noon and night. The food is mostly bannocks, made in a fryingpan [*sic*] over an open fire.

"Sunday—had a good rest, and sleep. Held service for the boys, and prayers in our tent.

"Started early, though quite cold. Mother and daughter, with the baggage and supplies, with a steersman, occupy the boat, while the rest of us pull on the towline, or wade alongside the boat, to steady it in the boiling rapids, or ease it over the many stones in the frequent shallows.

"We are making good progress, but the food is diminishing rapidly. We counted on reaching the Divide in ten days, with no mishaps. At noon, I addressed the crew, promising them eleven days' wages if they could make it in nine, and an extra day's pay for every day they could shorten the trip. They accepted with good will.

"Mrs. Whittaker, tired of long sitting in the boat, wished to walk along shore; so I carried Mabel, and we tramped, while the boys worked the boat. Soon our shore ended in a cut bank, and a tangle of willow. With Mabel on one arm, I picked up the wife on the other, and carried them about fifty yards across the shallows, where we were able to walk again till camping time. Flapjacks and dessicated [*sic*] potatoes for supper.

"The boys are doing wonderfully, having often to patch the boat, which means unloading everything, and overturning it on shore. This afternoon, as we approached a long hairpin bend in the river, the boys advised that I take the passengers across a short portage, while they took the boat around. We started, with veils over our faces, for the mosquitees [*sic*] are bad. Soon we came to a bog, with thick willows. I carried Mabel over, set her down on a mossy bed, then went back and carried the mother over. Then we climbed a hill, through clouds of mosquitoes, made our way through a rocky gully to the river bed again, and prepared to make a fire, only to find my matches were wet and useless. I had been in the river to my armpits, guiding the boat. We had to fight the enemy for about two hours, before the boat came up. They had ascended nineteen rapids rounding the bend. Then we made camp.

"My good Wellington boots have fallen to pieces, from water and stones. Some of the boys are wearing out two pairs of moccasins a day.

"Through many bad rapids to-day, but the stream is narrowing. After dinner we passed the last rapid, having reached the level plateau of the Divide. Now our travel is slower, having to pole or row the boat. The banks are very bad, snags many, and mendings frequent. Sometimes there is hardly room to take the boat round the bend, the rivulet being so crooked, though the water is deep. We are hemmed in by willows and alder on the banks.

"The stream winds interminably. We made a portage across a grassy plain to a lake, then to another—Bell Lake, crossing which we camped for dinner. Here I paid off three of the boys, with orders on the fort, and sent them home. Eight and a half days is good time.

"Sunday. We are very high, with mountains on three sides of us, and a mist all around. We take a well-earned rest, for there are more heavy days ahead. Usual services. One walk I saw mountain sheep high up among the rocks.

"Had to carry the boat, and luggage about a third of a mile, as the narrow stream running westward is so clogged with willows we cannot get through it. The two boys at one

end, and I at the other, found the boat a stiff burden!" ("Sunrise" 66-8)

(Vyvyan's misspelling—"Whitaker"—has been corrected throughout the book and field notes.)

we have to tie up to the river bank beside a pile of logs, in order to replenish fuel
According to Harold Innis, steam-powered vessels consumed almost one cord of wood per hour (348), but Sherwood Platt cites a different rate. He and his three companions, including Alfred E. "Jake" Driscoll (who went on to become governor of the state of New Jersey from 1947 to 1954), worked on the Slave and Mackenzie rivers aboard the SS *Distributor* in return for free passage from Fort Smith to the Rat River on the steamer's second trip of 1926. The work included hauling wood from the riverside piles to the ship's furnace, which, according to him, consumed it at a rate of "five cords an hour" (12).

Field Note for Thursday 3 June
3 or 4 RCCS
The Royal Canadian Corps of Signals operated the northern wireless stations. See the note, **"As for communications,"** under Chpt 11.

CHAPTER 6: DAYS ASHORE (6–13 JUNE)

In this chapter, both the accounts of the late-night visit to the wife of the factor (Leggo) at Fort Fitzgerald and the women's habit of breakfasting with coat thrown over nightgown are embellished, to emphasize Dorrien Smith's superior sense of propriety, which is allayed by Judge Dubuc's example. Also in the book but not in the field notes, Vyvyan compares the monotony of visiting women of the North with the monotony of visits paid to women in the Australian bush (36), which she described in more detail in her autobiography, *Roots and Stars* (154-56). There is no precedent in the field notes for the penultimate salutations and last paragraph of the chapter.

Fort Chipewyan
The oldest continuously occupied white settlement in Alberta, Fort Chipewyan was established in 1788 on the south shore of Lake Athabasca at Old Fort Point by NWC partner Roderick

McKenzie, cousin of Alexander Mackenzie. Two of its names in Native languages—*Yatheekwen* (Chipewyan) and *Yatseekwen* (Slavey)—mean "priest house," while the third—*Kaitekum* (Dogrib)—means "willow ground" (Aubrey to MacLaren). Located since 1804 on the north shore near the west end of the lake, it became a hub for exploration, trade, and travel to the north and west, earning the moniker "Emporium of the North." It came under the control of the HBC after that company's merger with the NWC in 1821. The Oblates of Mary Immaculate (omi), a French order founded in 1816, established a mission there in 1851, followed by the Anglicans in 1874. In 1898 the NWMP established a post there, and Treaty 8 was signed at Fort Chipewyan in 1899 (Parker). The "rocky surroundings" remarked on by Vyvyan are the first sight of the Canadian Shield that the women had had since their rail trip through northern Ontario to Winnipeg.

Fort Fitzgerald and Fort Smith
Fort Smith (*Tthebacha*) is the older of these two settlements. Located on the Slave River at 60° N, which marks the border between Alberta and the NWT, it was established by the HBC in 1874 in the former homeland of the Slavey Dene. During the 1870s, the Slavey were driven northward out of the Slave River valley by the Cree as they moved west with the expansion of the HBC. In 1876, the Roman Catholic Mission at Salt River moved to Fort Smith. In 1880, perceiving that steamboats would never manage to navigate the four rapids on the Slave River upriver from Fort Smith, the HBC built an outpost, called Smith's Landing, at the head of the portage around Cassette Rapids (Zaslow 188). In 1915, the RNWMP established a post at Smith's Landing, renaming the site Fort Fitzgerald, after Inspector Francis Joseph Fitzgerald (1867-1911), who perished on the Peel River in February 1911 while on the Fort McPherson-Dawson patrol (Holmgren and Holmgren 60). Unlike Fort Smith, NWT, Fort Fitzgerald is situated in the province of Alberta.

Fort Smith acquired a federal Department of Indian Affairs representative in 1911, a church-run hospital in 1914, a school in 1915, and an airstrip in 1928. In 1921, with all indications pointing to an oil stampede to Fort Norman on the Mackenzie River, the federal government's Department of the Interior concerned itself with "protecting the region and its native majority against the effects of too rapid changes" (Zaslow 188). Sitting at Ottawa, the Legislative Council for the NWT was a body consisting of seven high-ranking civil servants. Fort Smith, the traditional entry point to the North by Europeans and Euro-Canadians, was identified by the council as the logical territorial site for its administration of natural resources and other Canadian government business in the entire NWT, which, though huge in terms of space, boasted a population in the 1920s of only about 8,000 people (NWT). Consequently, administration buildings were erected that year, and Crown Timber, Land and Mining Recording offices were opened for the District of Mackenzie. Also in 1921, the first Court of Justice ever held in the Mackenzie convened at Fort Smith, and it was presided over by Judge Dubuc. In 1922, nearly 10,000 square kilometres became Wood Buffalo National Park, and wardens' offices were established at Fort Smith (*On the Banks* 40, 79). The settlement remained the administrative centre of the Mackenzie District until 1967 (*Northwest* 152); in that year, the Northern Transportation Company shifted freight operations from the Smith Portage to the newly-completed Great Slave Lake Railway at Hay River. "It was more than coincidence that the territorial capital was shortly moved from Fort Smith to Yellowknife" (Mackinnon 32).

where the Mackenzie, a vast brown river, ...
Vyvyan here means the Slave, not the Mackenzie, River.

We went to call on the factor's wife
From 1922 to 1930 and perhaps longer, the HBC post manager at Fort Fitzgerald was Charles Sydney Leggo (b. 1888 or 1889), whose employment with the concern began in 1908, but which was interrupted by a stint with the Department of the Attorney General in Regina. From 1932 to 1935, he was HBC post manager at Fort Smith. The peppery Jean Godsell, who was not at Fort Fitzgerald the year of Vyvyan and Dorrien Smith's trip, pictures him risibly, holding aloft a lighted lantern in order to watch as fire consumed the company's warehouse at Fort Fitzgerald in 1922 (145), and dismisses Mrs Edith Leggo because of her "general Ottawa-conscious intolerance" (147).

a peculiar man named Hornby
John Hornby (1880-1927) was born in Cheshire, England to an affluent middle-class family with interests in cotton. He was educated at Harrow, where he excelled at sports, but developed

no career interests until he emigrated to western Canada in 1904. There he made a living packing for the railway, trapping, and working with surveyors and prospectors. In 1908, he joined a small trading party going north to the Great Bear Lake area, where he remained, trapping, hunting, and trading. Until his return to England at his father's death in the winter of 1925-26, he lived in and travelled throughout the Arctic, from the Mackenzie River to Baker Lake, with time out only for the First World War and for a year guiding in the Rocky Mountains (1922-23). He lived by a combination of trading, trapping, prospecting, and hunting and fishing, with results that ranged from starvation to prosperity. In 1926, when he invited his eighteen-year-old nephew Edgar Christian to return to Canada from England with him, he had nearly two decades of experience of northern life, but his way of life was one that made the best of what came his way, not one guided by focused ambition or forward planning. In Edmonton, Hornby and Christian were joined by Harold Adlard, another young Englishman, and set out for the Thelon River, where they intended to build a cabin and spend the winter trapping on the Barrens. However, the men missed the caribou migration. Poorly provisioned to survive the winter, all three died of starvation before the next summer. Edgar Christian, the last to die, left a diary of his experience which was recovered by RCMP officers Trundle, Williams, and Kirk, who reached the cabin on 5 July 1929, after "eighteen months' persistent effort" (Steele 303). Initially titled *Unflinching*, Christian's diary went through several editions (Whalley in Christian, *Death* 5, 15-44); it was most recently republished as *Death in the Barren Ground*. There have been two biographies of Hornby (Waldron, Whalley).

Fort Fitzgerald was a gloomy place standing on slippery clay Philip Godsell described it similarly, as an "uninviting and squalid spot" (*Arctic* 187).

we got a little roadster car to take us to Fort Smith ... Our driver, half-Swede half-Eskimo, had driven buffalo teams over this portage as lately as 1911 It is doubtful that buffalo were ever used on Smith Portage; from the time of the cutting of the trail in 1882, the HBC freighted with oxen and Red River carts (Mackinnon 24-5; photo in Cameron, rev. ed. 190). Because these could complete "'about five full trips a week'," it seems doubtful that many trips required four days to complete (King and Weekes

164; qtd in Mackinnon 25). However, the ground was quickly turned to quagmire by spring thaws and summer rains. The "partial shift to teams of horses and wagons" resulted from the demand exerted suddenly in 1898 by the Klondike gold stampeders. The Ryan brothers introduced four-horse teams, and diminished these to two-horse units when road conditions deteriorated (Polyondi 68). In 1923, the American fur company Lamson and Hubbard brought Linn caterpillar tractors into service on the portage (Mackinnon 25, 29). The first automobiles were used in 1921 (*On the Banks* 78).

Somewhat surprising in connection with buffalo is Vyvyan's silence over the ongoing project at Wood Buffalo National Park. Beginning in the previous year and continuing until 1928, a total of 6,673 plains bison were shipped by rail and sternwheeler north to the park from Wainwright, Alberta to join the 1,500 wood bison already in the park (Kitto, *North West* 85, 86). Sherwood Platt recorded "250 live wild buffalo" on the train he took to Waterways on 6 July 1926 (6), so Vyvyan and Dorrien Smith must have been unlucky in the timing of their trip. This project was overseen by Colonel James K. "Peace River Jim" Cornwall, who was of the view, novel for the times, that "'the commercial prosperity of the country is in the hands of the Indians'" (Fumoleau 235). His name appears in Chpt 2 of Vyvyan's book, in Romanet's letter.

The confusion over buffalo being used on the portage might have been deliberate or accidental. The women's driver, identified as McNeil in Vyvyan's field note for 7 June, was William Georges Andes "Billy" McNeill (1891-1978), from Labrador, who went north in 1911 to help the federal government conduct its failed experiment with the grazing of reindeer. Later, he was appointed as the first park warden for Wood Buffalo National Park (Swanson). In the opinion of Kenneth Conibear, he was pulling no one's leg when he said he had driven teams over the Smith portage as late as 1911: "I think he meant reindeer, not buffalo, but the women knew that he was now a buffalo ranger and thought he meant buffalo. And possibly he was jesting. He had a great sense of humour, and was a delight to have around" (Conibear). Of Irish and possibly Métis descent, McNeill certainly was not mixed blood Swedish and Inuit. He operated W.G.A. McNeill Taxi out of Fort Smith from the mid-1920s to 1950. In 1916, he married Marie Celestine Squirrel (1904-24), daughter of chief Pierre Squirrel and Marguerite Mandeville; in December 1924, he married Eleonore Jeremie (Swanson).

we had supper at the hotel
Born in Devon, England, the oldest son of Lewis Gilbert and
Ada Mary Conibear, Frank Conibear (1896-1988) moved to
Fort Smith in 1916. He built Conibear House and a store in
1920 with his father and his brother Jack. In 1923, he built the
multi-storey hotel. With his wife, Cecelia Powell (whom he met
in Rochester, Minnesota on a hopeful trip in 1923 to treat his
loss of hearing, a complication from a bout of measles at the
age of two), Frank Conibear operated the establishment for
about ten years. Like his Rhodes Scholar bother, Kenneth,
Frank Conibear was also an author (*Along the Banks* 108, 109;
Bevington; Conibear). Lewis and Ada Conibear operated the
store where, according to her field note for 11 June, Vyvyan
"had soft drinks: rough place with Billiard Room attached: 'No
Treaty Indians allowed in.' 'No minors allowed.' 'No bad
language.'" Kenneth Conibear suggests the signs were posted at
the insistence of his mother, who was a very successful
merchant and trader (Conibear; Ellis, "Business").

how old Murphy of Fort Simpson missed the priesthood
Vyvyan's field note for 6 June (a day before the anecdote
appears in the book) attributes the story to *Harris* of Simpson.
Miriam Green Ellis' field notes from her trip in 1922 down the
Mackenzie River (M.G. Ellis Coll., Box 3—I) relate the same
story about Thomas William "Flynn" Harris, Indian agent at
Fort Simpson 1913-30 and at Fort Good Hope 1930-33
(Fumoleau 203), and Vyvyan's field note for 18 June repeats
this identification. Jean Godsell found Harris a character
sketcher's dream when, like Ellis, she met him at Fort Simpson
in 1922:

> … Magistrate and Indian Agent, a unique character if ever
> there was one. Of medium height, powerfully built, he was
> attired in a home-made khaki suit of semi-military cut
> which fitted where it touched, a pair of beaded moccasins,
> and a battered nautical cap which sat awkwardly upon his
> glistening bald pate. …
>
>   Fascinated, I gazed at his unbelievable, almost
> Neanderthal, homeliness, his frightful squint and low,
> receding forehead. So squint-eyed was he that his nose
> almost touched that of the person whom he was addressing.
> A master of English, French, German, Spanish, Esperanto,
> Cree, Chipewyan and one or two other languages, he could
> quote the classics verbatim, had gone to school with Sir

Robert Borden, … and would—but for his addiction to
John Barleycorn—have been one of the leading criminal
lawyers of his day. Now here he was—married to his second
Chipewyan squaw, and the father of I don't know how many
hybrid progeny.

>   Many were the stories told of him: of how he imbibed
> red ink, extracts, shoe polish, listerine—anything that was
> handiest, when his liquor permit was gone—and of how,
> when in his cups, he would conduct the business of the
> agency or the post office in his birthday suit, calling
> between splurges of work and copious draughts for
> Caroline, his wife, to slap him vigorously on the back and
> "*bust me gall*!"
>
>   Earlier that summer Flynn was seated by the river at Fort
> Fitzgerald with an opposition official from Edmonton who
> was bemoaning his bacchanalian indiscretions of the night
> before when he suddenly shot his face forward and exclaimed:
> "That was a swell trade we made last night, George."
>
>   "What do you mean trade?" George turned bleary eyes
> upon him. "You're crazy! We didn't do any *trading*."
>
>   "We sure did. Look!" Flynn flashed a wide grimace and
> pointed to his mouth. "Don't you remember *we traded false
> teeth*? Yours are the best fit I ever had. Just *try* and get them
> back!" (112-13)

For the protection of Dene from the unavoidable increase in
the numbers of whites coming north once the railway was
completed to Waterways, as early as 1914 Harris urged the
making of Treaty 11. He witnessed the signing of it at Fort
Simpson on 11 July 1921 (Fumoleau 138, 158, 174), and negotiated the signing of it at Fort Liard (*Echaot'j Koe*) on 17 July
1922. René Fumoleau offers a recapitulation of this side of the
man:

> he was well known for his understanding of the native
> people and he always remembered the spirit of friendship
> in which Treaty 11 was signed. The Territorial
> Administration complained continuously about "the
> leniency with which Mr Harris … has dealt with Indians and
> Half-breeds coming before him for contraventions of the
> Game Act." In his capacity as Justice of the Peace, "Flynn"
> Harris based his judgements not only on the letter of the
> white man's law, but also on the special promises made to
> the Indian people at Treaty time. (203; see also 244-45)

One day we visited the hospital
St Ann's Roman Catholic Hospital opened in 1914 and served a huge area of the North for sixty-five years before it was closed in 1979 ("Grey"). In the 1920s, all hospitals in the NWT were operated by the Anglican and Roman Catholic churches (Dickerson 44-5).

On Sunday we went to the Roman Catholic church
St Isidore Roman Catholic Church was built in 1923, three years before Vyvyan visited it.

the chief, whose name was Squirrel
Pierre Squirrel was the Slavey chief of the Fort Smith band. According to Philip Godsell, who met him in 1920, he spoke Cree as well as Slavey (*Arctic* 186). Local Fort Smith historian and genealogist Marie Swanson states that he was born in 1848. He married Marguerite Mandeville on 28 May 1878 in Fort Smith; they had eight children together, and adopted several more. After Marguerite's death, he became a newlywed again, when on 15 August 1924, at age seventy-six, he married Adele McKay in Hay River; they adopted one child. Squirrel died on 4 May 1939 and is buried in the cemetery at St Isidore Church, Fort Smith. Unlike Vyvyan, who seems to find him quaint if not risible, Agnes Deans Cameron considered him authoritative when she met him in 1908 (148-49; rev. ed. 114); however, Vyvyan accurately reported his appearance. Kenneth Conibear remembers that in the 1920s "Pierre Squirrel ... did indeed usually wear a blue serge suit and a yachting cap. I think we never saw him in full paint and feathers, and I do not recall ever seeing him with long grey hair. He was a good, and honest, customer at our store."

Chief Squirrel's political role in the emerging North was not insignificant. In 1920, "in addition to a number of white men," he told F.H. Kitto that "venereal diseases were introduced to the district, and the native population contaminated by them during the time of the Klondike rush" (Kitto, "Report" 27), and he asked Kitto to convey "his respects to the new Commissioner and to tell him that he would like to receive a warm suit of clothes for winter wear" (29). In 1922, he informed the Indian agent at Fort Smith of his people's alarm at the prospect of living on a reserve (Fumoleau 122). That same year, he voiced the opposition of the Fort Smith-Fort Fitzgerald Band to any plan to create a buffalo park if it impinged on his people's traditional hunting and trapping grounds (Fumoleau 255). In 1928, his expression of alarm over the feared effects on his people of the federal government's hastily initiated policy of closed seasons on fur and game animals issued in an alteration to the policy (Fumoleau 281-82), a policy which the bishops of both churches, as well as Department of Indian Affairs official (and poet) Duncan Campbell Scott, also opposed (Dickerson 52-3). However romanticized a picture of him Vyvyan is inclined to paint, Squirrel was of the generation of native leaders who made the transition from paint and feathers to yachting cap and other vestiges of bureaucracy.

A bearded French priest preached in French and then in Chipewyan
Rév Père Alphonse Mansoz omi was the supérieur oblat at the Hôpitale Ste-Anne and Maison provinciale du Térritoire du Nord-Ouest from 1924 to August 1926 ("Fort Smith Chroniques").

Mr Brabant arranged for a gas boat ... pulled close to an eddy below the rapids ... we landed on a flat pink granite islet ... there were waves with crests flung backward against the current, and rocky islets in mid-river, each one lonely and helpless as regret.
Vyvyan here conflates her account of an outing made in the boat on Saturday, 12 June—only in the middle of which did she learn that the place where she wanted to visit to see pelicans could be approached by boat only from Fort Fitzgerald—with her account of a walk that she took with Dorrien Smith to Mountain Rapids on Tuesday, 8 June; thereby, she creates the mistaken impression that she is describing the rapids nearest to Fort Smith. These are the Rapids of the Drowned, the sound of which had played on her ears during her stay at Fort Smith. By comparing her description of the rapids with a more detailed one of Mountain Rapids (two sets upstream), written by British naval explorer George Back 106 years earlier, one sees not only Vyvyan's narrative method but also her interest in the same details that captured the eye of the explorer-artist trained in the enduring English landscape conventions of the sublime and picturesque:

> On crossing the Mountain Portage there is an extremely fine view breaks upon the sight from the hill which you are ascending — The River is about 3 miles broad — perfectly

smooth in its course — and diversified by several islands so low that the trees on them appear to be growing out of the water — a little farther on is a fall of 15 feet over smooth rocks — which dashes against a number of high stones at the bottom and throws the spray to a considerable height whilst the high and wooded hills on each side form a romantic finish to the picture — but the spectators [sic] attention is mostly caught by the striking contrast between the calmness of the upper and the turbulency of the lower part of the fall. (67)

our long journey to Aklavik

In 1930, Kitto estimated the distance of the journey by water from Fort Smith to Aklavik at 1,297 mi (*North West* 57) or 2,088 km. The intermediate distances by water are as follows:

Fort Smith to Fort Resolution	203 mi or 327 km
Fort Resolution to Hay River	75 mi or 121 km
Hay River to Providence	78 mi or 126 km
Fort Providence to Fort Simpson	156 mi or 251 km
Fort Simpson to Wrigley	152 mi or 245 km
Wrigley to Fort Norman	150 mi or 241 km
Fort Norman to Fort Good Hope	171 mi or 275 km
Fort Good Hope to Arctic Red River	214 mi or 344 km
Arctic Red River to Fort McPherson, Peel River	55 mi or 86 km
Arctic Red River to Aklavik	98 mi or 158 km

Field Note for Monday 7 June
Mr Fletcher's talk interesting

Dorrien Smith's field note for this date mentions that RCMP Inspector Fletcher had been to the Isles of Scilly. George Frederick Fletcher (Fumoleau 125) supported District Agent John N.A. McDougal's call for the creation of game preserves for the Dene of the North (Fumoleau 245, 249). Generally, he was not hopeful about the welfare of the Dene in a North witnessing an influx of Euro-Canadians during the 1920s.

Field Note for Wednesday 9 June
Mr McDougall administrator for Dept. of Interior

This was John N.A. McDougal, district agent and head of government staff for the NWT and Yukon Branch of the federal Department of the Interior at Fort Smith (*On the Banks* 42; Zaslow 191). His responsibilities included paying annual

treaty annuities to Dene and Métis. It was McDougal who, in 1922, conceived the idea of establishing game preserves, not only to stave off the extermination of whole species, but also to make good on the promises contained in Treaties 8 and 11, that Dene would have the exclusive right to hunt and trap over the entire area of the Treaties, a right threatened by the increasing presence of white trappers in the near North (Fumoleau 209, 245).

Field Note for Friday 11 June
We visited the 2 schooners alongside 10 tons each + saw Mr Carel who is taking them down to the Arctic

This is likely A.A. Carroll, a sometime post manager for the HBC during the 1920s, who was born in Waco, Texas in 1876 ("Carroll"). Philip Godsell identified the same man as the post manager at Herschel Island in 1923 (*Arctic* 282); however, the index to his book lists this man as H.B, not A.A., Carroll (322). Explorer Knud Rasmussen remembered his expedition members being "excellently nursed" by Carroll in April 1924 (Rasmussen spells his name "Caroll" and identifies him as the "local manager" of the HBC at Herschel Island) (Ostermann 54). Vyvyan's note, in the material following the last dated entry of her field notes, recalls that Carroll's trip up the Rat River occurred "in 1913 in 11 days in scow with 1 ton stuff: 5 people" (227).

Field Note for Saturday 12 June
Mr. Moran with his Movie Kodak

John F. Moran, who boarded the train with the women in Edmonton and is first mentioned in the field note for 6 June, was chief inspector for the NWT and Yukon Branch of the Department of the Interior. His tour of inspection in 1926 kept him on the same Mackenzie River itinerary as Vyvyan and Dorrien Smith. His interest in photography resulted in a representative visual record of the North in the 1920s, fortunately preserved in the National Archives of Canada. His and his branch's negative view of native people often clashed with the views of Indian agents and the Department of Indian Affairs (Fumoleau 268). Jean Godsell remembered him as "a dapper, handsome Frenchman who was destined to become one of our staunchest, most devoted lifelong friends and an outstanding authority on the Arctic and the North" (99).

CHAPTER 7: GREAT SLAVE LAKE (14–17 JUNE)

The book expands the field notes' description of the women's afternoon on an island shore strewn with "boulders + piles of driftwood + soft 1/2 mouldy fibre" (15 June); a wider scope takes in those piles of driftwood and wood fibre, tracing them back to their origins on the Peace River. The chapter also expands the field notes' treatment of the "dream journey through Great Slave Lake" (17 June), creating characters, such as the man from Arizona, from among her fellow-passengers in order to invoke the North's effect on them during the journey across the lake and towards the northern wilderness. The chapter pays rather less attention than the field notes to the lives and concerns of the many people Vyvyan and Dorrien Smith met and the characteristics of the individual settlements.

Gwen made a sunset sketch, which I still possess
Vyvyan does not mention the sketch in her field note for 14 June, although the sunset is described in similar terms. It may have been the sketch now titled *Mission Is* (see above, 191).

We touched at Fort Resolution in the middle of the night
Located on the southern shore of Great Slave Lake, Fort Resolution (*Deninu Kue*) dates from 1876, when NWC traders Cuthbert Grant and Laurent Leroux erected Slave Fort (Philip Godsell, *Arctic* 191n). The HBC established a post in 1815, but the name, Fort Resolution, was initiated only after the merger of the two companies, in 1821 (Pool 2:822). A Roman Catholic mission was established in 1852, and it was joined in 1903 by a residential school run by the Grey Nuns until 1957. When the Oblates and Grey Nuns built a tuberculosis hospital in 1938-39, Fort Resolution became an important medical and educational centre, but, after the hospital was transferred to Edmonton in 1956, the settlement declined in importance as a regional centre (*Northwest* 148).

Two days later we came at dawn to Hay River
Hay River (*Xatt'o Dehe*) is situated in the homeland of the Slavey people. The HBC post was established in 1868, followed the next year by a Roman Catholic mission. The post was abandoned in 1875, but an Anglican mission opened in 1893, and in 1925 an RCMP detachment was established, to be followed by a hospital and church (*Northwest* 162).

Dorrien Smith's field note for 17 June reveals that the women went ashore in the company of "Canon Vale" while his wife stayed aboard the *Distributor*. This was Alfred James Vale (1876-1963), born in Waterloo, Ontario, who graduated from Wycliffe College, University of Toronto in 1906. In 1916, he was appointed canon of Mackenzie River and, in 1920, founded St Peter's Indian Residential School, Hay River, where he served as principal through 1927. His canonry then turned to the Indian Residential School at Chapleau, Ontario in the Diocese of Moosonee ("Vale").

the Mother Superior of the Grey Nuns of the North
Rév Mère Zoé Chartier Girouard (1867-1935) held the office of supérieure provinciale du Grand Nord from 1920 to 1927. Before then, her career had included seven years at St Boniface, Manitoba and eleven at St Albert, Alberta. She became rév mère locale at Fort Resolution in 1911, founded the Grey Nuns mission at Fort Simpson in 1916 (*Annales* [1936-37] 577), and, with Rév Mère Générale Octavie Dugas, travelled to Aklavik in 1924 to choose the site on which the hospital and mission were to be established the next year (see the notes to Chpt 10).

CHAPTER 8: IN AND OUT (17 JUNE)

This chapter does not follow the chronological organization of the field notes, but rather combines characters and anecdotes from various points in the women's northward journey, with no context more specific than "one day" and no identification other than "Mother Superior" or "one old-timer." For instance, the doctor described in the opening of the chapter is Dr McDonald, who was encountered at Fort Smith on 9 June; the discussion with the surveyor took place on 14 June before the women reached Resolution; and the mother superior's tale of having her teeth pulled before entering the North does not appear in the field notes at all. (Sœur Fernande Champagne, Archivist of the Grey Nuns Regional Centre, Edmonton, suggests that this detail is Vyvyan's invention.) The surveyor and the race between Roman Catholics and Anglicans to baptize native children *are* details presented in the field notes (13 and 14 June, respectively). Otherwise, the picture sketched by this chapter is of an undifferentiated North, a vast, stern wilderness full of picturesque, character *types* and adventurous or amusing anecdotes. The book, perhaps because of its retrospective nature, is less interested in the specifics of person and community than in types. Even the excerpt from Vyvyan's "diary" at the end of the chapter is a cobbled-together series of fragments taken out of context from various points in the journey. This style occurs in several chapters of the book. Here it contributes to the book's sense of timelessness at a point in the trip when neither their route nor their schedule lie under the women's control, and they are only passengers watching the North drift by.

we met a doctor who had been "in" for 15 years
A.L. McDonald (also MacDonald) was the doctor, appointed by the Department of Indian Affairs, who arrived in the North in 1913 (Fumoleau 114). Jean Godsell identifies him as "a kindly but rabid Scot from Glengarry, Ontario" (68). He was a witness to the signing of Treaty 11 at Fort Wrigley on 13 July 1921 (Fumoleau 177). This treaty did not make provision for Dene within the treaty boundaries to access regular medical attention, but McDonald's appointment represented an earnest attempt by federal authorities to make free and ongoing medical attention available. He travelled widely in the Mackenzie basin, but, as the remark quoted by Vyvyan clarifies, he had no pretensions to ubiquity. McDonald stayed in his job until 1931 (Fumoleau 331). Kenneth Conibear remembers him as follows:

> he lived in the Roman Catholic monastery, was reputed to spend most of his time playing solitaire with himself, other-wise kept busy bringing babies into the world in the nearby Roman Catholic hospital, and for all other ailments was reputed to keep a supply of pills in one of his pockets which he would pull out after hearing of your ailment, blow the fluff off them, pick one out and hand it to you with a hopeful "See how this works." Such was his reputation, but for my part I remember that he delivered my wife of her first child without any complications. (Conibear)

One of the Grey Nuns with whom we travelled
Described pejoratively in Vyvyan's field note for 11 June as "one wizened little Nut," the Grey Nun in question, according to historical records, is likely Sister Delphine Giroux-Pinsonneault (1865-1954), twenty years Vyvyan's senior. The two met at Fort Smith. Sister Pinsonneault served in missions at Fort Chipewyan 1892-96, Fort Resolution 1906-18, and Fort Smith 1919-38. Her year's rest had occurred in 1918;

hence her completion of thirty-two years' service by 1926. During her leave, she returned home to Napierville, Quebec to find that her parents and ten of her thirteen siblings had died since her departure. She had considered her first trip north too difficult to repeat immediately, and she found "life in the North, at least in those days, very favourable to one's union with God, in spite of and perhaps because of privation and the exhausting work that there was no choice about accepting" (*Annales* [1958] 493; translated from the French). She retired at the age of seventy-two, in 1938.

Lac la Biche
The literal translation of this name is "lake of the red doe." The name was given by fur traders, who encountered the lake on a route from the North Saskatchewan to Athabasca rivers that enjoyed greatest prominence in the late eighteenth and early nineteenth centuries (Betke; Holmgren and Holmgren 17). The first trading post established in the area was built by NWC explorer David Thompson in 1798. The railway began serving the community in 1915 (Hatcher, *Northern Alberta* 1), "bringing many settlers, the majority of whom were Catholic French Canadians" (Harrison 139).

Wonderful stillness
The content of Vyvyan's field note for 1 June is the same but the order of the words differs. None of the passages strung together in this quotation are exactly the same as the field notes from which they are allegedly quoted.

long chat with Canadian NW Policeman
Compare Vyvyan's field note for 4 June.

Never before met anyone who lives so near the North Pole, but he takes it as a matter of course
No field note offers a basis for this sentence.

These trappers talk as if they had nearly lost the power of linking one word to the next
A similar point of view is expressed in different words in Vyvyan's field note for 7 June.

Saw wax-wing and three-toed American Woodpecker with yellow crest
Compare Vyvyan's field note for 8 June.

Long walk in forest. Hard to realise the vast size of this country … Trees so monotonous
Compare Vyvyan's field note for 12 June.

No change ahead, only sometimes a glint of light between stems, light that may be sky or water
No field note provides a basis for this passage.

Begin to realise how a man might go mad … We came out suddenly on the river bank at last
Vyvyan's field note for 10 June provides the basis for this passage, but the exaggeration in the note—"a frantic futile struggle"—differs from the exaggeration in this revision.

an old-timer who had once walked 900 miles to stake his claim for gold and 900 miles back again
Compare Vyvyan's field note for 17 June. Born in Crediton, Devon, England, this old-timer, as the reference to "Conybeare" in the field note for 17 June clarifies, was Lewis Gilbert Conibear (1869–1941), father of Frank. Lewis was an officer in the Royal Navy when, in 1899, he, his wife Ada Mary (*née* Gribble; 1870–1954), and their two children emigrated to Kitchener, Ontario from Devon, not far from Vyvyan's home county. Three other children were born to them in Kitchener and Orrville, Ontario. In 1911, Conibear moved north when Polson Iron Works of Toronto, which had built a boat for the Roman Catholic missions in the North, received a letter from Bishop Gabriel Breynat asking for a competent engineer to be sent to repair and maintain the vessel. Conibear worked as an engineer maintaining the *Sainte Marie*, the boat used by the various Roman Catholic missions on the Mackenzie River before it was sold to the Northern Trading Company and was renamed the *Northern Trader*. In 1912, Ada Conibear took all five children from Ontario to Sawmill Snye, at the mouth of the Slave River. On this island Breynat had had a house built for the family near the RC brothers' sawmill, four miles from Fort Resolution. It proved a fortuitous location for the family:

> all the Indians who trapped in the lower Slave and the Eastern part of Great Slave Lake passed right in front of our door, winter and summer, on their way to and from visits to Fort Resolution for Christmas, Easter, and Treaty day. As was the custom, they invariably stopped, came inside for a cup of tea, and possibly for a change of clothing, and to see

whether Dad could mend some piece of broken equipment in his forge and, after a while, to see whether Mother would offer a better price for some of their furs or sell some articles at lower costs than they would have to pay the Hudson's Bay or private traders in Resolution. By the time we had to leave Sawmill Island Mother had established a good reputation as a fur trader and general merchant. (Conibear)

Thus did the Conibears become "the first independent white family to settle in the Northwest Territories" (Bevington 386). The Conibears moved to Fort Smith about 1916, when the Northern Trading Company decided to move its boat operation to Bell Rock, a few miles downstream of the settlement.

The "900 miles" walked by Lewis Conibear occurred in connection with oil, not gold. According to Kenneth Conibear (b. 1907), "the trip he is reported to have gone on was in fact from Fort Smith to Fort Norman and some fifty miles or so beyond that to the site of the Norman oil wells. He and my two brothers, Frank and Jack, made the trip in midwinter, by dog team, and staked claims over the wells. That, I believe, was in 1921. My father then spent a good portion of the following summer in the Outside, trying, without success, to sell the claims."

Several smiling girls, sly-faced and slit-eyed, going home from school
This refers to children at Hay River residential school. As far as the women's route is concerned, in the 1920s, Anglican missions operated day schools at forts Smith, Simpson, and McPherson, as well as at Aklavik, and a boarding school at Hay River. Roman Catholic missions operated day schools at forts Smith, Simpson, and Good Hope, a summer day-school at Wrigley, and boarding schools at Fort Resolution, Providence, and Aklavik. Both churches ran the schools with the aid of grants from the federal government's Department of Indian Affairs (Kitto, *North West* 62).

Mixed and interesting crowd
Apart from the sentence beginning, "Steamer hooted …," this long passage is very similar to Vyvyan's field note for 17 June; however, the chapter's re-creation is accorded a greater degree of ellipsis and more radical parataxis, which might be expected in field notes but which cannot actually be found in hers at this point.

Chapter 9: From Providence to Aklavik (17–23 June)

The women's excursion into the forest behind Providence is not referred to in the field notes, which focus on a description of the settlement and its people. Gwen sprained her ankle on this excursion but Vyvyan did not learn of the sprain until the next morning; thus, the details about the community would have dominated the day's field note entry, but the retrospective reconstruction in the chapter focuses on Gwen's ankle, omitting some of the description of Providence and its people, and deferring other details to a generalized description of a typical steamer landing at a northern settlement.

Providence in this case was the name of our first port of call after Great Slave Lake
The original Fort Providence was established on the north shore of Great Slave Lake. A Roman Catholic mission, called Notre dame de la providence, was built at the present site (*Zhahti Koe*) by Monseigneur Grandin in 1861 (*Northwest* 146). The Grey Nuns established a boarding school for Dene children in 1867, and the HBC, the NWMP, and federal government followed.

Fort Simpson, a beautifully sited place on a high bank at the mouth of the Liard River
Initially called Fort of the Forks when constructed by the NWC in 1804, Fort Simpson (*Liidli Koe*) was renamed for George Simpson, the inland governor of the HBC after the merger of the two concerns in 1821. Located on an island at the confluence of the Mackenzie and Liard rivers, it is the oldest continuously occupied post on the Mackenzie River and served as the HBC's district headquarters for many years. The Anglican mission was established in 1858, and the Roman Catholic mission came in 1894. When the HBC retired its York boat brigades in 1888 in favour of steamers, members of the brigades, who had often wintered over in the community, settled there. In 1910, the first Indian Agency was opened; a RNWMP detachment arrived in 1912, and a hospital in 1916. Until the Mackenzie Highway made possible regular deliveries of fresh food from the south, the Fort Simpson area produced livestock and vegetables for the North (*Northwest* 150).

Not only its situation but also the views from the settlement are often remarked on. Charles Camsell, who spent part of his boyhood there, considered "the view up stream … magnificent …, perhaps the best on the whole river" (9). The post was distinguished for the only billiard table in the Mackenzie district prior to the twentieth century, and an impressive lending library (Camsell 11-12). Eighteen months prior to Vyvyan's trip, an issue of *The Beaver* featured quotations from Agnes Deans Cameron's delighted description of the library, which she saw during her trip in 1908 ("Old Library"). Indian agent Flynn Harris had possession of it when Vyvyan met him there in 1926, and she marvelled over it in her field note for 18 June: "a fine library ~~Greek~~ (for these parts) Greek—Latin RLS—Dickens—Thackeray +c." Jean Godsell offers another description of Fort Simpson's library, assembled by Julian Camsell while he was HBC factor there: "seven or eight hundred volumes, some of which dated back to 1790, amongst them being Bohn's classics; sixteen volumes of *The Travellers Library*; Smithsonian Institute [*sic*] reports from 1858 to 1887; Grote's *History of Greece*; Plutarch's *Lives*; Barth's *Central Africa*; the works of Goethe, Chaucer and similar volumes of poetry, travel and philosophy, together with antiquated works of fiction" (114).

Dorrien Smith's field note for 18 June clarifies that Flynn Harris (Vyvyan's "old Murphy of Fort Simpson") embarked for a journey, not just a visit, while the *Distributor* moored at Fort Simpson. She did not record his destination.

the stark simplicity of this wooden building
Vyvyan's observation about the "strange contrast" between the "stark simplicity" of the wooden church at Fort Simpson and the great Gothic cathedrals of France and Italy (Chpt 9) is considerably more negative in the field note for 18 June, which sees the church as "pathetically out of place" in the wilderness.

At noon we came to Fort Wrigley
At least for part of each year, Slavey Dene dwelt on the site of present-day Wrigley (*Tthedzeh Koe*) prior to European contact. The NWC had a post there, called Fort Alexander, from 1817 to 1821; after it closed, the Slavey settled on Old Fort Island, near the present site of Wrigley. An HBC post was established there in 1870, but, following the 1900-05 famine and tuberculosis epidemic, the whole community moved forty-eight kilometres down the Mackenzie River to a site near Wrigley Rock, known as "Rocher qui trempe à l'eau." An airstrip was built in 1944, and the community acquired a church and one-

room school in the 1950s. In 1965, however, the wet terrain and extreme need for housing improvements led to a relocation at Hodgson Creek, the present site of the community (*Northwest* 224).

we heard a poor account of Stefansson's reputation in Arctic latitudes
Born in Gimli, Manitoba, Vilhjalmur Stefansson (1879-1962) travelled to the Arctic first in 1906 when he was appointed to the Anglo-American Arctic Expedition. His second expedition (1908-12) resulted in his "discovery" of the Copper Inuit ("Blond Eskimo") in the vicinity of Coronation Gulf and in his theory that they descended from the early Norse colonists of Greenland. His third expedition (1913-18) took him into the western islands of the Arctic Archipelago before he contracted typhoid fever and required nursing at the Anglican mission on Herschel Island (Story 777-78; see also notes to the next two chapters.)

After midnight we came to Fort Norman
Situated at the junction of the Mackenzie and Great Bear rivers in an area that has always been of seasonal importance to the Slavey Dene, Fort Norman (*Tulit'a*) was established in 1810 by the NWC, which arrived in the area in the late 1700s. The community was relocated several times after the fur trade companies merged in 1821, but by 1872 it was back at its original site. The post's strategic location made it a transportation centre for early exploration by Franklin, and, a century later, during the pitchblende discoveries beginning in 1919 (*Northwest* 144; Pool 2:822). Those discoveries resulted in a temporary boom in oil locations downriver from Fort Norman, but Vyvyan observed no great activity in 1926 because heavy initial expenditures and long waits for returns curtailed "the threatened stampede ... to a comparatively mild rush of a few hundred men" (Kitto, *North West* 78).

We were in the famous Ramparts
On 7 July 1789, Alexander Mackenzie and his exploration party passed the Sans Sault Rapids, reached the Ramparts Rapid, where the Mackenzie River has a width of more than three kilometres, and then came to the Ramparts, where the "River appeared quite shut up with high perpendicular White Rocks, this did not at all please us. ... We came between the steep Rock I mention as above but did not find the Current

stronger than elsewhere. We were still in Expectation of coming to the Rapid till they [local people who talked to Mackenzie's guide] told us there was no other but what we saw" (Mackenzie 190). W. Kaye Lamb, Mackenzie's modern editor, explains that the "sheer limestone cliffs 100 to 200 feet high confine the river for seven miles within a channel that is only a quarter of a mile wide at the entrance, but widens gradually to about half a mile" (Mackenzie 190).

We came to Fort Good Hope
Situated on the east bank of the Mackenzie River, Fort Good Hope (*Radili Ko*) was established by the NWC in 1805. It is the oldest fur trading post in the lower Mackenzie Basin. The Roman Catholic Mission was established there in 1859, and the settlement was known for its church, Our Lady of Good Hope, which was decorated with murals by a Roman Catholic priest in 1878 (Pool 2:820).

fish-nets where we found corny, jackfish and bluefish
No doubt, the fish seen was a conny (short for *poisson inconnu*), not, as Vyvyan heard the name, "corny."

Arctic Red River
Located at the junction of the Arctic Red and Mackenzie rivers, this site was probably a seasonal fishing camp for the Gwich'in before European contact. Roman Catholic members of the Fort McPherson Gwich'in were drawn to Arctic Red River (*Tsiigehtshik*) when a Roman Catholic mission was established in 1868. The HBC set up a post in the early 1870s, but the number of year-round permanent residents remained small until well into the 1960s, as families lived on the land trapping for part of the year (Pool 1:112). Not until the late 1970s, with the construction of the Dempster Highway and the ferry crossing associated with it, did the community have wage employment (*Northwest* 110).

up the Peel River to Fort McPherson
Located on the east bank of Peel River, Fort McPherson (*Teetl'it Zheh*) sits at the eastern edge of Gwich'in territory. The Gwich'in already had access to Russian trade goods by way of Alaska when Alexander Mackenzie passed through the region in 1789; later, they traded with the HBC at Fort Good Hope, until 1840. In that year, John Bell of the HBC established Peel River Post on a site known in Gwich'in as *Chii tsal dik* ("Gravel on

top"). Thereafter, it was known as *Teetl'it zheh* ("Head of the waters house"); the English name was later changed to Fort McPherson, after Murdoch McPherson, chief factor of the Mackenzie District. In 1852, a Dene village previously located on the Peel River flood plain moved to Fort McPherson because it offered a better view of the delta and approaching Inuit, who were occasional enemies. In 1860, Roman Catholic priest Père Henri Grollier baptised sixty-five people in the settlement, but this group subsequently moved to Arctic Red River, as an Anglican mission was established at Fort McPherson in 1860 and the remainder of the people followed that faith. With the flood of overlanders passing through Fort McPherson *en route* to the Klondike in 1898 and 1899, the need for law enforcement became evident. From 1894 to 1903, trader John Firth functioned as government law officer; then the NWMP set up a post. Fort McPherson was the northern-most location at which Treaty 11 was signed, on 28 July 1921 (Fumoleau 187; one witness to the signing was Jack Parsons, the HBC post manager at Aklavik who arranged a canoe for Vyvyan and Dorrien Smith and took them to Destruction City by motor boat). The first Dene member of the Territorial Council, Chief John Tetlichi (1967), and the first northern native member of parliament, Wally Firth (1972), were both from Fort McPherson (*Northwest* 142).

we came to Aklavik at 8
Aklavik, which in the Inuvialuktun dialect means "where there are bears," was established on the west side of the Mackenzie Delta by the HBC in 1911 (Krech, "Interethnic" 116) or 1912 (Bonnycastle, *Gentleman* 98). From the beginning, its popula-tion included Gwich'in, Inuit, and Métis (most were Scottish and Gwich'in). The HBC transferred its regional headquarters from Herschel Island to Aklavik in 1923 (Jean Godsell 128). During the 1920s, the settlement witnessed an increase in population when high fur prices attracted many transient whites to the region. The RCMP established a post at the settle-ment in 1922; by 1931, Aklavik "served a district containing 411 people, including 180 Indians and 140 Eskimo" (Honigmann and Honigmann 30). When, in 1961, as a result of serious flooding, the federal government established the community of Inuvik on the higher ground of the east side of the Delta, many native people chose to remain at Aklavik; thereby, it attracted the sobriquet of the "town that wouldn't die" (Pool 1:47). In her letter to her mother, begun on 20 June but continued for

a week, Vyvyan wrote, "sunny + place full of mosquitoes: but only 3 weeks ago they walked aX the river on ice."

Field Note for Thursday 17 June
the Rose of the North
The nickname is likely an affectionate play on the name of Eva Roy, Sœur Ste-Rose-de-Lima (1885-1932). Born the same year as Vyvyan in Lewiston, Maine, she served at La Laselle 1910-16 and at Fort Providence 1916-27, applying herself to the instruction and care of children. When illness cut short her career and forced her departure from the North the year after she showed the school to Vyvyan and Dorrien Smith, "les petits sauvages entourèrent leur maîtresse et lui dirent: 'Tu es malade parce que tu nous a trop aimés'" (*Annales* [1932-33] 672). A group photo of her and other nuns at Fort Providence, taken by Judge Dubuc in 1921, does confirm her comparatively larger size (Photo Scrapbook, recto, 4th leaf).

In 1922, Miriam Green Ellis, an Edmonton journalist, made a summer steamer trip to Aklavik. In her field notes, she recorded meeting Sœur Ste-Rose, whom she described as a gardener. Ellis' expression of admiration for her contrasts markedly with Vyvyan's pejorative description:

> But all the nuns are not small or pale faced. At Fort Providence was one of the jolliest brightest women one could meet. She was Sister St. Rose and perhaps I liked her specially because of the big piece of cake and the home made cookies she gave me with my tea when I visited the mission. She and many others are wholesouled [*sic*] women, living life as it comes and happy in the pleasure or the inci-dent of the moment. (M.G. Ellis Coll., Box 3—VII)

Told story of himself + Indian: Sunday morning
This anecdote puts on view an essential paradox of the North: on the one hand, institutional representatives such as this MP (Mounted Police) were sent north to enact the fervent desire of "civilized" Euro-Canada to bring native people out of their perceived cultural backwardness, and, on the other hand, the far from ideal example set by this particular mountie's drunk-enness, perhaps induced by the lonely life led by most of the institutional representatives stationed in the North but not native to it.

Field Note for Friday 18 June

G awoke with sprained or strained foot

In her characteristic understated style, Dorrien Smith wrote only the following in her field note for 18 June: "Fine but thunderstorm in p.m. I sprained my ankle yesterday somehow and could do nothing."

CHAPTER 10: ESKIMOS AT AKLAVIK (23–25 JUNE)

The field notes pertaining to the contents of this chapter make no mention of Sittichinli's "magnificent physique." The book creates suspense by making more than Vyvyan's field notes of both the doctor's examination of Dorrien Smith's sprained ankle and her contingency plan (using her brother's boots). As well, its focus on the murder trial expands the spate of dialogue recorded at the conclusion of the field notes; it includes information gathered about the Inuit at various points in the trip, including comments on Inuit customs and dress. No field note suggests that Inuit "must have been born smiling."

The first thing we had to do was to get the doctor. He came on board without delay

Dorrien Smith's field note for 23 June identifies this doctor as Cook; the Grey Nuns also refer to him only by his surname ("Aklavik" 26 May 1926). Vyvyan's letter to her mother of 30 June is slightly more specific about other details: "He said Gwen had strained 2 ankle tendons at Providence + put her into plaster of Paris all up one leg for 10 days."

Aklavik seemed to be a prosperous place

This positive statement is succeeded by a qualification that suggests that Vyvyan is likely underestimating the signs of material prosperity that she saw at Aklavik. Three groups of Inuit along the Arctic Coast at the beginning of the twentieth century were the Inupiat of the North Alaskan coast, the Kogmollicks or Inuvialuit of the Mackenzie Delta, and the Copper Inuit from Coronation Gulf, Victoria Island, and eastward. Inupiat began coming to the Mackenzie Delta in considerable numbers with the advent of American whaling at Herschel Island in 1888 (Ingram and Dobrowolsky 9), and especially after the collapse of the world price for whalebone and whale oil. Complete by 1907, this collapse resulted from the invention of artificial whalebone, steel springs, and kerosene. By 1924, fully seventy-five per cent of Inuit in the Delta were considered to be of Alaskan origin (Usher 1:25). The immigrant population continued to increase:

> The native Mackenzie Eskimos had never lived permanently in the wooded country of the Delta, and remained largely on the coast. The Delta people ... which consisted largely of the Alaskan immigrants ... were therefore the ablest and most energetic trappers, and indeed the most recent immigrants had come mainly for that purpose. ... By the early 1920s the value of both muskrat and white fox had increased twentyfold since the turn of the century, and the price of other furs had risen in similar fashion. Muskrats were taken by the hundred thousands, and mink was also a big crop in the Delta. Traders realized excellent profits, and the Delta trappers attained unprecedented prosperity; indeed many had far greater incomes than the average Canadian at the time. Although much of their money was dissipated in ephemeral luxuries, the Eskimos began to invest considerable sums in capital equipment. Gas powered whaleboats and schooners were the most popular items. In 1924 the Eskimo fleet at Aklavik consisted of 39 schooners (19 of which had auxiliary power), 28 whale boats and two other vessels. ... The Alaskan Eskimos were interested in producing a cash crop in order to amass wealth beyond the daily needs of shelter and food, and were willing and able to employ superior technology, greater commercial sophistication and increased geographical mobility to do so. The Mackenzie people resented these attitudes, and the distinction between the two groups on this basis persisted for at least fifty years after the initial immigration. Indeed, it continues today [1970] in modified form. (Usher 1:28, 30)

Kitto's "Report" of 1920 corroborates this view—"a layman is struck with two main thoughts, i.e. (1) that the Indian population has lost its vitality and the race in consequence is gradually dying out, and (2) that the Esquimo [*sic*] population on the other hand appears to be quite vigorous and healthy" (27)—and Knud Rasmussen's eyewitness account in the early months of 1924 echoes it: "the Mackenzie Eskimos had become an independent and prosperous people" (Ostermann 52). Six groups comprise the Mackenzie Delta Inuvialuit today: Kigirktayuk

(Herschel Is.), Kupugmiut (northern end of the Delta), Kigirktarugmiut (west side of the Delta, including Aklavik), Kittegaryumiut (southeast side of the Delta), Nuvorugmiut (northeast side of the Delta, extending up the Tuktoyaktuk peninsula), and Avvagmiut (Anderson River area) (Driscoll 172).

the Eskimo schooners ... had been brought in from the Arctic Ocean to be outfitted for the whaling season
Knud Rasmussen's observation of the schooners at Herschel Island in 1924 suggests that their use for whaling was strictly limited in the mid-1920s, by which time the Inuvialuit economy had switched principally to trapping:

> it was not surprising that these fur trappers addressed one another as "Captain"; in fact, they actually are the owners of schooners—flat-bottomed vessels which are sailed in about the great river deltas; they were obtainable for about 3,000 dollars, but were employed mainly on visiting trips in the summer season, whereas the business of trapping is carried on with the aid of the much more practical women's boats ["umiak" in Rasmussen, *Across* 294] or whaling sloops.
>
> Naturally there were motors in nearly all these schooners; in fact, machinery had been taken into use wherever possible. Whereas the [Fifth Thule] expedition up to this stage of its journey had had constant opportunities for admiring the great skill of the women at sewing skins, it was found here that the sewing machine was in use almost universally; many of the men had typewriters, though their correspondence of course was very small. Machine hair-clippers and safety razors too were looked upon as necessities, and people going about armed with cameras were quite common. The houses were illuminated with gasoline or, at a pinch, petroleum lamps, the ancient blubber lamps being regarded as antiquities and sold as such to tourists for up to 30 dollars each. (Ostermann 53)

the convent of the Grey Nuns
At the request of Gabriel Breynat, Roman Catholic bishop of the vicariat apostolique du Mackenzie, and Rév Père Alphonse Duport omi, director of the Oblates' mission at Aklavik, the Grey Nuns agreed to provide a hospital/mission/school at the settlement and arranged for its construction and completion in 1925. It was consecrated Mission de l'Immaculée

Conception in July of that year and operated until 1961, when it was replaced by the government-owned Grollier Hall in the newly created settlement of Inuvik. When Dorrien Smith was taken in by the nuns for the duration of her convalescence, sisters Ste Adelard, Obéline Pothier Firmin, Clara Gilbert, and Marie-Rose Poulin ran the hospital under the direction of the Rév Sœur locale Elizabeth McQuillan.

Lazarus Sittichinli ... a Loucheux Indian
Vyvyan's misspellings—"Loochoo" and "Sittichili"—have been corrected. The letter *n* in Lazarus' surname always escaped her. According to her letter to R. Hinks, the secretary of the RGS, 11 January 1929, she knew that "Loochoo" was a misspelling of the name of the northernmost Dene in Canada and requested that it be replaced by the correct spelling, but no correction was made before publication of her article later that year ("Rat River" 447) or, more than three decades later, before the publication of her book.

we were formally introduced to the murderer
Under this date, Dorrien Smith exclaimed that "one of the murderers came aboard ... and the judge introduced him to me and Clara. We shook hands!"

the judge, the prosecutor, the defence
Judge Lucien Dubuc, Crown Prosecutor Irving B. Howatt, Defence Attorney C. Gerald O'Connor, and Clerk R.F. Harris had travelled from Edmonton with Vyvyan and Dorrien Smith. (O'Connor is the man mistaken in Chpt 5 [23] for a gold prospector, full of exaggerated tales of Inuit.) Also, according to the *Edmonton Bulletin*, RCMP with the party included Sgt E.G. Baker and Const G.M. Wall, C.E. Wood, L.F. Fielder, A.J. Chartrand, C.E. Pounder, W.C. Tyack, A.J. Rayment, and H.W. Brinkworth ("Court"). Vyvyan's account of the murder trial at Aklavik is the most complete available, as no surviving records of the RCMP and the Department of Justice appear to make mention of this event. Edmonton newspapers offered limited coverage. The *Edmonton Bulletin* attributed the murder to "a shortage of wives" ("Arctic Killer" 1).

a policeman would act as interpreter
It is clear from the subsequent description that an Inuk who was not a member of the RCMP served as interpreter.

The accused had shot a neighbour's dog

The book's description of the murder case omits the information in Vyvyan's field note for 23 June—that the accused had stolen the victim's wife; the book states only what the field note for 1 June records—that he had shot the victim's dog. Another version of the circumstances of the crime is provided by RCMP historian Harwood Steele. It too makes no mention of the theft of a wife:

> Uluksak, the story went, had been bullying Ikayena. Then Ikayena shot one of Uluksak's dogs, "because it was old." He was said to have replaced the animal, but, in the Arctic, the action seemed "highly unfriendly." Some days later, while Ikayena and a friend were at cards "Uluksak hung around in front of the tent, playing around with some cartridges but saying nothing." The friend decamped, "the two principals remained eyeing each other." Suddenly two shots rang out—Ikayena had fired both, killing his enemy. He swore that Uluksak made the first hostile move and that the second shot was necessary, as Uluksak tried to reach his rifle, though witnesses disagreed and the first wound was very severe.
>
> So [Sgt F.A. Barnes] arrested Ikayena; and on February 23rd, after an 850-mile patrol, was back in Tree River. (254)

Quite properly, Vyvyan does not identify this man as one of the two men, named Uluksuk and Sinnisiak, who killed Roman Catholic priests Jean-Baptiste Rouvière and Guillaume Le Roux at Bloody Fall in 1913, and who faced trial—"the first involving Canadian Eskimos on a capital charge" (Steele 191)—in Edmonton and Calgary in August 1917. Death sentences were commuted to life imprisonment, but both Uluksuk and Sinnisiak were found to be model prisoners and were pardoned on 15 May 1919 (Moyles 85). This Uluksuk died of spinal tuberculosis in Coppermine 23 September 1929.

they are apt to kill off their old folk and their female babies in hard times

It is interesting that Vyvyan proceeds to qualify this assertion by O'Connor, the defense attorney. Another statement, again from a Euro-Canadian perspective, in support of it occurs in the Grey Nuns' history of their mission at Aklavik: "It was at this time, too, 1926, that the sisters at Aklavik begged their Superior and the Canadian government to open a 'creche' for new-born babies. Their reason was that baby girls were either crushed to death or left in the wilds to be devoured by bears or wolves. Their cause was well received" (Champagne). Different perspectives are offered by both the biographer and the wife of the then governor general of Canada. Julian Hedworth George, Viscount Byng of Vimy travelled down the Mackenzie in 1925 and, thanks to arrangements made at the last minute by Canon Edward Hester, met Inuvialuit at Kittigazuit: "One of [their] more endearing qualities," thought Byng, "was their obvious fondness for children—their name for them was 'noogiduks'" (Williams 299). Although she had travelled with him to the Yukon on an earlier trip, Lady Byng was advised against the Mackenzie River trip, "which was supposed to be too rough for me, though I shall always regret I didn't insist on going." She records her husband's impression of the Inuit view thus: "So long as a baby was a helpless piece of humanity it was everybody's job to help it, but the moment it was old enough to twist a rope, or do any work, it took its place in the scheme of things" (Byng 159). It is impossible to know if, without the opportunity of making her own observations, she might have detected a discrepancy in the treatment of boys and girls.

A somewhat more conclusive view of Inuit treatment of the elderly, nearly contemporary (1928) with the view heard by Vyvyan, is that of Anglican Archdeacon Archibald Fleming, who worked extensively with Inuit in both the eastern and western Arctic:

> From time immemorial the Eskimo had from sheer economic necessity but one solution to the problem of the aged and helpless: to wall them off during the cold of the winter into an igloo where death came quietly and alone. To us this seems cruel and terrible but in a land where constant traveling is essential and where hunger stalks each living thing, the burden of the handicapped makes an impossible demand. During the last thirty years [presumably, thirty years prior to 1956, the date of publication of Fleming's book] conditions in the Arctic have so changed that this problem, the pity of which lay on my heart like lead, has been largely solved. I think it is safe to say that no Eskimo or Indian now needs to feel the death knell tolling when he has had an accident or exceeds the normal span of life. (294)

Interpreter stands up ready for action, in reindeer parka, white wolverine collar, moccasins, blue trousers, a man with an aristocratic face and jutting chin, alert dark eyes, gold ring on one finger, half Kanaka, half Eskimo
By "Kanaka," Vyvyan refers specifically to someone from Hawaii or generally to someone from another South Seas island. To Vyvyan's eye, the man evidently possessed an exotic appearance, but another report of him, by one who knew him much better, does not accord with hers. Archdeacon Whittaker also attended the trial. Following is a portion of his account:

> At this trial, Billie Kemaksina, a native of mixed Eskimo and Portuguese blood, was the interpreter. I had known Billie as a small boy, an imp for mischief, but fairly attentive at school. Afterward he went to Point Barrow, where he had more schooling. Marrying there, he had returned to the Delta, having acquired a good working knowledge of English. Being a good hunter, and trapper, careful and honest, he was highly esteemed by the Hudson [*sic*] Bay Company, who had brought down for him an auxiliary power schooner, valued at $7,000, for which he had in hand a large down-payment of valuable furs.
>
> After the trial was over, Canon Hester, the resident missionary, secured the alleged murderer, with another from the same region, for attendance at the church, and Billie was put up to preach the Gospel to them. With a little book of notes in his hand, he began an address which presented to the minds of the pagan Eskimo, almost everything that the missionaries had spent thirty years in bringing to the consciousness of a people who were now in a high state of civilization, and of Christian living. Both as an interpreter of other men's words, and of the truths of the Christian religion, he had attained a high standard. I could gather enough, listening closely, to appreciate his loyalty to what he had been taught, and his native eloquence in delivering his message. (Whittaker, "Sunrise" 174)

The point about the expenditure of thirty years' effort echoes a statement by Bishop Stringer recorded in Vyvyan's field note for 29 May.

Nalonga is slit-eyed, tattooed lines on face
Generally, among Inuit of the region, pierced earlobes, pierced nasal septa, and facial tattoos were forms of ornamentation for both men and women. "Women's tattoos consisted of small blue crosses at the corners of the mouth and of several vertical blue lines on the chin," while "men's tattoos consisted of two or three transverse blue lines on the cheeks worn by homicides and of small blue crosses on the shoulder worn by whalers" (Smith 252-53).

like the dancer, I had left my own consciousness and gone back into some region of prehistoric time
In kind, Vyvyan's cultural disorientation is customary; in degree, it is rather remarkable, although Bishop Stringer found a similar dance "dreadful to behold" when he saw it at Kittigazuit in 1893 (qtd. in Frank Peake, *The Bishop* 27). One might be inclined to interpret "large village hall" as the local *kashim* (also transcribed as *qasgiq*—the communal men's clubhouse/assembly house [Smith 351; Ostermann 26; Fienup-Riordan 43]—and as *kajigi* [Frank Peake, *The Bishop* 26]); but, if it is, it is only a makeshift one, for Vyvyan's field note for 24 June establishes that it occurred in the mission house, and Dorrien Smith, who did not attend, specifies in her note for the same date that it was the Anglican, rather than the Roman Catholic, mission house. Vyvyan's basic description of the dance, aside from her response to it, is similar to earlier ones, including the one most often cited, by Roman Catholic missionary Émile-Fortuné-Stanilas-Joseph Petitot (1838-1916). Noted for the acuteness of his ethnographic observations, he visited Inuvialuit (Mackenzie Delta Inuit) four times between 1865 and 1877, and witnessed dances at both Fort McPherson and Fort Anderson, which, situated on the Anderson River east of the Mackenzie Delta, lay between Aklavik and Ikagena's home region. In noting how drummers using seal skin drums mark time and that a chorus of men and women always chant the words of a song (*ajajai*) to the beat of the drum, he recorded the following:

> their dances are characterized by mimic and rhythmed steps. Music makers and singers stand in around the dancers who, only a few at a time, gambol, gesticulate, and strike attitudes now with a terrible martial look, now with a gracious comical even burlesque stance. *Kréyouktark* started to imitate the behaviour, the little leaps, the contortions, the wingbeats and even the cawings of the crow. His song was tuned to the movements of the dance … He changed the theme of his dance and of his songs to represent the hunting of a

porpoise or of a sperm-whale, the pursuit in a kayak, the casting of the harpoon, the cetacean's writhings of pain, and his spurtings of blood-tinted water. (Savoie 1:193)

Depending upon how widespread the particular melody of the chanting was among Inuit groups, the tune heard by Vyvyan might have been the one recorded in Alaska by Charles Hoffman as "Song of the Seal" (23); another possibility might be that Ikagena enacted in dance the story of "The Man with a Scourge of Bearded-Sealskin," which Knud Rasmussen recorded in 1924 (Ostermann 130-32). "The Drum Dance" offers a salutary brief description of the drum dance, of which the seal dance is one example (O'Connell).

cotton dresses or fur-lined parkas with hoods … One old man wore two labrets in his lower lip
Alaskan Inupiat cultural practices, including clothing styles, came to the Inuvialuit of the Mackenzie Delta with the whaling trade in the late-nineteenth century. Generally, it had been traditionally the case that "the man's parka served as a metaphoric reference to the animal and to the man's role as hunter; the woman's parka, with its characteristic pouch (*amaut*), in which the wearer carried her infant, symbolized the maternal role of the woman" (Driscoll 176). On the new style of parka, made from caribou, "the hood was trimmed with wolverine instead of white caribou fur. The white insets on the side of the hood were smaller than on the old style. The white chest panels were replaced with tusk-like white-haired sections sewn on each side of the centre front. … These pieces are symbolic of walrus tusks. Walruses are honored for their strength and aggressive behavior. The new parka's hemline was about mid-thigh length. Instead of being cut straight across, the hem curved upwards at the hips. An authentic tail of the caribou was attached to the backs of parkas; … parkas were often trimmed with white caribou hair or wolverine" (Oakes and Pointe 102). While a colour illustration of the full man's outfit that Vyvyan likely saw is reproduced in Driscoll (180), it is noteworthy that Vyvyan's photographs of the interpreter, Billie Kemaksina, and of an unidentified woman at Aklavik show, respectively, shorter and longer versions of this design (see above, 59,62). The exaggerated "sunburst" effect of the trim around the hood of the parka seems to have been a later development (Oakes 8).

As to the cotton seen by Vyvyan on garments, Oakes and Pointe note that "the Alaskan Inupiat through traders obtained brightly colored fabric which was used to make a cloth shell for a skin parka. This style is currently known as the 'Mother Hubbard'. The Delta Inuvialuit, due to their interaction with the Alaskan Inupiat, were introduced to this colorful parka shell. … One way of displaying economic status [as a successful trapper] was to make the Mother Hubbard several inches longer than the skin outer parka. When wearing the outer parka, the fabric inner parka was visible designating one's ability to obtain trade goods" (102). Versions of these cotton garments apparently are represented in Dorrien Smith's watercolour sketch of Inuit outside a summer tent residence (see above, 196), and a photograph by Vyvyan appears in *Arctic Adventure*. One account of the inter-racial contact that issued in this fashion occurs in *Pursuing the Whale*, about the winter of 1900-01, which Capt John Cook and his wife, "the first and only white woman to winter as far north and east" (221), spent in the *Bowhead*, an American whaler, off Baillie Island, north-east of the Mackenzie Delta:

> As winter advanced, the Eskimo women became more acquainted with Mrs Cook and used to come aboard asking her to teach them how to sew calico, or cloth, for they call all cloth "calico," and they in turn would teach Mrs Cook to sew skins and furs, to make rugs and clothing. Although they quickly acquired the art of sewing clothing, Mrs Cook could not seem to stitch furs equal to them; and when her sewing of furs was examined by them, how they would laugh! (221)

Labrets are "buttons made of ivory worn as ornaments and inserted into cuts in the lower lip on either side of the mouth," but Archibald Fleming goes on from this description (294) to suggest that they were uncommon at Bernard Harbour by 1928, so it is perhaps not surprising that Vyvyan noticed that an "old" man wore them; in his book the next year, Rasmussen made the same observation (*Across* facing 292). Ethnographer Derek Smith explains that, among Inuvialuit, "paired cheek labrets were worn by men after puberty. These were usually made of polished stone or ivory, and in late times were ornamented with blue glass bead insets" (252).

one old woman who, as I learned later, was reputed to be a wife of the explorer Stefansson
According to Georgina Stefansson, who was a fifth-grade student at Inuvik Federal School in 1961, this woman was

Fannie Puniovaluk. She and Stefansson "had only one child, my father, who now lives at Aklavik, where he owns a freighter and hunts and traps in his spare time. My grandmother died many years ago. Since then my grandfather moved to the United States. ... Although I have never met him I have always been proud of him, and feel that I do know him because of the stories my dad has told me about him" (Georgina Stefansson 25). The explorer never did acknowledge his native offspring (Hunt 120), although in *My Life with the Eskimo* he mentioned that he travelled with "an elderly country-woman ... named Pannigabluk, whose husband had died the year before" (117).

Field Note for Wednesday 23 June
Not surprisingly, the first entry in Dorrien Smith's field note for this date reports on the doctor's house call to her aboard the steamer, as well as his verdict: "My foot keeps us here for a fortnight."

shupacks of fur or skin: babies tightly bound on backs in hoods
The latter are the women's *amaut*; the former are their footwear, which Vyvyan spelled phonetically, and which also is spelled "shoepak." This footwear consists of insulated rubber lowers and uppers of canvas or leather, or, as Vyvyan observed in Aklavik, caribou fur or seal skin. It is possible that a boot made entirely of rubber was introduced by the American whalers at Herschel Island and was modified for local use with a complement of warmer materials than rubber, leather, or felt.

CHAPTER 11: HARBOUR OF WRECKED MEN

While the field notes mention "city of the dead" (26 June) and "wrecked" men and women of the North (11 June), this chapter's extensive sketches are Vyvyan's later creations. Similar ruined figures appear in early adventure novels set in the North by writers such as Americans Rex Beach and Dillon Wallace and Canadian Gilbert Parker. Vyvyan's celebration of the RCMP as the exception to this pattern is typical of not only the anecdotes she records in the field notes about their exploits, but also the conventions of a long tradition of adventure novels featuring mounties, which portrayed the North as the proving ground of young manhood.

"The steamer brought in drink," he said. "The first liquor in nine months. They are all under the covers today. Dead drunk."
In her letter of 20 June to her mother, Vyvyan noted that "the drunkenness up here is something awful—among white men."

As for communications by wireless and airplane, both of them were, at the time of our journey, in their early stages of development in northern Canada
The situation was, indeed, about to change rapidly. The first airplanes were seen on the Mackenzie River in the winter of 1928-29, and thirty-year-old C.H. "Punch" Dickins, a veteran of the Royal Flying Corps in the First World War, reached Aklavik by air for the first time on Dominion Day 1929 (Bonnycastle, *Gentleman* 105). Reliable postal service quickly became the first regular cargo aboard northern flights; Richard Bonnycastle reported reading Winnipeg newspapers only three days old when in Fort Good Hope.

That Vyvyan mentions visits to the wireless stations at several posts might suggest that she was half-expecting a communication to be awaiting her. However, her apparently inordinate interest might also be attributable to their novelty. The NWT and Yukon Radio System had just come into being. Sheer distances had dissuaded the Department of the Interior from plans to erect and maintain a telegraph line, but radio-telegraph could function through air waves along a system of relay stations. The Royal Canadian Corps of Signals was assigned the task of erecting that system of stations. Led by Major W.A. Steel, a party of the RCCS installed stations at Mayo and Dawson, Yukon. With these, the System opened on 20 October 1923. In 1924, the terminal system at Edmonton and the control station at Fort Simpson were opened. In 1925, the equipment designated for the station at Fort Smith was seconded for the summer to the SS *Distributor* so that Governor General Byng could be supplied with continuous service. It was operational at Fort Smith once his return trip downriver was completed. After near-disaster delayed the installation at Herschel Island in 1924, Lt H.A. Young made his way from there to Aklavik in April 1925. As Jim Koe's memoir confirms, the system was installed and running there in October of that year, thus making possible Cunliffe's reservation, by way of Brabant in Edmonton and Parsons at Aklavik, of a canoe for the women, while the summer-only station at Herschel Island opened in 1926 (Moir 276-79). Young, who would go on to train Signals personnel in anticipation of the Second World War (Moir 64), is mentioned in Vyvyan's field note for 26 June. Only in her accounts, following the last dated entry in her field notes (227), does the information appear that she sent a wireless from Aklavik; it cost her $2.70, which, given the rate—"30 c[en]ts. a word"—listed in her field note for 2 July, must have represented a nine-word message.

the North-West Mounted Police
Vyvyan can hardly be blamed for erring in the name of the institution. Established as the North-West Mounted Police in 1873, the force was invited to add "Royal" to its name in 1904. On 1 February 1920, seven months after the Winnipeg General Strike (Kemp 69), "the RNWMP merged with the Dominion Police to form the Royal Canadian Mounted Police" ("North-West"). Acronyms, which do not show the hyphen, of the various forms of the name are used throughout the notes depending on the year referred to; in terms of strict accuracy, by 1926 all Vyvyan's references should have been to the RCMP.

CHAPTER 12: LA PIERRE HOUSE (23 JUNE)

Although Vyvyan's field note for 23 June records her meeting with Jack Parsons at Aklavik, the discovery that La Pierre House was abandoned is not mentioned. On 27 May, in Edmonton, Vyvyan was told that the women might be able to reprovision at La Pierre House, but since she discussed the Rat River with Archdeacon Whittaker on 2 June at Waterways, she likely knew well before she arrived in Aklavik that La Pierre House was abandoned; alternatively, since Whittaker's journey up the Rat had taken place "long ago" (as Vyvyan put it in her letter to her mother of 3 June), and he had been stationed in Penetanguishene since 1923, Vyvyan could have assumed that he was not *au courant* with its state.

In the published version of events, the discovery that the women would have to travel through the wilderness alone appears just as Dorrien Smith's ankle is healing, and Vyvyan's dramatic conversation with Parsons is followed by an anxious search for information about the route and for paddling lessons. Introduced in this chapter, then, the abandonment of La Pierre House heightens the narrative tension just as the women are about to embark on their wilderness adventure; Whittaker's qualified encouragement (Vyvyan's letter to her

mother of 3 June finds him "rather gloomy about our trip") and Sgt Anderton's confident encouragement are balanced by Vyvyan's own retrospective evaluation of the women's resources. The tension might be regarded as one between two identities, "mere tourists" (41) and "seasoned travellers" (73). Will the sprained ankle permit them to make themselves over into travellers now that they are on the brink of the wilderness? The interview with Anderton permits Vyvyan to move from "dream" to "sober fact," a progression they must make if they are to get up the Rat and over the Divide to the enchantment of three days alone on the Porcupine River.

Apart from the interview with Anderton, the contents of the chapter have no equal in the field notes.

the manager of the Hudson's Bay Company store, Mr Parsons
John Ambrose Parsons (1886-1974) was born in Codroy, Newfoundland, and served as a constable of the RNWMP from 1909 to 1916, taking his discharge after serving in Yorkton, Kamsack, Punnichy, Athabasca Landing, Fort McPherson, and Herschel Island (Zealley to MacLaren). The following year he joined the HBC, and throughout his career (1917-31) he worked as a post manager in the western Arctic. He was at Baillie Island 1917-20, at Fort McPherson 1920-24, and at Aklavik 1924-30, before returning to Fort McPherson for his final year in the company's service. He then became an independent trader at Aklavik ("Parsons"). In the winter of 1932, he was involved in the hunt for Albert Johnson, the "Mad Trapper" (Zealley to MacLaren).

a trader and also a trapper
It is possible that Vyvyan here preserves a distinction in the two terms as sometimes used in the North: "trader" refers to white trappers and "trapper" to non-whites.

our friend Sergeant Anderton
Sgt Frederick Anderton (1889-1974) was born in Leicestershire, England, and served with the Leicestershire Constabulary 1910-12 before emigrating to Canada. He joined the RNWMP in 1913 at Regina, served in France and Belgium during the First World War, and returned to the force after demobilization. Promoted to sergeant in 1920 and sergeant major in 1934, he served throughout the northwest and the Arctic from Regina and Edmonton to Herschel Island and

Aklavik. He was in charge of the schooner *St Roch* 1928-33, and resigned from the force in 1935 to assist in the organization of the Newfoundland Rangers. He retired in 1937, eventually settling in British Columbia ("Obituaries").

how Archdeacon Whittaker had exposed Stefansson and his "old hag of an Eskimo" wife

As in her field note for 27 June, Vyvyan proceeds in this paragraph to ask a somewhat elliptical question, which seems directed at the motives behind Whittaker's decision to expose Stefansson. It has been conjectured by Stefansson's biographers that Whittaker, who had befriended Stefansson at Herschel Island many years earlier, considered retaliation appropriate after Stefansson had "decried the unwholesome influence of missionary activity on the Eskimo in his book, *My Life With the Eskimo*" (Diubaldo 90), which had appeared in 1913 (see *My Life* 370-422, 428 for the relevant remarks). Anticipating that the marriage which appeared likely to issue from Stefansson's engagement to his American fiancée would make the explorer a bigamist, Whittaker claimed in public lecture and print in Toronto and Ottawa that "Stefansson had no use for religion and the Ten Commandments and charged that Stefansson had left a wife and child behind in the Arctic" (Diubaldo 90). In the 12 June 1913 issue of the *Toronto Globe*, he wrote, "We know the lives that abandoned men live away from the law and public opinion ... We should care as much about the Salvation of souls as Stefansson cares about the bodies" (qtd in Diubaldo 90; see also Hunt 120).

King William Land

If this error is Vyvyan's and not her publisher's, it is interesting to consider its significance: "King William Land" should be King William Island (as, indeed, Dorrien Smith's field note for 28 June puts it). Sir John Franklin, on his fourth and fateful voyage to the Canadian Arctic in 1845, understood that the island formed part of Boothia Peninsula, a northern extension of the continental mainland; his maps showed "King William Land" because British naval officer James Clark Ross, exploring in the early spring of 1830, did not discern the frozen strait (now known as James Ross Strait) between King William Island, Matty Islands, and Boothia Peninsula (Cooke and Holland 155). Although Roald Amundsen had sailed through the strait in 1903 and 1904 on his way to the first successful voyage through the Northwest Passage, his discovery

apparently occurred after the publication of the map to which Vyvyan had access. If it was in the same atlas that showed her La Pierre House and misled her into thinking it a settlement, both errors suggest that her atlas was published in the nineteenth century.

Field Note for Monday 28 June

Echoing the beginning of Vyvyan's, Dorrien Smith's note for this day ends with an apprehensive expression: "Snow on the Mts. up the Rat!"

Mr Karel just came in w. the 2 schooners after a rough trip

Dorrien Smith's field note clarifies that the women had first seen these two schooners at Fort Smith on 11 June.

CHAPTER 13: THE UNRELENTING NORTH (25, 26 JUNE, 1 JULY)

In 1935, an earlier version of this chapter appeared as an article, "The Unrelenting North." In both it and the book, Capt Cameron metamorphosed from the field notes' Capt McIntyre; he is one of the two people in the book whose name Vyvyan changed ("Murphy of Simpson" is the other). None of this description or the personal history related in the article and the chapter appear in the field notes. Mr Bloom the missionary is "Mr Gunn" in the article (179), and the article lacks any reference to Dorrien Smith's ailment.

Herschel Island

After 1860, whaling ships from the United States began arriving in the Beaufort Sea through Bering Strait; beginning in 1890, they adopted the practice of wintering over at Herschel Island (*Qikiqtaqruk*), which lies off the Yukon coast, 280 km or 175 mi north and west of Aklavik (Kitto, *North West* 57; Jenness 8-14; Philip Godsell, *Arctic* 259). This practice began to be curtailed after 1906 when the market for whalebone crashed; during the nearly two decades of vigorous commercial activity, as many as twenty ships wintered at the island.

Irving B. Howatt, K.C., counsel for the Crown, prosecuted the case in 1923 against Aligoomiak and Tetamagana, which resulted in their execution. Evidently, Capt McIntyre was a member of the jury panel (see photo above, 78).

Captain Cameron ... We found him on the shore
The identity of this man is uncertain, but it seems likely that he is Samuel "Scotty" McIntyre, who spent three years (1909-12) as an assistant to Ernest Leffingwell during his cartographical and geological survey of the Alaskan coastline west of Herschel Island. In August 1912, Leffingwell gave McIntyre the yawl, *Argo*, which had been used for their surveys. This was done "in payment of his wages, according to agreement, and a few days later he proceeded eastward with it into Canadian territory" (Leffingwell 16), provisioned for three years, apparently to become a trader with the Copper Inuit. Another reference locates him at Herschel Island on 26 August 1912 (Bockstoce). At Baillie Island, east of the Mackenzie Delta, on 22 August 1923, Arnold Liebes reported meeting "Capt. McIntyre." Liebes, whose father operated the Liebes Fur Company out of San Francisco along the Alaskan coast, sold him some trade goods and wrote, "McIntyre and Dr. Steffany will leave for Eastward in the morning. McIntyres schooner named Argo" (Liebes). McIntyre was then trading out of Tree River (Bockstoce), and this was at about the time of the murders in April 1922 for which Tatamagana and Aligoomiak were convicted by jury at Herschel Island in the summer of 1923. A photograph reproduced in this volume from Lucien Dubuc's scrapbook identifies McIntyre at Herschel Island with Judge Dubuc that summer, probably as a member of the jury panel. In the photograph, McIntyre's dress exhibits some of the features noted in Vyvyan's book: "knitted brown cap running to a point, ... mukluks made of seal-skin reaching to his knees," even an "old black pipe." In the photo, he would seem to be of about the right age to have come north in plenty of time to participate in the Klondike gold rush. Presumably, he was returning from the trial at Herschel Island when Liebes met him at Baillie Island.

According to Vyvyan's book, by the time the women met him three years later, McIntyre had lost the *Argo* as well as the *Bonny Belle* (perhaps they were one and the same "ship" and she changed its name as she had his surname, but the field notes offer no such evidence). Dorrien Smith's field note for 26 June includes more details about him: "Capt McIntyre, who has been in the North since '79 having come with the whaling schooners, came and had a yarn. He has spent most of his time with the Eskimos, and knew Uluksuk, the murdered man, intimately, and had great respect for him as a hunter with his three wives." McIntyre's knowledge of Uluksuk makes sense in light of the fact that both were in Tree River in 1923.

Captain Cameron ... held the most rigid notions about the impropriety of white men marrying Indians or Eskimos
The mixed-blood population of Aklavik originated in the liaisons of American whalers at Herschel Island with Inuit women, and, more significantly for Aklavik, fur-trade marriages between British men and Gwich'in women at Fort McPherson. According to Shepard Krech, the genesis of the latter

> can be traced mainly to three marriages. ... In 1858, a western Kutchin woman married Alexander Stewart, a Scotch [*sic*] Hebrides Islander who had arrived at Fort McPherson in 1852 as a laborer, carpenter and blacksmith for the HBC. In 1875, Stewart's halfbreed daughter married John Firth, an Orkney man who became renowned in the western Arctic during more than forty years (1872-1920) with the HBC. Firth managed the Fort McPherson post from 1893-1920, and his iron hand helped maintain order during the turbulent whaling era. The third important marriage of a White took place in 1912, when A.N. Blake, an Englishman who arrived in Fort McPherson as a member of the Royal North-West Mounted Police, and who subsequently worked both for the HBC and as an independent trader, married a Kutchin woman.... Stewart had four married sons [one of whom established Aklavik], one married daughter and approximately 20 grandchildren. Firth had 13 natural and four adopted children, at least seven of which raised families in the Mackenzie Delta. And six of Blake's sons, most of whom remained in the Fort McPherson region, fathered 46 children. ("Interethnic" 114-16)

Vyvyan has her Capt Cameron express an opinion about interethnic relations that is not uncommon among those northern men who experienced guilt over siring their own mixed-blood progeny (see, for example, MacLaren, "HBC's" 478-79 n23). Citing the published version of Vyvyan's interview as a case in point, Honigmann and Honigmann observed that

> despite some intermarriage between whites and natives, a two-part class structure consisting of whites and natives did tend to emerge in a large community like Aklavik where whites were numerous. The strongest proponents of social

exclusiveness were those white families who prempted [*sic*] power and held the highest prestige in the community. They relied on one another for sociability without need of the natives. ... These attitudes [of Cameron/McIntyre] sound overstated and may not have been entirely seriously uttered, but they reflect a real tendency to social exclusiveness. But we must also acknowledge the heterogeneity of the non-native population. While some whites were staid and abstemious embodiments of Victorian values, others regarded the North as a frontier where they could shuck many conventions. They chafed under the growth of regulation that seemed to pursue them north. (34-5)

In 1907 at Herschel Island, Archdeacon Whittaker and the RNWMP came to loggerheads over a mixed marriage. Francis Fitzgerald, after whom Fort Fitzgerald was named in 1911, was supported by Whittaker in his decision to marry Unalina, his Inuit common-law wife; however, Fitzgerald's superiors found his intentions unthinkable, disallowed the marriage, and rebuffed Whittaker (Coates and Morrison 135). Around the time of this event, McIntyre might have been a member of the Herschel Island community. He certainly was by 1909, if the Samuel McIntyre who was with Leffingwell at Flaxman Island is the same person. (It must be noted that no earlier mention of McIntyre occurs in the standard accounts of the time [Cook] or in lists of whaling captains [Frank Peake, *The Bishop* 36-7] and voyages [Bockstoce and Batchelder].) His negative attitudes towards intermarriage and the missionaries could have formed in response to this incident.

a modern Demosthenes or Bossuet
Demosthenes (384-22 BC) and Jacques Bénigne Bossuet (1627-1704) were renowned Greek and French orators of their respective ages.

CHAPTER 14: TWO IDLE WEEKS
(27 JUNE–6 JULY)

The visitors described by Vyvyan in this chapter appear in the field notes throughout the women's time in Aklavik. The difficult afternoon when both Archdeacon Whittaker and Capt Cameron appear was actually 1 July; according to both Vyvyan's and Dorrien Smith's field notes for that date, it was *Mrs*

Whittaker, the Archdeacon's wife, who visited the women at the same time as the captain. Mrs Whittaker, like many of the women mentioned, and admired, by Vyvyan in her field notes, does not appear in the book.

the doctor's wife with her new-born baby
According to "Aklavik Chroniques 1925-1941," the wife of Dr Cook had been admitted to the Grey Nuns infirmary for three weeks in late May; Vyvyan and Dorrien Smith's stay at the mission occurred during her second admittance. Vyvyan's mention of a "new-born baby" implies that the cause was a birth rather than an illness, and her letter to her mother of 30 June confirms this: "there are 6 Gray Nuns here some Indian children they are teaching Doctor's wife with new born baby."

Sister Firmin ... had hailed long ago from Ireland
The suggestion of the nun's connection to Ireland seems to arise from a misunderstanding by Vyvyan. Born Obéline Pothier in Eelbrook, Nova Scotia, Sœur Firmin (1878-1951) took the name Vyvyan knew her by when she joined the Grey Nuns in 1900, as a postulant of l'Association des Petites Sœurs Auxiliares. Her work in the North began in 1903 at Fort Resolution and continued for forty-five years, at Providence, Fort Simpson, Aklavik, Fort Chipewyan, and Fort Smith. Duchaussois, in *Grey Nuns in the Far North* (a book Vyvyan read, according to the list that appears following the last dated entry in her field notes [226]), lists her among the "Little Coadjutor Sisters" serving with the Grey Nuns in the North. She laboured chiefly in the kitchens of missions, although she also worked as a teacher. She was one of the founders of the Grey Nuns mission at Aklavik. She regained her birth name and became Sœur Obéline Pothier, a choir sister of the Grey Nuns, after the Petites Sœurs Auxiliares were amalgamated with the Grey Nuns proper in 1942. A victim of the influenza epidemic at Aklavik in 1951, she died that year (*Annales* [1955] 236-41; Duchaussois, *Grey Nuns* 277).

Lao-Tse's interpreter Kwang, of the 3rd century B.C.
Laotse or Lao-tzu (604?-531? BC), Chinese philosopher and mystic, is generally regarded as the founder of Taoism. Kwang or Chuang-tzu, who lived in the latter half of the fourth century BC and first years of the third, is the foremost interpreter of the *Tao te ching*. The quotation helps to clarify Vyvyan's allusion, which initially seems inappropriate to a list of quali-

ties that remind one rather more of the monastic tradition of Buddhism, especially in terms of denial and negation; the quotation seems intended to regard the characteristics of Aklavik that re-emerged after the departure of the *Distributor*, as ones that afforded the opportunity for reflection and spiritual growth.

One of our visitors, a trader, told us a story of an Indian
Vyvyan is mistaken in attributing this tale to a "trader"; her field note for 6 July states that she heard it from Anglican missionary William Archibald Geddes.

Canon Hester
Born in England, Edward Hester (1882–1945) undertook lay missionary work in Manchester and then in Ungava as a deacon in the Church of England. After his ordination, he served as missionary among the Inuit of the western Arctic from 1915 to 1927, travelling extensively between Herschel Island and Bathurst Inlet. In 1924, he met and travelled with Rasmussen during the Dane's Fifth Thule Expedition, and was remembered by him as "an energetic young man of 'the happy type', with a dominating laugh that comes just a little too often, otherwise a nice fellow of a practical turn of mind. Up here a missionary has to do everything himself—look after his dogs, procure dog-feed, tend his nets, build his own house, and knows nothing of the Kivfaks [servants] with which Danish missionaries in Greenland surround themselves. Small means—are glad of 'Fote' from the natives to help them in their work—which is often misunderstood" (Ostermann 32–3). In 1927, when he published his first book about the expedition, Rasmussen noted that, in 1924, Hester had had to move his mission work from Coronation Gulf nearer to the Mackenzie Delta, "as the missionary society which sent him out could not afford to keep him so far afield. Having in mind the sums spent on punishing criminals here in the wilds," Rasmussen went on, referring to the hanging at Herschel Island two months earlier of Tatamagana and Aligoomiak, "it seems a pity that it should be necessary to economize in a field of work which more than all else helps to prevent the growth of criminal tendencies" (*Across* 297). In 1927, Hester returned to England and married his fiancée, Hilda May Buckingham. He served in several English parishes until his death (Zealley, "Edward"). His mission work was the envy of the redoubtable Alaskan missionary, Archdeacon Hudson Stuck (*Winter* 326).

Although his purchase of several of her watercolour sketches alone might have created a fine impression on Dorrien Smith, her field note about Hester on 28 June is full of admiration: "Was most interesting. He had been all along the coast to King Williams Island etc. living with the Eskimos, and had been to Hudson Bay also and worked round there. Been in four years, now going out. I believe a very fine man."

an Irish friend named Tyrell who gave me daily lessons in his 17-foot canoe
Judge Dubuc's caption to the photograph of the Inuit trials in 1924 lists "Sam C. Tyrell, Aklavik, trader" as a member of the jury panel (Photo Scrapbook).

we went to an Eskimo service in the Church of England chapel
The first Anglican presence in the Mackenzie River basin occurred in 1858, when David Anderson, bishop of Rupert's Land, and the Church Missionary Society sent Archdeacon James Hunter to investigate the feasibility of missions in the area of Fort Simpson. The next year, Rev William West Kirkby was directed to the Mackenzie and thus began a more or less permanent Anglican presence in the region. The first mission at Aklavik was established in 1919 by Bishop Lucas, and construction on All Saints Anglican Church began in 1920 (*All* 1). (Construction began on All Saints Cathedral in 1937, and it was consecrated in 1939; for many years, Lazarus Sittichinli worked as the caretaker there.) In January 1924, Hester reported to Bishop Lucas that "the Church looks really fine now, everything that you have recommended has been done, and the mission plant is the best set up in the place and attended to. Be prepared to take some good photographs when you come" (Hester). From the beginning, separate services were held in the Gwich'in and Inuvialuktun languages.

We could not help thinking of that well-satisfied man who prayed with himself while he declared that he fasted twice in the week and gave tithes of all that he possessed
Vyvyan here alludes to Luke 18:10–14, which rehearses the parable told by Christ to his disciples about the Pharisee's self-exalted prayer, in contrast to the Publican's humble prayer for forgiveness. In her field note for 4 July, she clarifies that Whittaker's sermon put her in mind of the "Pharisee." The picture generally painted in the New Testament renders Pharisees, the strictest of

the Jewish sects (Acts 26:5), almost entirely negatively. Christ condemned especially their ostentation, their hypocrisy, their belief in salvation by works, their impenitence, and their loveless-ness (Bryant 453-54). Vyvyan's negative view of Whittaker's effectiveness, which is not so forcefully registered in the book as in the field note for 4 July, is not the only one. Whittaker's approach and personality seem not to have conduced to his winning over Inuvialuit or non-native northerners to the Christian message. One historical view sees Whittaker as "acerbic and inflexible" (Coates and Morrison 131), while another could locate "very few sympathetic accounts of Whittaker's character" (Ingram and Dobrowolsky 76). It may be, given her subsequent comments, that Vyvyan thought not only of Whittaker as the Pharisee, but also of Hester as the down-to-earth Publican.

He had translated the hymn "Jerusalem the Golden" for them, because he thought certain lines would appeal to their imagination
Hester was inspired in his choice of a hymn that imagined the future rather than described conditions in the world which might be foreign to the Inuit life experience. Written in English in 1851 and revised in 1859, this hymn by the Rev J.M. Neale translates one written in Latin in 1145 by Bernard of Cluny and based on The Revelation of St John the Divine 21:18: "And the building of the wall of it was of jasper: and the city was pure gold, like unto clear glass."

> Jerusalem the golden,
> With milk and honey blest,
> Beneath thy contemplation
> Sink heart and voice opprest.
> I know not, O I know not,
> What joys await us there,
> What radiancy of glory,
> What bliss beyond compare.
>
> They stand, those halls of Sion,
> All jubilant with song,
> And bright with many an angel,
> And all the martyr throng;
> The Prince is ever in them,
> The daylight is serene,
> The pastures of the blessèd
> Are decked in glorious sheen.

> There is the throne of David;
> And there, from care released,
> The shout of them that triumph,
> The song of them that feast;
> And they, who with their Leader
> Have conquered in the fight,
> For ever and for ever
> Are clad in robes of white.
>
> O sweet and blessèd country
> The home of God's elect!
> O sweet and blessèd country,
> That eager hearts expect!
> Jesu, in mercy bring us
> To that dear land of rest;
> Who art, with God the Father,
> And Spirit, ever blest.
> (*Book* no. 627)

Canon Hester. We always longed to know his subsequent history
Given her silence on the subject, it appears that Vyvyan did not learn, from Hester or anyone else in Aklavik, about his memo-rable and herculean winter trips along the Arctic coast, carrying his ministry east and west from Aklavik, or his removal in 1927 to England and subsequent appointments to Croscombe Church, Somerset, in 1927; St Saviour's, Retford, Nottinghamshire, in 1931; Ashampstead, Berkshire, in 1934; and St Helen's, Ipswich, Suffolk, in 1944 (Zealley, "Edward" 54).

Field Note for Thursday 1 July
Made assignations with Mr. West (H B Co inspector)
Born 23 March 1896, Vernon Weir West was an employee of the HBC 1906-07, 1914-19, and 1923-31. Until 1927, when he was relocated to James Bay, West served the HBC in northern Alberta and the western Arctic. As the field note clarifies, he was the inspector for the western Arctic in 1926 ("West"). Jean Godsell states that he was working for the competition, Lamson and Hubbard Company, in October 1920, when she travelled down the Athabasca River in his company; she found him "dour and taciturn" (22).

Field Note for Friday 2 July

Dorrien Smith's field note for this date states that she had sold "$200 worth or more" of her sketches by 2 July. Vyvyan's accounts, following the last dated entry in her field notes, show a record of sales; it is not known how complete this record is to this point, but it shows sales to people met prior to their arrival and during their stay at Aklavik totalling $252.50 (226). (In the last chapter of her book, Vyvyan remembers the figure of $600 as the total sales made during and as a result of the journey.) The young Richard Bonnycastle, in his diary entry for 4 June 1926, noted that Dorrien Smith also held a show of her work at the Macdonald Hotel in Edmonton: "the pictures were really awfully good," he wrote. "Scenes in England and on the continent. They were marekd [*sic*] at prices from 7.50 to 30.00 but I don't imagine they sold many at those prices although they were probably worth it" (Diary). As is clear from her letters to her mother of 15 and 28 August, Vyvyan also tried to arrange a showing while the women were in Vancouver.

Field Note for Saturday 3 July

All very down on HBC's methods in last years surly to own customers + keep free Traders out

Probably owing to all the help given her by the HBC, Vyvyan did not publish this negative view of the company in the 1920s, but it is known to have been widespread. It is echoed by Richard Bonnycastle (1903-68), an HBC employee who would be appointed district manager of the western Arctic on 29 June 1928 (Bonnycastle, *Gentleman* 97). In his diary, written as he steamed on the *Distributor* to Aklavik two summers after Vyvyan and Dorrien Smith, he observed that "the average traveller in the country resents the cheeky attitude of the Company clerks and other employees who think they are salt of the earth. Nothing puts the backs of the white population up more than this because they are powerless to do anything against the Company. It is easy for Company employees, safe in the fold, to take such an attitude" (*Gentleman* 25).

Field Note for Sunday 4 July

Mr Fry ... Mr Geddes

Rev W.H. Fry and his wife served at the Anglican missions at Herschel Island and Aklavik. When he visited Herschel in April 1919, Archdeacon Hudson Stuck praised Fry for his interest in arctic exploration (Stuck, *Winter* 326). In the same year, Mrs Fry nursed Vilhjalmur Stefansson back to health when he arrived during his third arctic expedition suffering from typhoid fever. A fiercely outspoken opponent of missionary work with Inuit, Stefansson was thought by Mrs Fry to have a worse bark than bite (Fleming 292).

Born on the Magdalen Islands and educated at Dalhousie University, William Archibald Geddes (1894-1947) began his arctic ministry in 1920, serving the first eight years at Herschel Island and Shingle Point. He was present at the hanging of Tatamagana and Aligoomiak at Herschel Island on 1 February 1924 (Frank Peake, *The Bishop* 145; Steele 241). A year after meeting Vyvyan and Dorrien Smith, Geddes was appointed archdeacon of Yukon Diocese. Eventually, he rose to bishop of Mackenzie River and bishop of the Yukon (Frank Peake, *The Bishop* 147n).

CHAPTER 15: PRELUDE TO ADVENTURE
(5–8 JULY)

In their initial encounter with the Rat River, Vyvyan seems, according to her field notes, to be more aware of the wildlife, the mosquitoes, and the rain than of the lonely sensation of the motor boat's departure, leaving them "completely at the mercy" of the guides (89). The field notes for the days prior to their departure are unpeopled by old-timers and the forebodings about the women's doom, while the sense of being "under a spell" in "a magic world" of "hippogriff or a dinosaur" or other miracles, on the threshold of "magic adventure," and accompanied by a guide with "an almost mystical union with his own country," also seems to be a function of Vyvyan's retrospective re-telling of the adventure. As a prelude to the adventure, however, this chapter's shift in tone from the field notes sets the stage for an excursion into a world unlike anything Vyvyan and Dorrien Smith had ever known.

she hopped downstairs and out to see the *Pioneer*, a Northern Trading vessel

Dorrien Smith's field note for 5 July confirms that Dr Cook cut her leg out of its plaster of Paris cast, freeing her to move about and make some sketches.

Rival to the HBC and Lamson and Hubbard, the Edmonton-based Northern Trading Company operated from 1913 to 1925. At its height, it captured an estimated fourteen per cent of the fur in the Mackenzie district. Financially strapped in 1925, it had to cease its transportation business at the close of the 1926 season, so Vyvyan was witnessing the company vessel's last trip to Aklavik as a freighter. The company avoided the HBC's takeover by acquiring backing from Winnipeg's Jewish traders. Under the name of Northern Traders, it survived from 1926 to 1930 before being crippled by the Depression (Ray 143, 161-63).

Gregorian chants, sung to celebrate the mother superior's feast day
The entry for 5 July 1926 in the Grey Nuns' "Akalvik Chroniques" reads: "Chant à la messe, fête toute la journée, puisse Ste Zoé patronne de Bonne Mère Provinciale nous la garder longtemps à notre affection." The reference is to Mother Superior Zoé Chartier Girouard.

I baked slabs of bannock
In the notes following the last dated entry in her field notes, Vyvyan listed the ingredients required for bannock and dough-nuts (226).

the reverend father and the two lay brothers
The identity of the lay brothers is uncertain but not that of the father: from 1926 to 1931, Père Joseph Trocellier omi presided at the Immaculate Conception Residential School and the Roman Catholic mission at Aklavik, both of which were established in 1924. He would become bishop of Mackenzie-Fort Smith later in his career.

The pemmican was to prove a standby … eating a lump no larger than a greengage
A greengage is a variety of sweet plum, having green skin and flesh.

Surely our puffing engine was the first mechanical sound that had ever broken the age-long silence of the river
Surely Vyvyan may be excused for expressing a view that over-comes most northern trippers, however much knowledge of a route's history they bring with them. Her quotation of English Romantic poet Samuel Taylor Coleridge's poem, *Rime of the Ancient Mariner* (l. 105), at the point when the voyage enters the Pacific Ocean, testifies to the ubiquity of the sensation, however illusory.

Destruction City … We looked about us in surprise. There was no sign that any human being had ever passed that way
Alden Hayes found more remains twelve years later than Vyvyan saw in 1926; either that or her book exaggerates the lack of evidence for effect (the field note for 7 July mentions "few remains"). Although Hayes called it a "ghost camp," he identified "the poles of four old lean-tos, two tipi frames, a few meat-drying racks, and axe marks on stumps where trees had been felled." (Perhaps some of these had been made between 1926 and 1938.) Unlike Vyvyan, Hayes does not exaggerate the loss of human life that occurred at Destruction City; mean-while, he correctly explains why more signs of the winter camp were not evident: "The Klondikers … stopped here at the beginning of the rapids, broke up their scows (hence the name of the camp), and used the lumber to make huts to winter in. In the spring they destroyed the huts and rebuilt the boats to continue the journey" (88-9).

As discussed in the Introduction, Emily Craig spent the winter of 1898-99 at Destruction City, before driving a dog team up the Rat River in April (Romig 93). Her first-hand account was not available until 1948. Born in Denmark in 1871 and orphaned (126, 75), she lived until 1957 (Mayer 235) and published her narrative under the name of Emily Craig Romig, having married again. Hers had been a prolonged adventure, beginning in Chicago in August 1897 (Romig 19) and concluding with her arrival in Dawson in August 1899 (107), too late to join in the gold rush. Those twenty-four months also included having to chop her way out of the icy embrace of her frozen sleeping bag (36); learning the culinary and domestic practices of native women (23, 45); adopting a more practical mode of dress—"Yesterday I started to wear Mr. Craig's overalls, because I could not be on the tracking line, and jump from one large rock to another, with skirts on. They all thought I made a very good boy" (70); meeting Bishop and Mrs Stringer (73), Emma, the wife of Archdeacon Whittaker (88), and Buffalo Jones (77); helping a "lady" (74) named Braund to travel and give birth to a child (88); bemoaning her and her husband's fate, "living like tramps, and moving from place to place" (79); watching as other men at Destruction City, following the example of American whalers at Herschel Island (Nagy 36), purchased Inuit women for their domestic comfort (73, 80); nursing scurvy-ridden Klondikers (85); sliding down a mountainside with Mrs Hoffman at the summit of McDougall Pass (95); baking and cooking at Fort Yukon and

Dawson for Klondikers, "discouraged men ... who wished they had stayed at home," and thereby earning cash for the first time (101); and feeling uncomfortable with her wilderness attire once she reached settlements again (104). Her narrative is otherwise remarkable for the little attention it pays to the clear inequality of the division of labour in her party. The responsibility for all the cooking fell to her, the only woman in a party of fourteen; her work began at the end of the day, after she had travelled as far as the men. The narrative seldom voices what Frances Backhouse calls "a common complaint among women on the trail[,] that men did not recognize that temperamental portable stoves, lack of ingredients, rain, and mosquitoes all made even simple meal preparation an onerous task" (22).

We felt like Shadrach, Meshach and Abednego clad in "their hosen, their tunics and their mantles, and their other garments," when, fully dressed, we crawled in under our mosquito bars
The reference is to Daniel 4:21, and the attempt by King Nebuchadnezzar of Babylon to burn the three Jews in a furnace for refusing to worship his gods. Like them but rather less miraculously, the women survived their ordeal.

Field Note for Monday 5 July
saw the Whitakers set off in gas boat
The Whittakers were conducting Arthur Creighton McCullum by way of Peel River Portage to the Yukon in order to meet Bishop Stringer. A graduate of Theology from Wycliffe College, Toronto in 1925, McCullum was ordained deacon by Bishop Lucas in the same year, and immediately took up the work of curate at Herschel Island with Shingle Point. After journeying over the mountains with the Whittakers, he was immediately ordained priest by Bishop Stringer. Vyvyan's oblique field note for 23 July suggests that McCullum's whereabouts were unknown but that she expected to meet up with him and the Whittakers on the other side of the mountains. Dorrien Smith's field note for 4 July is rather more explicit about a few of the details: "He is going across the portage to Old Crow to meet Bishop Stringer and be ordained. We may meet him again."

In his oral history, John Ross Tizya states that when he met up with him on the Bell River, Bishop Stringer ordained McCullum on his raft (*LaPierre* 65). Then he appointed McCullum missionary at Old Crow. Sherwood Platt's party

met him there on 25 August: "A new young minister, McCullum, recent graduate from Toronto and a peach of a fellow, was putting up a log church and was very interesting to talk to. He had just come over from Herschel Island where his powerful radio enabled him to amuse the Esquimos and also hear the Boston hockey games" (Platt 29). In 1929, McCullum moved to Mayo and then, as the incumbent, to Dawson from 1935 to 1940. Thereafter, his appointments were in Ontario, except during the Second World War, when he served as a military chaplain and earned the Order of the British Empire (*Crockford's*).

Field Note for Tuesday 6 July
a meal at English Mission with Miss Catt + Hackett
Ethel G. Catt went to Aklavik in 1926 from South America by way of a short stint at Fort Smith. At Aklavik, she served as housekeeper and assistant nurse at the Church of England Mission (Kealey). In 1927, Jean Godsell considered Miss Catt "one of the grandest people I ever met in the North. A small, dumpy Englishwoman, who wore her hair in a bun at the back of her head and dressed rather severely, she had done considerable missionary work in Lima, Peru, ere venturing into the frozen North to reopen the small, long-since-abandoned Anglican church" at Fort Smith (161). Her time in the North included a year at Fort Chipewyan (1928) and another stint at Aklavik (1929-30).

Minnie Hackett, RN, graduate of St Boniface Hospital, served several years at the Anglican mission in Aklavik beginning in 1926, facing her greatest challenge during the epidemic of influenza in 1927-28 when so many Gwich'in (including Edward Sittichinli, Lazarus' father) and Inuvialuit died (Simon, qtd in Sax and Linklater 74; Fleming 288). (As well, care had been handicapped in 1927-28 by a lack of drugs and supplies; they had all been burned in a warehouse fire at Edmonton where they were being collected for shipment north [Dickerson 45].) Although she is not mentioned by name in the field notes of either Vyvyan or Dorrien Smith until 6 July, it seems almost certain that the women had made her acquaintance much earlier. Because it is known from an article in the *Edmonton Bulletin* that Hackett attended a tea given in her honour by Mrs Gray, wife of the bishop of Edmonton, on Monday, 31 May ("Anglican Nurse" 6), her being in Aklavik likely resulted from her travelling by the same train and steamboats as Vyvyan and Dorrien Smith. She was at Hay River 1929-30 (Kealey).

Field Note for Wednesday 7 July

Mr. Parsons + Aberdeen boy in H.B.Co gas boat

Dorrien Smith's field note for this date names the gas boat, *Bluenose*, as well as the Aberdeen boy, Duncan, the mechanic; as well, it confirms that the ninety-five-mile trip took seventeen hours in the boat. Vyvyan's accounts following the last dated entry in her field notes show that the trip cost $30.00 (227).

CHAPTER 16: CHECK TO OUR PROGRESS (8–9 JULY)

Vyvyan's exaggeration about the origins of the name "Destruction City" accord well with the additional ominous statements and allusion to the failure of Laura Frazeur. Stronger than anything in the field notes is the chapter's sense that the women have embarked on an unknown and powerful wilderness, one which not only defeated many Klondike gold stampeders but, apparently, also effaced, in twenty-eight short years, any sign that humans had made a place of it. As the party is stopped by rising water, the field notes record only anxiety about the river. The book's repeated and anxious references to the woman whose guides refused to take her farther do not appear in the field notes, but if the women felt uncertain about their guides at the outset of the trip, perhaps they had other reasons than the spectre of Laura Frazeur.

CHAPTER 17: MOODS, RAPIDS AND ISLANDS (10 JULY)

This chapter's central episode, Vyvyan's sudden and fearful comprehension of their distance from human settlement and their helplessness in the face of the wilderness, occurs in the field notes (10 July) as well as the book. However, the book's shift in narrative point of view, from the field notes' first-person plural "we," which includes Dorrien Smith in the experience, to the first person-singular narrator, narrows the focus of the experience. The narrator is thus not only physically isolated in the wilderness, but also psychologically isolated, alone in her fear and uncertainty. It is interesting to note by contrast that Dorrien Smith's field note for this day expresses no alarm and attests very well, not only to Vyvyan's published implication that her own thoughts differed from

Gwen's, but also, perhaps, to her description of Gwen as lion-hearted: "Saturday 10th: Fine. Some thunder in the p.m. We left our camp in the spruce trees at 7 a.m. Clara + I walking on l. bank + climbing along as best we could, keeping view of the canoe on the opposite side till at last we got in touch. Boy lost axe + later p.m. we continued a short spell in their company + then had stiff climbing to do + eventually came down to them at the canoe + with them along a steep hillside + hard rapids. Had a meal at 6 + continued a little way, but canoe got into difficulties + Lazarus came after us + called us back to camp at 9 p.m." When in her book Vyvyan recounted the episode with heightened fear, she was doing so for the fourth time in print. The episode appeared similarly in the articles she published in 1931, 1933, and 1939, but not in the one published in 1929 in the *Geographical Journal* of the RGS. In it, the persona of a fearless male adventurer is emphatic.

All our strength and powers of endurance, are they to be snuffed out like a candle extinguished? Is the Rat a malignant enemy and are we unwelcome, fatally doomed intruders?

Eli MacLaren has noted that, although it has no equal in the field note for 10 July, the chapter's reference to the candle seems particularly apposite to the ominous mood of fatal doom which Vyvyan aims for in this passage. The women are reading aloud extracts from Shakespeare's tragedy *Macbeth*, in which the image of the extinguished candle occurs in Macbeth's speech at hearing the report of Lady Macbeth's death:

> To-morrow, and to-morrow, and to-morrow,
> Creeps in this petty pace from day to day,
> To the last syllable of recorded time;
> And all our yesterdays have lighted fools
> The way to dusty death. Out, out, brief candle!
> Life's but a walking shadow, a poor player,
> That struts and frets his hour upon the stage,
> And then is heard no more. It is a tale
> Told by an idiot, full of sound and fury,
> Signifying nothing. (5.5.19-28)

Then a vague fear took hold of me; at first it was like that little cloud in the Bible, no bigger than a man's hand

This evocative image does justice to the moment, if not to the original source. The biblical cloud brings a providential rain in answer to Elijah's prayer: "And it came to pass at the seventh time [of looking at the sea], that he [Elijah's servant] said, Behold, there ariseth a little cloud out of the sea, like a man's hand" (I Kings 18:44).

we knew now that Lazarus would take that care off our shoulders
There is no equal in the field notes for this chapter's last two and the next chapter's first two paragraphs; however, the statement of trust in Lazarus is echoed in a most praiseworthy, if racially conscious, evaluation made by Vyvyan in her letter to her mother of 3 August, once the canoe trip had been completed: "Our Indian guides were splendid, specially Lazarus the elder one. It was touch and go at first whether we turned back, for the water was very high and the current swift. I don't believe any other guide would have had the spirit to go on. … I can't see any white men doing the work they did. They cooked, pitched camp, made fires, ferried us across the river when we came to an impassable cliff, and were always cheerful even at the end of a long day. We were lucky in striking a good type of Indian, for they are a pretty poor lot as a rule. These 2 were undefeated and undefeatable." His race is not overtly referred to in an evaluation of him in one of Vyvyan's published articles: "Lazarus was indeed one of nature's gentlemen, silent, reliable, a watcher of signs, stalwart, with flat cheeks, wiry hair and power of endurance" ("On the Rat" 51).

CHAPTER 18: TO BARRIER RIVER (11 JULY)

No field note mentions the women's disagreement with Lazarus over the size and timing of the mid-day meal.

Field Note for Sunday 11 July
All day they shoved the canoe on, both waist deep in water pushing + pulling
Dorrien Smith's field note for this date clarifies the date of some of Vyvyan's photographs: "Clara got a good chance to Kodak the two guides toiling and sweating the canoe up the rapids."

CHAPTER 19: A TURNING POINT (11–12 JULY)

Although Vyvyan's field note for 12 July mentions brandy at tea, the description of the women's clandestine tippling in the willows appears only in the published version; there, it contributes to the book's ongoing reiteration of Vyvyan's anxieties over the guides' reliability. As well, of course, only the book's retrospective reconstruction of the journey makes the Barrier River camp a turning point in their ordeal on the Rat River.

"Short hours of sleep … are beginning to make us feel a bit empty."
Vyvyan's field note for 12 July is the source of this quotation.

we had to resume our scramble through white poplars and undergrowth
In her letter to her mother of 3 August, Vyvyan uses an interesting English expression to describe her progress through the bush: "We walked or rather scrambled through thick brush like beaters going through coverts." A beater is one who, in hunting, drives game from cover. Vyvyan used the simile again when she published her article in 1938 about the trip in *Blue Peter* (303).

CHAPTER 20: NEARING THE DIVIDE (13–14 JULY)

The first five paragraphs of this chapter are not based on field notes, and the paragraphs about a "heightened sense of adventure" and food cravings are additions.

Gwen … made up her mind to produce doughnuts
Vyvyan's description of Dorrien Smith's creation of "puftaloonas" and the comparison between her work and a blacksmith's hammering iron have no counterpart in either her or Dorrien Smith's field notes.

we had now come to niggerheads … a nightmare form of vegetation … you will fall into the space between your tuft and the next one
This is a fair description of a very common tundra phenomenon, but it neglects to emphasize that a thorough soaking

usually awaits the foot that treads among rather than atop hummocks. When thirteen men helped Lord Lonsdale cross the Peel River Portage from Fort McPherson to La Pierre House in September 1888, he found the hummocks "very very bad" (Krech, *Victorian* 69). The first day's trek westward on the portage had always elicited desperate descriptions from white travellers. Alexander Hunter Murray was reminded of the "'Slough of Dispond'" (22) in Edmund Spenser's *Faerie Queene* when he spent 11 June 1847 wading his way westward through the hummocky-laden lowlands of the Peel's drainage are. Elihu Stewart, who crossed the portage in July 1906, included this feature in his description: "The grass grows in hummocks known as *tête de femme* (woman's head). The trail is generally covered with some water, and one is often tempted to try to step from one to another of these tufts of grass, but as the somewhat larger head rests on a slender neck you will soon prefer to wade along the narrow path, after perhaps having a few tumbles" (117). Vyvyan saved her most interesting remark on the vegetation for her letter to her mother of 3 August: "these are grassy tussocks with a 2 ft. drop between each, and usually they are too small and wobbly for you to hop along the crests, so down you go up to the knee, also rather exhausting. How Gwen's ankle survived I don't know, but the Aklavik Doctor turned her out of that plaster cast sound as a bell."

CHAPTER 21: A DAY OF DAYS (15 JULY)

The chapter's first three paragraphs amplify the quotation of Vyvyan's field note for 15 July, and the sensation that the women were lords and conquerors appears only in the book.

There are some feelings too deep for tears
Vyvyan here paraphrases lines from English Romantic poet William Wordsworth's poem "Ode: Intimations of Immortality": "To me the meanest flower that blows can give / Thoughts that do often lie too deep for tears."

Loon Lake marks the Divide between Canada and Alaska
On the Department of Mines and Technical Surveys' modern map of the region—116P, Bell River—Vyvyan's "Loon Lake" is named Summit Lake. Her choice of name likely comes from Sittichinli, for "Loon" is the direct English translation of the Gwich'in name for the lake—*Daadzaii vàn* (GSCI no. 13). The

pertinent aerial photographs of McDougall Pass are A17622-135, from the three forks of the Rat River on the east to Long Lake on the west, and A17622-133, showing Long Lake, Summit Lake, and the stream flowing westward to connect to the Little Bell River (copies in Goering [33, 35]). Of course, Vyvyan means that Loon Lake straddles, *not* the Divide between Canada and Alaska (one does not exist), but, rather, the Divide between the Mackenzie River and Yukon River basins, which marks the boundary between the Northwest and Yukon territories.

CHAPTER 22: A GRIZZLY BEAR (16–17 JULY)

As Vyvyan notes, it is only with the book's retrospection that the hunt becomes both "the most exciting experience of the whole trip" and a shameful act. She could well feel shame for her own part—although her shot did not register—but her proprietary notion is misplaced. The desire for fresh meat comes from the men, they kill the bear, and it provides them with food for the trek back over the Peel River Portage to Fort McPherson; certainly, it is as much Gwich'in/Gwitchin river and country as it is an animal refuge. Vyvyan's subsequent use of the term "murder" seems a product of histrionic retrospection. Neither the sense of shame nor "murder" make an appearance in the field notes for 16 and 17 July; both tend to contradict her published assessment: "as the days went by we were filled with admiration for [Sittichinli's] knowledge of wild life which amounted to an almost mystical union with his own country" (99). The book alone includes her resentment of how high the men's wages are, although both field notes and book praise the men's work.

Perhaps because Vyvyan's own field notes do not mention when it was discarded, the lump of bear's meat stays with the women in the book much longer than it did in Dorrien Smith's field notes: her entry for Sunday, 18 July only the day after the men were paid off, mentions setting off from their "lovely" camp at 1 p.m., "leaving the sack of grizzly bear by the river."

American Margaret Murie, whose book of Alaskan travels appeared a year after Vyvyan's, travelled up the Porcupine River with her husband and young baby and with Jess Rust in June 1926, the previous month. Her published views contrast with Vyvyan's: "At the mouth of the Coleen River, on the lush goose-grass beach, we bagged a black bear. (The meat was delicious; we smoked some of it and it kept well)" (Murie 277; 2nd ed. 223).

La Pierre House

HBC employee La Pierre, "the man who built and ran the post for the first few years, was half Iroquois and half French-Canadian. The first post was probably at the junction of what [are] now the Little Bell and the Bell [r]ivers" (Coutts 155). Because, when he descended the Bell to establish Fort Yukon in 1847, Alexander Hunter Murray left his bride at La Pierre House, Anne Murray became the first woman to maintain the post (Holmes 541). The site of the post was later moved downriver, five bends below the mouth of the La Chute (formerly the confusingly named Rat) River.

La Pierre House was closed in summer and served a dual purpose in the fall and winter: as a strategically located point from which to intercept the migration of the Porcupine caribou herd in order to supply Peel River Post (Fort McPherson) with meat (Krech, "Eastern Kutchin" 222), and "to facilitate the transit of goods and furs across the mountains, although some trading [was] done both with the Loucheux and the Eskimo" (McConnell 121). The extent of the trading may not have been great, for *Zheh gwitsal*, the name for the post in Gwich'in, means "small house" (GSCI no. 22; "zzeh Gwutzul" in Gwitchin [*LaPierre* 30]), but this name also refers to the fact that it was smaller than Fort McPherson, the two being managed by the same factor. It was not, however, small in terms of food; indeed, it "supplied most of the caribou needed to provision Peel's River Post [Fort McPherson], as well as its own modest domestic requirements. It was also a fantastic source of fish for both establishments" (Allen Wright 85). When he spent the winter of 1859-60 at La Pierre House, American naturalist Robert Kennicott ate all the caribou he wished and noted that the daily ration for a dog at the post (then in the charge of Orkneyman James Flett) was "half a man's and the same as a wife's—that is, four pounds of fresh meat, one and a half pounds of dry meat, two fresh white fish, or two pounds of dry fish." Kennicott also reported that each fall Flett and his men, by erecting willow wicker fences across the rivers in the vicinity of the post, caught as many as 16,000 bluefish and whitefish (Kennicott 115-16, 111; qtd in Allen Wright 84, 85).

In 1862, the establishment of St Barnabas Mission at La Pierre House by Père Jean Séguin omi marked the first Roman Catholic enterprise in what became the Yukon Territory (Duchaussois 397). William Kirkby had visited it on behalf of the Church of England the year before (Kirkby; Frank Peake, "William" 267). It was abandoned as a fur post by 1890, by which time Rampart House could be supplied much more economically by Yukon River sternwheelers. La Pierre House was also known by HBC employees as "The Small House," and to Gwitchin as "Koahze" (Little House; Coutts 155).

When they canoed over the Rat River route and reached La Pierre House a decade later, on 4 September 1936, Bill and Sylva Bendy concluded "from various scraps of paper in the cabins ... that it was operated in 1931 and 1932 as a fur trading post of the Jackson Brothers from Dawson, who also operated a store in Old Crow. Apparently it has not been occupied since then. There are no footprints in the mud on the river bank and nothing at all to indicate that it has been visited this year" (75). One of those scraps of paper was a "Fur Trader's License for the Year 1931," made out to the Jackson Brothers of La Pierre House and signed by A.B. Thornthwaite, the RCMP officer then at Old Crow (Bendy, after 75). It was never the case, however, that the area in which the post was situated was without people: the oral histories of La Pierre House clarify as much; moreover, they indicate that the Jackson brothers, who, according to Moses Tizya, began operating a winter store at La Pierre house "around 1924," were, according to Mary Kassi, again in operation there from 1937 to 1939 (*LaPierre* 142, 7, 16).

Had they done more reading in preparation for their trip, Vyvyan and Dorrien Smith would have been disabused of the illusion that La Pierre House was anything other than abandoned; Fullerton Waldo confirmed its state in his book, published in 1923 (209). As well, a photo of it in an abandoned state appeared in Michael Mason's book, published in London in 1924 (facing 76; see above, 140). This book is mentioned by Vyvyan (169), and Mason's name appears in the field notes (27 July), but it appears that either it was brought to the travellers' attention only after they had passed La Pierre House, or Vyvyan chose to suppress her awareness of it in order not to undercut her effort to depict the North as empty. No doubt, it would have proved vexing to them to find the "liar" perpetuating itself: the name survived in at least one modern atlas (*e.g.*, Castner *et al.* 45), and into the fourth edition of the Canadian *Gazetteer* (Canada 1976, 27). Only in 1982, in a "Special Edition—Partial Names Update" of the *Northwest*

Territories and Yukon Territory map, did the name disappear from an official map (Canada 1982).

According to Vuntut Gwitchin Elder Mary Kassi, in the vicinity of La Pierre House the Gwitchin from the western slope and the Gwich'in from the eastern slope traditionally came together for hunting, gathering, and meeting (*LaPierre* 18, 22): "that place good for everything. It's good for caribou. It's good for moose. It's good for fish. It's good for porcupine, ducks, everything. It's really good country. Everything was there ... good for berries. Good for blueberries and good for cranberries in the fall" (*LaPierre* 9). Charlie Peter Charlie confirms that "people from all over gather there ... and hunt and that's the main place for caribou and that's where they stay and dry meat" (*LaPierre* 92). This image of plenty contrasts sharply with Vyvyan's telling view of La Pierre House as a symbol of abandonment and incapacity as a refuge.

Under the terms of the 1993 Gwitchin self-government agreement, the Yukon territorial government was required to establish La Pierre House and Rampart House as historic sites, and to schedule them for conservation and interpretation (*Vuntut* 190).

Now he answered Jimmy's question with a hoarse whisper. "Bear"
There is no basis in Vyvyan's field note for this verbal exchange between Jim and Lazarus; Vyvyan might have been prompted to it in order to maintain the strong distinction between their characters that she had earlier drawn. Certainly, Koe's memoir clarifies that, by 1926, although far from the best trapper and hunter, he had done his share of both for some years.

We landed on a spit full of boulders just below Shingle Rock
This place is not identified in other accounts of this route, yet, as has been seen, it was known to Whittaker and to Koe, and it appeared in both Vyvyan's (Shingle) and Dorrien Smith's (Sinclair) field notes for 17 July under one or another name. "Sinclair Rock" has been introduced on recent maps at 67°18'15" N., 137°01'00" W.; the Bell River makes a semi-circular loop around it as it flows across the 137th meridian, upstream from the mouth of Rock River (Canada 1989).

In her oral history, Gwitchin Lydia Thomas identifies "'single rock'" as the place where a spur of the summer trail from Fort McPherson to La Pierre House reaches the Bell River (*LaPierre* 39).

five days walking back to Fort McPherson
As discussed in the Introduction, Vyvyan probably knew the description of Elihu Stewart's trip across Peel River Portage in 1906. The account of the portage closest in time (1924) to the women's trip was Michael Mason's; with Harry Anthony and others, he crossed it in five days in June 1921 (206-13). Probably from their reading but also their discussion in Edmonton with Harry Warner (see field note for 27 May), and, no doubt, a discussion with the Whittakers about their past trip and proposed trip with McCullum over the portage that month, Vyvyan and Dorrien Smith knew their allowance of five days for the return to Aklavik was liberal; in the event, the men must have profited handsomely from the deal, if Koe's memory that they reached Fort McPherson in only "one long day" and Aklavik the next is correct (1:12).

CHAPTER 23: DOWN THE PORCUPINE (18–21 JULY)

a white man with an Indian family
David Low is Vyvyan's name for this man, but he was doubtless David Lord, after whom Lord Creek is named; it enters the Porcupine from the south about where the women met him. A Klondiker who chose to remain in the Yukon, Lord trapped in the vicinity of the creek mouth. He was there in 1910, when Edward and Lazarus Sittichinli visited him on their way to Rampart House, where Edward married him to Jennie Brule (qtd in Sax and Linklater 82). He died in Dawson in 1954 (Coutts 164).

We had arrived at Old Crow
Although "the first permanent log cabin dwelling at Old Crow is reported to have been built around the turn of the century by John Tizya, whose fishing camp was nearby, and who served as catechist for the band when the Anglican missionary was not present" (Acheson 695), according to Lazarus Sittichinli, there were still only three cabins there a decade later (qtd in Sax and Linklater 82). The greater part of the permanent settlement at the junction of the Old Crow and Porcupine rivers began forming in 1911-12, when Gwitchin from the Fort Yukon area who had moved up the Porcupine River to Rampart House in order to remain in British territory were forced to move again, both because of devastation from an

epidemic of smallpox, and, according to Hannah Netro, because enforcement of the newly surveyed international border constrained people's hunting patterns (*Rampart* 14, 15). In 1912, as well, two traders opened the first store at Old Crow (Acheson 695). "The new settlement took its name from a noted chief of the old days, 'Te-Tshim-Gevtik,' meaning 'Walking Crow.' He died in the 1870s, leaving his people a legacy of high standards and moral principles which have persisted to the present time. ... The word 'crow' here refers to the northern raven, as true crows are unknown this far north. ... The settlement is in the centre of the most prolific muskrat-breeding grounds in the entire northwest" (Coutts 200-01). Prices for muskrat pelts were strong in the mid-1920s (Balikci 41). Like Fort McPherson, Old Crow has been a staunch Anglican community from the time of the arrival of missionaries, although Christianity grafted on to, rather than wholly displaced, former beliefs (Balikci 52).

The people of this settlement now prefer the name Vuntut or Vantut, which means "the people of the lakes" and refers to Old Crow Flats, the wide area of lakes and marsh in their region (Leechman 64); hence, as well, the name of Vuntut National Park, located north of the settlement and Old Crow Flats Special Management Area (Weihs 234). When Vyvyan and Dorrien Smith reached Rampart House, the RCMP post was still situated there, but it was transferred to Old Crow in 1928 (Balikci 36). Old Crow is all but unique among northern communities in never having an HBC post (Acheson 695). In 1976, the community resisted the construction of an oil and gas pipeline through its region (Berger 36-8). One sign of Vyvyan's concern to make her published account reflect only what she knew of the communities when she visited them in 1926 is the lack of any mention in her book of the fame that Old Crow attained in the English press in 1945, when, on the suggestion of Chief Peter Moses, the community raised "several hundred dollars as a gift to the children of bomb-battered London" (McCourt 204). The gift was presented on 5 March 1942 by the Right Hon. Vincent Massey, high commissioner for Canada, and was gratefully acknowledged by the mayors of Bermondsey, Lambeth, and Southwark. Until recently, the letter of acknowledgement, which explains that the funds were spent on clothing for forty-six children orphaned in the air raids on London, was displayed at St Luke's Anglican Church, Old Crow.

Field Note for Sunday 18 July
Dorrien Smith's field note for this day, by mentioning their camp at night "between hills with rocks and steep banks; we sketched, canoe in foreground," locates the setting of one of her watercolour sketches (see above, 196).

Field Note for Tuesday 20 July
Unlike many of Dorrien Smith's field notes, the one for 20 July is not simply more understated and less detailed (except respecting flora) than Vyvyan's but also different in its point of view and choice of detail: "Sky cleared and it turned out a lovely day. Wind rather ahead. We had some shallows and islands to negotiate leaving our camp on the beach with a lovely glow on the mountains at 8:15, and paddled all day until 7:00, stopping for lunch at some Ramparts on high cliff, of which there were a good many today. Fine piece of rock with kestrels and young eagles. Camped tonight on muskeg above stony beach. Saw our old mountains behind and some new ones ahead today."

CHAPTER 24: FRIENDLY FACES (21–23 JULY)

The Indian chief came first
A photo taken by Douglas Leechman in 1946 shows the Gwitchin chief, Peter Moses, and his wife, Myra. A pencil portrait of Moses with yachting-cap, by W. Langdon Kihn, appears as the frontispiece in Leechman's book, *Indian Summer*. According to Richard Slobodin, "he has a visored cap with a badge lettered 'Chief'; the medal on his coat is also a sign of his office" (530). However, according to Sarah Abel Chitzi, Peter Moses was chief for only thirteen years, and so probably did not have that designation when met by Vyvyan and Dorrien Smith. Indeed, Chitzi states that Joe Kyakivichik (Joe Kay) preceded Moses and was "our first chief" (*Rampart* 10). The diary of Jess Rust, who visited Old Crow with the Muries in the same year as the Englishwomen, confirms that the chief then was "Big Joe" (23), "Chief Joseph" (72).

a youngish trader named Frost
Harold "Jack" Frost (1901-61), who was born in Owen Sound, Ontario, appears in a photograph with one of the Jackson brothers and RCMP constable Charlie Young (see above, 154).

"A young white trader and ex-policeman," he hosted Margaret, Olaus, and Martin Murie, and Jess Rust in June 1926. He gave breakfast to the Sherwood Platt party in his cabin on 25 August (Platt 29). Vyvyan's photo of him appeared in the articles about the trip that she published in 1931 (54) and 1938 (304). His widow Clara (*née* Moses) and several of the Frosts' ten children reside with their families in Old Crow. His son Stephen recently stated that, being a white person, his father "couldn't adapt to the trapping as well as the people who lived off the land" (*Rampart* 20).

David was a sturdy looking young Indian
Dorrien Smith's field note for 21 July supplies the guide's last name: Elias. At the very end of her field notes, in the accounts following the last dated entry (229), Vyvyan lists "David Elias (alias)" and payment to him as £10 10s, or $50, which must have been calculated at the rate of $5 per day for ten days, assuming the return trip would take Elias only as long as the trip downstream.

In that room we had the joy of sleeping in partial darkness
Vyvyan's field note for 22 July does not mention where the night was spent, but Dorrien Smith's note confirms that Frost "took us in, cooked us a meal, and let us bed down in his back room."

Martha, who had spent the night making our moccasins
The identity of this woman has not been established but she may have been the same person who, a month earlier, had made a pair of moccasins with similar haste for Martin Murie, Margaret's infant son. At the urging of the woman's four-year-old daughter, the moccasins were presented as a gift in the afternoon of the same day—26 June—that the Muries arrived at Old Crow (283; 2nd ed. 228).

"Those two women they came down the river paddling their canoe like a couple of squaws"
At first glance, there appears to be a basis for this sentence of dialogue in Vyvyan's field note for 21 July, but the seven words, "Came down the river like 2 squaws," are written in blue ink, not the black ink that Vyvyan invariably used to overwrite the original pencil, and there is no pencil underneath the words in blue ink. In combination with the fact that the handwriting of these seven words is not firm, this evidence suggests that Vyvyan

wrote the sentence later, perhaps as late as the time when she was preparing her book for publication in 1961. This bibliographical matter promises further significance, for the awe-struck response ascribed to the "the whole settlement" seems farfetched. The subsequent dialogue attributed to Frost *does* appear in pencil, as the last words of the original field note, and is overwritten in black ink.

the solitary cabin of a trader named Cadzow
Scottish by birth, Daniel Cadzow went to the Klondike in 1897 by way of Edmonton and the Rat River (Coutts 41). As an independent trader in 1906, he opened a store at Rampart House (Balikci 35). On 30 August 1907, during his trip from Fort McPherson to Fort Yukon, Stefansson met Cadzow there (Vilhjalmur Stefansson, *Hunters* 237). Bishop Isaac Stringer married Cadzow to Monica Njootli at Rampart House in November 1909 (Frank Peake, *The Bishop* 126; Hannah Netro and Mary Kassi gave her name as Veronica [*Rampart* 15, 58]). In January 1924, during his trip from Aklavik to Fort Yukon in the company of Lazarus Sittichinli, Philip Godsell also met the "grey-bearded American veteran of the Klondike days" at Rampart House (*Arctic* 291). According to Godsell, Cadzow died two years after their meeting, that is, sometime in the year of the women's visit to Rampart House (*Arctic* 292n). He was still alive in late June 1926, when Margaret Murie's husband, Olaus, found him "crippled with rheumatism" (280; 2nd ed. 226). He is remembered fondly by Hannah Netro: "He really took care of people" (*Rampart* 16).

Vyvyan's description of Cadzow's residence is surprising, for his two-storey house would easily have been the biggest building seen by the women since leaving Aklavik (see above, 157). In the oral history of Rampart House published in 1993, it is remembered fondly by many Vuntut Gwitchin (*Rampart*).

Rampart House … the international boundary of Canada and Alaska
When, in 1869, Americans took possession of Fort Yukon, its HBC servants moved east up the Porcupine River and erected Rampart House, it was thought, in British territory. There it stayed for three decades; however, when he surveyed its location in 1889, J.H. Turner found Rampart House some thirty miles downriver from the 141st meridian; the HBC agent took immediate action, dismantled the post, towed the logs upriver, and erected new Rampart House (*Rampart* 45) east of the survey stake

driven by Turner (Lain 16). It was this location that Vyvyan and Dorrien Smith reached. As a fur trade post, the new location "remained open for only three years, as the HBC withdrew from the area completely in 1893" (Coates 71). A regular Church of England mission was started there in 1882 (Hamilton 146). In 1893, Susan Mellet (1870-1962), with experience teaching in Ireland's Ragged Schools, arrived in the Yukon and was sent to Rampart House by the first bishop of Selkirk, William Carpenter Bompas. There she met and later married Rev R.J. Bowen, a young English clergyman (Backhouse 122). Charles Camsell, who met Cadzow when he reached Rampart House by the Rat River on 4 September 1905, found it "situated in a draw on the north side of the river. The location of the Post was characteristic of Arctic habitations, with its back to the hills on the north and facing south across the river in order to get the full benefit of the sunlight on the short winter days" (200). (Photographs of the settlement as it looked in the early 1970s appear in Harrington 42-3.) In the mid-1920s, Rampart House was ceding its centrality to Old Crow as the premier Gwitchin settlement. Robert Bruce suggests that after the death of Dan Cadzow, around 1926, "no one down there trading so that's why people moved I think" (*Rampart* 52, 53).

Thornthwaite and Allington

Sgt Arthur B. Thornthwaite was born in Surrey, England in 1901, and served with the force 1919-47. His service took him to the Yukon in the summer of 1924, and to the command of Rampart House in the summer of 1926, replacing Charlie Young. Young was the officer in charge in late June, when the Muries and Jess Rust visited the settlement (Rust 20), but they found Thornthwaite there and Young "gone to Dawson" when they passed on their return from Old Crow River on 15 August (Rust 76). In 1927, Thornthwaite married Helen, one of the two nurses at the Hudson Stuck Memorial Hospital in Fort Yukon, whom Vyvyan and Gwendolen Smith met later in the month. Thornthwaite's posting took the couple to Old Crow, where they remained until 1933. They retired to Victoria, where he was still living in 1992 (Batchelor; Glen Gordon).

   Under Thornthwaite's command at Rampart House in 1926 was Const Charles Ellingson, who had joined the RCMP in 1921. Vyvyan and Sherwood Platt, whose party was warmly hosted by him at Rampart House 26-7 August 1926, misspelled his name. Platt wrote it as "Ellington" (30). Margaret Murie described Ellingson as "a young Norwegian giant" whose

stature conformed to the depiction of mounties found in the stories of the American author James Oliver Curwood (278; 2nd ed. 225).

Mr Allington rigged up a mast and sail and we began to work across the current diagonally. I watched Gwen's face of horror

The statement that Dorrien Smith's knowledge of sailing was superior to Ellingson's appears only in the book, where it becomes one of a succession of incidents highlighting the women's competence and growing confidence once they had passed the test of the "malignant Rat," and once—indeed, for the first time since leaving England—they themselves began to navigate a craft in water. Vyvyan's observation that the bishop was unshaven also appears only in the book, where he becomes one of many eccentric northern characters who make up the substance of Vyvyan's adventure. Her field notes do not blame Ellingson for the idea of the mast and do not offer the basis for the paragraph about Sittichinli's idealism.

there was the *Moose*, ... one of the Jackson Brothers on board and also Bishop Stringer, the Bishop of the Yukon

The Jackson brother met on 23 July by Vyvyan and Dorrien Smith was perhaps Jim, for on 26 August just above Rampart House, Sherwood Platt's party met Frank Jackson coming upriver with "his huge outfit including 2 other white men and many Indians, dogs, and supplies" (Platt 30). Jim Jackson is mentioned by Mary Kassi in her oral history of La Pierre House; she also confirms that *Moose* was the name of their boat. Lydia Thomas, in her oral history, notes that Frank, who served on the patrol that hunted down Albert Johnson in February 1931, died at La Pierre House and Jim at Old Crow, but Moses Tizya claims that Jim died at Fort Yukon (*LaPierre* 17, 35, 145).

   Born in Bruce County, Ontario, Isaac O. Stringer (1866-1934) was ordained deacon in the Church of England after completing his B.A. at the University of Toronto in 1892. He worked as a missionary out of Fort McPherson from 1892 to 1893, travelling throughout the area, as far west as La Pierre House and as far north as Herschel Island. Ordained priest in 1893 and married to fellow Ontarion Sarah Ann Alexander (1869-1955; known as Sadie) in 1896, he first travelled to Herschel Island in 1893 and established a mission there the next year. In 1901, eye problems forced Stringer to accept the rectorship of Christ Church, Whitehorse. In 1905, he succeeded Bompas as bishop of Selkirk (the name of the diocese changed from Selkirk to Yukon in 1907). From 1907 to 1931, the Stringers lived in Dawson and travelled throughout the North, including trips together across Peel River Portage. It was in 1909 that, during a winter journey, he and a companion ran out of food and had to eat their moccasins, thus earning Stringer the sobriquet, "The Bishop who ate his boots." In 1931, he became Metropolitan of Rupert's Land, and he and his wife moved to Winnipeg for the remainder of their lives (Sovereign 3-21, 27-30). By Laura Berton, Sadie Stringer was remembered as "'the sort of woman who immediately hands you a piece of pie as soon as you cross her threshold'" (59; qtd in Backhouse 123). The standard biography of Bishop Stringer is by Frank Peake.

Field Note for Thursday 22 July
Gwen + our stalwart guide David are paddling
Dorrien Smith's field note for this date clarifies that "Clara and I [were] taking turns with the paddle at two-hour spells each."

CHAPTER 25: TO FORT YUKON (23–26 JULY)

"My name is Hely," said the man who had been steering the gas boat
When he visited Rampart House in August 1906, Elihu Stewart met "a French Canadian, bearing the Hibernian name of Healy, [who] ... was in charge of the store" (147). Perhaps this is the man in question. On 28 August, Platt met him coming upriver with his partner (31). The caption on an undated photo of Cadzow, Healy, and others at Rampart House lists Healy's first name as Henry (Alaska-Canada 65-31-76), and as Harry on the photo above, 158.

the Sheenjek River
Upstream from its confluence with the Yukon River, the Porcupine has four principal tributaries flowing in from the north; in order from east to west, they are the Bell, Old Crow, Coleen, and Sheenjek, the latter two being in Alaska. Flowing in from the south, the Black and Salmon rivers are the two principal tributaries, both in Alaska.

our arrival at Fort Yukon
In 1846, Fort Yukon was established on the east bank of the Yukon River just up from its confluence with the Porcupine River by Alexander Hunter Murray of the HBC. At 145°17' W., it stood well west of the 141st meridian, the international border officially set by the Anglo-Russian Treaty of 1825. (Fort Yukon, about eleven degrees of longitude west of Fort McPherson, was the HBC's second most westerly post—a short-lived post operated at Hawaii, another eleven degrees west of Fort Yukon.) Despite an "1839 agreement between the HBC and the Russian American Fur Company under which the former firm promised to refrain from trading on Russian territory" (Coates 61), the British found themselves unencumbered by Russian interference. Only after seventeen years of operation did the first Russian trader, Ivan Simonsen Lukeen, reach the fort from the sea (Wilson 47). The British operation thrived for two full decades, "returning profits as high as £4,200 in 1866" and consistently ranking "among the top three posts of the Mackenzie River District" (Coates 63).

In 1867, the annexation of Alaska by the Americans initiated a period of tension over the location of the fort, but, so profitable were its returns, the HBC was loathe to abandon it, even though it had to be supplied from across the mountains. In August 1869, not only did Capt Charles W. Raymond formally notify John Wilson, acting factor at the post, that Fort Yukon stood on American soil, but also he exceeded his written orders by taking possession of the fort in the name of the United States. At the time, it comprised a six-room house for the chief factor and six other buildings for a complement of seven HBC men and one Church of England clergyman (Dall 103). Rev William West Kirkby had visited the post first in 1861, and Fort Yukon featured an Anglican presence from that year onward (Allen Wright 87).

In due course, Fort Yukon became the property of the Northern Commercial Company, which continued the fur trade there for only a few years before trade declined and the post was abandoned, later to be torn down to supply wood for the Yukon steamers (Wilson 51): "By 1890, only a chimney, mounds of ashes, and a few graves marked the location .... Gold discoveries in the 1890's provided a measure of revival for the site as a supply depot and pilot station" (Lain 16).

Dr and Mrs Burke at the English mission

In 1908, Grafton Russ Burke (1882-1938) went to Fort Yukon as a medical doctor at the urging of his mentor, Archdeacon Hudson Stuck (1863-1920) of the U.S. Episcopal Church (Dean 133; Stuck, *Alaskan* 161; "Necrology" 536). Stuck assigned Burke to Fort Yukon, where the archdeacon had established a mission in 1904 ("Record" 14). In 1910, Burke married Clara Heintz, who had gone to Allakaket Mission in Alaska with the Episcopal Church in July 1907 (Burke 277). Both devoted the next three decades to the mission at Fort Yukon, where Dr Burke provided medical services and later served as justice of the peace, while Mrs Burke ran a small orphanage in addition to mission work (Hrdlička 159). In 1916, after a year's leave, the Burkes returned to Fort Yukon, where St Stephen's Hospital had been built during their absence; at the time, it was the only American hospital north of the Arctic Circle (Dean 206). In 1921, a year after the death of his mentor, Burke renamed the facility the Hudson Stuck Memorial Hospital, and himself was ordained to the diaconate of the Episcopal Church by the Rev Peter Trimble Rowe ("News" 607), who, in 1896, had become the first missionary bishop of Alaska. Burke was ordained priest in the Episcopal Church in 1938, six months before his death ("Record" 14).

The hospitable and congenial reception accorded Vyvyan and Dorrien Smith was no more or less than earlier travellers had received from the Burkes (*e.g.*, Philip Godsell, *Arctic* 293; Hrdlička 159). For her part, Clara Burke considered 1926 and 1927 among the couple's "happiest years" (Burke 275), in large part because their younger son, Grafton Jr, still lived at home, and their older son, Hudson, returned for the summers from boarding school. Dorrien Smith's field note for 26 July mentions that the Burkes' two sons were at home during their stay at Fort Yukon. Strictly speaking, Vyvyan is wrong to call it an "English mission"; the distinction is inappropriate for the Episcopal mission but it is understandable, since all previous settlements visited by her in the Arctic had either Roman Catholic or English (Anglican) missions.

Field Note for Monday 26 July

3 men from geological survey down from Scheneck river

Dorrien Smith's field note for this date identifies these three men as Merty, Hunter, and Kilmartin. Vyvyan's field notes mention these names later (29 July), but do not identify them in terms of the American geological survey.

CHAPTER 26: AT FORT YUKON
(27 JULY–2 AUGUST)

Harry Anthony. While he looked over Gwen's sketches with interest he told us of a trip that he made with Michael Mason

Michael Henry Mason (1900-82) was an explorer, sailor, linguist and author. He lived in the Canadian and Alaskan Arctic for three years. He wrote numerous travel books besides the one mentioned by Vyvyan, including *The Wild Ass Free*, *Where Tempests Blow*, and *Deserts Idle* ("Mason"). "About half the photographs" in his book *The Arctic Forests* "were taken by [his] friend, Harry Anthony" ([v]). Judging by the description in the field notes, the trip which Anthony recounted was the one made in 1921 and narrated by Mason in *Arctic Forests* (185-213).

On 26 August 1926 above Rampart House, Platt's party "saw a motor boat and barge coming up the river. It pulled into shore and we came up and found it to be Mr and Mrs Harry Anthony of Crow river in whose cabin Frost had received us. They were both extremely nice and we talked quite a while and pretty Mrs Anthony took pictures of us" (30).

we called one day on the matron of the hospital

Perhaps this matron was Winifred Dalziel, who had arrived at Fort Yukon in 1917 and who "divided her time between school and hospital, sometimes working 20 hours a day at the two jobs" (Phillips 2). As mentioned above, one of the two nurses met by the women during this visit was named Helen. Graduate of Pasadena General Hospital in California, she married Arthur Thornthwaite a year later, on 4 July 1927, and lived until 1956 (Batchelor).

a grand old man of 90 with a gangrenous leg

In 1936, this person became the subject of Vyvyan's article "Sunset on the Yukon," in which he is named William Burd. He is a dying old-timer whose memories of an adventurous life in the North are a composite of elements taken from various people described in the field notes, including Linklater and Guinness, the dog-sleigh driver (29 July), and various descriptions of the Rat-Bell-Porcupine route.

The doctor lingered by the grave of Archdeacon Hudson Stuck and told us much about his life and work and mountain climbing
Stuck was widely thought to be the first person to climb Denali (Mt McKinley), although Vyvyan's field note for 6 August reports meeting an old-timer in Nenana who claimed someone had beaten Stuck by a year.

Frank Foster and we had a long talk. He was a Yorkshireman
According to John Joe Kaye's oral history, Frank Foster worked in partnership with the Jackson brothers for a time (*LaPierre* 128). On 30 August 1926, Platt and friends met Foster at his cabin on the lower Porcupine River, only a day's downstream travel from Fort Yukon. "Though I'd believe it impossible," the young Platt wrote,

> he was the best man we've met yet. Surely treated us royally and gave us a huge supper of new potatoes and eggs. Stayed overnight at his cabin and slept inside on floor. We talked till after midnight. He was up on every subject and used perfect English. He took first boat over the Rat River in the gold rush of '98 and it was interesting to hear his experiences and find ours so comparable to them. He knew everybody, Jack London, Rex Beach, Service, Steffanson [*sic*], Michael Mason, and all. Most interesting and hospitable man I ever met. (32)

Bill and Sylva Bendy met Foster at Old Crow in September 1936 and reported as favourably on him. As well, they located his "permanent cabin on the Porcupine at Bootleg Bend, 65 miles above Fort Yukon" (89), and, when they passed it, found it had a garden and appeared "a nice looking place, with many little indications that there is a man with humor and imagination, something more than just enough interest to provide food and shelter. Many trappers' cabins are examples of how low a man can go when he lives alone in the woods, but not Foster's cabin" (100; a photograph of it appears in Bendy 102.).

Foster told them that his trip up the Rat River to the Klondike Gold Rush in 1898 involved burning his boat three times:

> Everybody started out with boats much too heavy to drag up the Rat. Many of them knew nothing better than to keep on

hauling them up through the rapids with block and tackle and were so delayed that they had to winter on the Rat. But a few, including Mr Foster and his partner, decided that lighter boats were necessary, burnt their old ones to recover the nails, hewed timbers and built lighter ones. As they went further and further up the Rat, the water became shallower and this process was repeated twice more. In this way they managed to cross the divide and reached Fort Yukon before the winter set in. (Bendy 89)

Tony...and Buffalo Jim of Crow River had rescued three men from the jaws of death in some canyon
Tony's tale of saving three men from drowning in a canyon does not appear in any field note. What remains in Vyvyan's book was apparently once part of a much longer anecdote, cut from the final version at the urging of her publishers (Vyvyan to Owen 2).

Mrs Burke, she had been the first woman missionary to go up to the Kobuk country
Clara Heintz's posting was not in Kobuk country, but at Allakaket, on the Koyukuk River, a northern tributary of the Yukon in north-central Alaska. North of the Yukon and not a tributary of it, the Kobuk River flows into Kotzebue Sound, north of Bering Strait.

a great vessel swung round the bend of the river and turned in towards our bank
The women steamed downriver aboard the inland sternwheel steamer, SS *Yukon*, which was built in Whitehorse and brought into service between Dawson and Nenana in 1913 by the British Yukon Navigation Company (Downs 151; "Yukon"). It was owned by several concerns before being retired in the late 1950s. Other photographs of it are reproduced in Anderson 83, 92, and Mason, facing 177).

The Burkes ... standing like beacon-lights in the lonely northland, keeping alive and shining the spirit of true Christianity
Michael Mason thought similarly of the Burkes after a much longer period of assessment: "If ever two people gave up their lives to ministering to the needs of others, it is Dr and Mrs Burke" (62).

Field Note for Wednesday 28 July
a swede Burgland woman
Dorrien Smith's field note for this date states that Mrs Burgland came from Wyoming.

Field Note for Thursday 29 July
to call on Linklater fine old-timer. H.B. servant
Likely this is the same man whom Michael Mason identified in 1924 as "Archie Linklater, born in Winnipeg, [who] has passed all his sixty-eight years in north latitudes" (6). His wife, Catherine, is another of those remarkable northern women over whom Vyvyan's field notes express wonder but who do not receive mention in the published version of her travels. Hannah Netro remembers Archie Linklater as the man who "built the church ... mission house, the store, that big house and the warehouse" at Rampart House (*Rampart* 14). Both Netro and Robert Bruce identified Linklater as a Cree (*Rampart* 16, 52), and Netro remembered him as "a fiddle player. He brought the music with him also. ... They (the Gwitchin) still dance to the same music today" (*Rampart* 16).

Field Note for Friday 30 July
the N.C. store
Descended from the Russian Fur Company, the Northern Commercial Company of Alaska came into being in 1867 when the territory came into American hands. It has operated more than one hundred stores in Alaska and three in the Yukon: at Dawson, Mayo, and Whitehorse (Kitchener 6, 7).

"Pecker" Mrs Heinz ie. Mrs Burke's M in law wandered down the beach as we were making tea + joined us
Vyvyan is mistaken: Mrs Heintz was Mrs Burke's step-mother (Dr Burke's mother was no longer alive). Whether or not "Pecker" and Mrs Heintz are, as this field note implies, one and the same person is not known for certain, but only "Mrs Pecker" walks down the beach in Vyvyan's book, and she, like Clara Heintz's family, comes from California.

Field Note for Sunday 1 August
Dr Burke read a sermon of Fosdicks
None of the six books that American minister Harry Emerson Fosdick (1878-1969) had published by the year 1926 were sermons *per se*, but evidently the texts could be modified for the requirements of that genre, or Burke had access to sermons through periodical literature.

Field Note for Monday 2 August
Dorrien Smith's field note for this date adds the detail, "We got three pairs of moccasins, made by Catherine Linklater, for the children at home," and states that the men of the American geological survey also embarked on the *Yukon*.

CHAPTER 27: TRAVELLERS, RIVERS AND MOUNTAINS (2–7 AUGUST)

Although the field notes of 2–4 August note the curiosity of the tourists on the steamer, the book chapter offers far more detail about Vyvyan and Dorrien Smith's reactions to their curiosity. Meanwhile, the curiosity of the book's tourists provides an intriguing counterpoint to the women's own curiosity about the northerners they had met.

The officers on board had, it appeared, been expecting us since April
Bill and Sylva Bendy made the same discovery ten years later. Their observation seems also to allude to the capture of the Mad Trapper, Albert Johnson, in the intervening decade:

> We thought we were going unknown and unnoticed through this 300 miles of isolated country [from Aklavik to Old Crow]. We saw nobody at LaPierre House, now 4 days and 130 miles behind. Yet the first man we met, Jimmie Hogg, knew all about us and so has every Indian we have met on the Porcupine. There is not much chance of anybody going through this country unnoticed, for the possible points of entry are so few. It is no hiding place for a criminal; New York would be better. (83)

as if we were still navigating the river alone ... we missed the rhythm of paddling our own canoe. An onlooker's life is no life at all, we thought
Vyvyan's description of what it means to travel a river is an addition to the field notes and acts as a form of closure to the portion of the journey undertaken under their own power through wilderness. Although the women are returning to the more distant role of tourists, they have been travellers intimately involved in a landscape, and it is the summation possible only in retrospect which attempts to describe what has been learned in the travel.

Professor Harold Innis of Toronto University and his companion was an undergraduate named Gibbs
Harold Adams Innis (1894-1952) was appointed a lecturer in economics at the University of Toronto in 1920. In the summer of 1926, Innis stood between his doctoral work on the CPR (1923) and his enduring study, *The Fur Trade in Canada* (1930). W.K. Gibb published an uninteresting account of his trip with Innis (Gibb).

We felt as Noah must have felt on the top of Mount Ararat
Of course, the allusion is to Genesis 8:13.

The heavens seemed to emit a crackling sound
The Northern Lights appear at a different place in this chapter than in the field notes, and only in their published form do they seem "to emit a crackling sound." Although regularly disproved by science, the notion that the Aurora Borealis makes a sound endures as a popular truth.

the poet's line: "When earth's foundations fled away"
The quotation is likely from the English poet Alfred Edward Housman's poem, "Epitaph on an Army of Mercenaries" (1896): "These, in the day when heaven was falling, / The hour when earth's foundations fled, / Followed their mercenary calling / And took their wages and are dead."

Field Note for Thursday 5 August
Nenana ... we got a room at Southern Hotel
Dorrien Smith's field note gives the name of the hotel as the Northern, not the Southern.

Field Note for Saturday 7 August
saw in Anchorage Hotel very fine picture by S. Lawrence of Mt. McKinley
Dorrien Smith's field note for this date adds a Christian name—Sydney—and notes his nationality—English. This is doubtless the American painter, Sydney Laurence (1865-1940), who did live and work in St Ives, Cornwall, England from 1890 to about 1904. During that time, he also travelled to Africa to cover the Zulu and Boer wars for *Black and White*, a London periodical. Perhaps because he also became a member of the Royal Society of British Artists, or perhaps because the hotel manager told her so, Dorrien Smith incorrectly gave his nationality as British. He was born and raised in New York,

and, after his sojourn to England, moved to Alaska, spending the remainder of his life between Anchorage and Los Angeles (Woodward and Burrus 123-27). He was the most highly regarded painter of Alaskan landscapes in the first half of the twentieth century, and his name was customarily mentioned particularly in terms of Mt McKinley (Francisco).

Seward for night + then to Restaurant + Cinema for show
According to Dorrien Smith's field note for this date, the departure from Rome of Amundsen's airship was the subject of the film at the cinema.

CHAPTER 28: THE JOURNEY HOME (8–15 AUGUST)

That the field notes end before the women reach Seattle suggests that Vyvyan considered the time spent in British Columbia of less interest than that spent in the North, less worthy of documentation. Certainly for the modern reader, the women's activities once they leave Alaska are far less interesting than their Rat River adventure. Perhaps because Dorothy Dashwood was her acquaintance, or perhaps because she kept a diary throughout her life, Dorrien Smith continued writing until the trip reached its conclusion.

embarking on the steamer for Seattle
The SS *Yukon* was built in 1899, and the Alaska Steamship Company operated it on the Seattle-Seward route from 1924 until it wrecked in 1946 (McDonald 140). It sailed the women south to Seattle with stops along the Alaskan coast at Port Ashton, Port Benny, Crab Bay, Latouche Island, Knight Island, Columbia Glacier, Valdez, Cordova, Port Althorp, Juneau, Petersburg, Wrangell, and Ketchikan. According to Vyvyan's field notes and letter of 15 August to her mother, the trip lasted from 8 to 16 August. (A photograph of the ship appears in McDonald 76.)

The best interview was with Sheriff Inkster, a fine upright old-timer aged 83, who loved talking about the Rat River
Colin Inkster (1843-1934) was born in the Red River colony, and in 1871 became a member of Manitoba's first legislative council. He was minister of agriculture and president of the Council 1874-76, was appointed speaker of the Legislative

Council in 1876, and served as sheriff of the East Judicial District of Manitoba 1876-1928 ("Inkster").

Field Note for Monday 9 August
Read Rex Beach's "The Silver Horde" all day
As its title might suggest, this novel tells the story of salmon. It is an adventure about a cannery in Alaska written by a contemporary of Robert Service who lived at the Ramparts on the Yukon River, and features an adventurous heroine, Cherry Malotte, who is as capable of swooning as of successfully undertaking dangerous wilderness travel to survive diabolical ruffians of the American frontier (Beach).

Field Note for Thursday 12 August
a Botanist Professor Harshberger from Philadelphia who named our plants for us
Dorrien Smith's field note for this date identifies him as John W. Harshberger (1869-1929), a professor of botany and

author of a *Phytogeographic Survey of North America* (1911). Evidently, the identification of the specimens in the women's collection of flora was much aided by this timely meeting.

Field Notes following last dated entry
Books read May-Oct. 1926
Citations of the non-canonical titles—by Cannan, Galsworthy, Masefield, Duchaussois, and Stewart—in this list are provided in the general list of references. The "Journal" is doubtless that of Alexander Mackenzie. As well, citations are provided for the eight titles of books about North American birds, which are listed towards the end of the field notes.

References

Books by Clara Coltman Vyvyan (née Rogers)
(arranged by year of publication)

Rogers, C.C. *Cornish Silhouettes*. London: John Lane at the
Bodley Head, 1924.
——. *Echoes in Cornwall*. London: John Lane at the Bodley Head,
1926.
—- (Lady Vyvyan). *Gwendra Cove and other Cornish Sketches*. Truro:
Jordan's Bookshop, 1931.
Vyvyan, C.C. (C.C. Rogers). *Bird Symphony: An Anthology compiled by
C.C. Vyvyan*. London: John Murray, 1933.
—— (C.C. Rogers). *Maria Pendragon*. Dawlish, England:
Channing, n.d.
——. *Cornish Cronies*. Dawlish, England: Channing, 1937.
Vyvyan, C.C. *Our Cornwall*. Illus. by Elizabeth Rivers. London:
Westaway Books, 1948.
——. *Amateur Gardening for Pleasure and Profit*. London: Museum
Press, 1951.
——. *The Dead Smile*. London: Carroll and Nicholson, 1952.
——. *The Old Place*. Illus. by Elizabeth Rivers. London: Museum
Press, 1952.
——. *The Scilly Isles*. London: Robert Hale, 1953, 1960.
——. *Down the Rhone on Foot*. London: Peter Owen, 1955.
——. *Temples and Flowers: A Journey to Greece*. London: Peter Owen,
1955.
——. *The Helford River*. London: Peter Owen, 1956.
——. *On Timeless Shores: Journeys in Ireland*. London: Peter Owen,
1957; Leicester: Ulverscroft, 1968.
——. *A Cornish Year*. London: Peter Owen, 1958.
——. *Random Journeys*. London: Peter Owen, 1960.
——. *Arctic Adventure*. London: Peter Owen, 1961.
——. *Roots and Stars: Reflections on the Past*. London: Peter Owen,
1962.
——. *Coloured Pebbles*. London: Peter Owen, 1964; London:
Country Book Club, 1965.
——. *Journey up the Years*. London: Peter Owen, 1966.
——. *Nothing Venture*. London: Peter Owen, 1967.
——. *Letters from a Cornish Garden*. Fwd. by Daphne du Maurier.
London: Michael Joseph, 1972.

Selected Articles by Vyvyan *(arranged alphabetically)*
"On the Rat River." *Canadian Geographical Journal* 2 (1931): 48-57.
"The Rat River." RGS, *Geographical Journal* 73 (1929): 447-52.
(published under maiden name: Rogers)
"The Rat River Route to Alaska." *Blue Peter* 18:196 (July 1938):
303-04.
"The Rat River Route to Alaska." *Discovery: A Monthly Journal of
Popular Knowledge* 14:162 (June 1933): 180-82.
"Sunset on the Yukon." *The Cornhill Magazine* 153 (1936): 206-
16.
"The Unrelenting North." *The Cornhill Magazine* 152 (1935): 176-
83.

Unpublished Sources by Vyvyan *(arranged alphabetically)*
"Alaska." Field Notes. 15 May-14 August 1926. 72 pp. Vyvyan
Papers, Private Collection, England.

"List of N. American plants collected by GD-S and C.C.R. May-July 1926" (with Gwendolen Dorrien Smith). 7 pp. Vyvyan Papers, Private Collection, England.

"Notes for the Sub-Editor." Typescript. 2 pp. Copy in Vyvyan Papers, Private Collection, England.

To R. Hinks, RGS. 13 December 1928; 11 January 1929. Archives, Royal Geographical Society, London.

To Peter Owen. 28 January 1960. Vyvyan Papers, Private Collection, England.

To Mrs Charlotte Rogers [mother]. 3 June, 20 June, 30 June, 3 August, 15 August, 28 August 1926. Vyvyan Papers, Private Collection, England.

To Edward Zealley. 6 January, 22 August 1975. Collection of Edward Zealley.

Other References

Acheson, Ann Welsh. "Old Crow, Yukon Territory." In *Handbook of North American Indians, Vol. 6: Subarctic.* Ed. by June Helm. Washington: Smithsonian Institution, 1981. 694-703.

"Aklavik Chroniques 1925-1941." Typescript. Archives générales des Sœurs de la Charité (Sœurs Grises) de l'Hôpital général de Montréal, Pierrefonds, Quebec. Copy, ed. by Sœur Lucrèce Vinet. Fort Smith, NWT: Grey Nuns Provincial Administration, 1971 (copy now held by the AGNRC).

Alaska-Canada Album. Alaska and Polar Regions Dept., Elmer E. Rasmuson Library, University of Alaska Fairbanks.

All Saints' Cathedral—Aklavik. Rev. ed. n.p. 1949. Copy in "Aklavik" File, ACC/GSA.

Anderson, Barry C. *Lifeline to the Yukon: A History of Yukon River Navigation.* [Seattle]: Superior Publishing, 1983.

"Anglican Nurse on Way to Arctic Is Expected Monday." *Edmonton Bulletin* 29 May 1926: 6.

Annales des Sœurs de la Charité (Sœurs Grises) de l'Hôpital général de Montréal desintées aux Maisons de l'Institut. 1876- .

"Arctic Killer Freed; Victim was Disliked." *Edmonton Bulletin* 9 July 1926: 1, 9.

Aubrey, Merrily K., to I.S. MacLaren, 28 April 1997.

——., ed. and introd. *Place Names of Alberta: Volume IV.* Calgary: Alberta Community Development, Friends of Geographical Names of Alberta Society, and University of Calgary Press, 1996.

Back, George. *Arctic Artist: The Journal and Paintings of George Back, Midshipman with Franklin 1819-1822.* Ed. by C. Stuart Houston; Commentary by I.S. MacLaren. Montreal and Kingston: McGill-Queen's University Press, 1994.

Backhouse, Frances. *Women of the Klondike.* Foreword by Pierre Berton. Vancouver and Toronto: Whitecap, 1995.

Balikci, Asen. *Vunta Kutchin Social Change: A Study of the People of Old Crow, Yukon Territory.* Ottawa: Northern Co-ordination and Research Centre, Department of Northern Affairs and Natural Resources, 1963.

Batchelor, Bruce. "Arthur B. Thornthwaite." May 1982. Yukon Archives, Miscellaneous MSS, Accession no. 82/549, Bruce T. Batchelor Collection.

Bayly, G.H.U. "Canoe Trip from Fort McPherson to Fort Yukon 1965." Typescript. 63 pp.

Beach, Rex. *The Silver Horde.* New York: A.L. Burt, 1909.

Beairsto, Colin, to I.S. MacLaren, 12 February 1997.

Bendy, W[illiam] R. "The Rat River and McDougall's Pass. 1936." Typescript. 116 pp. Ottawa: Library of the Geological Survey of Canada.

Benyk, Pearl, ed. *Fort McPherson: A Community Study.* Yellowknife: Department of Education, Government of Northwest Territories, 1987.

Berger, Justice Thomas R. *Northern Frontier Northern Homeland: The Report of the Mackenzie Valley Pipeline Inquiry: Volume One.* Ottawa: Ministry of Supplies and Services, 1977.

Betke, Carl. "Lac La Biche." In *The Canadian Encyclopedia.* 1987. 2nd ed. 4 vols. Edmonton: Hurtig, 1988: 2: 1161.

Bevington, Angie. "Frank Ralph Conibear (1896-)." *Arctic* 36 (1983): 386-87. Reprinted in *Aurora* (January 1984): 11.

Black, Martha Louise. *Yukon Wild Flowers.* Vancouver: Price, Templeton [n.d.].

Bockstoce, John, to I.S. MacLaren, 28 September 1997.

——, and Charles F. Batchelder. "A Chronological List of Whaling Voyages to the Bering Region and the Western Arctic of North America, 1850-1910. *Musk-Ox* 20 (1977): 3-8.

Bonnycastle, Richard Henry Gardyne. Diary. "1 June to 5 September 1926." PAM, HBCA E.154/3, fo.85-85d.

——. *A Gentleman Adventurer: The Arctic Diaries of R.H.G. Bonnycastle.* Ed. and Comp. by Heather Robertson. Toronto: Lester and Orpen Denys, 1984.

The Book of Common Praise: Being the Hymn Book of the Anglican Church of Canada. Toronto: Oxford University Press, [1938].

Boon, T.C.B. *The Anglican Church from the Bay to the Rockies: A History of the Ecclesiastical Province of Rupert's Land and its Dioceses from 1820 to 1950.* Toronto: Ryerson, 1962.

"Brabant, Angus." PAM, HBCA, Search File RG3/40C/2.

Bryant, T. Alton, ed. *The New Compact Bible Dictionary*. New York: Pillar, 1976.

Burke, Clara Heintz, and Adele Comandini. *Doctor Hap*. New York: Coward-McCann, 1961.

Byng of Vimy, Viscountess. *Up the Stream of Time*. Toronto: Macmillan, 1946.

Cameron, Agnes Deans. *The New North: Being Some Account of a Woman's Journey through Canada to the Arctic*. New York and London: D. Appleton and Co., 1912. Rev. ed. *The New North: An Account of a Woman's 1908 Journey ....* Ed. by David R. Richeson. Saskatoon: Western Producer Prairie Books, 1986.

Camsell, Charles. *Son of the North*. Toronto: Ryerson, 1954.

Canada. Dept. Energy, Mines and Resources. "Bell River." Sheet 116P. 3rd ed. 1:250,000. Ottawa: Canada Centre for Mapping, 1989.

——. Permanent Committee on Geographical Names. *Gazetteer of Canada. Yukon Territory*. 4th ed. Ottawa: Surveys and Mapping Branch, 1976.

——. Survey and Mapping Branch. *Northwest Territories and Yukon Territory*. 1:4,000,000. 1974. "Special Edition—Partial Names Update." Ottawa: Department of Energy, Mines and Resources, 1982.

Cannan, Gilbert. *Mendel: A Story of Youth*. London: T. Fisher Unwin, 1916.

"Carroll, A.A." PAM, HBCA, Search File RG3/40A/1.

Castner, Henry W. *et al.*, Consultants. *Atlas of Canada*. N.p.: Reader's Digest Assoc. (Canada), in conjunction with The Canadian Automobile Association, 1981.

Chalmers, John W. "Steamboats Round the Bend: Riverborne Traffic on the Athabasca." *The Land of Peter Pond*. Edmonton: Boreal Institute of Northern Studies, University of Alberta, 1974. 63-75.

Champagne, Sœur Fernande. "Histoires brèves des missions du Grand Nord." AGNRC.

Chapman, Frank M., and Chester A. Reed. *Color Key to North American Birds*. New York: Doubleday, Page, 1903.

Chekhov, Anton. "Across Siberia." 1890. In *The Unknown Chekhov: Stories and other Writings*. Transl. by Avrahm Yarmolinsky. London: Peter Owen, 1947. 268-308.

"Chief Judge Dubuc Dies." *Edmonton Sun* 8 March 1956.

Christian, Edgar. *Death in the Barren Grounds*. Ed. by George Whalley. [Ottawa]: Oberon, 1980.

——. *Unflinching: A Diary of Tragic Adventure*. 1937. Preface by Henry C. Link. Introd. and Concl. by B. Dew Roberts. London: John Murray, 1937; New York: Funk and Wagnalls, 1938.

Coates, Kenneth. "Furs Along the Yukon: Hudson's Bay Company-Native Trade in the Yukon River Basin, 1830-1893." *BC Studies* 55 (Autumn 1982): 50-79.

——, and William R. Morrison. *Land of the Midnight Sun: A History of the Yukon*. Edmonton: Hurtig, 1988.

Conibear, Kenneth and Marilyn, to I.S. MacLaren, 8 August 1996.

Cook, John A. *Pursuing the Whale: A Quarter-Century of Whaling in the Arctic*. Introd. by Allan Forbes. Boston: Riverside; New York: Houghton Mifflin, 1926.

Cooke, Alan and Clive Holland, eds. *The Exploration of Northern Canada 500 to 1920: A Chronology*. Toronto: Arctic History Press, 1978.

Cooke, Edgar D. "Boom and Bust, Bust and Boom: Fort McMurray and Waterways." In *The Land of Peter Pond*. Ed. by John W. Chalmers. Boreal Institute of Northern Studies Occasional Paper no. 12. Edmonton: Boreal Institute of Northern Studies, University of Alberta, 1974. 99-108.

Coues, Elliott. *Key to North American Birds*. 1872. 5th ed. 2 vols. Boston: D. Estes, 1903.

"Court Leaves for Far North." *Edmonton Bulletin* 1 June 1926: 9.

Coutts, R. *Yukon: Places & Names*. Sidney B.C.: Gray's Publishing, 1980.

Craig, Joan. "Bell, John." *Dictionary of Canadian Biography*. Vol. IX (1861-1870). Toronto and Buffalo: University of Toronto Press, 1976. 42-3.

Crockford's Clerical Directory, 1967-68. London: Oxford University Press, 1969.

Cunliffe, Leonard, to P.D. Stirling, November 1925-January 1926, PAM, HBCA A.92/128/1, fo. 47-49.

Dall, William H. *Alaska and Its Resources*. Boston: Lee and Shepard, 1870.

Dean, David M. *Breaking Trail: Hudson Stuck of Texas and Alaska*. Athens, Ohio: Ohio University Press, 1988.

Dickason, Olive Patricia. *Canada's First Nations: A History of Founding Peoples from Earliest Times*. Toronto: McClelland and Stewart, 1992.

Dickerson, Mark O. *Whose North? Political Change, Political Development, and Self-Government in the Northwest Territories*. Vancouver: University of British Columbia Press, 1992.

Diubaldo, Richard. *Stefansson and the Canadian Arctic*. Montreal: McGill-Queen's University Press, 1978.

Dorrien Smith, Gwendolen. Field Notes, 1926. Private Collection, England.

Douglas, George M. *Lands Forlorn: A Story of an Expedition to Hearne's Coppermine River*. Introd. by James Douglas. New York: G.P. Putnam's Sons, 1914.

Downs, Art. *Paddlewheels on the Frontier: The Story of British Columbia and Yukon Sternwheel Steamers*. Sidney, B.C.: Gray's Publishing, 1972.

Driscoll, Bernadette. "Pretending to be Caribou: The Inuit Parka as an Artistic Tradition." In *The Spirit Sings: Artistic Traditions of Canada's First Peoples*. Toronto: McClelland and Stewart; Calgary: Glenbow Museum, 1987. 169-200.

Dubuc, Lucien. "Généalogie de la Famille Dubuc, 1668-1918." Oblate Archives, Provincial Archives of Alberta, 84.400, Box 23.

———. "News Cuttings." 132 pp. Provincial Archives of Alberta 29.238/1.

———. Photo Scrapbook. 45 leaves. "Photo Souvenir of Trips to Forts Providence and McPherson, 1921; Herschel Island, 1923; Aklavik, 1924." Provincial Archives of Alberta 79.238.

Duchaussois, P[ierre Jean Baptiste]. *Aux Glaces Polaires: Indiens et Esquimaux*. Lyon: Œuvre Apostolique de Marie Immaculée; La Salle, Que.: Noviciat des Oblats, 1921.

———. *The Grey Nuns in the Far North*. Published in French as *Les Sœurs Grises dans l'extrême-nord: cinquante ans de missions*. Lyon: Œuvre Apostolique de Marie Immaculée; La Salle, Quebec: Noviciat des Oblats, 1919. Toronto: McClelland and Stewart, 1919.

Ederer, Bernard Francis. *Through Alaska's Back Door*. New York: Vantage, 1954.

Ellis, M[iriam]. G[reen]. "A Business Woman in the Far North." *The Canadian Countryman*, 12 December 1925: 1669, 1710.

———. M.G. Ellis Collection. Bruce Peel Special Collections Library, University of Alberta. 96-91, Boxes 1, 3.

"Englishwomen Brave Wilds in North Country." *Winnipeg Free Press Evening Bulletin* 22 September 1926.

"Englishwomen in the Arctic." *The Daily Express* 27 October 1926: 9.

"Eskimo Murder Trial Condemned by Bishop; All Arctic is Aroused." *Vancouver Daily Province* 15 September 1923. Copy in Dubuc, "News Cuttings." 74-5.

"Eskimos Executed." *News of the World* (London) 30 December 1923. Copy in Dubuc, "News Cuttings." 93.

Fienup-Riordan, Ann. *The Nelson Island Eskimo: Social Structure and Ritual Distribution*. Anchorage: Alaska Pacific University Press, 1983.

Fleming, Archibald Lang. *Archibald the Arctic*. New York: Appleton Century Crofts, 1956.

"Fort Smith Chroniques." Typescript. Archives générales des Sœurs de la Charité (Sœurs Grises) de l'Hôpital général de Montréal, Pierrefonds, Que. Fort Smith, NWT: Grey Nuns Provincial Administration, 1955 (copy now held by the AGNRC).

Francisco, Cyrus Peter. Foreword by Sue Burrus. *The Man and the Mountain: Sydney Laurence's Mt. McKinley*. Upland, California: Lynn F. Casella Communications, 1990.

Franklin, Capt John. *Narrative of a Second Expedition to the Shores of the Polar Sea, in the Years 1825, 1826, and 1827*. London: John Murray, 1828.

Frawley, Maria H. *A Wider Range: Travel Writing by Women in Victorian England*. Rutherford, New Jersey: Fairleigh Dickinson University Press, 1994.

Fumoleau, René omi. *As Long As This Land Shall Last: A History of Treaty 8 and Treaty 11 1870-1939*. Toronto: McClelland and Stewart, [1973].

Fussell, Paul. *Abroad: British Literary Traveling between the Wars*. New York and Oxford: Oxford University Press, 1980.

Galsworthy, John. *Captures*. London: W. Heinemann, 1923.

Gibb, W.K. "Eight Hundred Miles on the Yukon." *Canadian Geographical Journal* 8 (1934): 122-34.

Godsell, Jean. *I was no Lady ... I Followed the Call of the Wild: The Autobiography of a Fur Trader's Wife*. Toronto: Ryerson, 1959.

Godsell, Philip H. *Arctic Trader: The Account of Twenty Years with the Hudson's Bay Company*. New York: G.P. Putnam's Sons, 1934.

———. *The Vanishing Frontier: A Saga of Traders, Mounties and Men of the Last North West*. Toronto: Ryerson, 1939.

Goering, J.W.L. "Notes of a Canoe Trip from Fort McPherson, North West Territories to Fort Yukon, Alaska via the Peel, Rat, Little Bell, Bell, and Porcupine Rivers. 6 July 1965 to 27 July 1965." Typescript. 107 pp.

Gordon, Glen, to Lisa LaFramboise, 3 July 1996; 13 August 1996.

Gordon, Robert S., ed. *Union List of Manuscripts in Canadian Repositories*. Ottawa: Public Archives Canada, 1968.

"Grey Nuns in St Albert Province." Pamphlet. AGNRC, 1994.

GSCI. "Gwichya Gwich'in Place Names Project." Yellowknife: GSCI, 1992- .

Hamilton, Walter R. *The Yukon Story*. Vancouver: Mitchell, 1964.

Harrington, Richard. *Richard Harrington's Yukon*. N.p.: Alaska Northwest Publishing, 1974.

Harrison, Tracey, ed. and introd. *Place Names of Alberta: Volume III*. Calgary: Alberta Community Development, Friends of Geographical Names of Alberta Society, and University of Calgary Press, 1994.

Harshberger, John William. *Phytogeographic Survey of North America: A Consideration of the Phytogeography of the North American Continent, including Mexico, Central America, and the West Indies, together with the Evolution of North American Plant Distribution*. 1911. 2nd ed. Weinheim, W. Germany: H.R. Engelmann, 1958.

Hart, E.J. *Ambition and Reality: The French-Speaking Community of Edmonton 1795-1935*. Edmonton: Le Salon d'histoire de la francophonie albertaine, 1980.

Hart, James D. *The Oxford Companion to American Literature*. 4th ed. New York: Oxford University Press, 1965.

Hatcher, Colin K. *The Northern Alberta Railways*. Calgary: British Railway Modellers of North America, 1981.

——. *The Northern Alberta Railways (Volume 2)*. Calgary: British Railway Modellers of North America, 1987.

Hayes, Alden C. *Down North to the Sea: 2,000 Miles by Canoe to the Arctic Ocean*. Boulder, Colorado: Pruett Publishing, 1989.

Herzberg, Max J. *et al*. *The Reader's Encyclopedia of American Literature*. New York: Thomas Y. Crowell, 1962.

Hester, Rev Edward to [J.R. Lucas,] Bishop of Mackenzie River, January 1924. ACC/GSA Aklavik—E. Hester 1917-26 file.

Hodgins, Bruce W., and Gwyneth Hoyle, eds. *Canoeing North into the Unknown: A Record of River Travel 1874 to 1974*. Toronto: Natural Heritage/Natural History, 1994.

Hoffman, Charles. *Drum Dance: Legends, Ceremonies, Dances and Songs of the Eskimos*. n.p., 1974.

Holmes, Kenneth L. "Murray, Alexander Hunter." *Dictionary of Canadian Biography*. Vol. X (1871-1880). Toronto: University of Toronto Press, 1972. 540-41.

Holmgren, Eric J. and Patricia M. Holmgren. *2,000 Place-Names of Alberta*. Saskatoon: Modern Press, 1972.

Honigman, John J. and Irma Honigmann. *Arctic Townsmen: Ethnic Backgrounds and Modernization*. Ottawa: Canadian Research Centre for Anthropology, Saint Paul University, 1970.

Hrdlička, Aleš. *Alaska Diary 1926-31*. Lancaster, Pennsylvania: Jaques Cattell, 1943.

Hultén, Eric. *Flora of Alaska and Yukon*. 10 Parts. Lunds Universitets Årsskrift. N.F. Avd. 2. Bd 37. Nr. 1. Lund: C.W.K. Gleerup; Leipzig: Otto Harrassowitz, 1941.

Hunt, William R. *Stef: A Biography of Vilhjalmur Stefansson Canadian Arctic Explorer*. Vancouver: University of British Columbia Press, 1986.

Hutchison, Isobel Wylie. *North to the Rime-ringed Sun: Being the Record of an Alaskan-Canadian Journey made in 1933-34*. London: Blackie, 1934.

Ingram, Rob and Helene Dobrowolsky. *Waves Upon the Shore: An Historical Profile of Herschel Island*. Whitehorse: Government of Yukon, Department of Tourism, Heritage Branch, 1989.

"Inkster, Colin." *Macmillan Dictionary of Canadian Biography*. Ed. by W. Stewart Wallace. 4th ed. Toronto: Macmillan, 1978. 379.

Inman, Col. Henry, compiler. *Buffalo Jones' Forty Years of Adventure*. London: Sampson Low, Marston, 1899.

Innis, H.A. *The Fur Trade in Canada: An Introduction to Canadian Economic History*. 1930. Rev. Ed. by S.D. Clark and W.T. Easterbrook. Foreword by Robin W. Winks. Toronto: University of Toronto Press, 1956.

"Introducing Mr. F.E. Dynes." *The Beaver: A Journal of Progress* 6 (1925-26): 39.

Isbister, A[lexander]. K[ennedy]. "Some Account of Peel River, N. America." RGS, *Journal* 15 (1845): 332-45.

J.C.T. "Lady Vyvyan." *The Times* 4 March 1976.

Jason, Victoria. *Kabloona in the Yellow Kayak: One Woman's Journey through the Northwest Passage*. Winnipeg: Turnstone, 1995.

Jenness, Diamond. "Eskimo Administration." 5 vols. Vol. II: Technical Paper 14. Montreal: Arctic Institute of North America, 1964.

Job, Herbert Keightley. *How to Study Birds; a Practical Guide for Amateur Birdlovers and Camera-Hunters*. New York: Outing, 1910.

——. *The Sport of Bird-Study; A Book for Young or Active People*. New York: Macmillan, 1905.

——. *Wild Wings; Adventures of a Camera-Hunter among the larger wild Birds of North America on Sea and Land*. Introd. by Theodore Roosevelt. Boston and New York: Houghton, Mifflin; London: Constable, 1905.

Johnson, Beth. *Yukon Wild: The Adventures of Four Women Who Paddled 2,000 Miles Through America's Last Frontier*. Stockbridge, Massachusetts: Berkshire Traveller Press, 1984.

Kealey, Dorothy, to I.S. MacLaren, 22 July 1996; "Aklavik" File; ACC/GSA.

Kelcey, Barbara Eileen. "Jingo Belles, Jingo Belles, Dashing through the Snow: White Women and Empire on Canada's Arctic Frontier." Ph.D dissertation, Department of History, University of Manitoba, 1994.

Kemp, Vernon A.M. *Without Fear, Favour or Affection: Thirty-Five Years with the Royal Canadian Mounted Police*. Toronto, New York, London: Longmans, Green, 1958.

Kennicott, Robert. "Journal of Robert Kennicott, May 19, 1859-February 11, 1862" (1869). Rpt. in James Alton James, *The First Scientific Exploration of Russian America and the Purchase of Alaska*. Evanston, Illinois: Northwestern University Press, 1942.

King, William Cornwallis and Mary Weekes. *Trader King*. Regina: School Aids and Text Book Publishing, 1947, 1949.

Kinsman, Clara D., ed. *Contemporary Authors: Permanent Series: A Bio-Bibliographical Guide to Current Authors and their Works*. Vol. 1. Detroit: Gale, 1975.

Kirkby, William West. "A Journey to the Youcan, Russian America." *Nor' Wester* (Red River) 5 March 1862. Rpt. in *Annual Report of the Smithsonian Institution 1864*. Washington: Smithsonian Institution, 1865. 416-20.

Kitchener, L.D. *Flag over the North: The Story of the Northern Commercial Company*. Seattle: Superior, 1954.

Kitto, F[ranklin]. H[ugo]. *The North West Territories 1930*. Ottawa: F.A. Acland, for the Department of the Interior, 1930.

——. "Report of a Preliminary Investigation of the Natural Resources of Mackenzie District and their Economic Development, made during the Summer of 1920." Typescript. 32 pp. Ottawa: Department of the Interior, Natural Resources Intelligence Branch, 1920. NAC, RG10 vol. 4092, reel C-10187, file 548036.

Koe, James. "A Long Time Ago." Interview with Jim Koe, Parts One and Two and Three. Committee for Original Peoples' Entitlement (COPE); Oral History Project, 196- to 197-. Tape no. N-1992-253. Transcript provided by Fred E. Koe.

Krech, Shepard III. "The Eastern Kutchin and the Fur Trade, 1800-1860." *Ethnohistory* 23 (1976): 213-35.

——. "Interethnic Relations in the Lower Mackenzie River Region." *Arctic Anthropology* 16:2 (1979): 102-22.

——. *A Victorian Earl in the Arctic: The Travels and Collections of the Fifth Earl of Lonsdale 1888-89*. Biog. introd. by J.V. Beckett. Seattle: University of Washington Press, 1989.

Kritsch, Ingrid (GSCI), to I.S. MacLaren, 22 April, 29 September, 15 October 1996.

Lain, B.D. "The Fort Yukon Affair, 1869." *Alaska Journal* 7:1 (Winter 1977): 12-17.

LaPierre House Oral History: Interviews with Vuntut Gwitchin Elders. Transl. by Alice Frost and Roy Moses. Prepared for Parks Canada by the Vuntut Gwitchin First Nation, March 1995.

Lawrence, Karen. *Penelope Voyages: Women and Travel in the British Literary Tradition*. Ithaca and London: Cornell University Press, 1994.

Lea, Mrs Christopher (Susan), to I.S. MacLaren, 5 April 1996.

Leechman, Douglas. *Indian Summer*. Illus. by W. Langdon Kihn. Toronto: Ryerson, 1949.

Leffingwell, Ernest de K[oven]. *The Canning River Region of Northern Alaska*. United States Department of the Interior, United States Geological Survey, Professional Paper 109. Washington: Government Printing Office, 1919.

"Leggo, Charles Sydney." PAM, HBCA, Search File RG3/41A/3.

Liebes, Arnold. Diary for 1923 Trip to the Arctic. Special Collections, California Academy of Sciences, San Francisco.

McConnell, R.G. *Report on an Exploration in the Yukon and Mackenzie Basins, N.W.T.* Geological and Natural History Survey of Canada. Montreal: William Foster Brown, 1891.

McCourt, Edward. *The Yukon and Northwest Territories*. Toronto: Macmillan, 1969.

McDonald, Lucile. *Alaska Steam: A Pictorial History of the Alaska Steamship Company*. Introd. by D.E. Skinner. Published as *Alaska Geographic* 11:4 (1984).

MacGregor, J.G. *Edmonton: A History*. Edmonton: Hurtig, 1967.

——. *The Klondike Rush through Edmonton 1897-1898*. Toronto: McClelland and Stewart, 1970.

Mackenzie, Alexander. *The Journals and Letters of Sir Alexander Mackenzie*. Ed. by W. Kaye Lamb. Cambridge: Cambridge University Press for the Hakluyt Society, 1970.

Mackinnon, C.S. "Portaging on the Slave River (Fort Smith)." *Musk-Ox* 27 (1980): 20-35.

MacLaren, I.S. "The HBC's Arctic Expedition 1836-1839: Dease's Field Notes as compared to Simpson's *Narrative*." In *The Fur Trade Revisited: Selected Papers of the Sixth North American Fur Trade Conference, Mackinac Island, Michigan, 1991*. Ed. by Jennifer S.H. Brown, W.J. Eccles, and Donald P. Heldman. East Lansing, Michigan: Michigan State University Press; Mackinac Island, Michigan: Mackinac State Historic Parks, 1994. 465-79.

——. "Touring at High Speed: Fur-Trade Landscapes in the Writings of Frances and George Simpson." *Musk-Ox* 34 (1986): 78-87.

Mallory, Enid. *Coppermine: The Far North of George M. Douglas.* Fwd. by Frances Douglas. Peterborough, Ontario: Broadview, 1989.

Mardon, Ernest G. *Community Names of Alberta.* Lethbridge: University of Lethbridge, 1973.

Masefield, John. *Lost Endeavour.* London and New York: Macmillan, 1917.

Masik, August and Isobel Hutchison. *Arctic Nights' Entertainments: Being the Narrative of an Alaskan-Estonian Digger.* London and Glasgow: Blackie and Son, 1935.

Mason, Michael H. *The Arctic Forests.* London: Hodder and Stoughton, 1924.

"Mason, Michael Henry." *Contemporary Authors.* Vol. 108. 1983 ed. 307.

Masson, Louis François Rodrigue, ed. *Les bourgeois de la Compagnie du Nord-Quest: Récits de Voyages, Lettres et Rapports inédits relatifs au Nord-Ouest canadien.* 2 vols. Quebec: Coté, 1889-90.

Mathers, C.W. *The Far North.* Edmonton: C.W. Mathers, 1902.

Mayer, Melanie J. *Klondike Women: True Tales of 1897-98 Gold Rush.* [Athens, Ohio]: Swallow Press, Ohio University Press, 1989.

The Midnight Sun Route through Canada's Northwestern Waterways. Edmonton: Alberta and Arctic Transportation Co., n.d. Copy in Vyvyan Papers, Private Collection, England. Also PAM, HBCA RG3/10/2; and PP1973.

Moir, John S, ed., with Officers of the Corps. *History of the Royal Canadian Corps of Signals 1903-1961.* Ottawa: Royal Canadian Corps of Signals, 1962.

Morrison, Bruce and C. Roderick Wilson, eds. *Native Peoples: The Canadian Experience.* 1986. 2nd ed. Toronto: McClelland and Stewart, 1995.

Morrison, William R. *Showing the Flag: The Mounted Police and Canadian Sovereignty in the North 1894-1925.* Vancouver: University of British Columbia Press, 1985.

Morse, Eric W. *Freshwater Saga: Memoirs of a Lifetime of Wilderness Canoeing in Canada.* Foreword by Angus C. Scott. Toronto and London: University of Toronto Press, 1987

——. *Fur Trade Canoe Routes of Canada / Then and Now.* Toronto, Buffalo, London: University of Toronto Press, 1969.

——. "The Rat-Bell-McDougall Pass Canoe Trip." *The Arctic Circular* 17:3-4 (1968): 37-47.

Morton, Anne (PAM, HBCA), to I.S. MacLaren, 11 June 1996.

Moyles, R.G. *British Law and Arctic Men: The Celebrated 1917 Murder Trials of Sinnisiak and Uluksuk, First Inuit Tried under White Man's Law.* Saskatoon: Western Producer Prairie Books, 1979.

"Mrs. Frazeur, Crane College Teacher, is Dead." *Chicago Tribune* 26 April 1933.

Murie, Margaret E. *Two in the Far North.* Illus. by Olaus J. Murie. New York: Alfred A. Knopf, 1962. 2nd ed. Edmonds, Washington and Anchorage: Alaska Northwest Books, 1978.

Murray, Alexander Hunter. *Journal of the Yukon 1847-48.* Ed. and with notes by L.J. Burpee. Ottawa: Government Printing Bureau, 1910.

Nagy, Murielle Ida. *Yukon North Slope Inuvialuit Oral History.* Occasional Papers in Yukon History No. 1. Whitehorse: Yukon Tourism Heritage Branch, 1994.

"Necrology." *The Living Church Annual.* Episcopal Church of the United States of American, 1939. 536.

"News and Notes." *The Spirit of Missions* 86 (1921): 607.

"North-West Mounted Police." *The Canadian Encyclopedia.* 1987. 2nd ed. 4 vols. Edmonton: Hurtig, 1988. 2:1511.

Northwest Territories Data Book: A Complete Information Guide to the Northwest Territories and its Communities. Yellowknife: Outcrop, 1990.

NWT. "Northwest Territories Data Sheets, General Information Sheet." n.d.

Oakes, Jill. *Inuit Annuraangit Our Clothes: A Travelling Exhibition of Inuit Clothing.* Winnipeg: University of Manitoba, Department of Clothing and Textiles, 1986.

——, and Susan Pointe. "Social and Economic Factors influencing Mackenzie Delta Inuvialuit Parkas." *Canadian Home Economics Journal* 43:3 (Summer 1993): 99-104.

"Obituaries." *R.C.M.P. Quarterly* 40:1 (January 1975): 79-80.

O'Connell, Sheldon. "The Drum Dance." *North/Nord* 31:1 (1985): 32-8.

Ogilvie, William. *Exploratory Survey of Part of the Lewes, Tat-on-Duc, Porcupine, Bell, Trout, Peel and Mackenzie Rivers.* Ottawa: Printed by Brown Chamberlin, 1890. Reprinted as "Down the Yukon and up the Mackenzie: 3,200 Miles by Foot and Paddle." *Canadian Magazine* 1 (1893): 532-49, 642-59; 2 (1893-94): 45-58, 178-97.

"The Old Library of Fort Simpson." *The Beaver: A Journal of Progress* 5 (1924-25): 20-1.

On the Banks of the Slave: A History of the Community of Fort Smith Northwest Territories. Fort Smith, Alberta: Tourism Committee, 1979.

Osgood, Cornelius. *Contributions to the Ethnography of the Kutchin* Yale University Publications in Anthropology no. 14. New Haven, Connecticut: Yale University Press, 1936.

Ostermann, H[other], ed. *The Mackenzie Eskimos: After Knud Rasmussen's Posthumous Notes*. Report of the Fifth Thule Expedition 1921–24; the Danish Expedition to Arctic North America in Charge of Knud Rasmussen. Vol. X, no. 2. 1942. New York: AMS, 1976.

Parker, James M. "Fort Chipewyan." *The Canadian Encyclopedia*. 1987. 2nd ed. 4 vols. Edmonton: Hurtig, 1988. 2:819.

"Parsons, John Ambrose." PAM, HBCA, Search File RG3/40C/2.

Peake, Frank A. *The Bishop Who Ate His Boots: A Biography of Isaac O. Stringer*. [Toronto]: Anglican Church of Canada, 1966.

———. "William West Kirkby: Missionary from Alaska to Florida." *Historical Magazine of the Protestant Episcopal Church* 34 (1965): 265–76.

Peake, Geoffrey. "Across the Arctic Mountains." *Che-Mun: The Journal of Canadian Wilderness Canoeing* 78 (Autumn 1994): 6–8, 11.

Phillips, Carol. "Unsung Heroines." *Alaskan Epiphany* 17:1 (Spring 1996): 2–3.

Platt, Sherwood K. "Mackenzie Meanderings and Rat River Ramblings; Being the Diary Account of Sherwood K. Platt of Chicago, Illinois While Journeying down the Mackenzie river in Company with Alfred E. Driscoll of Haddonfield, New Jersey, Alexander P. Leete of Pittsburgh, Pennsylvania, and Pierce Onthank of Fitchburg, Massachusetts. Dedicated to the Millions of Mosquitoes that kept Us constantly on the Move." Typescript, prepared by Theodora P. Bobrinskoy. 43 pp. Collection of Sherwood Platt.

Polyondi, Barry. "How Mickey Ryan overcame the Smith Portage." *Canadian Geographic* 100:6 (December 1980–January 1981): 66–71.

Pool, Annelies. In *The Canadian Encyclopedia*. 1987. 2nd ed. 4 vols. Edmonton: Hurtig, 1988: "Aklavik" 1:47; "Arctic Red River" 1:112; "Fort Good Hope" 2:820; "Fort Norman" 2:822; "Fort Providence" 2:822; "Fort Resolution" 2:822.

Porsild, A. Erling and William J. Cody. *Vascular Plants of Continental Northwest Territories, Canada*. Ottawa: National Museum of Natural Sciences, 1980.

Rampart House: Stories told by our Elders. Ed. by Students at Te'sek Gehtr'oonatun Zzeh College. Old Crow: Te'sek Gehtr'oonatun Zzeh College, 1993.

Rasmussen, Knud. *Across Arctic America: Narrative of the Fifth Thule Expedition*. New York and London: G.P. Putnam's Sons, 1927.

———. *Intellectual Culture of the Copper Eskimos*. Report of the Fifth Thule Expedition 1921–24; the Danish Expedition to Arctic North America in Charge of Knud Rasmussen. Vol. IX. 1932. New York: AMS, 1976.

Ray, Arthur J. *The Canadian Fur Trade in the Industrial Age*. Toronto, Buffalo, London: University of Toronto Press, 1990.

Rayfield, Jo Ann, to Lisa LaFramboise, 25 November 1996.

"Record Book holds many Historical Facts about Early Days of St Stephen's Episcopal Church." *Alaskan Epiphany* 16:3 (Fall 1995): 14.

"Return from Northern Trip." *Manitoba Free Press* 23 September 1926: 4.

Romanet, Louis Auguste. Romanet Papers, University of Alberta Archives 72-81, 7/1/9. Incl. *A Guide to the Papers of Louis Auguste Romanet*. Manuscript Group 7. Edmonton: Boreal Institute of Northern Studies, University of Alberta, 1975.

Romig, Emily Craig. *A Pioneer Woman in Alaska*. 1945. Caldwell, Idaho: n.p., 1948.

Rust, Jess. "Diary kept by Mr. Jess Rust, Fairbanks, Alaska, … Boat Trip to and from the Old Crow River Region, Yukon Territory, Canada in 1926." VFMS—Rust, Jess—Old Crow River Trip Diary 1926, Archives, University of Alaska Fairbanks.

Savoie, Donat, ed. *The Amerindians of the Canadian Northwest in the 19th Century, as seen by Émile Petitot*. 2 vols. *Vol. 1: The Tchiglit Eskimos*. Ottawa: Northern Science Research Group, Department of Indian and Northern Affairs, 1970.

Sax, Lee and Effie Linklater. *Gikhyi, One Who Speaks The Word of God: The True and Remarkable Story of the Arctic Kutchin Christian Leaders*. Whitehorse: Diocese of Yukon, 1990.

Saxberg, Nancy. *The Archaeology and History of an Arctic Mission, Herschel Island, Yukon*. Occasional Papers in Archaeology No. 4. N.p.: Heritage Branch, Government of Yukon, 1993.

Schneider, Ena. *Ribbons of Steel: The Story of the Northern Alberta Railways*. Calgary: Detselig: 1989.

Scoggan, H.J. *The Flora of Canada*. 4 Parts. Publications in Botany no. 7(4). Ottawa: National Museum of Natural Sciences, 1979.

Service, Robert W. *Ballads of a Bohemian*. Toronto and New York: Barse and Hopkins, 1921.

——. "In from a Long Journey." *Daily News* (Dawson) 12 August 1911.

——. *Ploughman of the Moon: An Adventure into Memory*. New York: Dodd, Mead, 1945.

Simon, Sarah. Interview with I.S. MacLaren, 20 June 1994.

Slobodin, Richard. "Kutchin." In *Handbook of North American Indians, Vol. 6: Subarctic*. Ed. by June Helm. Washington: Smithsonian Institution, 1981. 514-32.

Smith, Derek G. "Mackenzie Delta Eskimo." In *Handbook of North American Indians, Vol. 5: Arctic*. Ed. by David Damas. Washington: Smithsonian Institution, 1984. 347-58.

Smyth, Heather. "'Lords of the World': Gender and Imperialism in C.C. Vyvyan's *Arctic Adventure*." Typescript.

"Social and Personal." *Manitoba Free Press* 22 September 1926: 8.

Sovereign, A. H., Rev. *Ambassador of the Frozen Way: Most Reverend Isaac O. Stringer, D.D., Archbishop of Rupert's Land*. N.p.: Centenary Committee of the Canadian Churches, n.d.

Spiller, Robert E. *et. al. Literary History of the United States*. 2 vols. Vol. 1: *History*. 3rd ed., rev. New York: Macmillan; London: Collier-Macmillan, 1963.

Steele, Harwood. *Policing the Arctic: The Story of the Conquest of the Arctic by the Royal Canadian (formerly North-West) Mounted Police*. London: Jarrolds; Toronto: Ryerson, 1936.

Stefansson, Georgina. "My Grandfather, Dr Vilhjalmur Stefansson." *North* 8:4 (July-August 1961): 25.

Stefansson, Vilhjalmur. *Hunters of the Great North*. New York: Harcourt, Brace, 1922.

——. *My Life with the Eskimo*. New York and London: Macmillan, 1913.

——. *Northwest to Fortune: The Search of Western Man for a Commercially Practical Route to the Far East*. New York: Duell, Sloan, and Pearce, 1958.

Stelter, Gilbert A. "What Kind of City is Edmonton?" In *Edmonton: The Life of a City*. Ed. by Bob Hesketh and Frances Swyripa. Edmonton: NeWest, 1995. 1-11.

Stevenson, Robert Louis. *Essays in the Art of Writing*. 1905. London: Chatto and Windus, 1925.

——. *An Inland Voyage*. 1878. Everyman's Library, no. 766. London: J.M. Dent; New York: E.P. Dutton, 1925.

Stewart, Elihu. *Down the Mackenzie and up the Yukon in 1906*. London: John Lane, The Bodley Head; New York: John Lane; Toronto: Bell and Cockburn, 1913.

Stewart, Ethel. "Early Days at Fort McPherson." *The Beaver* 285 (Winter 1954-55): 39-41.

——. "Kutchin Trade Prior to 1840." *The Beaver* 310 (Summer 1979): 54-8.

Story, Norah, ed. *The Oxford Companion to Canadian History and Literature*. Toronto: Oxford University Press, 1967.

Stuck, Hudson. *The Alaskan Missions of the Episcopal Church*. New York: Domestic and Foreign Missionary Society, 1920.

——. *A Winter Circuit of our Arctic Coast: A Narrative of a Journey with Dog-Sleds around the entire Arctic Coast of Alaska*. New York: Charles Scribner's Sons, 1920.

Swanson, Marie. Information regarding Chief Pierre Squirrel and Billy McNeill supplied through Gwen Rempel, Curator of Collections, Northern Lights Museum, Fort Smith, and directly, to I.S. MacLaren, 1 October 1996.

Taverner, Percy Algernon. *Birds of Eastern Canada*. Geological Survey of Canada, Memoir no. 104. Ottawa: Geological Survey of Canada, 1919. 2nd ed. Ottawa: F.A. Acland, 1922.

Taylor, Elizabeth R. "Up the Mackenzie River to the Polar Sea: A Lady's Journey in Arctic America." *Travel* 3 (April 1899): 559-64. Rpt. in *The Far Islands and Other Cold Places: Travel Essays by a Victorian Lady*. Ed. by James Taylor Dunn. N.p.: Pogo, 1997. 50-8.

——. "A Woman on the Mackenzie Delta." *Outing Magazine* 25:1 (October 1894): 44-55; 25:2 (November 1894): 120-32; 25:3 (December 1894): 229-35; 25:4 (January 1895): 304-11. Rpt. in *Tales of the Canadian Wilderness*. Secaucus, New Jersey: Castle, 1985. 69-110.

Thomas, Lowell. *Kabluk of the Eskimo*. London: Hutchinson; Boston: Little, Brown, 1932.

"To the Arctic and Back: A Summer's Trip through Canada's Northwestern Waterways." *The Beaver: A Journal of Progress* 6 (1925-26): 123.

Trelawny, John G. *Wildflowers of the Yukon and Northwestern Canada including Adjacent Alaska*. Victoria: Sono Nis, 1983.

"Two Englishwomen Start on Trip to Arctic Circle." *Manitoba Free Press* 28 May 1926: 9.

"Two Women on Arctic Jaunt to Use Canoe." *Edmonton Journal* 28 May 1926: 1.

Usher, Peter J. *The Bankslanders: Economy and Ecology of a Frontier Trapping Community*. 3 vols. Ottawa: Northern Science Research Group, Department of Indian Affairs, 1970.

"Vale, Alfred James." *Canadian Churchman* 90:8 (September 1963): 15.

Van Kirk, Sylvia. *"Many Tender Ties": Women in Fur Trade Society, 1670-1870*. Winnipeg: Watson and Dwyer, 1980.

Vuntut Gwitchin First Nation Final Agreement between the Government of Canada, the Vuntut Gwitchin First Nation, and the Government of the Yukon. Ottawa: Supply and Services Canada, 1993.

Vyvyan, C[lara]. C[oltman]. (*née* Rogers): Please see head of this list of References.

Waldo, Fullerton. *Down the Mackenzie through the Great Lone Land*. New York: Macmillan, 1923.

——. "Father Rovier Gets a Letter." *The Outlook* 133 (1923): 804-05.

——. "Fire." *The Outlook* 133 (1923): 267-68.

——. "The Freshman Class." *The Outlook* 133 (1923): 28-9.

——. "'Outside': A Study in the Point of View." *The Outlook* 133 (1923): 85-6.

——. "Running Water." *The Outlook* 132 (1922): 772-73.

——. "Soldiers of the Northern Cross." *The Outlook* 133 (1923): 221-22.

Waldron, Malcolm Thomas. *Snow Man: John Hornby in the Barren Lands*. Boston and New York: Houghton Mifflin, 1931.

Warner, H.A.O. "From the Mackenzie to the Yukon; Being a Description of a Trip across Arctic Mountains on a Route suitable for Tourists on extended Vacation. Edmonton, March 1926." Typescript. 15 pp. Copy in Vyvyan Papers, Private Collection, England.

——. "Re. Mackenzie River — Yukon Trip." Typescript. 7 pp. Copy in Vyvyan Papers, Private Collection, England.

Waterer, Alphonso. "Through the Great Loneland." [1947?] Typescript copy. 68 pp. NAC, MG30 C59, vol. 1.

[Watson, Robert]. "A Summer Trip to the Arctic." *The Beaver: A Journal of Progress* 5 (1924-25): 120-22.

Weihs, Jean. *Facts about Canada, Its Provinces and Territories*. Illus. by Cameron Riddle. [New York]: H.W. Wilson, 1995.

"West, Vernon Weir." PAM, HBCA, Search File RG3/40C/1.

Whalley, George. *The Legend of John Hornby*. Toronto: Macmillan; London: John Murray, 1962. Rpt. Toronto: Macmillan, 1977.

White, Robert and Sarah Baxter. *The Mac: Edmonton's Historic Hotel Macdonald*. Edmonton: Tree Frog, 1995.

Whittaker, Charles Edward. *Arctic Eskimo; A Record of Fifty Years' Experience and Observation Among the Eskimo*. London: Seeley, Service and Co., 1937.

——. Letter from Fort McPherson, October 1911. *The Letter Leaflet of the Woman's Auxiliary to the Missionary Society of the Church of England in Canada* (May 1912): 213.

——. "Sunrise in Eskimo Land or Dawn Among Eskimo: A Story of the Mission in the Mackenzie Delta By One Who Took Part in It; with Some Account of the Author's Life." Typescript. n.d. AGC/GSA M88-5.

"Whittaker, Rev Charles Edward." *The Canadian Who's Who*. Vol. 2. 1936-37. 1133.

Who was Who among North American Authors 1921-1939. 2 vols. Detroit: Gale Research, 1976.

Wiebe, Rudy. *Playing Dead: A Contemplation concerning the Arctic*. Edmonton: NeWest, 1989.

Williams, Jeffrey. *Byng of Vimy: General and Governor General*. London: Leo Cooper, and Secker and Warburg, 1983.

Wilson, Clifford. "The Surrender of Fort Yukon One Hundred Years Ago." *The Beaver* 300 (Autumn 1969): 47-51.

"Women to Go Hunting in Northland." "Women's Activities" Page. *Edmonton Journal* 28 May 1926: 13.

Wood, Samuel Thomas. *Rambles of a Canadian Naturalist*. London: J.M. Dent, 1916.

Woodward, Kesler E., and Sue Burrus. "Chronology." In Woodward, *Sydney Laurence, Painter of the North*. Seattle: University of Washington Press, in assoc. with the Anchorage Museum of History and Art, 1990. 123-30.

Wright, Allen A. *Prelude to Bonanza: The Discovery and Exploration of the Yukon*. Sidney, B.C.: Gray's Publishing, 1976.

Wright, Mabel Osgood. *Birdcraft; A Field Book of Two Hundred Song, Game, and Water Birds*. 1895. 9th ed. New York and London: Macmillan, 1925.

"Yukon." *Cariboo and Northwest Digest* (Spring 1949): 114.

Zaslow, Morris. *The Northward Expansion of Canada 1914-1967*. Toronto: McClelland and Stewart, 1988.

Zealley, Edward. "Edward Hester: Canon Husky of the Mackenzie." *North/Nord* 31:1 (1985): 46-54.

——. "Lazarus Sittichinli." *North/Nord* 26:1 (Spring 1979): 2-5.

——, to I.S. MacLaren, 15 July 1996 (with assistance from Glen Gordon, Historian's Office, RCMP).

Index *(Page numbers in italics refer to illustrations.)*